T0299898

Social Costs Today

This book deals with the causes of the present crises, but it claims that causes and policy implications cannot be properly assessed by focusing on allocative efficiency or income growth alone; it contends that a more general approach is called for, based on social costs. It does not deal with social costs according to the Pigouvian or the Coasian traditions. It draws on the work of Original Institutional Economics (OIE) such as Thorstein Veblen, Karl William Kapp and Karl Polanyi, on post-Keynesians such as Hyman Minsky and, in general, on authors who have provided insights beyond the conventional wisdom of economic thought.

The assumption underlying the book's social cost perspective is that social costs arise because the money-centered accounting of capitalist market economies is biased relative to social requirements and needs. Although social costs may sometimes have a monetary dimension, they cannot be dealt with in money terms alone. What is at issue at a more fundamental level is that (1) labor and knowledge, nature, money and finance, and problem-solving social institutions are treated as commodities, (2) our common knowledge is often distorted in order to favor vested interests, (3) whatever competition one might achieve, it cannot deal with the social dilemma between individualist profitability and societal serviceability and, finally, (4) when social costs rise and the quality of life declines, so does the ability of democratic collective action.

Social costs, in this perspective, identify the issues that need to be addressed if public policy would wish to prevent the economy from subsuming societal relations and freedom. Social costs, in this evolutionary-institutional perspective, particularly elaborated by Karl William Kapp, both precede and follow the crises, as causes and effects of the current financial, real economic, resources and food, energy and climate, social, political and moral crises. The sections in this book provide a framework that better allows us to situate the issues and to appreciate the crises.

Paolo Ramazzotti is Associate Professor of Public Policy at the University of Macerata, Italy.

Pietro Frigato received his PhD in Development Sociology from the University of Pisa, Italy.

Wolfram Elsner is Professor of Economics at the University of Bremen, Germany.

Routledge frontiers of political economy

Social Costs Today

Institutional analyses of the present crises

**Edited by Paolo Ramazzotti,
Pietro Frigato and Wolfram Elsner**

Routledge
Taylor & Francis Group

LONDON AND NEW YORK

First published 2012
by Routledge
2 Park Square, Milton Park, Abingdon, Oxon OX14 4RN

Simultaneously published in the USA and Canada
by Routledge
711 Third Avenue, New York, NY 10017

Routledge is an imprint of the Taylor & Francis Group, an informa business

British Library Cataloguing in Publication Data
A catalogue record for this book is available from the British Library

Library of Congress Cataloging in Publication Data
Social costs today: institutional analyses of the present crises/edited by
Wolfram Elsner, Pietro Frigato and Paolo Ramazzotti.
    p. cm.
    1. Externalities (Economics) 2. Institutional economics. I.Ramazzotti,
    Paolo. II. Frigato, Pietro. III. Elsner, Wolfram
    HB846.3.S685 2012
    330.15'52–dc23   2011051371

ISBN: 978-0-415-50846-9 (hbk)
ISBN: 978-0-203-11315-8 (ebk)

Typeset in Times New Roman
by Wearset Ltd, Boldon, Tyne and Wear

Contents

Illustrations

Figures

Tables

Contributors

Sebastian Berger, Dickinson College, USA.

Michele Cangiani, University of Venezia, Italy.

Manuel Couret Branco, Universidade de Évora, Portugal.

Pedro Damião Henriques, Universidade de Évora, Portugal.

Wolfram Elsner, University of Bremen, Germany.

Pietro Frigato, SPPIA 'Luigi Einaudi', Bolzano, Italy.

Spiridione Garbisa, University of Padova, Italy.

Valerio Gennaro, National Cancer Research Institute, Genova, Italy.

Frederic B. Jennings, Jr., Center for Ecological Economic and Ethical Education, USA.

Angelo Gino Levis, University of Padova, Italy.

Remi Maier-Rigaud, University of Cologne, Germany.

Özlem Onaran, University of Westminster, UK.

Paolo Ramazzotti, University of Macerata, Italy.

Roberto Rizza, University of Bologna, Italy.

Francisco Javier Santos-Arteaga, GRINEI, Universidad Complutense de Madrid, Spain.

Michael Sauer, University of Cologne, Germany.

Frank Schulz-Nieswandt, University of Cologne, Germany.

Arild Vatn, Norwegian University of Life Sciences, Norway.

L. Randall Wray, University of Missouri-Kansas City, USA.

Social costs today

Institutional analyses of the present crises – an introduction

Paolo Ramazzotti, Pietro Frigato and Wolfram Elsner

Pervasive social costs

One of the striking images of the financial and economic crises that broke out in 2007 was the employees of Lehman Brothers leaving their offices after the company's bankruptcy, carrying their personal belongings in cartons. This was a dramatic contrast to more traditional situations, where it is blue-collar workers who are laid off. Indeed, it seemed that the latter were not going to be the only ones to suffer the consequences of the crises. The social costs of financial business were affecting several sections of society.

Another things that made it surprising was that Lehman Brothers would have been expected to be 'too big to fail'. This unexpected consequence remains somewhat unique. As a general rule, financial institutions were not allowed to fail. Indeed, the risk that the whole world financial system might collapse in a domino-like fashion provided a reasonable justification for bailing them out. To some, however, this appeared to be inappropriate because it reinforced the moral hazard which they believed was at the root of the crisis. More generally, it accentuated what they claimed to be the cause of the financial crisis, namely state intervention in the financial system (Dowd 2009). From a different perspective, bail-outs could never solve the problems associated with the intrinsic financial instability of modern capitalism (Kregel 2009; Mirowski 2010). Furthermore, the financial system ought not to be viewed as the sole originator of the economic crisis, since its evolution went hand in hand with a major redistribution of income in most developed countries over the past 30 years (Petit 2010). Whether explicitly or implicitly, the underlying issue has been what policies were required to overcome the financial and economic crises and return to stable growth.

This book deals with the crises from a somewhat different perspective. Although it does deal with the causes of the present crises, it claims that causes and policy implications cannot be properly assessed by focusing on allocative efficiency or income growth alone; it contends that a more general approach is called for, based on social costs. Such a contention may appear to be somewhat awkward in that social costs are generally considered by conventional economists to be side-effects of the market, so focusing on them would seem to be a specific, rather than general, approach. The contributors to this book, however, do not deal with social costs according to the Pigouvian or the Coasian traditions. They draw on the work of Institutional economists such as Thorstein Veblen, Karl William Kapp and Karl Polanyi, on post-Keynesians such as Hyman Minsky and, in general, on authors who have provided insights beyond the conventional wisdom of economic thought.

The assumption underlying the book's social cost perspective is that social costs arise because the money-centered accounting of capitalist market economies is biased relative to social requirements and needs. Although social costs may sometimes have a monetary dimension, they cannot be dealt with in money terms alone. What is at issue at a more fundamental level is that labor power, nature, money and finance are treated as commodities, that knowledge is often distorted in order to favor vested interests, that whatever competition one might achieve, it cannot deal with the gap between profitability and serviceability and, finally, that when social costs rise and the quality of life declines, so does the ability of democratic collective action. Social costs, in this perspective, identify the issues that need to be addressed if public policy would wish to prevent the economy from subsuming societal relations and freedom.

The sections that follow attempt to provide a framework that may allow us to better situate the chapters and appreciate the general theme, as well as the interlocking issues.

The nature of social costs

The first group of chapters deals with social costs from a theoretical and methodological perspective. Their aim is not only to point out that the conventional view, centered on the notion of externality and market failure, is inadequate and misleading. They also discuss a common framework that may encompass specific issues. The framework is that social costs depend on institutional circumstances. They are a generalized and diffused phenomenon in market capitalist economies because of the specific functioning of business enterprises and of market competition.

Paolo Ramazzotti argues that the markets we are concerned with operate not only subject to specific rules defined at the societal level, but also according to a more general historically determined institutional setup, that of a capitalist economy. Its coordination of economic activity is centered on money gains and involves treating labor, nature, money and financial assets as commodities. Alternative forms of economic coordination exist, however, based on criteria such as solidarity or equity. They underlie the activities of institutions such as families, the welfare state, etc. The coexistence of these different coordinating instances reflects the systemic openness of the economy, and thereby requires a social accounting criterion that makes them mutually consistent and functional to complex societal priorities. Drawing on A. Sen, Ramazzotti suggests that such a meta-criterion and priority is provided by the ability for people to choose how to conduct their lives. This implies that policy must not only remove whatever constrains this ability. It must allow for a process of discovery of new societal setups. Economic inquiry, in turn, cannot rely on the identification of some coordinating rule based on once-and-for-all 'laws' of how the economy works; it requires awareness that, owing to its systemic openness and complexity, the economy may change in many ways. Following G. Myrdal, he stresses that what is at issue is not only how you study the economy, but what questions you ask.

In his discussion of institutions and social costs, Arild Vatn is particularly concerned with environmental issues, but his discussion is not restricted to these. He recalls that it is institutions that arrange the market, production and distribution. But he also points out that institutions determine the way people interpret information. They affect the roles that people resort to – e.g., whether they choose something as consumers or as citizens – their motivations and their preferences. Ultimately, they determine how the economy is coordinated and which social costs occur. Choice of the appropriate institutional setup therefore becomes crucial and, since technically 'there is no "fixed point" from where we can judge what is the better institutional solution', ethical issues come to the fore. The ethical views that the conventional approach favors are implicit in the institutions it purports, which lead to an individualization of economic relations to the neglect of (physical) interdependencies and, consequently, to the emergence of (environmental) social costs. Vatn argues that a cooperative rationality is required when interdependent choices that affect third parties are concerned. This calls for appropriate forms of coordination at the level of the basic units of the economy – e.g., not-for-profit firms and networks – but also at the level of public policy, so as to favor the collective learning and participation that are required in order to deal with the environmental uncertainties of innovation and change.

While Vatn discusses how the coordination of the economy depends on the framing effects of institutions, Frederic B. Jennings, Jr. provides a more specific analysis of the interpretative frameworks – one might say the mental models – that economic actors and theorists resort to. Drawing on H. Simon, he argues that, since dealing with reality requires a selection of what is relevant, everyone resorts to planning horizons – i.e., 'the range of consequences ... included in the imagined projections of outcomes among which we choose'. Although true uncertainty sets a limit to the features of reality that more extensive horizons can encompass, the latter nonetheless take into account direct interdependencies among individual actors, rather than just price-mediated indirect interaction. This has implications both for theory and for economic choice in general. From a theoretical perspective, it recalls Kaldor's emphasis on the irrelevance of approaches that focus on substitution alone. From the point of view of single actors, it suggests that many conflicts of interest arise because competition emphasizes substitution rather than complementarities; longer horizons would reduce conflicts of interest and lead to the identification of commonalities of interests. Social costs can therefore be traced back to the myopic view that both market institutions and prevailing theories provide. The conclusion is very much in line with Vatn's: Avoiding social costs requires not only a different approach to theory; it also requires institutions that favor longer planning horizons, thereby enhancing cooperation.

Jenning's emphasis on the need for an approach to the economy that broadens the scope of inquiry is consistent with A. Mayhew's (2000) distinction between fixed and open systems of analysis. This same distinction is the point of departure for Pietro Frigato and Francisco Santos-Arteaga's discussion of two strands of evolutionary theory: Richard Nelson's theory of the firm and Veblen's and Kapp's discussion of business. The authors provide an accurate overview of Nelson and Winter's famous book and of Nelson's subsequent depiction of institutions as social technologies. Although they acknowledge that these inquiries provided significant insights which are much in line with the Original Institutionalist tradition, they also stress that Nelson misses a key point in Veblen's and Kapp's analyses, namely the distinction between making things and making money. This leads Nelson to under-estimate the control that business exerts over scientific and technological research and the consequent predominance of money gains over serviceability. In order to stress the practical relevance of their critique, Frigato and Santos-Arteaga discuss two special cases: planned obsolescence and the manufacture of doubt. What they point out is that these practices consist of cost-shifting techniques based on those same routines that, according to Nelson, just ought to reduce transaction costs.

Similar themes appear in Sebastian Berger's reconstruction of Kapp's scientific dialogue with the community of economists who discussed social costs. Berger begins by recalling that Kapp wrote his dissertation as a critique of Mises and that his subsequent book on social costs was also critical of Hayek. Kapp's key issue – what Berger refers to as Kapp's 'impossibility thesis' – was that societal efficiency cannot be achieved through market-based accounting and that substantive criteria (in Weber's sense) are required to deal with human needs. The critiques provided by authors such as Knight, Stigler and Buchanan basically missed the point: they focused on market efficiency rather than human needs; they relied on the market to solve problems that the very existence of the market produced; while they emphasized the free market, they only implicitly acknowledged that the state had a role to play; and they denied the relevance of asymmetric economic power. Kapp's rejoinder dealt with these critiques by reasserting the inadequacy of exchange value when measuring human values and by pointing out that reliance on individual choice mechanisms in an environment characterized by complexity and uncertainty is simply misleading. Unfortunately, there was no substantial follow-up to this dialogue. It is often the case that it is easier to oblivionize heterodox critiques than to deal with them.

One of the conclusions the above discussions lead to is that it is not enough to argue that institutions matter. The key issue is *how* they matter and, possibly, to the advantage of whom. This general statement is qualified by the chapters that deal with the financial and economic crises. It should come as no surprise that they focus on those aspects of the economy that generate what K. Polanyi called fictitious commodities.

The social costs of the present crises

In her overview of the social costs of the economic crisis, Özlem Onaran focuses on distribution. She points out that the rise in inequality since the 1980s led to an increase in profits – at the expense of wages – but to no rise in investment. What prevailed was the mere exchange of assets so that growth declined in many countries, both developed and developing. The drop in the wage share reduced effective demand, thereby negatively affecting growth and profits. In the United States and other countries debt-led consumption provided a temporary solution to this problem but at the cost of growing financial instability. In the United States it also increased the current account deficit, which was financed by providing dollar-denominated reserves to exporting countries. Developing countries used them to prevent the negative consequences of speculative capital outflows rather than to support domestic growth, while developed countries used them to finance their neo-mercantilist debt-led export growth, thereby aggravating the foreign account of other countries. Drawing on the evidence from past crises in Mexico, Turkey, Korea and Japan, Onaran points out that present policies tend to accentuate distributional inequalities and that this reinforces the recession rather than solving it. An alternative policy framework is possible, however. It must, above all, abandon the commitment to satisfy the financiers that are speculating on public debt and revert the present distributive trends. It includes a range of other actions that may trouble market enthusiasts but basically provide the guidelines for a more humane institutional setup of the economy. In other words, there is nothing inevitable about social costs.

L. Randall Wray complements the chapter by Onaran with a detailed discussion of the financial aspects of the crisis. He describes institutional changes such as the original combination of lending and the payments system through private banks, the progressive reduction of relationship banking in favor of the market and the private management of that market not only through the use of privately owned asset pricing models but also through intentionally devised predatory (mortgage) contracts. He then relates them to the progressive erosion of underwriting standards, to innovations that render financial relations opaque and to the convergence of various types of banks. The result is not only a more advanced stage of 'casino capitalism', whereby shareholder value prevails over capital development, production and employment. It is the incentive for money managers to systematically prey on less informed actors, and even on the very firms they work for. Thus, financial fragility goes hand in hand with increasing fraud, despite the claimed efficiency of a 'deregulated' market. It is, however, important to note that, although Wray points out how policy measures – ranging from the establishment of government safety nets to Volcker's monetary experiment – affected this process, the transformation of the economy into what Minsky called money manager capitalism is, in his view, also the result of a triumphant trader mentality. So, although the social costs of the financial crisis are related to wrong policies and/or to policies that aimed to protect vested interests, there is more to the issue. Trader mentality basically means that what is misaligned is not the incentives but, as K.W. Kapp (1978) argued, the basic goals that business and society as a whole pursue. The implicit suggestion is that policy involves not only setting up a general institutional framework but acting on a day-by-day basis to contrast sectional interests.

Roberto Rizza looks at the distributional issues discussed by Onaran from a different perspective: changes in welfare and employment policies. In his discussion of the deregulation of working contracts in Europe he points out that it does not provide a solution to unemployment, that it increases the risk of poverty for less qualified and young workers and that it is progressively affecting the 25–49 age group, the group most concerned with long-term choices such as marriage and children. Activation policies, both in their 'welfare to work' and in their 'work for welfare' versions, support the view that unemployed workers need to be threatened: They will lose welfare provisions if they do not accept more or less any job they are offered. Thus, activation policies switch the rationale of traditional welfare policy: Whereas the latter was traditionally supposed to help people who suffered the effects of circumstances they did not control, activation policies shift the risk of unemployment on to the worker and, in so doing, they support the view that it is individuals who are to blame if they do not have a job. What this leads to is that people are likely to end up working for only a few hours per week while social protection declines and income insecurity rises. The result is that the weakest sections of society risk being trapped in precarious life-courses. Quite independently of the theoretical flaws underlying these welfare policies – whereby lower production costs ought to increase employment – what emerges from the above discussion is that they identify business priorities with the removal of economic constraints. Social costs turn out to be the outcome of a society that is embedded in the economy rather than the other way round (Polanyi 1944).

The neoliberal ideology that accompanies the above policies is formally in favor of the commodification of goods such as water on the grounds that this leads to greater efficiency. Manuel Couret Branco and Pedro Damião Henriques discuss this issue by acknowledging that, since access to water generally requires infrastructures, the provision of water may be made rivalrous and excludable, thereby turning a good that is essential for life into a generic private good. Commodification is fairly easy at this point and the supply of water may be made to depend on the willingness to pay. If a share of the population lacks the means to pay for it, however, the result is deprivation. Deprivation does not only clash with basic human rights. It is also inefficient in terms of economic growth in that it leads to diseases and poor health, which affect children in particular. This results in cognitive impairment and educational absenteeism and eventually feeds back on productivity and GDP. Furthermore, collecting water often requires so much time that it precludes going to school. This, along with other elements, affects girls more than boys, thus perpetuating gender biases. This social exclusion, however, is not the only social cost associated with the commodification of water. Other social costs arise because of the unconstrained – other than by willingness to pay – use of water. Such an unconstrained use feeds back either on the overall availability of water – when its extraction rate exceeds its recharge rate – or on its quality, as when irrigation disseminates chemicals and causes pollution. Thus, Couret Branco and Henriques conclude, the present crisis puts pressure on public finances and pushes governments to treat water as a commodity, but such a policy is going to clash with human rights, economic growth and ecological constraints.

The discussion of the commodification of water focused on the social costs that arise when a single good is subject to alternative uses. The chapter by Remi Maier-Rigaud, Michael Sauer and Frank Schulz-Nieswandt argues that problems arise also when a single good – private elderly care, in their case – has to be supplied by different actors. More specifically, the authors emphasize the social costs associated with inadequate coordination. The actors comprise families, private enterprises, public authorities and a 'third sector', which includes organizations such as the Red Cross or Caritas. Each actor differs in terms of its governance rationales – prices, reciprocity, legislation – and of the dominant features of the goals it may pursue: formal, informal or content. The authors believe that, owing to the complexity of the services required, interaction, cooperation and networking are better coordinating instances than competition or central planning. The absence of a coordinating body, however, may prevent the achievement of an adequate integration among these actors and may favor an 'economic rationality' that leads to missed opportunities, narrow optimization and substitution effects. Thus, social costs do not depend, here, on some technical ability to coordinate these different actors. The real issue is to acknowledge that the motives and rationales of each type of actor are different and that reliance on business-centered ones tends to be inadequate. Obviously, while it would be reassuring to rely on a single criterion – such as that of market efficiency – coordination of different rationales is problematic. It raises the ethical issue of the social priorities to be chosen, thereby forsaking the apparent technical neutrality of the coordinator.

Neoliberal reliance on the market tends to neglect the prevalence of oligopolistic markets in a great many industries. The most dramatic aspect of market power in these industries is less their control over prices than their control over knowledge. The chapter by Angelo Gino Levis, Valerio Gennaro and Spiridione Garbisa stresses this point by discussing how major companies carry out or finance studies in their fields. The authors provide an overview of epidemiological research that investigates the relation between exposure to electromagnetic fields – mainly those related to power lines and cell phones – and a range of diseases such as leukemias and tumors. They point out that there is a very large and statistically significant gap between the results of publicly and privately funded research: The results of the former show that EMFs significantly affect health, whereas the results of the latter tend to be much more reassuring. Drawing on the oncologist Lorenzo Tomatis, the authors contend that the method used in a great many privately funded studies is 'to raise background noise, increasing confusion thereby making assessment of risk more difficult'. They argue that it is important to critically assess the scientific validity of these studies and they also refer to some guidelines to this end. But the main issue they point out is that both single scientists and international journals are involved in conflicts of interest. The most likely reason is that this is the only way for them to gain information from expensive research projects that the reduction of public funds precludes. The implications are far reaching: It is not only that users of mobile phones are unaware of the risks of diseases and that inefficient scientific research cannot provide insights on potential future improvements. The most important consequence is that collective decisions concerning how these commodities should be produced and made available are precluded by the corrupted scientific knowledge that vested interests explicitly pursue.

Social costs and freedom

In his conclusive chapter, Michele Cangiani establishes a strong link between the first and the second group of chapters. His discussion is centered on how the range of social costs discussed up to now diminishes the ability of people to choose how to conduct their lives, thereby reducing their freedom.

Cangiani initially focuses on a specific case – that of the recent redefinition of contractual agreements that the automobile-producing firm Fiat has imposed on its workers. Although formally workers accepted them, the alternative they were faced with was to lose their jobs. This episode is dramatic in its own right, but what is particularly important about it is that it teaches us a great deal about the general loss of freedom that is occurring through the crises.

Fiat did not achieve its goals just because of its threats. It also managed to be convincing on ideological grounds. First, a pro-business culture prevails and presents Fiat's strategy as a necessary response to external constraints. This issue was already discussed with regard to other chapters. In Cangiani's chapter its importance emerges with all of its dramatic consequences. Second, lenders and investors constitute what Chomsky has termed a 'virtual senate', which contrasts – through capital flights and other actions – any policy that does not favor business. It is that same 'senate' that underlies the speculation on government bonds discussed by Onaran and that conventional wisdom labels with a much more appealing term: financial markets. Third, the ideology underlying dominant economic thought evaluates the economy's performance in terms of the economy's internal criteria. Its closed-system perspective prevents it from carrying out an evaluation in terms of criteria arising from the (social) system that the economy is a part of.

These circumstances allow technocratic and unaccountable institutions to prevail in the management of the economy, at the expense of all countervailing powers, thereby favoring a 'collusion between a political patronage system and private economic interests' and a 'growing connivance between neoliberal and illiberal tendencies'. Under these conditions it is no surprise that people lose interest in political issues, and that this further undermines the democratic process. The general conclusion is that Fiat and business in general are successful not only because they force their vested interests upon the rest of society. A major determinant of their power is that, in so doing, they also preclude public deliberation over possible alternatives. On the one hand this reinforces their ideological grip as there is no alternative. On the other, social disruption weakens the scaffolding that democratic deliberation requires.

Social costs and policy

Despite the peculiarities of each type of social cost examined by the contributors to this book, they all have some common features. First, they all affect a great number of people. Second, they do not relate to allocative efficiency alone but have dramatic consequences in terms of distribution, employment and the stability of the economy. Third, these consequences affect the ability people have to participate in collective decision-making. Under these circumstances, democracy becomes a merely formal procedure that reinforces vested interests, i.e., those same sections of the economy that gain from the existence of social costs. Fourth, as a consequence, social costs tend to feed back on the economy, thereby reinforcing their negative effects.

This cumulative process raises important policy questions. While it is fairly reasonable to acknowledge that these costs exist and that they must be dealt with, how to do so is a much more controversial issue. Conventional scholars of social costs believe that policy-makers should either remove the imperfections of the market or find the relatively most efficient (cost-effective) way to cope with them. The canonical argument is that it is not enough to identify a problem; it is necessary to assess what the most convenient solution is. So, the argument goes, we must check that solutions – e.g., a Pigouvian tax – are not more costly than the problem they are supposed to solve. Although it is apparently reasonable, this argument focuses only on efficiency. Furthermore, it is based on the assumption that we should assess which solution is preferable by using market prices, i.e., precisely what is originating the problem. It is difficult to say what the practical implications of this logical flaw might be. Even if we were to accept the conventional view that prices provide all the information that is required to formulate relevant choices, when something does not work with the price mechanism and prices provide wrong information, there is no reliable second best and many odd choices may be deemed reasonable. What is sure is that it is difficult to believe that wrong prices may lead to right choices concerning how to mend the situation.

Conventional economists would probably reply in a pragmatic way by arguing that even though this is logically true, the existing price structure is all we have: Any action will produce its consequences according to the however-faulty relative prices that prevail at a given moment. But this is precisely what the chapters in this book argue against: Relative prices are by no means all we have. The correct assessment of the benefits and costs of any action requires more than that. It requires societal goals.

Societal goals are ethical goals. They inevitably exist always and everywhere. They have to do with how members of society wish to organize human life. Human life has much to do with material welfare, but it cannot be restricted to it.

It involves choices that lie beyond that dimension and that cannot be assessed in terms of relative prices. This issue is pointed out by Berger when he recalls Kapp's contention that human rights cannot be priced.

Societal goals, and the non-economic values they include, are not mere constraints on how material welfare is achieved. The material reproduction of society may be achieved in many ways. This is not a subject for some future society. Economic activity today is characterized by different types of coordination, as Ramazzotti points out in his contribution. The choice among them, thus among different criteria to produce and distribute resources, is possible and, indeed, is what underlies present decisions concerning the welfare state, as the chapters by Rizza and by Maier-Rigaud *et al.* explain through detailed analyses.

Capitalist market mechanisms do prevail, but it is open to doubt that this is due to iron laws of the economy. Certainly, there are vested interests in favor of the status quo. Once these prevail, the economy takes on an evolution of its own, as Wray recalls in his reference to Minsky. But this does not mean that economic policy cannot change existing priorities: The list of actions that Onaran provides suggests that it is surely possible to deal with the crisis, its social costs and the circumstances that determined it, provided we agree on different goals from those that prevail today. Similar considerations emerge from Couret Branco and Henriques in their discussion of how to deal with a natural resource such as water.

Capitalist market mechanisms also prevail for a variety of ideological reasons. One prominent determinant of pro-market ideologies is vested interests, as Frigato and Santos-Arteaga explain on theoretical grounds and as Levis *et al.* describe with respect to electromagnetic fields. It is possible to contrast this situation at different levels: first, by acknowledging that firms pursue money gains quite independently of serviceability; second, by allowing for research to be carried out that is not subject to vested interests; and third, by assessing research in the light of possible conflicts of interest.

Pro-market ideology is also the result of intellectual activity and can be contrasted on those same grounds, i.e., by questioning the way the economy is investigated both by theory and by economic actors. Jenning's suggestion is that by expanding the way we look at the economy – from short-run to long-run, from individualistic to social, common, collective, and from rivalry to coordination and cooperation – we can identify a range of potential economic arrangements that the prevailing ideology excludes.

Pro-market ideology, Vatn argues, is also favored by institutions that enhance individualistic behavior. It is, however, possible to privilege alternative institutions, which to some extent already exist: consider not-for profit firms, for instance, or networks that favor cooperation. The aim is to center the valuation of economic coordination on societal requirements either by embedding market coordination within a broader socio-political process, through meritorization (Elsner 2001), or resorting to forms of non-market coordination of economic activity.

As Cangiani points out, pro-market ideologies prevail when people give up pursuing change because they realize they are deprived of the freedom to choose how to conduct their lives. Such a freedom involves the ability to choose out of a given choice context, e.g., how to work – or consume – given the requirements of a given institutionalized arrangement of the economy. It also involves being able to decide which choice context is appropriate, and thus whether a different arrangement is preferable. Such a freedom has a private but also a public dimension, which consists in the ability to co-determine, with other members of society, the boundaries of individual freedom as well as the organization and coordination of interdependent activities.

Openness and change

These themes underlie a straightforward assumption concerning the systemic openness of the economy and of society. The economy is an open system because it exchanges energy and matter with the surrounding environment, but also because it is organized by people. People are economic actors – in that they produce and consume – but they are more than that. Despite attempts to reduce them to passive adaptors, people are proactive. They use this ability to solve economic problems, but also to provide answers to other questions, such as why and how they should live. They build a more or less consistent set of beliefs that constitute their culture. All of this affects the way they act and react in all of their individual and social activities. Openness does not consist of their creativity alone. It relates to the impossibility of defining once-and-for-all boundaries between what is economic and what is not. It implies that there is no single way to arrange the economy and the society it is a part of.

The circumstances that determine social costs show that, although these different arrangements are possible, their realization does not occur just through willpower. The chapters identify different institutional tiers and hint at the resulting complexity of the social environment. While this does not warrant desirable self-organizing properties, it does suggest that change must take account of the different tiers and their interdependence.

It is within this framework that institutions are situated. The above framework implies that no separation can be assumed between economic or non-economic institutions. Similarly, their effects on knowledge cannot be restricted to one of these fields alone. Just as in the case of firms, institutions cannot be properly understood if the distinction between an economy centered on serviceability and one centered on money gains is disregarded. Institutions cannot be reduced to a solution to the shortcomings of the market. Their impact on knowledge cannot be restricted to business goals. Any claim to convergence among different theoretical approaches that dismisses these issues is likely to mislead rather than achieve clarity.

The notion of systemic openness provides an intuitive answer to what society the book refers to. The existing society obviously is not a homogeneous community. Conflicts of interest exist and generic reference to societal goals is not meant to disregard them. No welfare function that makes everybody happy is assumed. But it is possible to conceive of different societal arrangements, based on whatever long-term ends are deemed appropriate: Just as there are no iron laws for the economy, there are no such laws for society. The societal arrangement that underlies the book is based on a clear value judgment, which draws on K. Polanyi and A. Lowe, as recalled by Cangiani: Freedom, in its two-fold dimension – private and public – is both a means and an end for any humane form of community.

References

Dowd, K. (2009) 'Moral hazard and the financial crisis', *Cato Journal*, 29(1): 141–166.
Elsner, W. (2001) 'Interactive economic policy: toward a cooperative policy approach for a negotiated economy', *Journal of Economic Issues*, 35(1): 61–83.
Kapp, K.W. (1978) *Social Costs of Business Enterprise*, Nottingham: Spokesman.
Kregel, J. (2009) 'Why don't the bailouts work? Design of a new financial system versus a return to normalcy', *Cambridge Journal of Economics*, 33: 653–663.
Mayhew, A. (2000) 'Veblen and theories of the "firm"', in Louçã, F. and Perlman, M. (eds.), *Is Economics an Evolutionary Science: The Legacy of Thorstein Veblen*, Cheltenham: Elgar, pp. 54–63.
Mirowski, P. (2010) 'Inherent vice: Minsky, Markomata, and the tendency of markets to undermine themselves', *Journal of Institutional Economics*, 6(4): 415–443.
Petit, P. (2010) 'The systemic nature of the rise in inequality in developed economies', *International Review of Applied Economics*, 24(3): 251–267.
Polanyi, K. (1944) *The Great Transformation*, New York: Holt, Rinehart & Winston.

Part I

Social costs

At the core of the capitalist economy

1 Social costs and normative economics[1]

Paolo Ramazzotti

Introduction

The aim of this chapter is to assess the notion of social costs from an evolutionary institutionalist perspective. It argues that: (1) social costs can be defined as the difference between the actual outcome of a historically defined capitalist market economy and the outcome desired by the members of society; (2) markets are only one of the possible coordinating instances in such economies, albeit the prevalent one, the others including non-profit organizations, the welfare state, households, etc.; (3) under these circumstances, the assessment and organization of economic activities requires a meta-coordinating instance, and the extension of capabilities, as theorized by Amartya Sen, may provide such an instance.

The chapter is organized as follows. The section that follows briefly recalls some of the themes of, and problems related to, the conventional theory of social costs. It stresses that the theory's exclusive focus on the market neglects important issues concerning how the market is arranged in the first place. It points out that, for these issues to be properly treated, it is necessary to draw on external – with respect to the market – assessment criteria and rules.

The subsequent section specifies the context of the discussion by situating it in a historically defined economy: a capitalist market one. It contends that the rationale of such an economy involves treating labor, nature and money as 'fictitious commodities', and that the existence of social costs ultimately depends on this central feature. Based on this approach, it discusses Kapp's suggestion that policy should focus on minimal social requirements. It points out, in this respect, that any policy that does not aim merely to constrain the market but wishes to take account of the criteria underlying other coordinating instances – such as the welfare state, non-profit organizations, families, etc. – must consider that each one functions according to a specific metric. Thus, a meta-metric is required to assess the economy as a whole and to coordinate the interaction among the different coordinating instances.

The fourth section, on social costs and society, discusses the nature of the required meta-metric. Its point of departure is Sen's presentation of the different criteria people resort to when they must choose. The discussion stresses that choices cannot be reduced to a single dimension – such as (economic) welfare – and that the economic context may preclude the freedom to choose how to conduct one's life. The implication is a qualification of the definition of social costs: They are determined by economic activities that prevent people from achieving the capabilities they need to choose how to conduct their lives. In this perspective, capabilities can be conceived of as a meta-metric to assess the performance of the economy.

The section on compatibilities and economists discusses the implications that an open-systems approach, such as the one the chapter leads to, has for public policy and for scholars wishing to devise the required measures. It contends that systemic openness is likely to involve more alternatives to the status quo than systemic closure. At the same time, it makes their identification difficult, owing to the complexity of the interdependence among sub-systems. In the light of these features, the discussion reasserts the need for a normative approach to economic inquiry. The final section draws the main conclusions.

Social costs and 'the market'

The conventional approach to social costs was to consider them as externalities. In so far as the market did not register all the effects of economic activity, some of these effects remained external to it. Externalities were the result of an imperfect price mechanism. The implication therefore was to make up for this failure. Whereas the Pigouvian solution consisted of government action to correct prices, given that they did not function properly, Coase argued that the market could be made to work properly.[2] The reason why the market did not work was that some property rights were not assigned. Once this problem was solved – i.e., once property rights were assigned – the market could resume its key function.[3]

This solution raised a problem, however. Who was to obtain the property rights? One answer was that they were to be assigned in order to achieve the most efficient outcome. Obviously, this answer would not make any sense in a perfect Walrasian market because any initial endowment allows a Pareto optimum to be achieved. In other words, it would not make any difference to assign a property right to one agent rather than another because efficiency would always follow.

Truly, owing to transaction costs, markets were claimed not to be perfect.[4] Given this imperfection, how can the potentially most efficient outcome be assessed? How do we know whether the output achieved through one solution will be higher than the one we would have achieved through an alternative one? The answer would seem to be that you assess efficiency according to existing relative prices. But those relative prices are biased. They reflect the inefficient allocation of resources achieved by an imperfect market, so they do not provide an appropriate criterion. In other words, when the allocation mechanism is imperfect, it is conducive to prices that provide inadequate information, and you cannot rely on them to correct the mechanism.

This problem was dismissed by stating quite simply that you should not try to fit actual markets to some ideal. In other words, it would be pointless to rely on what Demsetz (1969) labeled the 'Nirvana approach'.[5] What you could do was 'use an ideal norm to provide standards from which divergences are assessed for all practical alternatives of interest and select as efficient that alternative which seems most likely to minimize the divergence' (ibid.: 1). While this sounds reasonable, it does not say anything about what the ideal norm is or is supposed to be. If the norm still refers to the same notion of optimal allocation that is under attack, with the mere proviso that 'perfection is not of this world', this sounds sensible, but it certainly is not a theoretical innovation: anything is justifiable on these grounds. Conversely, if that notion of optimal allocation is discarded altogether, what are the grounds for a claim such as: 'The foundation of a private-ownership, market-based economy is its generally superior ability to work with resources as compared with central planners' (Demsetz 2008: 116), or even 'the state has a role to play' (ibid.)?

In the absence of an appropriate criterion, pragmatic reliance on 'relative' efficiency turns out to have no meaning whatsoever. Plausibly, it will refer to the mere convenience of self-interested agents, but such a criterion is not an alternative to the Nirvana approach: It simply denies that any phenomenon other than the immediate convenience of single agents is relevant. Paradoxically, the ultimate implication is that there simply is no scope for social costs: 'Society might be better off if the "problem" of social cost had never been discovered' (Rowley 1978: 13).

The above approaches are centered on the assumption that social costs exist because some things do not have a price tag. There are two reasons that may account for such a situation. The first one, which underlies the above approaches, is that the market does not function properly. The second one is that the market is simply unable to register some phenomena. An important example of this case occurs when some circumstances transcend the very rationale of the market. Consider human rights. Although we may conceive of a market where children are allowed to work so that a price (a wage) is determined for the 'child workforce' commodity, this situation clashes with the generally acknowledged right of children not to work. Thus, even though a price tag exists, it is still possible to claim that the way the market is arranged leads to a specific social cost on the grounds that child labor is inconsistent with social values.[6]

Whether child labor is allowed or not, the market functions subject to rules concerning the overall setup of the economy: Some transactions may be forbidden, some property rights may be denied, some other rights may be acknowledged. These rules underlie the legal–economic nexus which determines the boundaries and the specific features of the market.[7] Under these circumstances, there actually is no market as such, but a wide range of possible markets, each one defined by its legal–economic nexus. Furthermore, whatever the criterion used to define allocative efficiency, the latter will depend on the specific characteristics of the market as they are determined by the nexus. You cannot compare the efficiency of these different market setups, just as you cannot compare consumer choices associated to different lexicographic preferences. Another way to state this is that you cannot assess the efficiency of resource allocation independently of value judgments concerning the way that allocation should be arranged.[8]

While the more conventional views attach social costs to the malfunctioning of a given market, the approach outlined here stresses that the latter must meet requirements that are defined by society, i.e., that are independent of the market as such. In the traditional approach, social costs occur because of imperfections within the market; in the legal–economic nexus approach they occur because the external criteria that determine the way the market is arranged do not adequately reflect social values. Let us see why this may occur.

Social costs and the capitalist market economy

What market?

What metric do markets use? In general, markets tend to be considered coordinating instances based on relative prices. Even when we refer to markets in terms of contracted exchange, however, relative prices need not be the only possible, or indeed the actual, metric used. In order to continue our discussion, we therefore need to specify what kind of market we are talking about.

In what follows we refer to a capitalist market economy. In such an economy commodities are produced in order to obtain a money profit. Businesses acquire money that they use to pay for the materials and labor force required for production. Their aim is to sell the resulting commodities in order to gain an amount of money greater than the one originally advanced.[9] Businesses must make money. What they do with the money they gain is a secondary – and in the first instance, irrelevant – issue: indeed, the main goal is to increase the value of existing capital, not that of gaining access to ever more consumption goods.

Since the ultimate goal is to achieve a money gain, a commodity must be profitable to manufacture and sell: it must have an exchange value, which is conceptually distinct from its use value. If a commodity ceases to be profitable – if its exchange value is inadequate – it eventually will stop being produced. It is no surprise, therefore, that people may lack nutrition, shelter or health. Basic goods required to ensure these conditions may not be supplied because, although they may be desperately needed, it just may not be profitable to produce and sell them.

Three key commodities in capitalist economies – labor, nature and money – do not match this requirement: their supply does not reflect their profitability.[10] When the availability of workers exceeds their demand from businesses, workers do not cease to be produced and the price for labor may drop below subsistence or, alternatively, unemployment may ensue. The case may be that the economy's overall wage bill is not sufficient to pay for the subsistence of all available workers. Under these circumstances three situations may occur: people live in dire conditions and may even starve to death; people disrupt society in order to survive; or society somehow bears the cost of their subsistence. In the latter case there is a gap between the wage bill and the (overhead) cost that society must bear (Clark 1923; Stabile 1996). Obviously this would be labeled a social cost and it is no surprise that on many historical occasions the effort was made to restrict the 'allocation' of people as if they were a commodity.

Similar considerations apply to nature and money. Because the supply of natural resources is not determined as it is for normal commodities, their prices may lead to the irreversible depletion of the environment required for survival. Society will inevitably suffer the feedback of nature's disruption by bearing a cost that the economy does not take into account. Finally, the price of liquidity – thus, not only money but also financial assets – is often characterized by positive, rather than negative, feedbacks: As prices for these assets go up, their demand does not drop but rises along with supply, leading to the financial bubbles that have become so frequent over the past decades. The consequences may be both the over- or under-production of financial assets, and the resulting financial instability (Minsky 1957) will produce social costs such as lower incomes and unemployment.

Another feature of a capitalist market economy is worth pointing out. The pursuit of money gains involves continuous innovative activity. Innovation concerns production (in achieving economies of scale or scope, as well as gaining strategic control over the high value added phases), technology (through process and product innovation), marketing (through the identification of unsatisfied wants as well as through their very creation), finance (through the creation of new financial instruments, often with the aim of circumventing extant regulations)[11] and the 'rules of the game' underlying the legal–economic nexus. While innovative activity qualifies our discussion of how social costs arise, what is most important about it is that it continuously changes the boundaries of specific markets and of the market as a whole. Business constantly redefines not only property rights but the overall features of the legal–economic nexus.[12] It is therefore somewhat of an understatement to consider social costs as the consequences that bear on society because of economic activity. It is more appropriate to consider them as resulting from the specific features of the money-making rationale of the capitalist market. They are not just determined by the (insufficient or inappropriate) assignment of property rights or by an inadequate recognition of distributional issues by the legal–economic nexus. They result from the inconsistency between the constant attempt by business to maintain the commodity status of labor, nature and money and the persistence, over time, of a socially inclusive society. This is why Kapp's book deals with the social costs of *business enterprise*.

Business and minimal social requirements

Given these general premises, however, how are we to deal with the social costs that a capitalist market economy leads to? Kapp's (1978) suggestion is to define minimal social requirements that act as constraints on market practices. In practice, this prescription remains important and viable even though many oppose it on strictly ideological grounds. It suggests that the definition of a legal–economic nexus that avoids social costs basically is a matter of ethical choice.

On more general grounds, however, this suggestion may require a few qualifications. What are the minimal social requirements for pollution, for instance:

the probability of any minor affects or the probability of serious illness? Are only human concerns taken into account or should other forms of life be considered? What are the relevant probability intervals to decide when there actually is a risk? These are not strictly technical issues; they involve a value judgment, and who is to decide over these matters is a critical issue.

How to decide about these issues in no less a problem. Consider, for instance, the income-related cost of being unemployed. This can be dealt with in a variety of ways: workers may enjoy some type of private – for profit – insurance; the welfare state may provide them with subsidies by redistributing income; their families may support them; they may be assisted by some charitable – non-profit – association. Each type of solution affects the size and the arrangement of the market. When the scope of the market is restricted – i.e., when it does not coordinate all economic activities – alternative forms of coordination are required, based on criteria different from those underlying the market: families and charitable organizations generally operate on the basis of solidarity; welfare states may operate on the basis of solidarity and/or equity; central planning may resort to some notion of efficiency. Each type of coordination, in turn, requires an appropriate metric.

Although the market has a dominant role in a capitalist market economy, if other coordinating instances are assigned specific tasks, the issue arises of how these coordinating instances relate to each other. Obviously, if the goals pursued – and the criteria to assess them – differ, it is not appropriate to compare different coordinating instances. Thus, while it may be sensible to compare a private and a government-owned company in terms of their profitability when the sole task they are assigned is to make a profit, the same comparison is misleading if the two companies are assigned different tasks – for instance, if a government-owned company is assigned the task of establishing an infant industry that a private, profit-pursuing one would not deem convenient to set up. In the unemployment-related example above, while the company that provides private insurance needs to be profitable, a public agency may need, at the very least, to balance its budget and, under some circumstances, may even be a channel for a deficit-spending fiscal policy.

The relevance of this issue emerges especially when different goals – associated to different metrics – clash.[13] Indeed, a great deal of opposition to non-market coordinating instances is that they preclude the proper functioning of the market; consider, for instance, Okun's (1975) open bucket metaphor whereby there is a trade-off between equity and efficiency.[14]

A more relevant case is provided by Kalecki (1943), who argues that full employment policies eventually undermine the bargaining power of capitalists, thereby leading to negative expectations and a drop in investment. Whether the choice is between the desired goals (private profitability and full employment) or between alternative solutions to the clash, a criterion is required to choose. Granted that the clash arises because the goals pursued are based on different coordinating criteria and metrics, a meta-metric is required to judge what the best way to proceed is. In the limit case where no solutions to the clash exist, the choice may be between private profits (with unemployment) and full employment (with socialized investment).[15] The conventional view is to use the market metric as the meta-metric, which would lead to the choice of private investment. But while the choice of this metric is legitimate, it is neither the only one nor, a priori, the best one.

The clash between the rationale of the market and societal values is a distinctive feature of K. Polanyi's studies and of his notion of the double movement. According to Polanyi (1944; 1957), the self-regulating mechanism of contracted exchange renders the market autonomous relative to the society it is a part of. This autonomy eventually leads to the subordination of societal values and to a situation where the market is not embedded in society anymore; quite the contrary, it is society that is embedded in the market. The autonomy of the market determines a reaction from within society and the attempt to restore the subordination of the former to the latter. In some instances, this attempt may produce a stalemate that disrupts the polity and society. Although the implication is that the above problems tend to be less economical than political, some specifically economic considerations may be worth focusing on.

As I mentioned above, Kapp's (1978) and Polanyi's (1944) suggestion is that there are commonly accepted social priorities which should not be subordinated to the rationale of the market. They are not reducible to the money metric, so that economic accounts, whether of micro units or of a country as a whole, are inadequate when it comes to assessing social welfare. Indeed, if we think of nutrition, shelter or health, this would seem to be reasonable, although even these fundamental living conditions are far from being generally acknowledged to be social priorities.

This is where our discussion of the meta-metric is important. A criterion is required to identify societal priorities, i.e., what is wanted and what is not. It must not be bound to specific coordinating instances but it must take account of their existence. It must acknowledge that societal priorities may constrain the functioning of the market to the point that a clash is envisaged between the market metric – money profit – and non-market constraints. The function of a meta-metric, therefore, is to assess the overall priorities in the light of the different goals that markets and society pursue.

A meta-metric also allows the assessment of priorities when – as envisaged by Kapp – distinct social requirements are identified and coexist, each one dealing with a specific issue. This is particularly important when we take into account issues that are not strictly related to basic goods or elemental living conditions, such as urban congestion or car accidents.

As I shall argue later, the systemic openness of the economy does not warrant a mechanistic view of the market, whereby social constraints either allow or preclude its ability to coordinate some activities. Nonetheless, a coordination of different coordinating instances – e.g., markets, welfare state, non-profit organizations, households, etc. – is important to achieve consistency for the economy as a whole.

From the perspective here outlined, social costs can be depicted as the effects of business-related activities that are not only unwanted – according to some societal criterion – but also avoidable. The problem is how to assess what is unwanted and whether it is avoidable. I will discuss these issues in the following and subsequent sections.

Social costs and society

Economic agents or members of communities?

In conventional theory social costs may be deemed unwanted if a gap exists between individual and social welfare. Although it may be difficult in practice to measure these two types of welfare, they are conceptually clear in so far as they reflect utility maximization with given preferences.[16] While the origin of such preferences remains an open issue, the true problem with this approach is the restrictiveness of the assumption that only preferences matter for choice.

Sen (1982; see also Sen 1993; 1999) argues that there is no reason to believe that individuals choose on the basis of their preferences alone. Other criteria act upon choice. Thus, whereas I may want to smoke, so that utility maximization would require me to do precisely that, I may also be concerned that it is bad for my health or that it may be inappropriate to force other people to breathe my smoke.

Sen (1982) points out, in this respect, that individuals may be egoistic but they may also be concerned about other people's conditions. One type of concern is sympathy, which involves that the individual's personal welfare is directly affected by those conditions. In order to increase her personal welfare, the individual will behave so as to increase/reduce the welfare of the people she likes/ dislikes. Another type of concern is commitment. In this case, the individual's personal welfare is not directly involved. Her behavior depends on what she deems appropriate, independently of whether it will affect her welfare in one way or another.[17] This means that her general views of what is right and what is wrong may make her behave in a way that is inconsistent with her personal welfare.

Sympathy involves caring about others. Some people may care about human- ity as a whole, while others may care for nobody at all. In general, however, it is likely that sympathy will depend on how many people someone is in touch with, i.e., the number of people in her family, at work and in the other communities – religious, political, recreational, etc. – she is a member of. It will also depend on the intensity of her interaction with those people. Thus, her 'sympathetic' – as opposed to strictly egoistic – behavior will depend on the network of social rela- tions that she is embedded in.

Commitment involves a less emotional relationship between the individual and her surrounding environment. She need not care about other people but she does judge whether the world she lives in meets her moral expectations. What- ever her views of how things should be, they affect her behavior. In other words, once commitment is a possible feature of behavior, the individual inevitably chooses – explicitly or implicitly – whether to take account of circumstances that transcend her personal welfare. Commitment, however, depends not only on the moral conceptions of the individual – thus her views concerning how things should be – but on her understanding of how things actually are. For instance, her commitment against on-job mortality is likely to depend on how informed she is about such phenomena, thus on the availability of information and on her degree of literacy. Interaction with others – communication, dialogue, etc. – is also likely to affect her views. Just as for sympathy, her behavior depends on the social environment she is embedded in.

Given the above-depicted features of individual behavior, the criteria people resort to in order to assess the economy may depend on their egoistic wants but also on their views concerning what is appropriate for them (their needs), for their acquaintances or for society as a whole. Following the textbook representation of consumer behavior, for instance, a hungry individual may choose whether to eat meat or vegetables according to her taste for these types of food and to their (relative) price. She may also wish to take account of their nutritional characteristics, however, which means that, although she likes one type of food more than the other, she may eventually choose the other because it is healthier. On similar grounds, the consumer may like one type of food very much but may feel concerned, on humane or moral grounds, about working conditions in that industry: For instance, she might prefer to eat junk food because of its orga-noleptic qualities, but chooses not to eat it because the companies that supply it operate like sweatshops.

Thus, the consumer may choose in relation to quite a few variables. Depending on which variables she deems important, she may rank all her actions in more than one way. In other words, what she chooses to do depends not only on her preferences but on her meta-preferences as well.

Let us continue to look at our consumer. Given her moral views concerning how workers are treated, her behavior need not be restricted to the choice between eating junk food or substituting it with some other food. In order to make sure that the food people buy meets her humane requirements, she may choose to involve public opinion. She may also act in order to have new laws passed against working conditions she deems unacceptable.

The same applies to a worker. She may bargain over the money that the firm must pay her, but she may also be concerned about the real value of her wage, with all that this implies in terms of business strategy as well as industrial and macroeconomic policy. Her concern may even transcend her direct gain and include what the firm does: whether the products it manufactures are safe; whether it carries out strategies that may be harmful to the community (e.g., the way it builds and manages an oil rig in the Gulf of Mexico); whether it invests in oil-derived fuels rather than in less polluting types of energy.

This leads us to the conclusion that the classical separation between the individual as a consumer and the individual as a citizen does not hold. When people do not like a commodity simply because it does not meet their preferences, they choose not to buy it. When they believe that the same commodity may be harmful for the health of the community or that it may clash with the moral concerns of others, they may well choose to inform and convince others not to buy those goods. In this case they are neither just voting with their money, i.e., by buying one good rather that another, nor are they (necessarily) acting through the polity, i.e., choosing policy-makers who will eventually change the market according to what meta-preferences – values, in this case – prevail. They are conducting direct actions to promote a different understanding – and, eventually, a different arrangement – of the economy. They are disrupting the conventional separation between economy and polity.

Three points are worth noting, here. First, since individuals choose according to different criteria – strict self-interest, sympathy, commitment – it is not possible to draw conclusions concerning their personal welfare from what they buy. Furthermore, precisely because they may be concerned about circumstances that lie beyond the price and quality of the goods they can buy – when someone thinks about switching the television on in order to relax, she may also be concerned about whether the required electricity is generated with a polluting technology – their choices may involve more information than the market is fit to supply. Extra-market information is just as important as market information. In fact, in many cases people not only need information *from* the market, they also need information *about* the market.

The second point is that, since people cannot formulate satisfactory decisions on the basis of preferences alone, the very criteria underlying choice need not be mutually consistent,[18] so that there is more to choosing than just processing information in order to achieve maximization. It is no wonder, therefore, that, according to Sen (2004: 4): 'Rationality is interpreted here, broadly, as the discipline of subjecting one's choices – of actions as well as of objectives, values and priorities – to reasoned scrutiny.' This 'loose' conception of rationality reflects the condition whereby people may have a bounded understanding of the world they live in, especially if their social and institutional environment prevents them from taking advantage of all possible opportunities.

An extreme case of bounded understanding is provided by Sen's (1999) example of a woman who, having internalized her subordinate role in society, cannot imagine that an alternative to the status quo is possible – she will be content with what she has rather than lamenting the situation she is in. Truly, she does not suffer any dilemma. She is unaware of her unawareness. But this is not the outcome of a choice of hers; her bounded understanding prevents her from identifying an appropriate choice context.

It is important to consider that the same type of problem may prevent people from identifying social costs, i.e., they may be unable to realize that some unwanted effects of business-related activity are also avoidable. Whether an individual is obliged to take the status quo for granted or is able to conceive of possible alternatives depends on her capabilities, i.e., on the set of possible combinations of actions that she can take.

The final point is that the conceptual distinction between the economic and the ethical dimensions does not mean that they are separated in practice. Business does not just comply with the wants of its customers. It also tries to change those wants by acting on how customers understand their choice context. In so far as it wishes to direct the polity to its advantage, it acts on the ethical and political views of the citizenry. More generally, people – be they businessmen or plain citizens – do not only vote for policy-makers so that the latter set the rules of the game that those same people will eventually play as economic agents. People interact by communicating, discussing and scrutinizing each others' views in order to assess whether the economy – and the polity – match their overall views and concerns. They may act directly to change the existing setup of the economy, in its factual if not legal aspects. The distinction between 'rules of the game' and 'game' should not be mistaken for a separation; the rules of the game are determined *while* the game is played, sometimes by *how* the game is played. They may reflect egoism, sympathy, commitment.

These three points are different ways to look at one issue: Markets are not systemically closed and what economic agents do cannot be understood independently of the more general (historical, social and natural) environment they are a part of. The relevance from the perspective of social costs is that these costs cannot be identified in terms of market-related welfare as in the conventional approach. Pigou's (1932) original distinction between economic and general welfare is misleading even as a working hypothesis. What people view as their welfare depends on how they relate to the world they live in.

Capabilities and social costs

This leads us to a rather important conclusion. The definition of social costs, in terms of a gap between potential and actual welfare, implicitly acknowledges that, as I mentioned above, they must be unwanted and avoidable. But in order to be unwanted, they must be identified, and in order to be identified people must have the appropriate capabilities. So, along with the social costs Kapp and Polanyi had in mind, which were basically related to elemental living conditions, a new category emerges from the above discussion. Social costs include the lack of capabilities that prevents people from being aware of possible welfare improvements. We might refer to this as the lack of capabilities that prevents people from being aware of that very lack of capabilities.

When people have the capabilities that allow them to find out what their potential welfare is, another category of social costs can be identified. These costs are associated to negative effects that were not previously perceived or that were considered as the inevitable side-effects of some desired goal. Let us consider these in greater detail by going back to a question asked before: are car accidents a social cost?

From a conventional perspective, it is possible to argue that the probability of a car accident can be computed, or at least figured out. Whoever chooses to use a car therefore knows that she is taking that risk and is, even if implicitly, assessing the costs and benefits of such a choice. In other words, she is aware that, although cars have (potentially) negative effects, it may nonetheless be worthwhile to use them. The question this approach does not address is whether an alternative is possible. Are less dangerous cars possible? Could public transport substitute private transport and reduce the risk of accidents?

Obviously, I am not concerned with these questions as such. What I wish to point out is that people need not be – and often are not – concerned with the 'here and now' alone. They may want to think about possible alternatives and pursue them. Under these circumstances, even though people currently use cars and, given the present circumstances, would not think of doing without them, it makes sense to ask whether some different arrangement of economic activity would be more desirable. If we acknowledge that cars have negative effects and that some envisaged alternative may be less damaging, then it is appropriate to classify car accidents as a social cost; the envisaged alternative may change people's views as to the inevitability of their use.

Alternatives that appear to be better than the status quo may eventually turn out not to be so. Decisions are taken *ex ante*, which always implies some degree of uncertainty. This applies in all cases, including the choice of maintaining cars rather than opting for the alternatives. What is important, however, is that people must be able to question the status quo, seek alternatives, assess them in terms of a meta-metric they deem appropriate and, finally, choose how to proceed. The identification of these types of social costs, therefore, is the outcome of a deliberative process. People must be able to understand what is at stake and to judge according to their value systems. In this sense, while the previous types of social cost can be classified as 'basic' social costs, in that they preclude the very possibility to choose how to conduct one's life, this type of cost can be classified as a 'freedom-related' cost, in that it emerges as a result of the freedom that people acquire.

The distinction between these two types of social costs may give the impression that they can be dealt with independently of one another and, possibly, that the 'freedom-related' ones are not as important as the basic ones. The fact is that basic social costs can be identified precisely because they prevent people from choosing how to conduct their lives. In other words, they prevent the identification of freedom-related social costs. In this perspective, the freedom to choose how to conduct one's life – and to identify freedom-related costs – is an end in terms of which it is possible to identify basic social costs. It is a term of reference to assess the performance of the economy and of economic policy.

The removal of social costs requires a decision concerning which coordinating instance is more appropriate to carry out each type of economic activity. The decision does not involve a mere reorganization of the market but a redefinition of the relation between the market and other components of the economy such as the welfare state, non-profit organizations, families, etc. By defining the boundaries of the market and how it must interact with these other components, it therefore determines what is deemed the appropriate degree of systemic openness of the market. In Polanyian terms, this involves determining not only whether, but also *how*, the market must be embedded in society. In so far as the removal of social costs affects the way that distinct components of society interact, it impacts on the social, as well as on the material, reproduction of society.

Compatibilities and economists

In the previous section I argued that it is possible to decide whether and how some features of the economy are unwanted. Let us now consider whether they can be deemed avoidable.

Economic theory has long discussed the failure of a capitalist market economy to achieve desired goals such as full employment, growth stability, a socially just distribution of income and wealth, ecological sustainability and other aspects of economic welfare. In most instances what emerged was that public action was required and that, in some instances, it led to positive sum outcomes: full employment policies would provide more jobs to workers but would also raise the profits of firms; welfare provisions improved the living standards of people but, in so doing, increased social cohesion, thereby leading to higher productivity and to positive expectations by investors. In many cases the relationship between efficiency and equity turned out to be a synergy rather than a trade-off. Market-centered criteria were consistent with the ends derived from other, non-market, criteria.[19]

Granted that these issues are very important, it is also important to consider that social goals may be more far reaching and/or that, in some instances, they may be inconsistent with market goals. What conventional economists connote as trade-offs do occur. What is wrong with the notion of trade-off is not that different goals may clash, but the a priori pretense that the choice between them should be based on relative prices, i.e., on a market metric.

The theoretical suggestion underlying the approach of this chapter is that social accounting should be based on a criterion – the social inclusion and empowerment of all the members of a community – that is distinct from the conventional market-centered one. More specifically, the key contention is that social costs arise precisely when the use of the latter criterion contrasts the goals that the former would put forward. It is not possible to separate the areas that these criteria refer to because, although, as I argued above, a capitalist market economy has a rationale of its own, it is nonetheless part of an open (nearly decomposable; Simon 1981) system and, in one way or another, interacts with the other sub-systems. What is at issue, therefore, is – following Polanyi (1944) – what kind of interaction should prevail, i.e., whether social priorities should subsume the economy or the other way round.

The conventional view considers that some problems may be solved either by constraining the economy (usually at a cost) or by relying on the resources that the economy makes available. Systemic openness,[20] on the other hand, suggests that this mechanistic view is misleading, and that the economy may be arranged in a variety of ways. It suggests that we may grasp a broader view of how the economy affects the social and natural environment. An economic system is open because it interacts with its surrounding environment, through the exchange of matter, energy or information. Consequently, the economy affects the quality of life not only through prices and the supply of goods and services. It also affects it through the feedbacks of the social and natural environment. Racism, as Myrdal (1962) pointed out years ago, is an economic phenomenon not just because it reflects the way the economy is organized, but also because it feeds back on the quality of life either by acting on strictly economic variables such as prices and the provision of goods and services or by determining undesired consequences such as a shorter life expectancy. The same applies to completely different phenomena such as the depletion of the ozone layer or what is generally called international peace keeping.

Precisely because of systemic openness, the effects of economic policy may affect the overall quality of life. Given the strong relation between the material and the social reproduction of society, it is most likely that different arrangements will affect sections of society in different ways.[21] Negative reactions to change are definitely possible. Actions that aim to protect vested interests, however, should not be confused with technical impediments to change. The dynamic nature of a capitalist market economy implies that whenever business is constrained it seeks new ways to achieve its money gains. In some instances they consist of new economic activities that overcome the constraints, in others they consist of rent seeking to bypass them. The evolutionary nature of this process entails that there is no arrangement that avoids social costs once and for all, but, as Stanfield and Carrol (2009: 11) point out, 'While it is true that any regulatory scheme tends to bring forth efforts to evade control, this only means that regulation must be continuously reformed not that it must be abandoned.'

A critical issue, however, is whether – quite apart from social and political reactions – technical impediments to economic change exist and what they consist of. In order to clearly understand what is at issue, note that the openness of the economy involves myriad possible variables which may or may not interact in a variety of ways at any given moment. In other words, the openness we are concerned with is characterized by complexity,[22] whereby 'An open system is one where not all of the constituent variables and structural relationships are known or knowable, and thus the boundaries of the system are not known or knowable' (Dow 1996: 14).

This specific aspect of systemic openness provides quite a few insights. First, since the boundaries of a system are never given once and for all,[23] it is not possible to provide a once and for all assessment of how constraining a given structure actually is. More specifically, in so far as the system is engrained in a historical process, these boundaries are subject to change in rather unpredictable ways. As Schumpeter (1911) argued a century ago, capitalism involves a process of creative destruction – that is, a constant rearrangement not only of how available resources are used but also of how they are produced. Although his analysis was restricted to business in a capitalist market economy, it does suggest that change occurs, and sometimes in most unpredictable ways. Indeed, the a priori assumption that technical impediments cannot be overcome is at odds with the historical record of the evolution of technology.

Second, aside from how it affects a system's boundaries, it is the very nature of novelty that is unpredictable. The learning process, whereby the structural relationships become knowable, is itself an open system. This means that human learning allows people to identify connections, relations and potential innovations as it proceeds. Human learning need not be bounded by the extant boundaries of the economy, it may transcend them, thereby affecting society as a whole. Market-oriented entrepreneurs need not be the only innovators. What appears to be an impediment today may turn out not to be so in a subsequent period.

Third, systemic openness involves the need to establish heuristic boundaries in order to make sense of reality: Although everything is connected to everything else, you must eventually choose when to conclude – if momentarily – your inquiry, thus what will fit in and what will be left out of it. Hence, when you choose to investigate an issue and you attempt to identify what is relevant to that end, you can never be sure that you are not missing something. Models that depict the economy are possible only in so far as they formulate assumptions on some structural features of the economy. These assumptions allow us to grasp aspects of the economy but the extent to which we should take them for granted depends on how far we are willing to go in order to achieve our goals. In other words, while in a closed system one may expect no other structure to be possible, in an open system such a belief would be unwarranted. The acceptance of a given structure – which ultimately means that one chooses to abstain from further investigations on possible alternatives – is discretionary; it is a matter of value judgment. It depends on the questions we ask and the priorities we set. It ultimately reflects our (moral) value judgments, concerning what we wish to achieve, and our (cognitive) value judgments,[24] concerning how we expect to grasp the reality we live in: 'Valuations are always with us. Disinterested research there has never been and can never be. Prior to answers there must be questions. There can be no view except from a viewpoint. In the questions raised and the viewpoint chosen, valuations are implied' (Myrdal 1978: 778–779).

Systemic openness suggests that alternatives to the status quo may exist, but the very nature of openness prevents us from identifying them in terms of an organic and consistent arrangement. Owing to the great many interdependencies there are in a society, a new societal setup may be difficult, if not impossible, to envisage.

In most instances the existing organization of the economy and of society simply does not allow people to envisage possible changes, thereby leading to a view of the world which very much resembles that of the subordinate woman discussed by Sen. Even if we leave aside this extreme case, it is worthwhile to recall that the above discussion of sympathy and commitment emphasized that these types of behavior – thus, the choices they involve – depend on the social environment individuals are embedded in. This embeddedness, in turn, depends on the capabilities that the environment warrants.[25]

Viewed from this perspective, social costs are not the peculiarities or theoretical conundrums that lie at the margins of economics. They are the key issues for whoever investigates the economy in order to establish a more humane society. They have to do not with marginal changes in an otherwise 'well behaved' economy, but with issues such as unemployment, lack of basic education, unhealthy living conditions, on-job accidents, lack of proper housing and unfair income and wealth distribution[26] that prevent people from choosing how to conduct their lives.

Efforts to remove social costs and the structural constraints that are associated with them greatly depend on the willingness of scholars to consider these issues as the points of reference for any change in the direction of a more humane society. In other words, only a normative approach to economics will allow scholars to go beyond the boundaries that conventional knowledge sets and to deal with Keynes' remark that 'The difficulty lies, not in the new ideas, but in escaping from the old ones, which ramify [...] into every corner of our minds' (Keynes 1936: xxiii).

Conclusion

The notion of social cost is still open to debate. Different theoretical approaches tend to look at the issue in different ways. This would not be a problem if it testified to the liveliness of economic thought and debate. Unfortunately, this is not always the case. The variety of treatments of the social cost issue reflects the neglect of some approaches, thus the persistence of open issues. It is somewhat daunting that Kapp's work should be ignored by well-known scholars, despite his important contribution to this topic.

This chapter has tried to put together some of the key issues that emerge from the literature. It did not pretend to provide a full-fledged survey. It did try to point out some major shortcomings in the theoretical debate which remain to be discussed. The key issue the chapter focused on is the need for a criterion to assess the performance of the economy. Given the internal inconsistencies of the mainstream approaches outlined at the outset, it focused on the contributions of Kapp, Polanyi and Sen. It pointed out that while it is important to understand how markets function in a capitalist market economy, the latter cannot be reduced to them. Economic activity is coordinated by a range of other subsystems, each one according to its priorities and criteria. This raises coordination problems for whoever wishes to carry out a policy that avoids social costs. It also raises the question: What are the priorities of society as a whole?

Amartya Sen's notion of capabilities provides important insights on what public policy should be concerned about, which provides the basis for a depiction of social costs as the negative effects that the capitalist market economy has on capabilities. This notion of social costs encompasses Kapp's, and in practical terms it would be difficult, today, to distinguish the policy implications that the two approaches would have for most countries. It goes beyond Kapp's notion of minimal social requirements, however. On the one hand, it suggests that the struggle against social costs should not consist only of constraining markets, but that it involves an active coordination of the economy as a whole. On the other, it suggests that, given the present economic and environmental crises, a clearer view of what the policy objectives are – from the social cost perspective – will contribute to the avoidance of the dramatic stalemate – pointed out by Polanyi – that the clash between market requirements and societal values may lead to.

Notes

1 A preliminary version of this chapter was presented at recent EAEPE, STOREP and AISSEC conferences. I wish to thank all the participants who commented on it. I also wish to thank Michele Cangiani, Wolfram Elsner, Vinicio Guidi and Pietro Frigato for their comments. The usual disclaimer applies.

2 Aguilera Klink (1994), however, argues that the antagonism between Pigou and Coase is overstated and should be traced back to how Coase's followers interpreted his views.

3 Even when this was not possible, institutional setups were to reflect the market requirements of the actors involved (cf. Coase 1988a).

4

> What I showed in 'The Problem of Social Cost' was that, in the absence of trans-action costs, it does not matter what the law is, since people can always negotiate without cost to acquire, subdivide, and combine rights whenever this would increase the value of production.... Cheung has even argued that, if transaction costs are zero, 'the assumption of private property rights can be dropped without in the least negating the Coase Theorem' and he is no doubt right.
>
> (Coase 1988b: 14–15)

5

> In practice, those who adopt the nirvana viewpoint seek to discover discrepancies between the ideal and the real and if discrepancies are found, they deduce that the real is inefficient. Users of the comparative institution approach attempt to assess which alternative real institutional arrangement seems best able to cope with the economic problem.
>
> (Demsetz 1969: 1)

6 Passas and Goodwin (2004) provide an extensive treatment of situations such as the ones discussed here. The title of their book – *It's Legal but it Ain't Right* – vividly stresses the inconsistency between various economic practices and the values of society.

7

> There are no absolute or given costs, only a cost–price structure which is a func-tion of the interplay of demand and supply, which in turn is a function of the opportunity–set structure which in turn is a function of the power (rights) structure.
>
> (Samuels and Schmid 1997: 234; see also Bromley 1989)

8 Based on this view, the reason why the assignment of a property right was problem-atic in the Coasian case was that no such value judgment was formulated.

9 Marx referred to this as an expanded economic reproduction, i.e., one based on an M–C–M' (Money–Commodity–Money + surplus) process. You begin with money that you use to buy commodities which will have to be transformed into new commodi-ties. These will eventually be sold in order to obtain a greater amount of money. This process is contrasted to simple reproduction, i.e., a C–M–C process, where commodi-ties are turned into money only to obtain other commodities. Note that a third process is also possible where production is left out because the ultimate goal of making money may be achieved without it. The process then becomes M–M', financial specu-lation being a special, if prominent, example. A major implication of these qualifica-tions is that the goal that business pursues is not profit alone but wealth, where the latter includes all other money gains that are not associated to production.

10 Polanyi (1944) refers to them as 'fictitious commodities'.

11 Innovation in production is generally associated with the pursuit of profit through changes in technology and in the impact of transaction costs. An insightful alternative approach, from a business-oriented perspective, is provided by Jacobides and Winter

(2007), who stress that money profit is only one possible type of money gain and that the pursuit of rents may be much more important than action on technology and costs. For innovation in finance, see Minsky (1957).

12 Under these circumstances, reliance on *ex ante* restrictions reflects a substantial neglect of the key role that innovation has in modern capitalism.

13 Different goals and different coordinating instances need not clash, as I will argue later. Such a circumstance, however, is not warranted.

14 Despite its importance in the literature and its intuitive appeal, the metaphor is based on an assumption that is seldom made explicit and that greatly reduces its generality: While different goals may happen to be mutually inconsistent – or at least, they may cause friction – the notion of a trade-off implicitly assumes that the metric required to assess the problem is relative prices. It therefore takes the extant distribution as the terms of reference, whereas what the equity issue suggests is that it is precisely that specific distribution which is at the root of the problem.

15 On strictly economic grounds, private profits would be enhanced by a higher level of aggregate demand, so that there would seem to be no reason to claim that full employment clashes with private profitability. This is why Kalecki specifically refers to these issues as *political aspects* of full employment.

16 I do not wish to downplay the difficulties associated with the dramatic conclusions of Arrow's Impossibility Theorem. What I wish to argue is that major problems lie elsewhere.

17 Sen (1982) provides the example of torture. If we are against it because we suffer for the people who are tortured, that is sympathy. If we believe that torture should be banned because it is wrong, even though we may not be affected by what tortured people must bear, that is commitment.

18 As Hirschman (1984) points out, an individual's views on some action – such as smoking – generally reflect different types of judgment.

19 One of the reasons why Italian industrial districts intrigued many scholars is that they seemed to allow for the convergence of interests between a community of people and a population of firms (Becattini 1990). The fragility of this convergence is discussed in Ramazzotti (2010).

20 See Kapp (1976) for a discussion of the 'open-system character of the economy and its implications'.

21 As Etzioni points out, conflict is indeed possible but, while it does lead to change, it need not be disruptive of a social community:

> We see room for conflicts *within* a community; classes *within* society. And while any other societal structure or equilibrium may be upset, society as a community needs to be maintained as a context for the particular collectivities, to encapsulate conflict, to avoid total war. In short, structures may be changed but society cannot be avoided.
>
> (Etzioni 1988: 216; emphases in the original).

22 'Roughly, by a complex system I mean one made up of a large number of parts that interact in a nonsimple way' (Simon 1981: 195).

23 'An open system is one where not all of the constituent variables and structural relationships are known or knowable, and thus the boundaries of the system are not known or knowable' (Dow 1996: 14).

24 A discussion of these two types of value judgments can be found in Ramazzotti (2012).

25 This issue is stressed from a different but interesting perspective by Davis (2009).

26 In a nutshell, one could simply refer to the Universal Declaration of Human Rights, especially from article 20 onwards (cf. United Nations 1948).

References

Aguilera Klink, F. (1994) 'Pigou and Coase reconsidered', *Land Economics*, 70(3): 386–390.

Becattini, G. (1990) 'The Marshallian industrial district as a socio-economic notion', in Pyke, F., Becattini, G. and Sengenberger, W. (eds.), *Industrial Districts and Inter-firm Cooperation in Italy*, Geneva: International Institute for Labour Studies.

Bromley, D.W. (1989) *Economic Interests and Institutions: The Conceptual Foundations of Public Policy*, New York: Blackwell.

Clark, J.M. (1923) *Studies in the Economics of Overhead Cost*, Chicago: University of Chicago Press.

Coase, R.H. (1988a) 'The lighthouse in economics', in *The Firm, the Market, and the Law*, Chicago: University of Chicago Press.

Coase, R.H. (1988b) 'The firm, the market, and the law', in *The Firm, the Market, and the Law*, Chicago: University of Chicago Press.

Davis, J.B. (2009) 'The capabilities conception of the individual', *Review of Social Economy*, 67(4): 413–429.

Demsetz, H. (1969) 'Information and efficiency: another viewpoint', *The Journal of Law and Economics*, 12(1): 1–22; reprinted in (1991) *Efficiency, Competition and Policy: The Organization of Economic Activity*, Cambridge, MA: Blackwell.

Demsetz, H. (2008) *From Economic Man to Economic System: Essays on Human Behavior and the Institutions of Capitalism*, Cambridge: Cambridge University Press.

Dow, S.C. (1996) *The Methodology of Macroeconomic Thought*, Cheltenham: Edward Elgar.

Etzioni, A. (1988) *The Moral Dimension: Toward a New Economics*, New York: The Free Press.

Hirschman, A.O. (1984) 'Against parsimony: three easy ways of complicating some categories of economic discourse', *The American Economic Review*, 74(2): 89–96.

Jacobides, M.G. and Winter, S.G. (2007) 'Entrepreneurship and firm boundaries: the theory of a firm', *Journal of Management Studies*, 44: 7.

Kalecki, M. (1943) 'Political aspects of full employment' *Political Quarterly*, 14(4): 322–330.

Kapp, K.W. (1976) 'The open-system character of the economy and its implications', in Dopfer, K. (ed.), *Economics in the Future: Towards a New Paradigm*, London: Macmillan; reprinted in Kapp, K.W. (1985) *The Humanization of the Social Sciences*, edited by Ulman, J.E. and Preiswerk, R., Lanham: University Press of America.

Kapp, K.W. (1978) *Social Costs of Business Enterprise*, Nottingham: Spokesman.

Keynes, J.M. (1936 [1973]) *The General Theory of Employment, Interest and Money*, London: Macmillan.

Minsky, H.P. (1957) 'Central banking and the money market', *Quarterly Journal of Economics*, 71(2): 171–187; reprinted as in Minsky, H.P. (1982) 'Central banking and money market changes', in *Can 'It' Happen Again? Essays on Instability and Finance*, New York: M.E. Sharpe.

Myrdal, G. (1962) *An American Dilemma: The Negro Problem and Modern Democracy*, New York: Harper & Row.

Myrdal, G. (1978) 'Institutional economics', *Journal of Economic Issues*, 12(4): 771–784.

Okun, A.M. (1975) *Equality and Efficiency: The Big Tradeoff*, Washington, DC: The Brookings Institution.

Passas, N. and Goodwin, N. (eds.) (2004) *It's Legal but it Ain't Right: Harmful Consequences of Legal Industries*, Ann Arbor: University of Michigan Press.

Pigou, A.C. (1920 [2009]) *The Economics of Welfare*, New Brunswick: Transaction Publishers.

Polanyi, K. (1944) *The Great Transformation*, New York: Holt, Rinehart & Winston.

Polanyi, K. (1957) 'The economy as instituted process', in Polanyi, K., Arensberg, C.M. and Pearson, H.W. (eds.), *Trade and Market in the Early Empires: Economies in History and Theory*, Glencoe: The Free Press.

Ramazzotti, P. (2010) 'Industrial districts and economic decline in Italy', *Cambridge Journal of Economics*, 34(6): 955–974.

Ramazzotti, P. (2012) 'The "solitude of the reformist": public policy and value judgments in the work of Federico Caffè', *History of Economic Ideas*, 1.

Rowley, C.K. (1978) 'Prologue', in Cheung, S.N.S., *The Myth of Social Cost: A Critique of Welfare Economics and the Implications for Public Policy*, London: The Institute of Economic Affairs.

Samuels, W.J. and Schmid, A.A. (1997) 'The concept of cost in economics', *The Economy as a Process of Valuation*, Cheltenham: Edward Elgar.

Schumpeter, J.A. (1911) *Theorie der wirtschaftlichen Entwicklung*, Leipzig: Duncker & Humblot. Reprinted as (1961) *The Theory of Economic Development: An Inquiry into Profits, Capital, Credit, Interest and the Business Cycle*, New York: Oxford University Press.

Sen, A. (1982) 'Rational fools: a critique of the behavioural foundations of economic theory', in *Choice, Welfare and Measurement*, Oxford: Basil Blackwell, pp. 84–106.

Sen, A. (1993) 'Capability and well-being', in Nussbaum, M.C. and Sen, A. (eds.), *The Quality of Life*, Oxford: Clarendon Press.

Sen, A. (1999) *Development as Freedom*, New York: Alfred Knopf.

Sen, A. (2004) 'Introduction: rationality and freedom', in *Rationality and Freedom*, Cambridge, MA: Harvard University Press.

Simon, H.A. (1981) 'The architecture of complexity', in *The Sciences of the Artificial*, Cambridge, MA: MIT Press.

Stabile, D.R. (1996) *Work and Welfare: The Social Costs of Labor in the History of Economic Thought*, Westport: Greenwood Press.

Stanfield, J.R. and Carroll, M.C. (2009) 'The social economics of neoliberal globalization', *Forum for Social Economics*, 38: 1–18.

United Nations (1948) *The Universal Declaration of Human Rights*, www.un.org/en/documents/udhr/index.shtml (accessed 21 September 2010).

2   Institutions, rationality and social costs[1]

Arild Vatn

Introduction

As the economy expands, the interdependencies between the economy and its environment are becoming more and more evident. We have now reached a situation where the size and form of our activities may endanger core functionalities of the environment – e.g., climate change and biodiversity loss – potentially threatening the long-term sustainability of the economy itself.

A core question related to this is whether we have organized the economy in a way that allows us to treat these issues in a good manner. As problems are mounting, we need to ask what is causing them and what alternatives are available to avoid them or handle them better. The aim of this chapter is to shed some light on how the way we structure the economy and its interface with wider society influences the magnitude and treatment of social costs. I will also try to outline a direction we could take to effectively reduce the level of such costs.

Fundamentally, the environment in which our economy operates is a system of interlinked processes. This is an essential aspect of the biosphere, exchanging matter and energy through an extensive set of processes. When we utilize environmental resources – both when we extract resources and when we release matter and energy back into the environment as waste – the effects of our actions are therefore spread far beyond the bounds of our immediate activities. Hence, human actions are interdependent. There is no way we can avoid this. We may, however, be better at institutionally connecting actions that are physically connected by necessity.

As the environment is common to humanity, using it demands coordination of the various activities we undertake. This concerns both which interests and values we decide to protect and how demanding it is to coordinate our actions to ensure that protection. These issues are foremost institutional questions. I will start by briefly presenting a perspective on the economy as an institutional system, emphasizing aspects that are important when we try to handle interdependencies. Next I will use these insights in an analysis of how institutional structures influence what becomes efficient or alternatively what becomes a social cost. Thereafter I will discuss the role of institutions in fostering cooperation. Finally, I will try to bring the different elements together in a discussion about which direction to take when forming institutions that could seriously reduce the level of social costs.

Before I start, a brief comment on language is required. The present book is based on understanding social costs as the difference between exchange/ market value and social value – e.g., Kapp (1971). It departs from standard 'externality theory' in seeing external costs not just as some accidental or peripheral 'add on' to the core of the economic process, but as costs defined by the firm-market system itself. Using markets as the reference point is certainly relevant, given present institutions and the state of theory. Nevertheless, one should acknowledge that any system will face difficulties with ensuring that all costs are properly included when making decisions. A more universal defini- tion would hence be to see social costs as social value that is not captured by the system in place. The general challenge is to ensure these costs are minimized.

Institutions and the economy

Institutions can be defined as the conventions, norms and legal rules of a society (Scott 1995; Vatn 2005). One may distinguish between the three categories, emphasizing the dimensions of coordination and conflict. Conventions can be seen as pure coordination devices – e.g., measurement scales of time and space. Norms, on the other hand, distinguish themselves by protecting values through emphasizing what should or should not be done – e.g., the value of equality as protected by norms of sharing. Values and interests may be in conflict. If norms are found to be too weak to handle such conflicts, we may observe a turn to legal rules – e.g., rules backed by the power of the state (third person).

Institutions are important in structuring economies. They define a common set of conventions that make interaction possible – e.g., money and measurement of weight and volume. They define norms about, e.g., honesty and what informa- tion about products and their qualities one may or may not withhold. Finally, institutions define who has access to which resources and how the actions between resource holders are coordinated, including the flow of both products and waste.

The institutions of an economy shape its dynamics and outcomes. In relation to that I would like to start by emphasizing four core issues. First, we have the question of *rights and responsibilities*. A central aspect here is property rights defining who has access to various resources or benefit streams and on what basis. Typically, we distinguish between private property, state property and common property. A society may similarly define responsibilities for various rights holders in, e.g., the form of liability rules. Holding property does not imply a right to harm others (Honoré 1961). Certainly, in relation to the issue of social costs, it becomes crucial how the responsibilities for 'side-effects' of eco- nomic activities are treated – such as effects on the environment. Rights struc- tures protect, but also form interests. This concerns property rights, but holds also for rights and responsibilities more generally as they shape different positions or roles as part of various institutionalized systems like the firm, university or bureaucracy.

Second, we have the issue of *information*. This concerns both descriptive and normative aspects. The world – both its physical and social spheres – is inherently complex. Description demands development of models that are 'images' of the real world. This requires simplification. Hence, our descriptions – their format and content – are influenced by the state of practical knowledge and of science. The normative or evaluative aspects concern how we institutionalize processes of decision-making, which information is to be taken into account and in what form. While the physical world and its capacities exist independently from our observations, which aspects we decide to focus on is influenced by institutional structures. We observe this not least if we look at decisions made by firms, where what is relevant information is described by the legal system defining these entities and what responsibilities they have for, e.g., share-holders and the wider society. Also, the evaluative processing of information is strongly dependent on the 'rules' (Vatn 2005). Typically, decisions related to profit-making and decisions made on the basis of cost–benefit analysis (CBA) demand values to be expressed in commensurable (money) terms.

Third, we have the *costs of coordinating* the actions of the various agents involved, such as the property-holding units. In a world of interdependencies the capacity to coordinate is core. The literature has mainly focused on whether coordination should take place in markets or internally in firms (Coase 1937; Williamson 1985; 2005). What should be chosen is seen to depend on the level of coordination or transaction costs as defined by the characteristics of the goods involved (e.g., asset specificity; uncertainty). In the case of environmental resources, demarcating goods and bads is especially difficult. Hence, coordinating action in this realm may be very demanding if based on separate decision units.

Finally, there is the issue of *motivation*. Here a core question concerns whether human motivation and preferences are independent of the institutional system or not. Recently there has been an increasing focus in the literature on endogenous preferences (Bowles 1998; 2008; O'Hara and Stagl 2002; Vatn 2009a). If motivation and preferences are endogenous, there is a second-order issue of importance to coordination: to structure the economy in a way so that agents' own motivations to coordinate actions are strengthened. This would reduce both needs for and costs of external coordination. Hence, coordination can be facilitated both by choosing systems with the lowest possible coordination costs and systems that facilitate a 'cooperative spirit'.

Actually, the second-order issue spans all four dimensions above. Fundamentally, if interests, information, coordination (transaction) costs and motivation/the will to cooperate are all influenced by the institutional structures, there is no 'fixed point' from where we can judge what is the better institutional solution. Nevertheless, such judgments must be done; better understanding of the dynamics of various institutional structures is therefore crucial.

Efficiency: an artifact of institutions

Efficiency is a core concept of economics. It forms the basis for the dominant tradition – the neoclassical position. This tradition has delivered the arguments for why the market is the most efficient institutional structure for allocating resources (the first welfare theorem). Given the assumptions, the conclusion is sound. Preferences are seen as exogenous and coordination costs/transaction costs are assumed to be zero. Moreover, information is complete or uncertainty can at least be treated in risk terms.[2] Choices – including social choices – should finally be made on the basis of individual preferences. While being a normative aspect of the model, it is taken to be a rather trivial assumption. Since preferences are understood as purely individual (context independency), choices not based on the individual himself would have to be based on somebody else's preferences. Hence, the principle of 'consumer sovereignty' guards against what is considered paternalistic decision-making.

Certainly, it is observed that markets may not lend themselves to treat all kinds of goods. There is focus on public goods, where both non-excludability and non-rivalry cause problems. There is focus on 'externalities' where non-excludability alone implies a difference between private and social costs. To restore optima, all resource use has to be priced according to the marginal costs that such use creates. While markets are unable to deliver such information, it is nevertheless taken for granted that decisions should be made on the basis of information available as if such markets had existed. Social optimum is restored if one is able to measure 'external costs' in terms of market prices – e.g., willingness to pay – and correct market allocations by making agents face these prices in the form of taxes. Hence, a role of the public or the state is admitted as soon as there is 'market failure'.

The alternative perspective is to see costs not as a neutral measure of preferences, but as systems-dependent themselves. In the following sections I will show how the firm–consumer–market nexus itself defines what becomes a cost and for whom. While the issues raised here concerns all kinds of social costs, I will in the rest of the chapter restrict myself to look only at costs related to the use of environmental resources.

Institutions, distribution and efficiency

Market prices both reflect preferences and ability to pay. The latter is not least related to distribution of resources – to the rights structure of a society concerning access to, e.g., material resources, education and health care. So, the most insignificant desire of a rich person could be fulfilled while the basic needs of a poor individual could go unsatisfied. The problem in our case is that new welfare economics cannot differentiate between a state where just a few own most resources of a society and a state where resources are more equally distributed. While the standard utilitarian position from Bentham, Mill and Marshall included 'sum-ranking' – i.e., that individual utility could be measured in cardinal terms and added together – the new welfare theory denies this aspect of the utilitarian calculus. So while the utilitarians could reach the conclusion that redistribution toward more equal access to resources would increase overall welfare of a society, the ordinalist revolution of the 1920s denied the (implicit) comparison of individual utilities inherent in such a calculus. This move was thought to reduce the value assumptions underlying economics to a bare minimum.

Certainly, neoclassical theory observes that the initial distribution of endowments influence which of the potentially efficient resource allocations the market produces – i.e., where on the utility frontier one ends up. This issue was, however, removed from economics itself. By adapting the principle of Pareto optimality (PO), one pledged for value neutrality. The only value assumption one thought was left concerned the 'innocent' notion that 'more is better than less'. This way welfare calculations could be made without taking a stand on normative issues. While it is in many senses a good move to leave normative issues to the political process, economics still pertains to be able to offer answers to what is the better thing to do – i.e., what is efficient. Here the value issues creep back into the analysis. The formal language cannot guard against the real consequences of efficiency claims.

First, the effect of the PO rule becomes an implicit defense of status quo distribution. This follows from defining efficiency in non-distributive terms. Hence, something that is not neutral – the existing distribution – acquires neutrality in the policy discourse that economic analyses inform. Being able to refer to what is efficient increases your position in the political debate. Who will go against efficiency?

Second, and more important in our case, environmental consequences of market trades are themselves normally non-neutral in distributive terms. In this case we face issues that do not lend themselves to be treated by the PO criterion. It is only in rare situations that environmental effects of economic activities do not put net costs upon somebody. Hence, there will normally be losers. To avoid this, one could argue that environmental issues should also be included in markets and made accessible to voluntary trades (Coase 1960). This is, however, typically not possible due to high transaction costs (see the section on 'Institutions, transaction costs and efficiency'), and one has to 'retreat' to the potential Pareto improvement (PPI) rule as in CBA and Pigouvian tax solutions. Both imply redistribution, as 'victims' are not compensated. So while Baumol and Oates (1988) may argue that the tax offers the only necessary incentive to restore efficiency, this reasoning cannot avoid the fact that someone has to carry uncompensated costs – i.e., the costs related to the Pareto irrelevant externalities. Hence, the implicit right to not compensate 'victims' will next influence the market prices for ordinary commodities.[3]

While potentially a small issue if 'external effects' were insignificant, the present level of economic activities does not make this rescue of the neutrality of the policy prescription in welfare terms sensible. Rather – like Kapp (1971) and Martinez-Alier (1987) – we should see 'externalities' as successful cost shifting that systematically hits the economically weak or future generations. The logic is simple in economic terms. As the poor have less capacity to pay, their environments appear less valuable than the environments of the rich. Hence, most of the environmental degradations they face become 'Pareto irrelevant'. So while the problems are mainly caused by the capacity of the rich to consume, the effects will systematically hit the poor. Over time this could result in substantial cumulative effects on human well-being where an optimal path in economic (PPI) terms creates losers in a systematic way.

This relates to the distinction between formal and substantive rationality. Weber (1922) introduced this distinction, emphasizing the difference between what can be numerically assessed through prices and what is the real influence on humans and their well-being. So while prices measure willingness to pay, they say little about the satisfaction of human needs. While the ordinalist revolution commencing at the time when Weber wrote was intended to guard against having to take a value position, he showed that this was possible only by retreating to a formal notion of rationality. Another way of ensuring value neutrality of the economic discipline could be to accept that the aims of economic policy are all truly political – i.e., to let the political level define environmental goals in substantive terms. Weber hence emphasized that the role of economics should be that of studying which means could best realize these goals (Weber 1949).

Kapp (1961; 1967)[4] was influenced by Weber's analysis, but he also departed from it in his various elaborations. He took an objectivist position on human needs, emphasizing their universality as based on the biological structure of the human organism. This offers content to concepts like social value as something going beyond the subjectivist sum of willingness to pay and allowed for scientific analyses of goals and standards of value. His 'rational humanism' does not demand that human needs are fixed. It is nevertheless possible to study implications of different policies on human well-being. This implies that the effect of various distributional schemes can be assessed in terms of substantive consequences.

Institutions, information and efficiency

Decisions should be informed. We would generally see it as problematic if the decision-maker is unable to assess the consequences of different alternatives. Certainly, if the information problem is independent of who makes the assessment and under what conditions, we just have to acknowledge the difficulty. If, however, the format of the decision-making process itself influences how the issue is understood and treated, the non-neutrality of the institutions is once again evident.

Choices in the realm of the environment dominantly concern very complex issues. Assuming full information, even assuming that people can calculate the risks involved – i.e., know all possible outcomes and their probabilities – is a very strong position to take. Nevertheless, basing environmental priorities on information from markets or market surrogate processes like contingent valuation must presume this for choices made on the basis of such data to be efficient.

A pertinent critique of market-based environmental valuation and its associated CBA is hence that the monetary values obtained are inadequate and ineffective (Kapp 1972). A specific issue concerns how to handle discrepancies between expert knowledge and knowledge among respondents to monetary valuation studies (Spash 2008). Moreover, it is argued that people are not used to thinking about environmental issues in monetary terms, and being asked to inform decision-making via such a construct could be confusing (Diamond and Hausman 1994; Clark *et al.* 2000). Finally, it is questioned whether values – especially environmental values – can be treated in commensurable (monetary) terms (Vatn and Bromley 1994; O'Neill *et al.* 2008). Concerning the latter, it is particularly emphasized that environmental questions typically raise issues that are fundamentally ethical, rendering monetary assessments incoherent with the underlying value dimensions.

Alternatives to CBA are multi-criteria analysis (MCA) and deliberative methods (DM). While CBA demands data to be based on consumer evaluations and values to be measured along one scale, the latter methods are based on different assumptions concerning both value commensurability and the role of experts. Typically, MCA and DM grant a different role to expert statements and judgments than CBA. In many types of DM, expertise is called to inform and discuss with a group of lay people/citizens who then assess this information and propose a solution or a prioritized list of solutions to the problem at hand.

The above-mentioned methods can be viewed as value-articulating institutions (Jacobs 1997; Vatn 2009b). This concept emphasizes that the valuation methods are defined by a set of rules concerning who should participate and on which premises/according to which role – e.g., consumers or citizens. They also define how people are supposed to participate and what kind of inputs they should deliver – e.g., price bids, arguments, etc. Next, there are rules concerning how and what information should be conveyed to participants – e.g., the role of expertise. Finally, there are rules concerning how conclusions are to be reached – e.g., aggregation, voting, consensus. This is not the place for an assessment of these methods or institutions (see Vatn 2005; 2009b for this kind of analysis). The point is that various ways of organizing the assessment process emphasize various aspects of the decision problem and which institutional structure is used may strongly influence the outcome of the process. This has to do with what kind of information is allowed and how it is to be treated.

It should be noted that the issue of climate change seems to be moving mainstream economists beyond the perspective of treating environmental consequences in risk terms. Hence, the concept of ambiguity is invoked. In this literature ambiguity is describing a situation in which probabilities are not known or can only be described as falling within certain ranges (e.g., Heal 2009).[5] Certainly, this development may have the power to substantially alter the neoclassical or mainstream economic model itself.

Institutions, transaction costs and efficiency

The neoclassical economic model assumes zero transaction costs (Becker 1976; Eggertsson 1990). This is problematic already for the analysis of markets (e.g., Williamson 1985). Moving to environmental resources, the problems increase. Certainly, if transaction costs were zero, Coase (1960) is right when emphasizing that markets will treat 'externalities' efficiently as the concept is defined. No 'Pareto relevant externalities' will appear as the market will be able to costlessly make the necessary trades between the parties involved. Certainly, rights need to be defined, but given these rights, direct bargains between the parties will result in efficient outcomes. There will be no distinction to make between environmental services and ordinary commodities. It is therefore quite confusing to find a whole branch of environmental economics emphasizing the role of the state in internalizing 'external effects', but at the same time ignoring transaction costs.

Including transaction costs into the analysis changes its direction quite fundamentally. Then a comparative study of which institutional structures are offering the lowest costs of transaction or coordinating becomes a core issue. State regulations become interesting exactly because of the reduced level of transaction costs following from the hierarchical structure invoked – i.e., Simon (1973) and his emphasis on the simplification of information flows and the concentration of decision power. Moreover, a range of new issues appear for the policy analyst that are overlooked if transaction costs are not included in the analysis. This concerns which instruments are the better to use, where in the chain from inputs to emissions an instrument should be applied,[6] and how policies should best be administered (Vatn 1998; 2005).

Certainly, it is argued that letting the state regulate implies that economic agents no longer are 'free' to negotiate over environmental issues themselves. The general observation that 'external effects' more and more are spread across a large amount of 'receivers' renders negotiated results infeasible. The high level of transaction costs related to market (horizontal) bargains would make most 'externalities' Pareto irrelevant. All potential gain would be consumed by the transaction costs. Hence the 'freedom' of bargained outcomes becomes illusory and in practice protect the interests of the producers of 'externalities'.

Externality theory is confusing (Vatn and Bromley 1997). One reason seems to be that the internal – i.e., the competitive market – actually is the cause of the external diseconomies. They are a systems feature and not a kind of accidental side-effect. Bromley (1991: 60) puts it the following way:

> The individualization of the world – its atomization really – is argued to be the very best means of individuals to be made better off and, by simple aggregation, for the collection of all individuals (call it society) to be better off. Now, if externalities arise at the boundary of decision units, and if theory and policy celebrate and sanctify atomization, then theory and policy would seem to advocate the maximization of decision units and, *ipso facto*, the number of boundaries across which costs might travel. Bluntly put, atomization ensures potential externalities.

In our language, what makes competition in the market work is at the same time creating a level of transaction costs that makes the market itself infeasible to treat the 'externalities' it produces.

Institutions, preferences and efficiency

Similar to transaction costs, there is quite strong evidence that even preferences or motivations depend on institutions. Kapp emphasizes this in his analysis of the social costs of private enterprise. He notes that

> a system of decision-making operating in accordance with the principle of investment for profit cannot be expected to proceed in any way other than by trying to reduce its costs whenever possible and by ignoring those losses that can be shifted to third persons or to society at large.
>
> (Kapp 1971: xiii)

Hence, externalities are a 'wanted' outcome of production for profits, not just 'accidental side-effects' as is the standard perspective (e.g., Baumol and Oates 1988). Like Bromley above, Kapp turns the focus around, seeing externalities not as external to the system, but as an expected result of it.

In the wider social science literature, the effects of institutions on preferences are seen as core (Berger and Luckmann 1967; Etzioni 1988). Through enculturation people learn the conventions and norms of a society. Becoming internalized, these institutions moreover move from operating as external constraints to become formative of the person. This does not imply that 'all is culture'. Certainly, enculturation or socialization processes cannot do away with physical and biological needs. They influence, however, in which form they are satisfied. More importantly, socialization adds a new dimension to the possibility to study and explain the preferences or goals of humans in objectivist terms. Typically, agents' goals or preferences are strongly influenced by the roles they have taken on. Hence, being a mother, a CEO of a firm, a teacher or a bureaucrat implies emphasizing different goals and values. Even what becomes self-interest is itself influenced by institutional structures like that of the family, the firm, the school and the bureaucracy (see also O'Neill 1998). How institutional contexts form our actions therefore becomes an important area of study.

There are many issues involved in the above. Here I will look at two aspects. First, I will delve into a rather specific issue concerning how rights influence preferences – i.e., the observed discrepancy between willingness to pay (WTP) and willingness to accept compensation (WTA) measures in environmental valuation studies. Second, I will look at a more fundamental question – that of plural preferences, especially individual vs. social preferences.

The distinction between WTP and WTA refers to different institutional structures – i.e., rights structures. If rights are with the polluter, WTP is the right measure to use. If they are with the victims, the proper measure is WTA. Standard theory implies that if payment estimates are not amounting to a large fraction of one's income, the difference between WTA and WTP measures should be insignificant (Willig 1976). Several authors have acknowledged that this is not the case in reality (Gregory 1986; Knetsch 2000; Horowitz and McConnell 2002). The latter source is a quite comprehensive literature review concluding that WTA measures on average are about three times larger than WTP measures even in cases where the value of the good equals a very low fraction of the respondents' income.

This observation illustrates that in the case of environmental costs, what rights situation is assumed will strongly influence 'what becomes efficient'. Following a WTA rule would give a much higher environmental cost of a certain nuisance than using WTP. Mainstream economics is again confusing. While typically embracing the polluter-pays principle (PPP) as the politically legitimized rule, it is nevertheless advised that WTP should be used to assess environmental costs (Arrow *et al.* 1993). The argument is that this will yield more 'realistic' estimates as WTP is bound by the individual's income constraint, while WTA is not. This mixes up a practical problem with a principal one. The PPP rule implies that the right is with the victim and a consistent implementation demands analysis is based on WTA estimates. Certainly, one could argue that the WTP–WTA discrepancy is a sign of irrationality among respondents. Then, however, the whole model collapses.

Mainstream economics assumes preferences to be context independent. As indicated above, this is not a good description of what is observed. Rather, preferences change as the context changes. One specific issue in this is the distinction made in the literature between individual and social preferences. The issue goes at least as far back as Smith, with his focus both on moral sentiments and self-interest (Smith 1759; 1776). More lately, the issue is raised by many authors (Swaney 1987; Sagoff 1988; Bowles 1998; Bowles and Hwang 2008).

The understanding of what social preferences are and imply varies across the literature. In relation to our focus, the distinction between the consumer and the citizen (Sagoff 1988) is especially important. We are not only consumers maximizing utility. We may also act as citizens. The priorities we make under these conditions refer to different sets of preferences. While the market emphasizes what is the better for the individual, the forum puts larger emphasis on what is best for the group.

Concerning decisions over environmental goods, one observes that they are decisions about goods that to a large extent are common. That follows from the interdependencies of the physical environment. Hence, the preferences that A holds will influence the opportunities of B and vice versa. If A wants development and B wants protection, the interest that wins in the political process will influence the situation for both. It is therefore a distinct social dimension to environmental choices. This does not only offer a noticeable explanation of why we may hold different preferences in private as opposed to social settings. It also supports the view that choices in the realm of the environment should rather be made on the basis of evaluating the soundness of arguments – the substantivist view – than on summarizing individual price bids – the formal procedure. So moving away from the subjectivist 'consumer sovereignty' to social choice by collective reasoning is not to become paternalistic, but to emphasize a different logic.

Institutions, rationality and action

In the previous section I have shown how institutional structures influence distribution, production and processing of information, transaction costs and preferences. Hence, what 'becomes efficient' is an artifact of the institutional structures established. This implies that using the market as the 'yard stick' against which solutions to social choices should be measured is circular to its assumptions. Rather, the argument for the market must be empirically based and founded on a comparative analysis with other institutional structures. One must therefore ask if the market is good at handling distributional issues, if it fosters development and distribution of information well, if it is good at treating uncertainties, if transaction costs are low and if it fosters the kind of preferences we would like to emphasize.

In this section I shall go one step further, discussing more specifically the role institutions play in forming human motivation. Handling environmental problems well demands not only that the issues are prioritized in the right way when choosing among conflicting interests. It also demands a capacity to act cooperatively that goes beyond what we have presently been able to institutionalize. Moving forward on this issue demands institutions that can better foster cooperative will. I shall start by a short review of recent publications on cooperative action.

Observing cooperative action

It becomes more and more evident that the human capacity and will to cooperate goes far beyond what can be expected from the standard model of individual utility maximization. This is observed in sociology (Etzioni 1988), ethnography and anthropology (Murdoch 1967) and the literature on common-pool resource management (Ostrom 1990; 1998). During the last years a substantial literature in social psychology and experimental economics has added to this picture – offering more detail to an otherwise quite coherent set of findings (Gintis *et al.* 2003; Ostrom 1998).

The experimental literature has not least focused on sharing and the will to invest in common pools that render gains to the group. In ultimatum and dictator games sharing is observed to a degree that cannot be explained by the standard model of individual utility maximization (Güth *et al.* 1982; Hoffmann *et al.* 1994; Gintis 2000; Frohlich *et al.* 2004). Similar observations are made in the so-called public goods games. Here participants to the game are offered a sum of money which they may keep or invest in a common pool. Typically, if one invests a dollar in the pool, each player receives 50 cents. Hence, if the number of participants is three or more, investments in the common pool pay for the group. It is still not individually rational to do so. Despite this, quite substantial levels of cooperation are observed (Ledyard 1995; Gintis 2000). Biel and Thøgersen (2007) conclude, after reviewing the literature, that even in one-shot public goods games 40–60 percent of participants cooperate. Moreover, Ostrom (2000) refers to results from public goods games showing that 30–40 percent of the participants rank the cooperative result as better than the situation that offers the most to themselves (i.e., a situation where they themselves defect and all others cooperate); 25–30 percent of the participants were indifferent between these two outcomes.

In some experiments monetary reward is included in a context where cooperation already exists. This has been done to see if it increases cooperative will. The effect is rather the opposite (Frey 1997; Gneezy and Rustichini 2000a; 2000b; Bowles 2008). In the case documented in Gneezy and Rustichini (2000a), they studied the effect of including a monetary reward to students collecting money for a charity. The students used every year to collect money without any specific pay for their efforts. In their study Gneezy and Rustichini divided the students into three groups; one that did as before (no individual reward); one that was paid 1 percent of what they collected; and one that was given 10 percent of what they collected. The group with no pay collected the most; the group paid 1 percent the least; and the group paid 10 percent came in the middle. The differences between the groups were significant. The latter two observations show that economic incentives may work as expected. The higher level of the non-paid group cannot be understood using this kind of explanation. Actually, the fact that money was collected under a non-compensation scheme is impossible to explain if referring to the standard version of the utility maximization model.

Explaining cooperative action: institutions as rationality contexts[7]

Different efforts have been undertaken to explain the above observations. Most of the proposals delivered by economists are based on expanding the utility function, including, e.g., the 'warm glow of giving' (Andreoni 1990), intrinsic motivation where the reward comes from the activity itself (Frey 1997) and the self-image model of Brekke *et al.* (2003). All of these explanations are focused on individual motivation only. Ostrom (1998) takes a similar route when developing her 'second generation model of (bounded) rationality'. Here a set of 'delta parameters' are included in the utility function. She goes a step further than the previous authors, though, by linking these parameters to norms of the society. Following a norm yields pride (positive delta), while breaking it brings a feeling of shame (negative delta). By referring to norms, Ostrom brings the collective into 'play'. Society develops norms that people internalize and next follow due to the 'pleasure and pain' that is created. This mechanism creates and sustains cooperation.

While being a very important step, there are also some limitations to such a model. One of these was discussed by Hume.[8] He noted

They found, that every act of virtue or friendship was attended by a secret pleasure; whence they concluded, that friendship and virtue could not be disinterested. But the fallacy is obvious. The virtuous sentiment or passion produces the pleasure, and does not arise from it. I feel a pleasure in doing good to my friend, because I love him; but do not love him for the sake of that pleasure.

(Hume 1742: 85–86)

Sen (1977) develops a similar reasoning when making the distinction between commitment and sympathy. Again the argument is that reducing all other-regarding preferences to a concern only for own utility is problematic.

Noting this, one could take Ostrom further and argue that different institutional settings are built around different logics or rationalities. The treatment of a friend is different from the treatment of a competitor simply because friendship and competition are 'governed' by different rationalities. Collecting money for a charity without pay is to serve duty to society, while as soon as pay is introduced, the logic (may) shift to think about own income. A lousy pay – just 1 percent – may result in low interest in collecting money. Hence, it makes sense to distinguish between individual rationality (what is best for the individual) and social or cooperative rationality (what is best for the group/society). The latter concerns norms about what is the right thing to do in a group setting, where the role of the norm is to offer a solution to the coordination problem.

From this follows that institutions can be seen as rationality contexts. The idea is that individuals, when entering a specific setting, will first look for clues to help define what the situation is all about. Is it about exchange? Is it about group coordination, and if so, which specific logic is meant to govern it? Institutions are generally seen as human constructs developed to provide meaning to the situation. More specifically they are remedies to support cooperative action as such action is hard to establish based on individual reasoning alone (Vatn 2005; 2009a).

Human history is filled with situations that can be characterized as coordination problems. That is the case with all kinds of pollution problems, taking the form of prisoners' dilemmas. That is the case with all gains from cooperation typified in the public goods game described above. What is best for the individual is detrimental to the group. At the same time, if cooperation was established, all could gain compared to the non-cooperative solution.[9] Hence, one may argue that if institutions had the capacity to secure cooperation, a lot of gains to those involved could follow.

Ostrom (2000) offers some interesting observations in relation to this. She reviews much of the literature on how our capacity to learn norms may have evolved. She suggests that in the long period during which individuals operated in small groups as hunters and gatherers, survival was

dependent not only on aggressively seeking individual returns but also on solving many day-to-day collective action problems. Those of our ancestors who solved these problems most effectively, and learned how to recognize who was deceitful and who was a trustworthy reciprocator, had a selective advantage over those who did not.

(Ostrom 2000: 143)

Certainly, we cannot prove whether institutions work through shifting the logic of the situation or by switching on and off various 'delta parameters' in the utility function. While the perspective of Hume and Sen seems to be the most reasonable – that it is about different logics – the Batson and Shaw (1991) experiments aimed at proving the existence of 'true' altruism failed to deliver a waterproof test. Whenever they had managed to set up an experiment that supported the hypothesis of true altruism – i.e., the act was not based on increased utility for the one acting – economists could show that by adding an element of intrinsic motivation to the utility function, what was observed could be equally well explained in individual utility terms as by claiming the existence of true altruism – see also Sober and Wilson (1998) on this.[10]

These 'counter attacks' on Batson and Shaw come at a high price for economic theory. Introducing intrinsic motivations actually renders the utility model non-testable. It may, however, not be important – at least for practical policy purposes – which understanding of how norms work is the right one.[11] The important point is that institutions have the capacity to influence which rationality pertains. There is overwhelming empirical evidence that this is the case.

Institutions, policy and social costs

Over the last 200 years we have developed institutions that have vastly strengthened the capacity of the economy to grow. Not least through the creation of the corporation – the stock-holding company – the dynamism of the system was substantially expanded as individual capitals could be easily pooled. Together with the expansion of market interactions – e.g., various trade liberalization efforts – this has created an arrangement producing a level of economic growth that is historically unprecedented.

A core element in this has been to foster *separation of decisions*. The system may function well for the aspect of environmental resources that can be equally separated – the creation of commodities. It does not work well for the interactive aspects of environmental resources. Splitting up nature in pieces as is demanded by separation of decision-making can only be made in formal terms. It cannot circumvent interruptions into the web of interdependencies that fundamentally characterize environmental resources. Rather, it has exaggerated the problems by establishing a structure that makes it extra difficult to institutionally reconnect what is already physically connected.

The future seems to demand a system that can integrate rather than separate. What could such a system look like? In the following I will discuss some aspects of this issue organized around the four dimensions of institutional analysis as developed in the section on 'institutions and the economy'. Certainly, both space restrictions and the present level of insight force the analysis to be very sketchy. Nevertheless, the above material – not least that on cooperation – points toward some novel options.

Rights and responsibilities: toward ex ante *regulation*

The dominant way of handling environmental consequences of economic activity is presently through governmental regulation of harms. It mostly takes the form of *ex post* regulations. Firms are generally free to establish. If at some point harm is observed and the cause can be proven, restrictions may be instituted to reduce the extent of this harm, such as emission standards, environmental taxes. This grants a right to establish economic activity assuming that no harm will appear. However, as all economic activity demands material resources, some harm is inevitable.

However, it normally takes a lot of time from when a new activity or production process is established for the harm to be observed and proven. Hence, the activity causing the problem may have grown to substantial proportions before any action is put in place. Moreover, at that point in time, huge investments are often made under the presumption of no harm, and the economic loss following from changing to a less harmful process or product could be substantial. Following the logic of the PPI rule/CBA it could deem no-regulation to be the optimal choice.

An alternative structure would be to demand *ex ante* proof of no harm. In this situation the authorities have the right to deny establishment of any production if proof of safety/acceptable levels of safety cannot be delivered. Certainly, such definitive proofs will not be possible to deliver in most cases, and there will be a high risk that the limitations and uncertainties created for the production sector would result in unnecessarily low production/high unemployment rates. A way out of this would be to include some flexibility around the limits set. This could be done by institutionalizing a learning procedure beyond the initial evaluation; hence combining weaker *ex ante* regulation with a continuous evaluation of consequences, facilitating learning both for the state and the firms.

In relation to the above it should be noted that strict liability is now included both in US and EU environmental law. Liability regulation was first established for private goods, but has been extended to environmental issues. It is a form of *ex post* regulation – i.e., demands *ex post* proof of harm – but should offer *ex ante* incentives to avoid harm, hence be closer to the above proposal. The experiences with this type of regulation offer important insights into the dynamics around environmental regulation. First of all, this system works best for clearly defined harms with mainly local consequences. Moreover, it fits reversible harms best. As already emphasized, environmental harms are rather systemic, characterized by complex cause–effect relationships, large time lags, asymmetric information, and damage caused by multiple sources. This makes identification of harm difficult (Ulph and Valentini 2004; Feess *et al.* 2009). Moreover, it is argued that firms tend to ignore low-probability risks when deciding (Katzman

1985; Sunstein 2008). Hence, risks will go unnoticed. Certainly, the competitive environment of decision-making may also influence this situation. Due to this, the success of environmental liability laws in the United States has been heavily disputed (Schoemaker and Schoemaker 1995) as most natural resource damage payments have been rather small (Environmental Protection Agency 1996). In line with this, Bohme *et al.* (2005) show how all kinds of uncertainties can be utilized by firms to 'confuse' the situation to the extent that a final proof of harm that holds in the court becomes difficult to deliver. They refer to various strategies that firms may take on, like funding scientists to produce counter evidence, establishing front groups/think tanks, influencing media, etc., all for the purpose of producing doubt. We see this in the area of industrial hazards – e.g., campaigns against tobacco, lead and asbestos as harmful substances – and recently climate change.

Information: toward adaptive learning

The above corporate strategies exploit the fact that environmental systems are complex and therefore hard to understand. They also utilize that they are quite resilient. While resilience is a good thing as it offers time to adapt if we are on a wrong track, it may also create an illusion of 'no limits'. Our actions work mainly through reducing the resilience of natural systems. This increases the chance for abrupt and unexpected changes, such as when a lake 'flips' due to nutrient inflows over many years. Hence, we may observe that things are developing fine, while suddenly they are not anymore. This is certainly a difficult issue to handle if decision-making is separated as emphasized above. There is no incentive in the system to explore where potential limits may be.

A potential solution could be found in the idea of adaptive management as advocated among scholars in the field of ecosystem management (Folke *et al.* 2005). Learning is accumulated through careful testing of the consequences of different strategies. The idea is that one cannot establish *ex ante* what will happen with certainty. Rather, one has to test what the consequences are by systematically trying out various strategies. The idea is to expand what is acceptably safe and what is not and gradually build a firmer basis for what one can and cannot accept.

The challenges for instituting such a system in a private property-market setting are several. Certainly, to avoid large irreversibilities from such searches, the speed of change would have to be rather low. This challenges the very logic of a growth-based system like our economy. As Sonntag (2000) shows, a core element of present corporate strategies to keep competitive is to accelerate product cycles. Rapid economic growth is the 'lubricant' that secures the success of this strategy. This creates a context where adaptive management is actually not possible.

Moreover, this kind of learning process must be collective as the consequences are experienced in common environments. It implies that the state must play a core role both in knowledge production and setting limits for economic agents. This will create a specific type of uncertainty as there will be negotiations over how to adapt as one learns. Negotiating could be challenging as the aims of the firms and the coordinating state are pulling in opposite directions – cf. the above discussion about the corporate strategy of confusing knowledge. Adaptive management could in this setting just be captured by various strategic games between the state and business agents.

Coordination costs: more hierarchy

The above illustrates that the challenge is foremost one of coordination in a state of conflict. The issues we face are fundamentally about separated but interdependent choices influencing a wide range of third persons. In such situations the literature advises bringing decision-making under one authority structure with the implied reduction in coordination costs. Expanding the insights from Coase (1937) and Williamson (1985) one could conclude that the solution would be to establish one firm owning all environmental resources, having the power to take all interdependencies into account.

Certainly, one may rather like to give such power to a unit under democratic control – e.g., the state – than to a structure like a firm. The problem with both solutions is, however, the established monopoly of power. Hence, the strength is also the greatest weakness. Moreover, monopolizing decision-power would most probably result in vast information overload. A successful use of environmental resources would demand sensitivity to local conditions that state management has often proven to not possess (Ostrom 1990). Some level of decentralization and some kind of separated decision-making seems necessary despite the need to strengthen coordination.

Motivation: more cooperative rationality

To find a solution to all the above incompatibilities is very demanding. One route that seems promising would be to strengthen the role of social or cooperative rationality at the level of the basic economic unit itself, be it the firm or some other construct. Given the findings reported in the section on 'Institutions, reality and action', cooperative will is a capacity that is sensitive to institutional structures. The idea here is that the goal structure of the constructed economic agents should be developed away from standard profit maximization and toward social and environmental responsibility – toward a 'cooperative spirit'. This could only happen through changing the rules for the basic units of the economy – e.g., through changing property rights structures including more community ownership, ownership by environmental groups, etc. and by strengthening the position of not-for-profit type firms. The logic of economic decision-making could hence be changed to include a greater sensitivity to social costs.

The point is not that by doing this we will create a system that is self-coordinating. The issue is rather to create a situation where the strengthening of the hierarchical power of the common authority – the state – becomes meaningful.

This power can focus more on the overall restrictions to be set for the use of environmental resources. Moreover, the increased level of cooperative will at the level
of firms is crucial when instituting adaptive learning. It simply reduces the motive
to play strategic games between higher and lower systems levels.

At a conceptual or theoretical level it seems quite obvious that we need to
strengthen the capacity to coordinate. At a practical level we will still face many
challenges when trying to turn that concept into reality. Information asymmetries
will not disappear. Strategic motivations will not vanish. The issue is rather to
'tip the balance' such that it becomes much more meaningful to act cooperatively and avoid that cooperative will to be ruined by strategic action.

Conclusion

Throughout this chapter the role institutions play in the economic process has
been explored. The profound importance of institutions for what 'becomes efficient' has been emphasized. In this we have especially discussed the effect of the
institutional structures at the level of social costs and the kind of human motivations involved. The structure of the present system seems to facilitate maximization of social costs. Certainly, public regulations are set up to curtail such a
development. While having produced some progress, the resulting institutional
'blend' is characterized with several shortcomings and conflicts.

There is urgent need for developing alternatives. The thrust of this chapter is
that progress lies in strengthening the room for cooperative rationality. This will
demand construction of new institutions. So far we have just been able to define
what the challenge is about. Substantial amounts of research and practical learning
is necessary to even get the process of institutional change up and running.
Humanity has, however, shown a lot of ingenuity when it comes to constructing
new institutions. The corporation is an example of such a product. It will certainly
take more than shifting a letter or two to change the corporation into a cooperation.
While being a vastly demanding task, it is nevertheless a very important one.

Notes

1 The author thanks two anonymous reviewers for very good input. They have helped
  me both to ensure greater clarity and expanded my insights into the importance of
  industrial organization for environmental issues.
2 If information is not seen as complete, it is assumed that it can be treated in risk terms.
  As defined by Knight (1921), risk implies that while the outcome may not be known
  with certainty, both possible outcomes and their probabilities are known. This makes
  it possible to still optimize, in this case in terms of expected utility.
3 Certainly, as already emphasized, the politically defined distribution of endowments
  makes any price non-neutral. The point here is that it is the economic policy measure
  that is itself influencing distribution, here even in the sense of creating a situation
  where some party will lose.
4 I am indebted to Berger (2008) for parts of this analysis.
5 Ambiguity is, hence, defined similar to Knight's concept of uncertainty (Knight
  1921).

6 Mainstream environmental economics emphasizes regulation on emissions or actually on the effect of the emissions. With positive transaction costs this is no longer obvious. Other points of instrument application like regulations of inputs or technology may be better.

7 For the interested reader, note that the ideas presented here are developed more completely in Vatn (2009a).

8 I am indebted to John O'Neill for becoming aware of Hume's position.

9 Certainly, in many situations, only some will gain from cooperation. The above argument is simplified; it does not go against the fact that in many situations cooperation cannot be established due to uneven distribution of the gains.

10 The point is not that the Batson and Shaw experiments were flawed. The issue is about what can and cannot be proven by behavioral experiments when introducing intrinsic motivations. What we see here is a case where authors agree that there are intrinsic motivations – altruism or 'delta parameters' of the utility function – but that they disagree about their kind. So far at least, no methods exist to differentiate with certainty between the two perspectives.

11 Certainly, if it is impossible to test which of the two models of norm-based motivations are the better description, it does not matter for policy which is 'right'. Put the other way around, if the explanation matters for policy, it should be possible to define test implications that could differentiate between the two models. To avoid misunderstanding: What is not provable (yet) is how norms work – i.e., as defining what is right to do as opposed to changing what yields the highest individual utility through changing, e.g., 'delta parameters'. What is already well documented, though, is how institutional factors like norms change behavior or action. Hence, outcomes will certainly be different if a policy puts emphasis on individual/egoistic motivations as opposed to social/normative ones – cf. the Gneezy and Rustichini case.

References

Andreoni, J. (1990) 'Impure altruism and the donations to public goods: a theory of warm glow giving', *The Economic Journal*, 100: 467–477.

Arrow, K., Solow, R., Portney, P.R., Leamer, E.E., Radner, R. and Schuman, H. (1993) 'Report of the NOAA panel on contingent valuation', *Federal Register*, 58: 4601–4614.

Batson, C.D. and Shaw, L.L. (1991) 'Evidence for altruism: toward a pluralism of prosocial motives', *Psychological Inquiry*, 2(2): 107–122.

Baumol, W.J. and Oates, W.E. (1988) *The Theory of Environmental Policy*, New Jersey: Prentice Hall Inc.

Becker, G. (1976) *The Economic Approach to Human Behavior*, Chicago: University of Chicago Press.

Berger, P. and Luckmann, T. (1967 [1991]) *The Social Construction of Reality: A Treatise in the Sociology of Knowledge*, London: Penguin Books.

Berger, S. (2008) 'K. William Kapp's theory of social costs and environmental policy: towards political ecological economics', *Ecological Economics*, 67: 244–252.

Biel, A. and Thøgersen, J. (2007) 'Activation of social norms in social dilemmas: a review of the evidence and reflections on the implications for environmental behavior', *Journal of Economic Psychology*, 28: 93–112.

Bohme, S.R., Zorabedian, J. and Egilman, D.S. (2005) 'Maximizing profits and endangering health: corporate strategies to avoid litigation and regulation', *International Journal of Occupational and Environmental Health*, 11(4): 338–348.

Bowles, B. and Hwang, S.H. (2008) 'Social preferences and public economics: mechanism design when social preferences depend on incentives', *Journal of Public Economics*, 92: 1811–1820.

Bowles, S. (1998) 'Endogenous preferences: the cultural consequences of markets and other economic institutions', *Journal of Economic Literature*, 36 (March): 75–111.

Bowles, S. (2008) 'Policies designed for self-interested citizens may undermine 'the moral sentiments': evidence from economic experiments', *Science*, 320: 1605–1609.

Brekke, K.A., Kverndokk, S. and Nyborg, K. (2003) 'An economic model of moral motivation', *Journal of Public Economics*, 87(9–10): 1967–1983.

Bromley, D.W. (1991) *Environment and Economy: Property Rights and Public Policy*, Oxford: Basil Blackwell.

Clark, J., Burgess, J. and Harrisson, C.M. (2000) ' "I struggled with this money business": respondents' perspectives on contingent valuation', *Ecological Economics*, 33: 45–62.

Coase, R.H. (1937) 'The nature of the firm', *Economica*, 4: 386–405.

Coase, R.H. (1960) 'The problem of social cost', *The Journal of Law and Economics*, 3: 1–44.

Diamond, P.A. and Hausman, J.H. (1994) 'Contingent valuation: is some number better than no number?', *Journal of Economic Perspectives*, 8(4): 45–64.

Eggertsson, T. (1990) *Economic Behavior and Institutions*, Cambridge: Cambridge University Press.

Environmental Protection Agency (1996) 'Valuing potential environmental liabilities for managerial decision-making: a review of available techniques', Available at: www.epa. gov/oppt/library/pubs/archive/acct-archive/pubs/liabilities.pdf.

Etzioni, A. (1988) *The Moral Dimension: Toward a New Economics*, New York: The Free Press.

Feess, E., Muehlheusser, G. and Wohlschlegel, A. (2009) 'Environmental liability under uncertain causation', *European Journal of Law and Economics*, 28: 133–148.

Folke, C., Hahn, T., Olsson, P. and Norberg, J. (2005) 'Adaptive governance of social-ecological systems', *Annual Review of Environmental Resources*, 30: 441–473.

Frey, B.S. (1997) *Not Just For the Money: An Economic Theory of Personal Motivation*, Cheltenham: Edward Elgar.

Frohlich, N., Oppenheimer, J. and Kurki, A. (2004) 'Modeling other-regarding preferences and an experimental test', *Public Choice*, 119: 91–117.

Gintis, H. (2000) 'Beyond *Homo economicus*: evidence from experimental economics', *Ecological Economics*, 35: 311–322.

Gintis, H., Bowles, S., Boyd, R. and Fehr, E. (2003) 'Explaining altruistic behavior in humans', *Evolution and Human Behavior*, 24: 153–172.

Gneezy, U. and Rustichini, A. (2000a) 'Pay enough or don't pay at all', *Journal of Economic Behavior and Organization*, 39: 341–369.

Gneezy, U. and Rustichini, A. (2000b) 'A fine is a price', *The Journal of Legal Studies*, 29: 1–17.

Gregory, R. (1986) 'Interpreting measures of economic loss: evidence from contingent valuation and experimental studies', *Journal of Environmental Economics and Management*, 13: 325–337.

Güth, W., Schmittberger, R. and Schwarze, B. (1982) 'An experimental analysis of ultimatum bargaining', *Journal of Economic Behavior and Organization*, 3: 367–388.

Heal, G. (2009) 'The economics of climate change: a post-Stern perspective', *Climatic Change*, 96: 275–297.

Hoffman, E., McCabe, K., Shachat, K. and Smith, V. (1994) 'Preferences, property rights, and anonymity in bargaining games', *Games and Economic Behavior*, 7: 346–380.

Honoré, A.M. (1961) 'Ownership', in Guest, A.G. (ed.), *Oxford Essays in Jurisprudence*, Oxford: Clarendon Press.

Horowitz, J.K. and McConnell, K.E. (2002) 'A review of WTA/WTP studies', *Journal of Environmental Economics and Management*, 44: 426–447.

Hume, D. (1742 [1985]) *Of the Dignity or Meanness of Human Nature: In Essays Moral, Political, and Literary*, Vol I., Indianapolis: Liberty Press.

Jacobs, M. (1997) 'Environmental valuation, deliberative democracy and public decision-making', in Foster, J. (ed.), *Valuing Nature? Economics, Ethics and Environment*, London: Routledge.

Kapp, K.W. (1961) *Toward a Science of Man in Society: A Positive Approach to the Integration of Social Knowledge*, The Hague: Martinus Nijhoff.

Kapp, K.W. (1967 [1985]) 'Economics and rational humanism', in Ullmann, J.E. and Preiswerk, R. (eds.), *The Humanization of the Social Sciences*, Lanham: University Press of America.

Kapp, K.W. (1971) *The Social Costs of Private Enterprise*, New York: Schoken Books.

Kapp, K.W. (1972) 'Social costs, neo-classical economics, environmental planning: a reply', *Social Science Information*, 11(1): 17–28.

Katzman, M.T. (1985) *Chemical Catastrophes: Regulating Environmental Risk through Pollution Liability Insurance*, Homewood: Richard D. Irwin.

Knetsch, J. (2000) 'Environmental valuation and standard theory: behavioural findings, context dependence and implications', in Tietenberg, T. and Folmer, H. (eds.), *The International Yearbook of Environment and Resource Economics 2000/2001: A Survey of Current Issues*, Cheltenham: Edward Elgar.

Knight, F.H. (1921 [1933]) *Risk, Uncertainty and Profits*, London: London School of Economics.

Ledyard, J.O. (1995) 'Public goods: a survey of experimental research', in Kagel, J.H. and A.E. Roth (eds.), *The Handbook of Experimental Economics*, Princeton: Princeton University Press.

Martinez-Alier, J. (1987) *Ecological Economics: Energy, Environment and Society*, Oxford: Basil Blackwell.

Murdoch, G.P. (1967) *Ethnographic Atlas*, Pittsburg: University of Pittsburg Press.

O'Hara, S. and Stagl, S. (2002) 'Endogenous preferences and sustainable development', *Journal of Socio-Economics*, 31(5): 511–527.

O'Neill, J. (1998) *The Market: Ethics, Knowledge and Politics*, London: Routledge.

O'Neill, J., Holland, A. and Light, A. (2008) *Environmental Values*, London: Routledge.

Ostrom, E. (1990) *Governing the Commons: The Evolution of Institutions for Collective Action*, Cambridge: Cambridge University Press.

Ostrom, E. (1998) 'A behavioral approach to the rational choice theory of collective action: presidential address, American Political Science Association, 1997', *American Political Science Review*, 92(1): 1–22.

Ostrom, E. (2000) 'Collective action and the evolution of social norms', *Journal of Economic Perspectives*, 14(3): 137–158.

Sagoff, M. (1988) *The Economy of the Earth: Philosophy, Law and Environment*, Cambridge: Cambridge University Press.

Schoemaker, P.J.H. and Schoemaker, J.A. (1995) 'Estimating environmental liability: quantifying the unknown', *California Management Review* 37(3): 29–61.

Scott, W.R. (1995) *Institutions and Organizations*, California: Sage Publications.

Sen, A. (1977) 'Rational fools: a critique of the behavioral foundations of economic theory', *Philosophy and Public Affairs*, 6(4): 317–344.

Simon, H.A. (1973) 'The organization of complex systems', in Patte, H.H. (eds.), *Hierarchy Theory: The Challenge of Complex Systems*, New York: George Braziller.

Smith, A. (1759 [1976]) *The Theory of Moral Sentiments*, edited by E. Cannan, London: Methuen.

Smith, A. (1776 [1976]) *An Inquiry into the Nature and Causes of the Wealth of Nations*, Chicago: University of Chicago Press.

Sober, E. and Wilson, D.S. (1998) *Onto Others: The Evolution and Psychology of Unselfish Behavior*, Cambridge, MA: Harvard University Press.

Sonntag, V. (2000) 'Sustainability: in light of competitiveness', *Ecological Economics*: 34: 101–113.

Spash, C.L. (2008) 'How much is that ecosystem in the window? The one with the biodiverse trail', *Environmental Values*, 17(2): 259–284.

Sunstein, C.R. (2008) 'Two conceptions of irreversible environmental harm', University of Chicago, Law & Economics, Olin Working Paper No. 407. Available at: www.law.uchicago.edu/files/files/407.pdf.

Swaney, J.A. (1987) 'Elements of a neoinstitutional environmental economics', *Journal of Economic Issues*, 21: 1739–1779.

Ulph, A. and Valentini, L. (2004) 'Environmental liability and the capital structure of firms', *Resource and Energy Economics*, 26(4): 393–410.

Vatn, A. (1998) 'Input vs. emission taxes: environmental taxes in a mass balance and transactions cost perspective', *Land Economics*, 74(4): 514–525.

Vatn, A. (2005) *Institutions and the Environment*, Cheltenham: Edward Elgar.

Vatn, A. (2009a) 'Cooperative behavior and institutions', *Journal of Socio-Economics*, 38: 188–196.

Vatn, A. (2009b) 'An institutional analysis of methods for environmental appraisal', *Ecological Economics*, 68: 2207–2215.

Vatn, A. and Bromley, D.W. (1994) 'Choices without prices without apologies', *Journal for Environmental Economics and Management*, 26: 129–148.

Vatn, A. and Bromley, D.W. (1997) 'Externalities: a market model failure', *Journal of Environmental and Resource Economics*, 9(2): 135–151.

Weber, M. (1922 [1978]) *Wirtschaft und Gesellschaft*, In English: *Economy and Society: An Outline of Interpretive Sociology*, edited by G. Roth and C. Wittich, Berkeley: University of California Press.

Weber, M. (1949) *The Methodology of Social Sciences*, Glencoe: The Free Press.

Williamson, O.E. (1985) *The Economic Institutions of Capitalism*, New York: The Free Press.

Williamson, O.E. (2005) 'The economics of governance', *American Economic Review*, 95(2): 1–18.

Willig, R.D. (1976) 'Consumer surplus without apology', *The American Economic Review*, 66(4): 589–597.

3 Social costs and the horizonal approach to ecological economics

Frederic B. Jennings, Jr.

> The history of every science, including that of economics, teaches us that the elementary is the hotbed of the errors that count most.
>
> Nicholas Georgescu-Roegen (1970: 9)

Introduction

K. William Kapp's (1963: 264–266) theory of social costs shows how unregulated market systems of pricing, cost accounting and profit tend to impose social costs on the public of various sorts, including

> air and water pollution ... exploitation of both renewable (flow) and non-renewable (stock) resources or natural wealth ... industrial accidents and occupational diseases ... technical change and unemployment ... duplication of capital facilities and excess capacity ... cutthroat competition, planned obsolescence and sales promotion ... retardation of technical efficiency and the overconcentration or 'mislocation' of economic activities

saying that 'these social costs ... pervade the entire economic process and their avoidance would call for the most far-reaching measures of social legislation and structural reform'. He criticized standard theory in economics for being too narrow, ignoring effects that are hard to price or value in monetary terms. He also spurned equilibrium models based on substitution assumptions and closed systems with negative feedbacks in favor of ecological frames showing complementarity, cumulative causation and positive feedbacks in dynamically open systems. Kapp's theory of social costs shows how private profit incentives strongly imply an avoidance – if not the actuation – of costs spilling on others now and in the future radiating outward forever. He advocated strict tolerance thresholds and minimum standards as a means of at least partial prevention of these likely irreversible losses.

Kapp's approach to economics was both institutional and ecological, recognizing unbounded interdependence as central to a proper economic analysis. As Myrdal (1978: 774) put it: 'There is no one basic factor; everything causes

everything else. This implies *interdependence* within the whole social process.'
Standard theory in economics sidesteps the issue of interdependence; unbounded
economic causality offers no place to stand. Joan Robinson (1941: 8) captured
the point: 'In order to know anything it is necessary to know everything, but in
order to talk about anything it is necessary to neglect a great deal.' According to
Kapp, the failures of traditional economic conceptions show in neglect of fundamental issues of social cost that extend well beyond the Pigovian notion of
simple 'externalities'. So orthodox standards simply opt to shun interdependence, shaping their rigors around demands of closure (Mirowski 1986: 193) and
equilibrium models (Kaldor 1972; Reder 1982). Simplistic constructions shall
not suffice in dealing with dynamic complex systems such as are found throughout all ecologies with diverse social effects spreading outward to others.

   If all we do ripples outward forever in social and physical space, Simon's
theory of 'bounded rationality' opens a route through the maze (Simon
1982–1997). Social effects of individual actions spread out forever, while our
rational anticipation of those effects is strictly contained by understanding, conscience, effort and the stability of our decision environments. Decisions are
made on imagined projections of outcomes framed in our minds; the range of
these projections should be known as the *planning horizon* embedded in a particular choice. A way to look at Kapp's theory of social cost is in terms of planning horizons as an index of the 'boundedness' of our reasoned deliberations
underlying choice. Social costs, ignored, are reflections of outcomes set beyond
the range of those accounted for in decisions; short horizons are related to
radiant externalities which a longer horizon might internalize to a greater extent.
These are matters of degree, where raising the length and breadth of horizons
signifies improvement, though irreversible losses should be avoided wherever
realistically possible. The introduction of planning horizons into economic analysis suggests a means to expand Kapp's theory into a larger frame of the sort
that Kapp persuasively advocated.

   The planning horizon in any decision denotes the range of consequences –
social, physical and ecological – included in the imagined projections of outcomes among which we choose. But reality always has the last word: the
planning horizon needs to be seen as the range of *accurate* anticipation, trun-
cated by 'surprise' wherever reality yields some other result than intended or
expected. This makes the planning horizon a measure of foresight, rationality
and the 'fit' between theory and truth or between models' suppositions and the
context of their application. Boulding (1968) captured its substance as an index
of organization that has value in measuring progress and development in economics. But planning horizons serve also as an index of social 'conscience' in
the sense that horizonal lengthening captures a greater range of social costs so
more 'externalities' are internalized into our private decisions.

   But economics should be about observable manifestations, and we cannot see
or measure our planning horizons in direct ways; no metric counts the 'wits'
(Boulding 1966: 22–23) embodied in any discrete decision. Think of the planning horizon as an ordinal measure of rationality, and of personal conscience in

the internalization of 'externalities' stemming from any action. The planning horizon also relates to time preference or 'future mindedness', such that long-term effects weigh more in current decisions with longer horizons. So will the incidence and nature of social costs in Kapp's sense shift with horizon effects – with longer or shorter horizons, for better or for worse – showing a role for this notion in Kapp's theory. When horizons extend or retract, they yield *horizon effects*. Horizon effects should be found at the core of any institutional or ecological economics.

The process of choice

Every choice is a normative process of multidimensional causal projection in the mind of the agent, where expectations stretch as far as they can to embrace our results. The range of anticipated projection into the fog of future and distant effects should be seen in horizonal terms; every act displays or embodies an agent's planning horizon. In any interdependent domain, every choice sets in motion a spreading array of ever-expanding social and ecological impacts. The welfare question about these social effects is whether they do good or ill. In any event, these social and ecological economic connections should be understood. Every avoidable ecological and social loss is horizontal, lying in failures of foresight and conscience; we are all prisoners of this dilemma if our fortunes are wholly entwined in a complementary universe of cumulative causation. As Kapp says, separation of phenomena into narrow or 'partial' analyses simply is insufficient in this setting of fully interdependent and irreversible outcomes spilling from private decisions.

Indeed, horizon effects suggest a novel form of social linkage, as planning horizons interact directly in complementary ways. If you are in my decision environment, any expansion of your horizon will likely open mine too; horizon effects spread contagiously outward through any group. Private horizonal changes stimulate similar social effects, called 'interhorizonal complementarity'. Planning horizons slowly extend with understanding, conscience and trust; their range is sensitive to the reliability of other agents. In this respect, we are role models for each others' behavior, especially if individual learning is imitative and socially based. The rates of horizonal growth and decline are asymmetrically different, however: plans can collapse in the wink of an eye if any condition is breached. The impact of planning horizons on economic behavior should be explored as a means of framing social costs in relation to private decisions.

Horizon effects supply an elemental linkage between economic and ecological interdependence by emphasizing complementarity in our social relations. Standard theory in economics stresses substitution at its axiomatic core, allowing equilibrium models and diverse static constructions; rejection or refutation thereof is simply not an option in neoclassical economics (Blaug 1976: 156–157). Krupp (1982: 388) remarked that: 'Axioms of independence ... lead directly to the laws of substitution.... Independence means that the behavior of the elementary unit can be described without reference to the behavior of other units.' Indeed, as suggested below, economic relations are also *horizonal*; horizon effects shift the balance of substitution and complementarity in a predictable way in any economic context. If so, where and how horizon effects emerge from mainstream models shall be important to understanding their impact on social costs.

A horizonal theory of pricing

Standard theories of price-setting have it that prices stem from some measure of unit cost multiplied by a mark-up based on demand elasticity. In neoclassical theory, a unique and determinate price emerges under standard assumptions of independence, substitution and decreasing returns so long as planning horizons are fixed, such that there are no horizon effects at play in an application. If planning horizons shorten or lengthen, price shifts upward or downward (Jennings 2008a). In a broader social context, the Marshallian scissors of supply and demand cut outward and downward as planning horizons extend (and inward and upward as they retract). Margolis (1960: 531–532) said it best, regarding an individual price-setter: 'The greater the uncertainty ... the shorter will be the planning horizon.... The implications ... are that the greater the ignorance of the market the higher will be the estimate of the costs and the more inelastic the estimate of demand.'

A useful way to think about it is that economists' static graphs – subject to *ceteris paribus* claims – occur in horizonal families in a file drawer full of transparencies sequenced by planning horizons. All longer-horizon constructs are at the back of the drawer, with more myopic conceptions in front. The price-setting decision involves selection of one transparency, that for the agent's planning horizon, determining how these relations are represented. The larger our frame of analysis or reflection, the more effects are considered (not only in time but across social and physical space as well).

But it is also important to understand that the planning horizon – as instantiated in private decisions – is not a matter of belief, but rather exists as an ordinal 'measure of fit' between the model on which we base our imagined projections of outcomes (among which we choose) and the real world to which we have no direct (epistemological) access. So planning horizons reflect not only the range but also the *accuracy* of our representations; surprises set the bounds of our rationality in this sense. We may think our horizons are long, if all our anticipated depictions of the effects of our actions stretch well ahead in time and penetrate deeply through the fog around us. But if what truly occurs spins off in some unexpected direction then our horizons were actually short, despite the effort we thought we had made. The planning horizon is an inductive ordinal measure of rational bounds, where reality has the last word.

In sum, the longer the planning horizon, the lower the price and the better the understanding of the social reactions to and outcomes of our decisions. If so, then horizon effects – namely ordinal changes in planning horizons in economic decisions – show predictable economic effects, including the range and impact of social costs spreading from private decisions in Kapp's sense of the term. These are some of the economic consequences of horizon effects, but 'private' horizon effects generate 'social' horizon effects in turn due to their interpersonal linkage.

Interhorizonal complementarity and its economic effects

The previous section only considered individual pricing decisions. Any economic construction based on interdependent decisions should address social effects. Standard theory in economics supposes substitution as our primary human relation: trade-offs, scarcity and opposition often define its subject from a far too narrow perspective. Complementarities are simply shunned, like increasing returns (Waldrop 1992: 18). Simon (1976: 140–141) called this 'the permanent and ineradicable scandal of economic theory', in which claims that complementarity 'is far more important' (Kaldor 1975: 348) are ignored (cf. Mueller 1984: 160) on the premise that 'there is ... no satisfactory alternative to neoclassical theory' (Hart 1984: 189; cf. Hahn 1981: 129), to which Simon (1979: 510) had noted that 'there is an embarrassing richness of alternatives'. As Kapp put it, describing the impact of competition on academics:

> Instead of testing our solutions by trying to disprove them we tend to defend them against evidence to the contrary.... Theoretical systems are not easily abandoned in the social sciences.... Social analysis and economic theory are no exceptions in this respect. In fact ... the social sciences encounter special difficulties when it comes to the necessary weeding out of untenable propositions ... due to the abundance and complexity of social evidence and the extreme difficulty of disproving 'experimentally' ... any particular social theory.
>
> (Kapp 1963: 1–2)

That being said, the persistence of substitution assumptions in economics – especially in the face of arguments and evidence for increasing returns in the long-run technical sense – illustrates what Kapp says. The point is that the dominant form of interdependence for all long-term material output (due to increasing returns) and for all intangible goods and horizonal change is complementarity (Jennings 2008a, 2010a). In the horizonal realm, your horizon effects impact others' in a similar manner (interhorizonal complementarity). When your horizons extend, those of others around you will lengthen as well; horizon effects are contagious, spreading from private to social milieux. If so, any horizon effects shift economic relations of interdependence in a predictable way. Consider the interrelation of maximum-profit prices in any group of firms with respect to their radiant externalities on the profits of others, or even the simple correlation of your well-being with mine. 'Market' theory – in its aggregation of firms into 'industries' – supposes substitution, overlooking complementarity. Any rule of composition or 'grouping' ought to include them both (Krupp 1963).

Indeed, in network contexts substitution and complementarity exist together in non-decomposable links, akin to the difference of parallel lines and end-to-end ties in transportation (Jennings 1985; 2006). But here as well, one trip's substitutes are another's complements, so even these specific connections are purpose- and context-bound. The grouping of firms or agents in a more general way than by 'industry' implies that substitution and complementarity always occur together in an often indeterminate balance in terms of their relative weight. But that balance seems to adjust in an orderly way with horizon effects: socioeconomic connections shift toward complementarity (concerts of value) and away from substitution (conflicts of value) with horizonal lengthening. For example, longer horizons mean lower prices and higher output and growth, increasing the size of the pie for everyone in a Pareto improvement. Furthermore, a greater range of foresight and conscience also reduces conflicts of interest directly, as people take into account – as horizons extend – more of their impact on others (hopefully in a considerate way). Longer horizons thereby increase the commonality of our interests and decrease strife and discord throughout social relations. Social costs are therefore reduced in the presence of longer horizons; such is the economic effect of interhorizonal complementarity, and it has many important institutional implications.

Competition and cooperation

The economic case for competition rests on substitution, where collusion raises price through restriction of output, decreasing social welfare. Inversely, complementarity yields a reciprocal case for cooperation; here, competition reduces output and so induces scarcity, just like collusion of substitutes. Substitution necessitates competition, but complementarity yields a case for cooperation as our route to economic efficiency. All the welfare implications of market structure reverse with complementary interdependence. Competition, although encouraging substitutes, stifles complements (starving all intangible goods and truncating horizons). If so, then competition is spawning a myopic culture resulting in an array of social costs better reduced through cooperation.

If longer planning horizons shift our relations toward complementarity, institutions should also evolve, favoring cooperation, to support economic advancement (Jennings 2009a). Otherwise, with longer horizons, competition impedes development and economic growth as the composition of output demand transforms in favor of mutual gains away from rival interests. The failure of institutions to adjust to this shift of interdependence stifles output and welfare, resulting in shorter planning horizons. Competition among complements spurs their reciprocal loss. In sum, due to social designs applied outside their assumed domain, threatened people get selfish, short-sighted and materialistic under this sort of organizational stress (Argyris 1971); such are signs of competitive failure rising from poorly structured incentives. Cooperation encourages output of complementary goods such as learning, love and human community, and the resulting horizonal lengthening into broader perspectives and knowledge also reduces social costs by increasing conscience in our decisions.

Substitution assumptions showing competition as efficient do not apply among complementarities where cooperation is sought. This is how and why competition is spawning a fearsome myopic culture, resulting in ethical and ecological losses along with a failure of vital media to inform a voting public so that democracy can thrive and the political process function (Jennings 2010a). These shortcomings are all due to competitive frames and their social effects, shrinking horizontal length, thus spreading a careless and socially ignorant culture evident to us all.

Learning environments stand as a ready example of complementarity: economists long have seen knowledge as a public good. Thus is it no surprise that competition discourages growth and the sharing of knowledge in educational settings. Ecologies serve as another realm of complementary interdependencies: see what economic competition is doing to them! Many economists say increasing returns substantiates complementarity as the dominant form of socioeconomic connection; this claim makes suspect the whole case for competitive virtue applied throughout economics. Kaldor (1975: 348) opined that: 'The principle of substitution ... ignores the essential complementarity between ... different types of activities ... which is far more important for an understanding ... of the economy than the substitution aspect.' Myrdal (1978: 774) explained the same thing in terms of 'cumulative effects' in a positive feedback process of circular causation. The importance of complementarity yields a different type of economics, similar to what Kapp proposed:

> The present investigation must thus be understood as part of a larger inquiry the purpose of which is ... to lay the foundation for a reformulation of economic analysis.... Such a new science of economics will have to recognize that a partial view of the economy can never lead to a rational (i.e. critical and scientific) view of the economic process ... which will always call for a comprehensive interpretation.... Only by overcoming the present compartmentalization of our knowledge in the social sciences ... will we be able to construct a new science of economics.
>
> (Kapp 1963: 11–12)

Economists' substitution assumptions have forced us into a box. Substitution derives from materialistic constructions in economics, while competition for love in a family setting erodes the total for all (McCloskey 1990: 142–143), to pick just one example. Love is a complementary good: the way to get more is to give it away (Jennings 2009c). Information is similar in its economic effects (Jennings 2008c). As Boulding (1968: 133–134) put it: '[T]eaching ... is the one clearly observable process in the universe where the strict laws of conservation do not hold.... Teaching is in no sense an exchange, in which what the student gets the teacher loses.' Indeed, the whole development process involves a shift from material goods to higher-order intangibles as sources of value in trade

(Maslow 1954; 1968). If so, wants shift away from material substitutes to intangible complements with economic advancement (Jennings 2009a). Longer horizons also reduce price, so increase the size of the pie, yielding greater complementarities and easing conflicts of interest; these are some of the ways in which longer horizons shape human relations in favor of greater community and reduced social costs. If so, our institutions should adapt to favor cooperation or economic growth will be stifled. The effects of competition – in creating a myopic culture – risk our health and general well-being as social costs spoil lives (Jennings 2010b). Kapp's (1963: 20) theory of social costs described the dangers so well: '[S]ocial costs threaten the life and health not only of the individual but of all humanity and play havoc with a rational use of our resources.' If competition truncates horizons, then it directly augments social costs spilling from private decisions.

Social and economic growth through horizon effects

Competition in complementary settings is doomed to fail. Look at the educational system as an example of this: science so opposed to new learning has self-defeating effects (Jennings 2008d). As Kapp put it regarding our scientific research establishment:

> Extreme secrecy, duplication, lack of coordination, absence of provision for the exchange of data and results achieved are all inherent in the normal organization of research under present conditions....
> These inefficiencies in the organization of science can have only one effect: a substantial proportion of the money and effort devoted to research is wasted and the progress of science is retarded.
>
> (Kapp 1963: 254)

Economics has been in a state of arrested development for many years (Leontief 1982); another academic case of fighting against new ideas is the long resistance to chaos theory (or non-linearity models) in physics (Gleick 1987; Waldrop 1992). As Kapp (1963: 289) said, disheartedly:

> So far, however, this broadening of the scope of economic analysis has not taken place. Traditional definitions of wealth and production, of productiveness and efficiency ... are among the most important obstacles to an understanding of the socio-economic issues of the twentieth century.

The problem is that the basic character of ecological interdependence in complex societies is not substitution but complementarity: only in narrow applications do rivalries seem to pertain (Jennings 2008b). Universal increasing returns suggest the same for economies (Kaldor 1972, 1975): If so, then competition is keeping our private and social horizons short, disrupting ecologies and defeating growth through organizational learning (Jennings 2009a). All is the counterproductive fault of economists' substitution assumptions.

In any advanced economic society, substitution is not our most general form of social interdependence; complementarity is. Increasing returns support this contention even in static contexts. Horizon effects strengthen the argument through interaction of planning horizons. Interhorizonal complementarity yields a case for cooperation not only in its direct effects but also by shaping our interdependence. If longer horizons always enhance the importance of complementarity over substitution in human affairs, economists should take heed. The general nature of interdependence – for all long-run material outputs, as well as for all intangible goods and throughout the realm of horizonal change – is not substitution but complementarity, yielding a case for cooperation as an efficiency standard and not one for competition. If so, then neoclassical economics, standing on substitution and decreasing returns, seems to have failed dramatically. The process of economic development changes social relations to enhance the importance of complementarity over substitution, negating orthodox standards and tools (Jennings 2009a).

This is not a point that Kapp raised, save with his call for a broadening of social science and economic analysis. However, this shift to complementarity away from substitution is so resonant with his ideas – since complementarity is almost synonymous with the twin notions of 'positive feedback' and 'cumulative causation' – that the horizonal theories suggested here offer new insight to Kapp's approach. They also offer another resolution to widespread social costs: that of an institutional adaptation to cooperation as a means to lengthen horizons and thus encourage a greater internalization of social losses such as Kapp propounds.

Indeed, the unraveling of our cultural and ecological fabric caused by our rivalrous social systems seems so evident at this juncture – one needs no detailed justification of this opinion nowadays – that Kapp's social cost theories should be center stage in the current study of economics. These signs of competitive failure reveal themselves in many ways: social, ethical, ecological, organizational and even cultural crises surround us at every turn. The cause is an economic claim ill-fit to its sphere of use. Social and economic growth is being cut off by short horizons; competition is keeping us socially and economically immature (Kohn 1986; Wachtel 1989). As some wise soul once said: 'Fish discover water last' (McGregor 1971: 317). We cannot see outside this box until we relax substitution assumptions for a broader representation of our interdependence and the social costs spilling on us from profit-seeking activity. Economics – in Kapp's view – will need to adopt a broader frame:

> In fact any attempt to delimit the scope of economic analysis is likely to yield only a distorted picture of the manifold problems with which economic science actually has to deal. It is not surprising, therefore, that most previous attempts to define the subject matter of economic science have failed to convey an adequate idea of the actual scope of economic analysis....

In fact a delimitation of the scope of economic science is not only unnecessary but actually harmful.... In the first place, it tends to make economics a closed system of thought.... Secondly, the specifically Robbinsian definition of the subject matter of economics in terms which do not transcend the horizon of a market economy, permits the drawing of the 'scientific' conclusion that any alternative form of economic organization would be incompatible with the principles of a rational utilization of scarce means for the attainment of competing ends.... Thirdly, the endeavor to delimit the subject matter of economics and of other social sciences has so far led only to the multiplication of artificial boundaries between the social disciplines and their compartmentalization. The resulting specialization and fragmentation of social inquiry tends to obstruct and defeat the search for knowledge and truth by restricting the scope and horizon of scholarly investigations. This is the road to futility in social inquiry which must be concerned with the analysis of a fundamentally interdependent socio-economic and political reality.

Indeed, scientific method in social and economic research calls for the progressive elimination of all boundaries which past generations of scholars have created for scholastical, pedagogical and other reasons. The ultimate aim is not merely 'collaboration' but the closest possible integration and ultimate synthesis of the social sciences.

(Kapp 1963: 285–287)

In any application dominated by complementarity – and it is argued here that this is the case for most economic connections – substitution assumptions, so any model built thereon, do not fit these settings, so will lead to other results than predicted by such theories. This is surely observable and true in the ecological sphere, as well as in many other realms of economic activity. Our myopic culture is reflected in media, education, politics and the ethical and ecological losses seen everywhere (Jennings 2010a); is it not time to address our myopia as a horizonal problem, in the spirit of Kapp's call for broadening economic analysis?

The ecological implications of horizon effects and myopic cultures

If every act ripples outward forever, an interdependent world demands a theory of planning horizons to address social costs and their resistance to regulation. In fully interdependent domains, we cannot see the effects of our actions beyond a horizonal limit depicting the bounds of our rationality (Simon 1982–1997). It is our range of foresight that determines social health and well-being. The short horizons stemming from competition disrupt any higher level of organizational effort better reflecting our interdependence. Such implies a case for cooperation to curb ecological loss and other social ills. We act, our consequences endure, and they always stretch beyond sight. Learning cooperation is our route to a healthy ecology, in its effect on horizonal length and the resulting internalization of social costs through ethics and broadening conscience.

Internalizing the cost of vital incursions on the environment through the price system makes a worthy start in the battle to save our resources (Kapp 1963; Hawken 1994). But this is only a holding action without an extension of planning horizons. Such myopic concerns, stemming from competitive forces – and thus with institutional roots – serve as the origin of ecological loss and the associated dispersion of various social costs so well described by Kapp. Slowing our pattern of value depletion necessitates shifting our institutions to favor cooperation and away from competitive frames. Such will lengthen horizons, so address the actual source of these problems of ecological loss and other related social costs.

The social costs of myopic cultures spawned by institutions standing on incorrect deductions from erroneous suppositions show no measure or bound, just as Kapp pointed out. The role of substitution assumptions serves to confine economic research to partial analyses of phenomena as if fenced off from other reactions in an interdependent domain. Substitution allows separation of forces treated in isolation; complementarity yields a process of 'cumulative causation' in which all is connected in a wholly interactive frame, mandating economic constructions based on dynamic complex systems such as Kapp proposed. Substitution assumptions have forestalled the development of economics into a more realistic confrontation with complementarity as an alternative form of interdependence. Few orthodox standards and tools survive in the absence of substitution and decreasing returns, such that an economics of fully dynamic complex systems is still undeveloped. This is the unmet challenge for economists of our time.

The very nature of an ecology – in its system manifestations and largest dimensions – shows in its interactive vitality and dynamic complexity. Each part ties to all others and changes spread in chaotic cascades of unpredictable outcomes wholly unbounded in their ramifications. Such a realm makes substitution assumptions – so theories standing thereon – untenable and destructive for realistic guidance in choice. So rivalry would yield tragedies stemming from opposition imposed on organizations where integration is needed for active functionality and to regulate social costs. Decentralization does not work in a complementary setting; cooperation and trust are required.

All learning – horizontal lengthening – calls for cooperation as the institutional form encouraging complementary goods. Such is the only ongoing answer to ecological loss, sustainable lives, social harmony and the long-term maintenance of the planet. There is no obvious solution other than dealing with the myopic culture resulting from competition as an institutional form. Even the effort to internalize social costs through regulation cannot prevail in a democratic culture lacking horizontal lengthening. Organizational – or individual – learning, growth and development turn on designs suited to an exchange of complementary goods subject to mutual losses and gains. Substitution does not apply in this setting: cooperation encourages output while competition creates scarcity, especially in the learning process. Indeed, the very viability of our life-support system – planet-wide – depends on adopting appropriate theories of economic connection based on complementarity as our most essential linkage.

In sum, mainstream models in economics have failed to specify our relations of interdependence sufficiently, properly or correctly. As a result, we soil our own nest, generating runaway social costs that threaten us all. Independence, substitution, trade-offs, scarcity and decreasing returns suppositions only apply to short-term material output, due to fixed or 'cranky' input factors; all long-term material outputs – subject to increasing returns – imply economic complementarity across social relations (Jennings 2008a; 2009b). Such is also the case for intangible goods and horizonal linkages, so our interdependence in every instance (save for short-term material outputs) is not defined by substitution but by complementarity, yielding the latter – and not the former – as our most general form of relation (Jennings 2010a). So efficiency characteristics would adapt away from competition to favor cooperation (Jennings 2005), especially in economic development (due to a change in the composition of output demand toward intangibles as civilizations advance), such that the balance of interdependence shifts toward complementarity with the horizonal lengthening consequent to economic cooperation in a self-reinforcing process.

Symptoms of organizational stress arising from inappropriate theories ill-fit to their realms of use include disintegration of effort (through turf wars and other pathologies), short-sightedness (myopia) and materialistic consumption, all observable features of our unhealthy social milieux. Indeed, the failure of corporate news to inform public debate directly threatens political liberty and democratic society. Even the educational process, saturated by rivalry, habituates us through avoidance of error to a fear of learning, as a potential explanation for the unbearable lightness of our communications media. Further, politics are so mired in noxious opposition that the regulations sought to forestall abuse of market power and to thwart ethical and ecological losses are often ineffective. Vast dangers stemming from our erroneous substitution assumptions and their institutional legacy are risking all we hold dear. Is it not time to deal with them before additional losses occur? Kapp (1963) posed these sorts of concerns and the social losses associated therewith in his prescient book. But Kapp did not develop planning horizons as a concept or include directly any explicit endorsement of complementarity, although it is almost synonymous with the ideas of cumulative causation and positive feedback which he used.

So what is needed at this point is a marriage of Kapp's theory of social costs with the notion of planning horizons and 'horizon effects'. This will extend the scope of Kapp's theory, enriching his very insightful discussion of social costs with a new understanding of how competition has failed due to its substitution assumptions: applied to complementary realms, they promulgate tragic consequences for ecological and human health (Jennings 1999; 2003; 2010b). The pathological symptoms of competitive failures surround us; such will always show wherever rivalrous substitution assumptions are wrongly applied to organizational settings steeped in complementarities. Social losses spreading outward across society and the ecology are a result of horizon effects stemming from incorrect theories applied to realms where they have no place. Substitution and competition do not pertain among complementarities; if complementarity – cumulative causation, to use Kapp's term adopted from Myrdal and Veblen – is our most general form of interdependence, then the economics of competition is wrongly used in these settings. So economists sorely need the reformulation proposed by Kapp in his statement above.

Indeed, the ecological economics of horizon effects is a research program in need of attention. All avoidable losses of vital living ecologies are horizontal; longer planning horizons are the key to both their rescue and the internalization of social costs through conscience and public finance (via taxes and other well-structured incentives). Institutions supporting competition do not tolerate any relief from myopic concerns. The only way environmental losses shall be curbed is through a wrenching cultural shift to cooperation, away from competition – if that can be done. No other remedy is sustainable, even with Kapp's suggested development of minimum standards as a means to reduce social costs. Somewhat assuring is the fact that cooperation will sell itself, given a chance to work, capturing gains for all in a less stressed domain. The role learning and knowledge play in economic efficiencies sought through successful collaboration is the primary implication of a horizonal economics. Such an approach should dovetail well with Kapp's theory of social costs.

Conclusion

Orthodox economics stands on its substitution assumptions, which support the case for competition as an efficient design. Substitution depicts societies shaped by *conflicts of value*: efficiency eases scarcity and an inherent trade-off of wants. If you do better, I do worse: our gains are always opposed. This view is supported by a reliance on economic convexity and closed-system models seen as central to rigorous science by many academic economists. But in its practical workings, competition does not produce the outcomes so richly offered in theory. Instead, dangerous symptoms of ill economic and ecological health are radiating outward in the form of social costs simply ignored by intransigent theorists sequestered in academic cloisters. So little has changed in the 50 years since Kapp (1963) presented the second edition of his book on social costs that his words still apply – as do Veblen's (1898) – to economics today. Is that not a testament to the lack of progress both men assailed? There is something terribly wrong with academic competition that appears increasingly evident in the behavior rampant therein. The core of the problem manifests in economists' substitution assumptions in their application to a complementary setting of academic creation and transfers of knowledge as an intangible good.

Proper recognition of an alternative form of interdependence should change our institutional understanding of how we organize academic communities for effective performance and development. The case for increasing returns and horizon effects suggests that economic relations show *concerts of value*, with our ambitions aligned. If fortunes are linked, we rise and fall together; and I wish you well, not ill. There is no limit to economic growth and well-being in this scenario, emphasizing intangibles and learning over conflicts of interest. The main constraint on development is our rivalrous system and culture: 'We have met the enemy, and he is us.' Social costs stemming from inappropriate theories of competition applied where they have no proper relevance shorten horizons and divert attention from meaningful lessons and truths.

Short horizons stand as a primary cause of ecological loss. Short horizons are remedied by a shift to cooperation and away from competitive frames. Competition does not yield growth in a complementary universe, such as in education, communications, politics or ecology; instead, the effects are arrested development, stress and systemic collapse. Such is not a conclusion afforded by orthodox substitution assumptions or any arguments standing thereon. Kapp's theory of social cost describes such problems well, limning preventive and practical means addressed to minimum tolerance limits along with thresholds for regulation based on human needs. But this approach shall have more promise combined with horizonal theory and the case for an institutional shift toward cooperation and away from competition due to its harmful social effects. This strategic combination ought to enrich both theories, supporting further research on how each might be extended effectively.

Evolving our institutional setting in favor of cooperation, especially in those spheres where complementarities show in bolder relief, forces serious sociocultural changes on us for which we are ill-prepared. The forceful internalization of social costs through regulation is equally risky in a democracy imbued with short horizons along with a woeful level of voter apathy. Yet the urgency of this situation can hardly be overstated. The losses of biodiversity in an age of rapid climate change, runaway population growth and the rapid pace of change in our lives shall be catastrophic if we continue on our present course. The social and natural losses implied by ethical and ecological failures shall become irreversible if we do not turn our myopic culture around to embrace institutional learning and more cohesive forms of economic organization, along with a fuller accounting of social costs. The promise of longer horizons cannot be met in conditions of fear, relentless strife, insecure rage, ongoing crisis or tragic collapse, nor can Kapp's theory of social costs be effectively applied in this context. We must act before these dangers consume us along with our options.

References

Argyris, C. (1971) 'The impact of the organization on the individual', in Pugh, D.S. (ed.), *Organization Theory*, New York: Penguin.

Blaug, M. (1976) 'Kuhn versus Lakatos or paradigms versus research programmes in the history of economics', in Latsis, S.J. (ed.), *Method and Appraisal in Economics*, Cambridge: Cambridge University Press.

Boulding, K.E. (1966) 'The economics of knowledge and the knowledge of economics', *American Economic Review, Papers and Proceedings*, 56(2): 1–13.

Boulding, K.E. (1968) 'Some questions on the measurement and evaluation of organization', in *Beyond Ethics: Essays on Society, Religion and Ethics*, Ann Arbor: University of Michigan Press.

Georgescu-Roegen, N. (1970) 'The economics of production', *American Economic Review, Papers and Proceedings*, 60(2): 1–9.

Gleick, J. (1987) *Chaos: Making a New Science*, New York: Viking Penguin.

Hahn, F. (1981) 'General equilibrium theory', in Bell, D. and Kristol, I. (eds.), *The Crisis in Economic Theory*, New York: Basic Books.

Hart, O. (1984) 'Comment' on Mueller, in Wiles, P. and Routh, G. (eds.), *Economics in Disarray*, Oxford: Basil Blackwell.

Hawken, P. (1994) *The Ecology of Commerce: A Declaration of Sustainability*, New York: HarperBusiness.

Jennings, F.B. Jr. (1985) 'Public policy, planning horizons and organizational breakdown: a post-mortem on British canals and their failure', Ph.D. dissertation, Stanford University.

Jennings, F.B. Jr. (1999) *'Scaring the Fish': A Critique of the NRC's Justification for Individual Transferable Quotas (ITQs) and a Systems Analysis of their Likely Effects*, Washington, DC and Ipswich, MA: Greenpeace USA and CEEEE.

Jennings, F.B. Jr. (2003) 'Ecology, economics and values', *Environmental Health*, 3(2): 40–57.

Jennings, F.B. Jr. (2005) 'How efficiency/equity tradeoffs resolve through horizon effects', *Journal of Economic Issues*, 39(2): 365–373.

Jennings, F.B. Jr. (2006) 'A horizonal challenge to orthodox theory: competition and cooperation in transportation networks', in Pickhardt, M. and Sarda Pons, J. (eds.), *Perspectives on Competition in Transportation*, Berlin: LIT Verlag.

Jennings, F.B. Jr. (2008a) 'A new economics of complementarity, increasing returns and planning horizons', in Elsner, W. and Hanappi, H. (eds.), *Varieties of Capitalism and New Institutional Deals*, Cheltenham: Edward Elgar.

Jennings, F.B. Jr. (2008b) 'A cognitive view of scale and growth', in Chapman, R.L. (ed.), *Creating Sustainability Within Our Midst: Challenges for the 21st Century*, New York: Pace University Press.

Jennings, F.B. Jr. (2008c) 'A horizonal theory of pricing in the new information economy', in Richter, C. (ed.), *Bounded Rationality in Economics and Finance*, Berlin: LIT Verlag.

Jennings, F.B. Jr. (2008d) 'Hammers, nails and new constructions: orthodoxy or pluralism – an institutional view', presented at the Association for Institutional Thought (AFIT) Conference, Denver, CO, April, and at the International Consortium of Associations for Pluralism in Economics (ICAPE) Conference, University of Utah, Salt Lake City, UT, June 2007.

Jennings, F.B. Jr. (2009a) 'Does competition advance or retard economic development? An institutional view', presented at the AFIT (WSSA) Conference, Albuquerque, NM, April.

Jennings, F.B. Jr. (2009b) ''The Hicksian Getaway' and 'The Hirshleifer Rescue': increasing returns from Clapham to Kaldor', presented at the AFIT (WSSA) Conference, Albuquerque, NM, April.

Jennings, F.B. Jr. (2009c) 'The economics of love', in Richter, C., Calero, A., Vieira, C. and Vieira, I. (eds.), *Challenges for Economic Policy Design: Lessons from the Financial Crisis*, Saarbrucken: Lambert Academic Publishing.

Jennings, F.B. Jr. (2010a) 'Atoms, bits and wits: the elements of economics', presented at the AFIT (WSSA) Conference, Reno, NV, April.

Jennings, F.B. Jr. (2010b) 'The economic cultures of fear and love', presented at the Association for Social Economics (ASE) 13th World Congress, Montreal, June.

Kaldor, N. (1972) 'The irrelevance of equilibrium economics', *Economic Journal*, 82: 1237–1255.

Kaldor, N. (1975) 'What is wrong with economic theory', *Quarterly Journal of Economics*, 89(3): 347–357.

Kapp, K.W. (1963) *Social Costs of Business Enterprise*, Bombay: Asia Publishing House.

Kohn, A. (1986) *No Contest: The Case Against Competition*, Boston, MA: Houghton Mifflin.

Krupp, S.R. (1963) 'Analytic economics and the logic of external effects', *American Economic Review, Papers and Proceedings*, 53(2): 220–226.

Krupp, S.R. (1982) 'Axioms of economics and the claim to efficiency', in Samuels, W.J. (ed.), *The Methodology of Economic Thought: Critical Papers from the Journal of Economic Issues*, New Brunswick: Transaction Books.

Leontief, W. (1982) 'Academic economics', *Science*, 217(9): 104–107; also appearing as the Foreword in Eichner, A.S. (ed.) (1983) *Why Economics is Not Yet a Science*, Armonk: M.E. Sharpe.

McCloskey, D.N. (1990) *If You're So Smart: The Narrative of Economic Expertise*, Chicago: University of Chicago Press.

McGregor, D. (1971) 'Theory X and theory Y', in Pugh, D.S. (ed.), *Organization Theory*, New York: Penguin.

Margolis, J. (1960) 'Sequential decision making in the firm', *American Economic Review, Papers and Proceedings*, 50(2): 526–533.

Maslow, A. (1954) *Motivation and Personality*, New York : Harper and Row.

Maslow, A. (1968) *Toward a Psychology of Being*, New York: Van Nostrand.

Mirowski, P. (1986) 'Mathematical formalism and economic explanation', in Mirowski, P. (ed.), *The Reconstruction of Economic Theory*, Boston, MA: Kluwer-Nijhoff.

Mueller, D. (1984) 'Further reflections on the invisible-hand theorem', in Wiles, P. and Routh, G. (eds.), *Economics in Disarray*, Oxford: Basil Blackwell.

Myrdal, G. (1978) 'Institutional economics', *Journal of Economic Issues*, 12(4): 771–783.

Reder, M.W. (1982) 'Chicago economics: permanence and change', *Journal of Economic Literature*, 20(1): 1–38.

Robinson, J. (1941) 'Rising supply price', *Economica*, 8: 1–8; reprinted in (1952) *A.E.A. Readings in Price Theory*, Chicago: Irwin

Simon, H.A. (1976) 'From substantive to procedural rationality', in Latsis, S.J. (ed.), *Method and Appraisal in Economics*, Cambridge: Cambridge University Press.

Simon, H.A. (1979) 'Rational decision making in business organizations', *American Economic Review*, 69(4): 493–513.

Simon, H.A. (1982–1997) *Models of Bounded Rationality*, Vols. 1–3, Cambridge, MA: MIT Press.

Veblen, T.B. (1898) 'Why is economics not an evolutionary science?', *Quarterly Journal of Economics*, 12(3): 373–397; reproduced in Veblen, T. (1990) *The Place of Science in Modern Civilization and Other Essays*, New Brunswick: Transaction Publishers, pp. 56–81.

Wachtel, P. (1989) *The Poverty of Affluence: A Psychological Portrait of the American Way of Life*, Philadelphia: New Society Publishers.

Waldrop, M.M. (1992) *Complexity: The Emerging Science at the Edge of Order and Chaos*, New York: Simon and Schuster.

4 Planned obsolescence and the manufacture of doubt

On social costs and the evolutionary theory of the firm

Pietro Frigato and
Francisco Javier Santos-Arteaga

In this chapter we adopt and extend in a precise direction Mayhew's critical arguments against the evolutionary theory of the firm as elaborated by Nelson and Winter (Mayhew 2000). Focusing on the distinction between 'fixed and open systems of analysis', Mayhew emphasizes the sharp difference between Veblen's theory of business enterprise and the 'truncating' view of Nelson and Winter (ibid.: 57).

There are, of course, a number of problems connected with this broad theoretical issue. We may, just passing through, call attention to the clear inconsistency between Mayhew's position and Hodgson's well-known interpretation, according to which Nelson and Winter's work is largely compatible with Veblenian institutionalism. Nelson's receipt of the Veblen-Commons award in 2007, Hodgson has pointed out, 'is in recognition for his great and hugely inspiring contribution to a modern evolutionary and institutional economics' (Hodgson 2007). Such assumed theoretical convergence is further confirmed by the fact that Nelson himself 'has fully acknowledged his affinity with the original institutionalism' (ibid.). Indeed, Nelson deliberately accepts both Veblen's concept of institutions and Veblen's focus on how things are done (Nelson 2007: 314; Nelson 2008: 2).

We clarify a well-specified aspect of this neglected compatibility issue. In particular, we address the theoretical relationship between the theories of social costs of business enterprise of the 'old' institutionalists – Veblen and Kapp – and the most up-to-date version of the evolutionary theory of the firm elaborated by Richard R. Nelson. Starting from Nelson and Winter's treatment of production routines in their seminal book, *An Evolutionary Theory of Economic Change* (1982), we discuss Nelson's recent work on the concept of 'social technologies' in the context of the Veblenian–Kappian critique of business enterprise and the competitive mechanism.

We show that Nelson's evolutionary approach to the firm sharply differs from the Veblenian–Kappian approach. Although pertinently focusing on firms' 'knowing how to do' (and 'to choose') (Nelson and Winter 1982: 52), Nelson's competence-based theory completely disregards the fundamental distinction between *making things* and *making money* or, put another way, the 'controlling dichotomy' of business and industry (Tsuru 1997: 61). This neglect explains two sanitizing elements underlying Nelson's and Winter's evolutionary theory of the firm and Nelson's more recent work on the coevolution between 'physical' and 'social' technologies: the equation between technological innovation under business and market guidance, and technological advance or progress; the assimilation of economic growth to economic progress.

We start by briefly reconstructing the evolutionary theory of the firm elaborated by Nelson and Winter. We then turn to Nelson's recent effort to integrate a useful concept of institutions (dominant social technologies) in their original theoretical framework. The next step will be to illustrate the core arguments of Veblen and Kapp concerning how the business management of industry tends to favor the institutionalization of various forms of disservices. This was Veblen's and Kapp's central thesis. After recalling the former's path-breaking position we sketch out Kapp's theory of social costs of business enterprise. For their relevance to the present discussion, we illustrate Kapp's treatment of planned obsolescence and his critique of GDP as an indicator of economic performance.

Selected recent theoretical and empirical research concerning the deliberate shortening of the lifespan of products and the limits of GDP as an indicator of progress in terms of human welfare shows the enduring relevance of these early institutional arguments. We contextually discuss the well-settled and today highly sophisticated organizational routine among big businesses, which goes under the name of 'scientific misunderstanding'. Albeit apparently unforeseen by Veblen and Kapp, this type of misbehavior adds to the argument that business principles and practices might entail criminal elements and be extremely wasteful from a social point of view.

Doubtlessly, Nelson provides some useful insights in business decision-making analysis that are compatible with the old institutional legacy. Indeed, the very emphasis he puts on 'how things are done' both in terms of physical and social technologies (see the section on Nelson's recent work, below) is, in our view, typically institutionalist. However, his complete disregard of the Veblenian distinction between business and industry has a far-reaching negative implication: In accordance with his previous work with Winter, Nelson's more recent analysis of physical and social technologies and his definition of the very goals of economic science continue to be based upon a sanitized and unrealistic conception of the firm and economic calculus.

Thus, if one accepts Nelson's view of the capitalist firm then he must necessarily acknowledge that the converging analyses of social costs of business enterprise of Veblen and Kapp are outdated and irrelevant for fruitful economic theorizing. Contemporary discussions on the building blocks of old institutionalism and the theory of the firm tell the story of a silent removal of the theory of social costs among present-day original institutionalists.

A short reconstruction of *An Evolutionary Theory of Economic Change*

Richard Nelson and Sidney Winter have developed an evolutionary theory of the behavior of business firms competing in a market environment (Nelson and Winter 1982: 3). Their main interest concerns 'the dynamic process by which firm behaviour patterns and market outcomes are jointly determined over time' (ibid.: 18).

Firms are regarded as 'motivated by profit and engaged in search for ways to improve their profits' (ibid.: 4). Firms nevertheless are not assumed to be profit maximizing over exogenously well-defined possibility sets. Thus, Nelson and Winter's maximization hypothesis is by no means the optimal maximization assumed by the orthodox view. Evolutionary theory accepts 'an assumption of "profit-seeking" or "profit-motivated striving", but certainly not of profit maximization' (ibid.: 31). Following Simon's bounded rationality concept, 'firms cannot maximize', 'firms satisfice' (ibid.: 35).

In their search for profits, business enterprises can rely upon context-specific capabilities and decision rules. These competencies and procedures evolve. They

> are modified as a result of both deliberate problem-solving efforts and random events. And, over time, the analogue of natural selection operates as the market determines which firms are profitable and which are unprofitable, and tends to winnow out the latter.
>
> (Ibid.: 4)

To put it differently, 'market environments provide a definition of success for business firms, and the definition is very closely related to their ability to survive and grow' (ibid.: 9). Market competition in the different sectors operates as the selection environment. According to Schumpeter, a major source of inspiration for Nelson and Winter, competition provides

> both a carrot and a stick to motivate firms to introduce better production methods or products. 'Better' here has an unambiguous meaning: lower cost of production, or a new product that consumers are willing to buy at a price above the cost. In either case the criterion boils down to a higher monetary profit. Successful innovation leads to both higher profit for the innovator and to profitable investment opportunities. Thus, profitable firms grow. In so doing they cut away the market for the noninnovators and reduce their profitability, which, in turn, will force these firms to contract. Both the visible profits of the innovators and the losses experienced by the laggers stimulate the latter to try to imitate.
>
> (Ibid.: 266)

Another beneficial consequence of competition, in a Schumpeterian perspective, is 'to reward and enhance the choices that prove good in practice and suppress the bad ones' (ibid.: 276). Over the long term, this positively affects the overall efficiency of the system: 'The competitive system would promote firms that choose well on the average and would eliminate, or force reform upon, firms that consistently make mistakes.... This is very much the position taken by Schumpeter more than seventy years ago' (ibid.: 276–277).

The concept of 'routine' provides an essential theoretical tool for the understanding of the evolutionary process by which firm behavior patterns and market outcomes are co-determined over time. Production or organization routines determine the behavior of firms in the same way genes define that of living organisms in biological evolutionary theory. In this sense, routines are heritable and selectable, allowing those firms with superior-performing routines to increase their relative importance in their corresponding industries (ibid.: 14).[1]

Moreover, 'profitability operates, through firm investment rules, as one major determinant of rates of expansion and contraction' (ibid.: 18–19). Accordingly, in Nelson's and Winter's models 'profit is the only business objective explicitly recognized' (ibid.: 30).

Operationally, the concept of routine encompasses

> characteristics of firms that range from well-specified technical routines for producing things, through procedures for hiring and firing, ordering new inventory, or stepping up production of items in high demand, to policies regarding investment, research and development (R&D), or advertising, and business strategies about product diversification and overseas investment.
>
> (Ibid.: 14)

Successful businesses '*remember* by *doing*' (ibid.: 99) through the reiteration of their satisficingly profitable activities:

> When this is the case, the routine (in its smoothly functioning version) takes on the quality of a norm or target, and managers concern themselves with trying to deal with actual or threatened disruptions of the routine. That is, they try to keep the routine under control.
>
> (Ibid.: 112)

Thus, satisficingly profitable routines are relatively durable and stable, since the surviving organizations to which they belong to will tend to resist mutations over those presenting themselves as 'desirable innovations' (ibid.: 116; see also 134–135).

Successful business firms' control systems 'struggle' against environmental 'potentially mutagenic events' (ibid.: 117). This conservative tendency can be rather easily explained: Profit satisficing routines tend to be replicated due to the evolutionary advantage they confer to the firms adopting them. Hence,

> if an existing routine is a success, replication of that success is likely to be desired. In particular, in the models to follow, the organization in question is

a business firm for which success is roughly measured by profits, and replication of productive routines is motivated by a desire to replicate the profit
flows that those routines make possible.

(Ibid.: 121)

As a consequence, when confronted with environmental obstacles and adver-
sities, profitable firms tend to remain firmly committed to their 'existing ways of
doing things': 'the only "search" that goes on is for the resources to continue to
finance the existing routine' (ibid.: 122).

Given these operational rigidities, how is it possible for innovation to
occur? As concrete, 'useful questions arise in the form of puzzles or anomalies
relating to prevailing routines', innovations emerge, in large part from 'new
combinations of existing routines' (ibid.: 129–130). Of course, R&D done by
business firms is dominated by profit-seeking too – 'and the more profit the
better' (ibid.: 250).

Technological advance, as a result of private business innovation, is cumulative, in the sense that 'as the product evolves, so do the processes of production'
(ibid.: 258); and 'the new is not just better than the old; in some sense the new
evolves out of the old' (ibid.: 255). The examples of aviation and petroleum-
refining technology tell stories of product cycles characterized by 'a flow of subsequent improvements' and a 'hunting for marginal improvements' (ibid.:
256–258).

Both products and production processes evolve in the direction of cumulative
upgrading. Nelson and Winter assume that 'learning curves' lead to simultaneous improvements in workers' activities, management decision-making and
engineering practices (ibid.: 258). Satisficing profitability becoming a widespread target of the business management of industry in specific productive
branches allows for the institutionalization of 'technological regimes' and 'trajectories' (ibid.: 258–259):

> While natural trajectories almost invariably have special elements associ-
> ated with the particular technology in question, in any era there appear to be
> certain natural trajectories that are common to a wide range of technologies.
> Two of these have been relatively well identified in the literature: progres-
> sive exploitation of latent economies of scale and increasing mechanization
> of operations that have been done by hand.

(Ibid.: 259)

Other examples of 'widely used natural trajectories' inaugurated in the twentieth century are: 'First, the exploitation of an understanding of electricity and
the resulting creation and improvement of electrical and later electronic components, and, second, similar developments regarding chemical technologies'
(ibid.: 261).

Nelson and Winter make clear that underlying these industrial developments
'is a body of knowledge held by the technicians, engineers, and scientists

involved in the relevant inventive activity' (ibid.: 261). They also point out that 'often an innovation is produced by a firm for sale to customers who will use it' (ibid.: 263). The disciplining role of business management over scientific and technological research is nevertheless treated as irrelevant for the study of technological regimes or paradigms in the neo-Schumpeterian framework elaborated by Nelson and Winter. This omission occurs despite their focus on the 'industrial research laboratory that is represented as central to the innovation process' (ibid.: 278).

Nelson and Winter explicitly address 'the issue of the strengths and weaknesses of free enterprise' in their discussion of contemporary welfare economic theory (ibid.: 22). They admit that social costs of business enterprise are pervasive. They nevertheless specify that an evolutionary perspective on welfare economics does not aim at 'a radical departure' from the standard neoclassical interventionist view (ibid.: 362). Market failures are 'partially remediable with ancillary organizational machinery', leading to a 'patched-up system' (ibid.: 358). Through their discussion of Environmental Protection Agency regulations which 'took the form of particular required standards' imposed upon business producers they convincingly show that these forms of intervention did not try to come to grips with the trade-offs that specified standards implied, and disregarded the potential usefulness of a range of possible alternative measures (ibid.: 374). In order to overcome these typical rigidities, Nelson and Winter advocate for policies that comprehensively acknowledge the complexity of the public–private interactions resulting from their implementation (ibid.: 385). As a consequence they refuse 'simple (and simple-minded) arguments about the optimality of private enterprise, or simple pointing to market failures' (ibid.: 385). In particular, in the case of social costs, 'the unique organizational characteristics of a particular sector ought to come to the fore in the analysis of policy toward that sector' (ibid.: 364). These last types of arguments are coherently re-evoked in the recent work of Nelson, *The Limits of Market Organization* (Nelson 2005: 2, ch. 14).

Nelson's recent work on 'social technologies' and institutions

Although it was based on the concept of productive or organizational routines, the original analysis of Nelson and Winter almost exclusively focused on the evolution of 'physical technologies' while not assigning a definite role to the concept of institutions.[2] The need to incorporate a useful concept of institutions in the evolutionary theory of the firm, elaborated with Winter, has been explicitly recognized by Nelson for the first time in a paper with Sampat (Nelson and Sampat 2001; Nelson 2007: 315).

In Nelson and Sampat (2001) we find the general formulation of this integrative effort. Coherently with their acceptance of the 'broadly shared conception' among economists according to which 'institutions influence, or define, the ways in which economic actors get things done' (ibid.: 39), Nelson and Sampat aim at elaborating 'a concept of institutions that is useful for analysis of factors molding economic performance, and long run economic growth in particular' (ibid.: 33).

How, then, do you bring institutions into a theory of production and economic growth? Elaborating on the concept of an 'economic activity', in order to disclose the multi-party interaction that characterizes most production activities, Nelson and Sampat focus on *how activities are carried out*: 'While that notion is presumed to involve a description of the "physical" technology involved, here we propose also to include a characterization of the "social" technologies' (ibid.: 40). The notions of 'social technologies' and 'physical technologies' are quite similar. However, whereas the former involve 'patterned human interaction', the latter have to deal with 'physical engineering' (ibid.: 40). In particular, social technologies focus on the effective coordination of interactions among different people as a basic requisite for accomplishment (ibid.: 40). Thus,

> Sampat and I proposed that it might be useful to call the recipe aspect of an activity its 'physical' technology, and the way work is divided and coordinated its 'social' technology. From this perspective, virtually all economic activities involve the use of both physical and social technologies. The productivity or effectiveness of an activity is determined by both aspects.
>
> (Nelson 2008: 3)

The intimate intertwining of the development of physical and social technologies, i.e., their coevolution, is highly problematic, since 'the process of evolution of social technologies and their supporting institutions is erratic, compared to the way physical technologies evolve' (ibid.: 7). The main reason explaining this diversity is that 'physical technologies are amenable to sharp specification and control' and 'easier to replicate and imitate' than social technologies:

> The performance of physical technologies, including the nature of the output they produce, tends to be relatively tightly constrained by the physical inputs and processing equipment used in their operation. On the other hand social technologies are much more open to the vagaries of human motivations, and understandings regarding what is to be done, which seldom can be controlled closely.
>
> (Ibid.: 8)

Whereas physical technologies can be tested through deliberate experimentation in controlled settings, social technologies cannot be easily isolated 'from the influences of a wide variety of other variables that bear on the profitability of a firm' (ibid.: 8). 'Progressive cumulative learning' is typical in the case of engineers and designers; this is not the case for 'business or research organization' (ibid.: 9). That is, obtaining reliable evidence on the efficacy of a new institution or social technology constitutes a much more difficult task than measuring the performance of a new physical technology (ibid.: 8). This discrepancy in assessment possibilities explains why social technologies 'develop much more erratically and slowly than do physical technologies' (ibid.: 10). Effectiveness, in both cases, is measured as 'economic viability' or as the capacity of a business enterprise to make money satisfyingly (ibid.: 10).

Of course, this intrinsic difficulty in evaluating the economic performance of social technologies does not impede their selection and institutionalization. We may note in this respect that, once determined social technologies become so diffused that they are 'a standard and expected thing to do, given the objectives and the setting', they become institutions (Nelson and Sampat 2001: 40, 44; see also Nelson 2007: 316).[3] 'Standardized social technologies' do indeed prevail as the interacting modes for getting things done in a society (ibid.: 316).

In other words, in as much as ' "social technologies" come to be regarded by the relevant social group as standard in the context' they become institutions: 'Under our proposed language, not all social technologies are institutions, but rather only those that have become a standard and expected thing to do, given the objectives and the setting' (Nelson and Sampat 2001: 40)[4] This formulation of the problem of social technologies and institutions allows Nelson and Sampat to recognize that 'our institutions concept corresponds to Veblen's "widespread habits of action", and to Schotter's "way the game is played" ' (ibid.: 40).

Of course, a 'widely used social technology' (i.e., an institution) requires flexibility in order to be implemented in a range of specific contexts:

> Thus, our concept of institutions as social technologies is consonant with the notion that institutions are 'the rules of the game' when these are regarded as defining relatively closely, but with discretionary room, what people do when they play the game.
>
> (Ibid.: 40)

Building on their concept of institutions, Nelson and Sampat propose a theoretical and empirical research program emphasizing the relative rigidity associated with the actual institutional dynamics:

> Once they become institutionalized, they become attractive ways to do something. We can couch our proposal in the language of transaction costs. Institutionalized social technologies define low transaction cost ways of doing things that involve human interaction. Note that, under this conception, on the one hand, institutions are constraints. They in effect define the particular ways things must be done if they are to be done parsimoniously. But, on the other hand, effective institutions, like effective physical technologies, define productive pathways for doing things. Absent of an effective institutionalized social technology for doing something, it may be very costly to do that thing, or doing it may be impossible.
>
> (Ibid.: 41)

Standard social technologies, or institutions, are at a single time organizations, governing rules and prevailing customary attitudes:

In addition to being embodied in and molded by particular organizational and governance structures, standardized social technologies are formed, and held in place, in the context of the broad system of norms, beliefs, and rules of the game, that prevail in a society. We propose that our social technologies concept is a useful generalization of North's notion of the variety of particular kinds of institutional arrangements that are allowed by the institutional environment. The language we are using here associates the term institutions with the specific behavioural (and organizational) structures, and uses the term institutional environment for the more general molding forces.

(Ibid.: 41)

The theoretical relationship between routines and physical and social technologies is explicitly addressed by Nelson and Sampat.

We believe that the language of routines, as developed in Nelson and Winter (1982), is a useful vehicle for characterizing social technologies, and we begin our analysis with a general discussion of the 'routines' concept. A routine involves a collection of procedures which, taken together, result in a predictable and specifiable outcome. Complex routines, of the sort associated with the production of goods and services, almost always can be analytically broken down into a collection of subroutines.

(Ibid.: 42)

Productive routines include at once 'a recipe that is anonymous regarding any division of labor, and a division of labor plus a mode of coordination' (ibid.: 44). The first aspect concerns the physical technology involved, whereas the second deals with the organizational aspect, i.e., the social technology.

When analyzing concrete industrial sectors and businesses it can be observed that

prevailing physical and social technology limit choices regarding how to do things.... Available inputs – machinery and materials – generally are tailored for use in prevailing routines, and to try to do something significantly different may require hand crafting the inputs, perhaps at considerable cost and risk of failure ... innovation is risky for exactly the reasons put forth.

(Ibid.: 44)

Thus, while the detailed operation of a routine by a business organization leaves considerable room for variation and idiosyncratic elements (differences in the details), 'at its core almost always are elements that are broadly similar to what other competent parties would do in the same context' (ibid.: 43). In this sense, 'particular routines tend to be parts of systems of routines' (ibid.: 43).

The relative stability of sector-specific production routines explains why physical and social technologies operate both 'as constraints and as productive pathways' (ibid.: 44). Of course, prevalent social technologies may be 'highly inefficient compared with other ways of organizing transactions' (ibid.: 44). They may obstruct the introduction or smooth functioning of new physical technologies or impede an efficient allocation of resources as market conditions change (ibid.: 44).

'Prevailing institutions', 'defined in terms of generally employed ways to get things done where the doing involves coordinating the actions of independent individuals or organizations', tend nevertheless to characterize the functioning of markets (ibid.: 45). The concept of market can indeed be 'modelled as a set of processes or routines' (ibid.: 45) and actual competitive struggles are heavily influenced by 'the institutionalized social technologies' that take on 'the character of norms' among competitors (ibid.: 45): 'Major deviation from them is, at least, cause for notice and surprise, and likely will lead to inadequate outcomes' (ibid.: 46).

In the language of transaction costs, Nelson and Sampat argue, 'institutions define and provide low transaction cost ways of doing things that require coordinated interaction with other parties' (ibid.: 47). Hence, 'developing an institutionalized way of doing something may be the only way to achieve a low transaction cost way of doing it' (ibid.: 47). In this respect, we may note that these transaction cost minimizing practices do not automatically help reduce social costs to a minimum. Reality seems to offer a dramatic picture concerning the social repercussions of the social technologies employed in most settled productive branches.

Like any other social technology, specific cost-shifting techniques and maneuvers (including criminal activities) also tend to be forms of learned behavior, and tend to exhibit contagion-like patterns with very high concentrations in particular sectors – the petrochemical, automobile and pharmaceutical industries representing prominent examples in this respect (Heath 2008: 601; Clinard 2005). Organizational theorist Charles Perrow, an inspiring source for the works of Nelson, points out that 'organizations sometimes lie to protect themselves and hope they won't be found out' (Perrow 1992: 374). 'False documents can be institutionalized as true documents' and 'documents that lie about how disasters will be limited or averted are special kinds of social constructions', 'carefully designed with the law in mind', that help corporations in limiting legal liability and regulation (ibid.: 374). As we have mentioned above, a good illustration of these 'techniques of neutralization' (Heath 2008: 605–610), largely employed in business as plausible-sounding excuses and disguises for misconduct, is provided by 'scientific misunderstanding'. The question concerning 'efficiency for whom' becomes decisive once one accepts the existence of these institutionalized cost-shifting practices (Perrow 1992: 374).

Veblen and Kapp: the social costs of 'prevailing social and physical technologies' in business

The coevolution of markets and production systems, at the core of Nelson's theory of the firm, can have widespread adverse societal repercussions. Viki

Sonntag has recently shown that, in order to stay competitive, firms adopt strategies that through the growing recourse to the new manufacturing technologies favor product obsolescence (Sonntag 2000). Although Sonntag's analysis is explicitly formulated within the framework of the evolutionary theory of the firm, we may note that planned obsolescence and other adverse social repercussions associated with market organization are rarely taken into account by Nelson and by the large majority of evolutionary economists.

We point out the deep motives underlying this analytical flaw by resorting to the critical inquiries into business organization and market competition originally conduced by Veblen and systematically developed by Kapp. Both Veblen and Kapp share the view that the prevailing decision-making routines of business enterprises inherently tend to be socially disserviceable and wasteful. They accept the existence of a structural conflict between the principal goal of business enterprises (profit maximization) and the basic imperatives of technical efficiency and serviceability. The institutionalization of a range of ordinary forms of sabotage on production is the natural outcome of the business-like control of industry.

A crucial divergence emerges between Veblen and Nelson in the handling of how things get done within and between capitalist firms. According to the former, as a consequence of the general acceptance in the economic profession of the 'theorem of equivalence',

> Pecuniary activities, in short, are handled as incidental features of the process of social production and consumption, as details incident to the method whereby the social interests are served, instead of being dealt with as the controlling factor about which the modern economic process turns.
>
> (Veblen 1919: 286)[5]

This relegation of pecuniary motives and practices to the background of economic theorizing explains why 'the economic process is rated primarily as a process for the provision of the aggregate material means of life' (ibid.: 285). This is, however, a highly misleading view according to Veblen. He insists on the neglected fact that the businessman manages industry through pecuniary dispositions and that 'his superintendence is a superintendence of the pecuniary affairs of the concern, rather than of the industrial plant', especially 'in the higher development of the modern captain of industry' (ibid.: 292). What about the implications of this business-like management of industry?

For their being 'lucrative without being serviceable to the community', pecuniary employments and business management 'are concerned primarily with the phenomena of value – with exchange or market values and with purchase and sell – and only indirectly and secondarily, if at all, with mechanical processes' (ibid.: 293).[6]

This means, in the first place, that in Veblen's view the business control of industry is not to be classified as an industrial or productive activity at all. Actually, the businessman's attempt at altering the distribution of wealth may, or may not, indirectly result in enhanced production (ibid.: 296–297).[7]

Under these conditions, the 'pecuniary dispositions' of the entrepreneur determine

> whether and which of the known processes and industrial arts shall be practiced, and to what extent. Industry must be conducted to suit the business man in his quest for gain; which is not the same as saying that it must be conducted to suit the needs or the convenience of the community at large.
>
> (Ibid.: 298)

Industrial organization is closely conditioned by the competitive pecuniary struggle among businesses. It is a struggle for survival in which the selective process rewards those economic units that are fit for pecuniary gain. Hence, market competition between businesses tends to reward fitness for serviceability only incidentally and, as a general rule, inhibits its diffusion in every case in which it interferes with the business goal of profit maximization (ibid.: 299).

Veblen is quite explicit in this respect when he states:

> It happens so frequently that it might fairly be said to be the common run that business interests and undertaker's manoeuvres delay consolidation, combination, coordination, for some appreciable time after they have become patently advisable on industrial grounds. The industrial advisability or practicability is not the decisive point. Industrial advisability must wait on the eventual convergence of jarring pecuniary interests and on the strategical moves of business men playing for the position.
>
> (Ibid.: 300)

It follows that an 'ordinary line of business strategy' consists of 'manoeuvres of restriction, delay, and hindrance' adopted 'by competitive business concerns to get the better of their business rivals or to secure their own advantage' (Veblen 1921: 3). In order to warrant that the rate and volume of output are 'regulated with a view to what the traffic will bear' and avoid over-production businessmen systematically recur to 'a conscientious withdrawal of efficiency', i.e., 'sabotage' (ibid.: 8–9). Businessmen's 'day's work has come to center about a running adjustment of sabotage on production' (ibid.: 39). In their quest for 'a reasonable profit'[8] business enterprises are forced to make large use of sabotage:

> Should the business men in charge, by any chance aberration, stray from this straight and narrow path of business integrity, and allow the community's needs unduly to influence their management of the community's industry, they would presently find themselves discredited and would probably face insolvency.
>
> (Ibid.: 14)

The work and main objective of the businessman consists of allocating the values under his hand 'from the less to the more gainful point of investment'

(Veblen 1919: 307). Therefore, economic theory should not concentrate on his serviceability or on his contribution to the improvement of human welfare as his main defining characteristic. It is just the undertaker's ability to uncover gainful investments that actually matters for a correct description (ibid.: 301, 303–304, 307).

Veblen's analysis of the deleterious impact of the business-like management of industry had a crucial influence on the work of Kapp, who indeed changed the title of *The Social Costs of Private Enterprise* (1950) to *Social Costs of Business Enterprise* (Kapp 1963).

Following Veblen,

> The author holds the view that the institutionalized system of decision-making in a system of business enterprise has a built-in tendency to disregard those negative effects on the environment that are 'external' to the decision-making unit. Even if an individual firm intended (and would be in a financial position, as oligopolists obviously are) to avoid the negative effects of its applied technology, it can do so only by raising its costs; that is, by deliberately reducing its profit margin and its profit-earning capacity. Hence, a system of decision-making operating in accordance with the principle of investment for profit cannot be expected to proceed in any way other than by trying to reduce its costs whenever possible and by ignoring those losses that can be shifted to third persons or to society at large.
>
> (Kapp 1971: xiii)

Making an explicit reference to Kapp, Vatn and Bromley clarify why there exists a cost-shifting mechanism inherent to the functioning of the market

> While it is not necessary to allege that all externalities are the clear result of intended cost-shifting, it is clearly incoherent and incorrect to assert that the opposite is universally so. Certainly, if costs can be shifted – and done so without violating any previously established and enforceable rights – then it will happen under conventional assumptions about the objectives and motivations of the relevant economic agents.
>
> (Vatn and Bromley 1997: 147)

It follows that,

> Indeed, one will need to be on constant lookout for the creation of new cost-shifting possibilities as competition intensifies. While the 'invisible hand' clearly conduces to efficiency within the 'internal' economy, it must – with the same ruthless logic – conduce to the shifting of costs throughout the 'external' sphere.
>
> (Ibid.: 147)

In this regard, a specific line of social damage that emerges as a consequence of the routinized business-like control and management of industry can be highlighted: the social costs of planned obsolescence. These costs, being at the core of the business-like control of the modern industrial laboratory, are particularly well-suited for a demonstration of our main argument: the unbridgeable divergence between the theories of business enterprise of Nelson, and of Veblen and Kapp. The latter two put at the core of their institutional analyses the prevailing productive routines by businesses – i.e., 'physical and social technologies' in Nelson's own terms. Veblen and Kapp are mainly interested in *how things get done* within the decision-making routines of business enterprises. While sharing the same focus, Nelson does not explicitly recognize the socially adverse consequences of the pecuniary or business-like management of industry. Conceptually he does not need to employ the notion of business: the reference point can simply be the firm. In Nelson's view, firms will automatically tend to introduce socially serviceable productive processes, as well as goods and services, in their attempt at reaching satisficing levels of profits. The subservience of the industrial process to the profit motive remains essentially unproblematic.

Kapp deals with the social costs of planned obsolescence in chapter 12, 'The social costs of cutthroat competition, planned obsolescence and sales promotion' of his *Social Costs of Business Enterprise* (Kapp 1963: 224–247). He states that: 'The phenomenon of planned or accelerated obsolescence is a relatively new phenomenon anticipated only partially by Veblen's earlier discussion of "sabotage" and "the conscientious withdrawal of efficiency in modern industry"' (ibid.: 224, quotations from Veblen 1921: 20)

Kapp illustrates how the typical non-price competition existing in the oligopolistic sectors of modern economies may take 'various forms of competition in disservices' (Kapp 1963: 229). It follows that

> It is fair to assume that there have been many oligopolistic firms who have failed to see any reason why they should not reduce the quality and average 'life expectancy' of their products if by doing so they could increase the volume of their sales. In fact, such reduction of quality and planned obsolescence of both the physical serviceability and the desirability of consumers' goods is the aim and effect of many sales promotional activities.
>
> (Ibid.: 230)

There is indeed an apparent self-reinforcing trend toward built-in obsolescence in many industrial branches in which oligopolistic competition is characteristic:

> Both the obsolescence of desirability and the obsolescence of quality seem to have undergone rapid development since Veblen first spoke of sabotage and the conscientious withdrawal of efficiency in modern industry. Automobiles, automotive parts, tires, home appliances from washing machines to television sets, and floor coverings, draperies and furniture have been increasingly the object of complaints on the ground of deliberate quality deterioration.
>
> (Ibid.: 231)

Kapp suggests that 'product and quality designs and the deliberate spacing of the lifespan of different parts in such a fashion that the need for replacement is increased, are commercially profitable in oligopolistic market structures' (ibid.: 232). In general, from the point of view of an oligopolistic market context, 'an industry with excess capacity and high overhead charges has much to gain from an accelerated obsolescence' (ibid.: 233). Deliberate quality deterioration or shortening of the life-span of products increases the sales of oligopolistic firms, in markets in which each competitor, in order to commercially survive 'depends upon his ability to increase the demand for his particular product and to make this demand as inelastic as pos-sible' (ibid.: 233). In this sense, the intentional reduction or destruction of the useful-ness of durable (and semi-durable) goods constitutes an opportunity (and social) cost reflected in the unnecessary repair and earlier replacement of goods resulting from their purposefully accelerated obsolescence (ibid.: 232–233, 242–243).

Beyond the specific examples of social losses associated with planned obsol-escence and aggressive sales promotion, in Kapp's open-systems view social costs are widespread, heterogeneous and often latent harmful effects of private business activities in a competitive economy. Therefore, in order to evaluate the effective social efficiency of business productive activities, their real total impacts (both physical and monetary) matter. What is most needed is a substan-tial *ex ante* evaluation of the input mix and the output pattern. Operationally, this could mean the creation of

> Institutionalized agencies [that] would have the function and responsibility to anticipate, appraise, and judge beforehand the hazards and benefits of alternative technologies, techniques and locations. On the basis of such an assessment it would be possible to direct investments with respect to both permissible choice of factor inputs and the location of specific industries, in accordance with criteria that take account of the full range of the costs and consequences of new techniques for the individual and society as well as the world community.
>
> (Kapp 1971: xxi)

The reality of social costs of business enterprise tells us that 'the conventional measurements of the performance and "growth" of the economy in terms of national income indicators are inadequate and hence misleading' (ibid.: vii):

> They leave out of account important social costs of production borne by third persons and future generations. In fact, in their present form, national income indices not only fail to subtract these social costs, but include money spent to repair the damages caused by productive activities of the past and present.
>
> (Ibid.: vii)

With these critiques the successive debate on the need to revise and extend the System of National Accounts based on GNP figures is clearly anticipated. Kapp invokes the need for a comprehensive approach to economic accounting, in which both defensive expenditures and real damages can be faithfully and reliably reflected. Since the late 1960s, research on the extension of the national accounts in order to better reflect monetizable detrimental components and distributive effects has consistently progressed:

> Extended accounting is approaching official recognition. Following two decades of research and consultation, in its last revision of the SNA, the United Nations introduced guidelines for an optional set of 'satellite' environmental accounts, designed to integrate with the main core SNA.
>
> (Offer 2000: 11)[9]

Notwithstanding the importance of several analytical and operational limitations, the enduring research efforts in alternatives to GDP as measures of welfare reflect a gradual shift of policy priorities away from the established and exclusive preoccupation with growth. An increasing number of professional economists are changing their view on economic growth and social progress. A prominent figure among them, Robert U. Ayres, observes in this respect:

> I now think (along with many others) that economic growth as measured by increasing GDP, at least in the developed countries, is mostly an illusion. It reflects increasingly frantic activity, especially trade, but little or no progress in terms of human welfare in 'real' terms (health, diet, housing, education, etc.).
>
> (Ayres 1996: 117)

Ayres recognizes that much of the background of this critical re-examination is not new (ibid.: 118), and, following Shigeto Tsuru, we may just add that its theoretical foundations were laid by the old institutionalists (Tsuru 1997: 83–99). Quoting Myrdal, Tsuru explains the enduring relevance of old institutionalism through its realistic outlook:

> Institutional economics is destined to be winning ground at the expense of conventional economics, according to Myrdal not only because of the strength of its logic, but also 'because a broader approach will be needed for dealing in an effective way with the practical and political problems that are now towering and threatening to overwhelm us'.
>
> (Ibid.: 75; quotation from Myrdal 1979)

Some prevailing social and physical technologies in today's business: planned obsolescence and the manufacture of doubt

Planned obsolescence consists of a 'set of product development practices' that tends to become 'ubiquitous among durable goods manufacturers' (Guiltinan

2009: 20). Planned obsolescence routines aim at stimulating replacement buying by consumers. In their effort to shorten the usable life of their products, producers can recur to well-established '*physical* obsolescence mechanisms'. These amount to settled production practices such as 'limited functional life design ('death dating')', 'design for limited repair', 'design aesthetics that lead to reduced satisfaction' or 'design for fashion', and 'design for functional enhancement through adding or upgrading product features' (ibid.: 20).

Planned obsolescence has a long industrial tradition. With the introduction in 1913 of the electric starter in automobiles, 'obsolescence due to technological innovation' obtained for the first time nation-wide attention in the United States (Slade 2006: 4; on the electric starter see also p. 35). 'Psychological, progressive, or dynamic obsolescence' was inaugurated soon after by the success of 'GM's cosmetic changes to the 1923 Chevrolet' (ibid.: 4). Consumers were clearly willing to 'trade up for style, not just for technological improvements, long before their old cars wore out' (ibid.: 4). This 'discovery' was quickly imitated by 'many other American industries, such as watches and radios' (ibid.: 4).

The Depression promoted a further development in the same direction: 'The Depression gave manufacturers a new incentive to systematize their strategies of adulteration and apply scientific research methods to the practice of death dating or planned obsolescence in order to increase repetitive consumption' (ibid.: 78). A further refinement of the various forms of 'adulteration' (ibid.: 77) has been actively promoted since the 1930s: Producers progressively achieved the capability to 'manipulate the failure rate of manufactured materials' (ibid.: 5). An early illuminating example in this respect is provided by General Electric laboratories' experimentation concerning how to shorten the lifespan of its flashlight bulbs 'in order to increase demand by as much as 60 percent' (ibid.: 5). From a memorandum from the files of the General Electric Company, dated 1932, we know that the proponent company engineer concluded by stating: 'We can see no logical reason either from our view point or that of the battery manufacturer why such a change should not be made at this time' (Kapp 1963: 230; Slade 2006: 80–81).

Death-dating was, however, one among different possible instruments to encourage repetitive consumption:

> Solutions to the problem of how to promote repetitive consumption would eventually include a wide range of manufacturing strategies, from branding, packaging, and creating disposable products to continuously changing the styles of non disposable products so that they became psychologically obsolete.
>
> (Slade 2006: 10–11)

While not drawing a prohibitive general picture of the diffusion of this practice in the different oligopolistic sectors, we may briefly call attention to the impressive picture of today's e-waste due to the hastening of product extinction in the sector of electronic durables:

Today, the mounting numbers of functioning durable goods ending up in landfills have led to renewed criticism of product obsolescence. Sources indicate that in North America over 100 million cell phones and 300 million personal computers are discarded each year, and only 20,000 televisions are refurbished each year while 20 million are sold, resulting in tremendous environmental damage from lead, mercury, and toxic glass.

(Guiltinan 2009: 19)

Slade has recently pointed out that

as federal regulations mandating HDTV come into effect in 2009, an unknown but substantially larger number of analog TVs will join the hundred of millions of computer monitors entering America's overcrowded, pre-toxic waste stream. Just this one-time disposal of 'brown goods' will, alone, more than double the hazardous waste problem in North America.

(Slade 2006: 2–3)

Beyond the risk of overcapacity faced by oligopolists, which is generally recognized as the conditioning threat causing planned obsolescence, Viki Sonntag has recently emphasized the role of competition in the 'knowledge-based economy' in 'the past few decades' (Sonntag 2000: 101). In particular, 'computer-based, flexible production technologies', i.e., 'the latest advanced manufacturing technologies', tend to favor the institutionalization of one domi-nant technological trajectory in production systems: 'One such trajectory, faster product cycles, has serious implications for achieving sustainability for the reason that firms with fast-to-market strategies must "grow in order to compete", resulting in the need for ever larger effective market demand' (ibid.: 102). 'Current generation production technologies' or 'new manufacturing technolo-gies', according to Sonntag, 'are radically changing the terms of market com-petition' (ibid.: 101, 102). They favor the emergence of coevolving 'distinctive patterns in market organization' and firms' behaviors to stay competitive based on accelerating product cycles: 'Faster product cycles presage new product vari-ants and faster product obsolescence linked to intensified customers' needs' (ibid.: 101, 109). The pressure to reduce the durability of goods explains why 'there is cause for concern that many current practices in the strategic use of advanced technologies are unsustainable since they lead to increasing resource consumption in the aggregate by increasing market demand' (ibid.: 101).'

Another highly sophisticated maneuvering social technology, widely employed in business, is the manufacture of doubt. The tactic was initially elab-orated as an answer to the observable links between exposure to chemicals and adverse health effects in workers and consumers: 'As early as the 1930s petro-leum and chemical companies recognized that exposure to chemicals they pro-duced (as well as to substances like asbestos) in production plants could cause cancer, pneumoconiosis, and other health problems' (Ludwig *et al.* 2001: 524). The industry response was to orchestrate the obfuscation of the links between exposures and harmful effects. 'An aura of "controversy"' was deliberately created,

> concerning the scientific basis for the alleged effects by confusing the epistemology of causation, and corrupting medical literature through intentional misdesign, suppression and misrepresentation of research. The companies, their lawyers and consultants fabricated a debate concerning the issues whether or not disease increases in exposed populations were real or 'controversial.'

> (Ibid.: 524)

This sponsoring of manipulated studies and the attentive management of their diffusion among the public has progressively evolved into a prevailing social technology in several industrial branches. Asbestos provides a well-documented example of the high profitability of 'the corruption of science from within' (McCulloch 2006: 610). Although 'evidence of the risks of working with asbestos was well established in the early 1930s', and medical proof of the adverse health impacts of exposure to airborne fiber since 1960, the industry was able to gain a reprieve of some decades before being banned in industrial states. Asbestos production and manufacturing is still a highly profitable line of industry in the developing world, 'where in countries like India, Kazakhstan, and Thailand, industry-sponsored research is used to justify the continued mining of asbestos and the manufacture of asbestos-based products' (ibid.: 613). In sum, it was the industry's shrewd 'management of medical knowledge' that 'has been the key to the continued use of asbestos' (McCulloch 2005: 398). What seems most disturbing about failure to regulate (i.e., ban) asbestos production is that the 'magic mineral' that came to be recognized as a 'killer dust', as Geoffrey Tweedale makes clear, 'is only one of a number of potential hazards – radioactivity, pesticides, lead, and air pollution, to name only a few – that may result in insidious, long-term damage to our health' (Tweedale 2003a: xi).

Based on previously secret internal business documents produced in toxic tort litigations, it is today possible to get a reliable picture of 'the modus operandi of at least a large proportion of corporations in the United States' (Rankin Bohme *et al.* 2005: 338). A thorough documentation of 'the strategies employed by various tobacco, asbestos, beryllium, plastic and chemical companies, their industry organizations, front groups, and industry-funded scientists' (ibid.: 338) is now available. These tactics, 'social technologies' or 'prevailing production routines' are both intentional and socially destructive, and entail the funding of scientists in order to manufacture doubt over the risks of production processes or products (Rankin Bohme *et al.* 2005; Tweedale 2003b: 77–82). While limiting both liability and regulation, they allow firms to obtain their (expected) huge 'satisficing' profits.

Recently, Geoffrey Tweedale has lamented the 'striking' fact that there is 'no tradition of dealing with this type of subject-matter in business history' (Tweedale 2003b: 70). This lacuna seems even more troubling if one considers that 'the empirical work that does exist on business crime shows that it is far from marginal; it also shows that it has *deep* historical roots' (ibid.: 73; emphasis in the original). These social technologies are dominant modes to avoid sustaining social costs that corporations either cannot or do not want to compensate for or prevent.

As pointed out in the present text, planned obsolescence and the manufacturing of doubt through scientific misunderstanding occur through well-settled productive routines and are at the origin of serious and widespread social losses. They have undergone a process of institutionalization and progressive refinement in both traditional and new industrial branches. Hence, evidence does not support a comforting view of business and market competition. Any theory of the capitalist firm that does not pay attention to these settled practices in modern oligopolistic sectors shares the embarrassing limit attributed by Geoffrey Tweedale to business historians: 'Their almost complete failure to address those areas of business activity that one might label corporate crime or misconduct' (ibid.: 70). Understandably, this limit is evident in the evolutionary theory of the firm. However, both planned obsolescence and corporate corruption of science can be properly explained and understood as special cases of cost-shifting routine practices by capitalist firms within the theory of social costs of Veblen and Kapp.

Final remarks

One of the truly innovative and lasting insights from old institutionalism was its theory of social costs. It was the most persistent theoretical interest of both Veblen and Kapp. Although the theory of social costs is lucidly and eloquently developed in their works, this fundamental piece of institutional theory is wholly neglected by the 'Veblenian' Nelson.

It is a subtle irony that, both Nelson and Winter, and Nelson more recently, share the basic assumptions of Veblen and Kapp concerning business firms' behavior. They indeed assume that capitalist firms are profit-seeking organizations that, in order to stay competitive, submit their production and decision-making routines to the pursuit of satisficing net returns. The market mechanism rewards successful firms and penalizes non-profitable production units. Prevailing productive routines – investment decisions, 'well-specified technical routines for producing things' and 'research and development' – are strictly keyed to the firm's profitability. Under these circumstances, it is reasonable to assume, as Nelson and Winter do in their models, that 'replication of productive routines is motivated by a desire to replicate the profit flows that those routines make possible' (Nelson and Winter 1982: 121). As a consequence, profitable productive routines tend to be persistent: Profitable firms tend to remain firmly committed to their 'existing ways of doing things' and to resist major changes (ibid.: 122). This relatively rigid superintendence of the profit motive over industrial practices (scientific and technological research) is by no means disturbing. Accordingly, technological innovation under business-like management is a matter of cumulative and progressive improvements in both production processes (management decision-making and engineering practices) and products (ibid.: 258).

Nelson's more recent interest in institutions and social technologies does not change this apparently inescapable limit of the evolutionary or competence-based theory of the firm. Profitability remains the efficiency test for both physical and social technologies.

In other words, Nelson risks 'ignoring all the costs of profits or growth that are silently borne by the community and by employees' (Perrow 1992: 373). Only a too 'narrow view of efficiency' (ibid.: 371) can equate technological and organizational innovation by business with actual progress or socially serviceable discoveries and inventions. Planned obsolescence, as we have seen, represents a well-documented example in this respect. The advocated need to encourage entrepreneurship in order to advance technology seems highly disputable as it is the idea that 'As Schumpeter argued long ago, by far the principal benefit that society gets from market organization of economic activity and competition, is innovation and economic progress' (Nelson 2007: 320). The neo-Schumpeterian or evolutionary theory of the firm elaborated by Nelson espouses this highly positive, largely apologetic, vision of the role of the competitive mechanism. According to this view, the discipline of the market tends to be inherently pro-social; private business costs and efficiency provide reliable, synthetic measures of social costs and efficiency.

The contextual neglect of the social costs of settled production practices as planned obsolescence and the manufacture of doubt sufficiently explain why Nelson can consider economic growth the most reasonable objective of economic policy, despite the fruitful and illuminating critiques of GDP as a measure of real human welfare in the post-war period.

In sharp contrast with Nelson's comforting view of business and market competition, Veblen and Kapp have provided a general analytical framework that can help to address in a realistic way the prevailing organizational and productive routines of business enterprises. Based on the fundamental distinction between profitability (making money) and serviceability (making things in order to achieve social efficiency goals), their critique of business enterprise and the market still offers an ideal framework of analysis to understand the actual behavior of competing businesses.

Notes

1 Conceptually, routines can be distinguished in 'operating characteristics' ('the routines that govern short-run behaviour') and 'actual investment behaviour', both 'keyed to the firm's profitability', since 'profitable firms will grow and unprofitable ones will contract, and the operating characteristics of the more profitable firms therefore will account for a growing share of the industry's activity' (Nelson and Winter 1982: 16–17).

2 Among professional economists

there is widespread recognition that powerful 'physical technologies' generally are involved centrally in productive routines. Under neoclassical theory, at least, there has been less explicit and systematic reflection on the roles of effective 'social technologies' in productive activity, although as we have noted this is what much of the new discussion of institutions seems to be mostly about. This is our focus here. It is apparent that 'knowing' prevailing social technologies, and what they allow and deny, and how to operate within them, is just as important as 'knowing' available physical technologies in determining the available range of 'choice' facing a particular actor.

(Nelson and Sampat 2001: 45)

3 'A standard and expected thing to do, given the objectives and the setting' refers both to dominant 'modes of organizing work' and 'appropriate practice' (Nelson and Sampat 2001: 44).
4 As examples of social technologies evolving into institutions (i.e., dominant social technologies), Nelson and Sampat offer 'Chandler's M-form' and the preference for strong intellectual property rights in pharmaceuticals (Nelson and Sampat 2001: 41).
5 In other words, pecuniary employments and allocation criteria are handled by mainstream economists as 'auxiliary to the process of production, and the gains from such employments are still explained as being due to a productive effect imputed to them' (Veblen 1919: 287). In the scheme of productive factors the undertaker's activity has 'the function of coordinating and directing industrial processes' (Veblen 1919: 288–289). In the realm of distribution his income is dealt with 'as a peculiar kind of wages, proportioned to the heightened productivity given to the industrial process by his work'. Thus, 'his income has been reconciled with the tacitly accepted natural law of equivalence' (Veblen 1919: 289).
6 According to Veblen, pecuniary dispositions are the sole motives underlying investment and allocation activities by business enterprises. As a consequence any good or service produced and distributed under business guidance can be, at best, only incidentally serviceable for consumers and society at large.
7 'Enhanced production' means here a socially efficient way of producing goods and services, i.e., a way that minimizes social costs (Veblen 1921; Kapp 1963).
8 'A reasonable profit always means, in effect, the largest obtainable profit' (Veblen 1921: 13).
9 Despite UN approval of the Human Development Index and the UN standard based on a 15-item 'minimum national social data set', research on social and ecological indicators remains more problematic and less promising in its present stage of development (Offer 2000: 18).

References

Ayres, R.U. (1996) 'Limits to the growth paradigm', *Ecological Economics*, 19: 117–134.
Clinard, M.B. (2005) 'Corporate crime: yesterday and today – a comparison', in Clinard, M.B. and Yeager, P.C. (eds.), *Corporate Crime*, New Brunswick and London: Transaction Publishers.
Guiltinan, J. (2009) 'Creative destruction and destructive creations: environmental ethics and planned obsolescence', *Journal of Business Ethics*, 89: 19–28.
Heath, J. (2008) 'Business ethics and moral motivation: a criminological perspective', *Journal of Business Ethics*, 83: 595–614.
Hodgson, G. (2007) 'The 2007 Veblen-Commons award recipient: Richard R. Nelson', *Journal of Economic Issues*, 41(2): 311.
Kapp, K.W. (1963) *Social Costs of Business Enterprise*, Bombay, London and New York: Asia Publishing House.

Kapp, K.W. (1971) 'Introduction to the 1971 edition', in *The Social Costs of Private Enterprise*, New York: Schocken Books.

Ludwig, E.R., Madeksho, L. and Egilman, D. (2001) 'RE: mesothelioma and lung tumors attributable to asbestos among petroleum workers', *American Journal of Industrial Medicine*, 39: 524–527.

McCulloch, J. (2005) 'Mining and mendacity, or how to keep a product in the marketplace', *International Journal of Occupational and Environmental Health*, 11: 398–403.

McCulloch, J. (2006) 'Public health chronicles', *Public Health Reports*, 121: 609–614.

Mayhew, A. (2000) 'Veblen and theories of the 'firm'', in Louça, F. and Perlman, M. (eds.), *Is Economics an Evolutionary Science? The Legacy of Thorstein Veblen*, Cheltenham and Northampton, MA: Edward Elgar.

Myrdal, G. (1979) *Essays and Lectures After 1975*, Kyoto: Keibunsha.

Nelson, R.R. (2005) 'Introduction', in *The Limits of Market Organization*, New York: Russel Sage Foundation.

Nelson, R.R. (2007) 'Institutions and economic growth: sharpening the research agenda', *Journal of Economic Issues*, 41(2): 313–323.

Nelson, R.R. (2008) 'What enables rapid economic progress: what are the needed institutions?', *Research Policy*, 37: 1–11.

Nelson, R.R. and Sampat, B.N. (2001) 'Making sense of institutions as factors shaping economic performance', *Journal of Economic Behavior & Organization*, 44: 31–54.

Nelson, R.R. and Winter, S. (1982) *An Evolutionary Theory of Economic Change*, Cambridge, MA: Harvard University Press.

Offer, A. (2000) 'Economic welfare measurements and human well-being', *Discussion Papers in Economic and Social History*, 34: 1–34.

Perrow, C. (1992) 'Organizational theorists in a society of organizations', *International Sociology*, 7(3): 371–380.

Rankin Bohme, S., Zorabedian, J. and Egilman, G.S. (2005) 'Maximizing profits and endangering health: corporate strategies to avoid litigation and regulation', *International Journal of Occupational and Environmental Health*, 11: 338–348.

Slade, G. (2006) *Made to Break: Technology and Obsolescence in America*, Cambridge, MA: Harvard University Press.

Sonntag, V. (2000) 'Sustainability: in light of competitiveness', *Ecological Economics*, 34: 101–113.

Tsuru, S. (1997) *Institutional Economics Revisited*, Cambridge: Cambridge University Press.

Tweedale, G. (2003a) *Magic Mineral to Killer Dust: Turner & Newall and the Asbestos Hazard*, Oxford and New York: Oxford University Press.

Tweedale, G. (2003b) 'Researching corporate crime: a business historian's perspective', in Tombs, S. and Whyte, D. (eds.), *Unmasking the Crimes of the Powerful: Scrutinizing States and Corporations*, New York: Peter Lang.

Vatn, A. and Bromley, D. (1997) 'Externalities: a market model failure', *Environmental and Resource Economics*, 9: 135–151.

Veblen, T. (1919 [2002]) 'Industrial and pecuniary employments', *The Place of Science in Modern Civilization*, New Brunswick and London: Transaction Publishers.

Veblen, T. (1921 [1965]) *The Engineers and the Price System*, New York: Augustus M. Kelley Bookseller.

5 The discourse on social costs

Kapp's 'impossibility thesis' vs. neoliberalism[1]

Sebastian Berger

Introduction

Economists have tried for a long time to shape the mode of thinking about damages that arise from economic activity. As 'social costs' or 'externalities' these damages were assigned a specific place in modern society. According to historians of economic thought: 'It is now well established that the boundaries of the modern analysis of externalities were defined by A.C. Pigou's Economics of Welfare ([1920] 1932) and Ronald H. Coase's "Problem of Social Cost" (1960)' (Aslanbeigui and Medema 1998: 1).

This intellectual history is quite symptomatic for contemporary economic discourse, in that only neoclassical and neoliberal theories are considered while K. William Kapp's fundamental critique of both of these theories is omitted. His work once received recognition even by his staunch neoliberal critic, Wilfred Beckerman:

> The economics profession in general, and those who are interested in environmental problems in particular, owe a great debt to Professor Kapp. It was he who first drew our attention to the widespread nature of external costs imposed by many productive activities and the way in which these impaired the environment, in his book on The social costs of business enterprise. This work was not duly appreciated at the time it was published because this was before concern with the environment became fashionable.
>
> (Beckerman 1972: 1)

In the words of Kapp's colleague, the institutional economist Marc Tool:

> Dr. K. William Kapp and his forty-year career as a front rank institutional economist ... [established] the relevance of the holistic, institutional mode of thinking to the complex and urgent problems of environmental deterioration and economic development. Indeed, Kapp was among the first to explore the interdependent significance of these two problems.
>
> (Tool 1978: 1)

Much has changed in economic discourse since the 1970s, and Kapp's arguments are – with few exceptions (Franzini 2006) – no longer part of the discourse on social costs. This chapter provides a rational reconstruction (Rorty 1984) of Kapp's argument to complement the concept's intellectual history and to broaden economic discourse beyond the limits of neoclassical and neoliberal arguments.

Kapp's 'impossibility thesis' vs. liberalism a là Mises and Hayek

Kapp's argument about social costs emerged in his dissertation, 'The planned economy and international trade' (1936), as a critique of the doctrine of liberalism and an economic accounting system based on market exchange value. Given the book's argument, it is surprising that it was written at the Postgraduate Institute of International Studies in Geneva and at the London School of Economics. According to Plehwe, the Geneva institute was an interwar institution that provided an organizational haven for 'concerned and committed liberals', such as Ludwig von Mises, who later became a founding member of neoliberal organizations, such as the Mont Pelerin Society in 1947 (Plehwe 2009). In fact, Kapp's preface even thanks Mises for the 'friendly interest' he took in the dissertation.

Kapp began his argument by addressing Mises' thesis that 'a rational economy under conditions of a centrally organized community is impossible because the removal of the means of production from the market makes their exact valuation impossible in the decisions of the central economic authorities' (Kapp 1936: 27). According to Mises, without the market and a common denominator for valuation there cannot be any economy because there is no way to determine what is rational and because production cannot be 'economical' (ibid.: 30–31). Kapp argued that this thesis is the focal point in the discourse on economic accounting, which in turn reflects differences in the theories of value. While he was not surprised that economists adopting a subjectivist theory of value argue that valuation becomes impossible in a planned economy, Kapp considered the socialists' reactions problematic because they mainly tried to prove Mises' thesis wrong. Instead, Kapp argued, a countervailing thesis about the market economy was needed, as well as an inquiry into the actual effects of a pure economic accounting system based on the valuation of single individuals – i.e., market exchange value (ibid.: 34).

Chapter 3 of the dissertation took up this task. Kapp built his argument upon previous contributions made by Arthur C. Pigou, Carl Menger and Karl Polanyi. The third subchapter of chapter 3, entitled 'The impossibility of reaching societal efficiency[2] based on an economic accounting of market values', argued that economic accounting based on market values does not and cannot account for the *societal* disadvantages and damages of an economic decision. Kapp used Pigou's account (Pigou 1929) of how societal disadvantages arise from economic decisions of private enterprises, referring to societal disadvantages such as health effects on workers, crime, etc., but also environmental damages caused by smoke. Kapp added to this the question about the losses due to the premature depletion of non-renewable energy and raw materials. Importantly, Kapp already outlined his future research project (*The Social Costs of Private Enterprise*, henceforth *Social Costs*) that would elaborate the different kinds of social costs more rigorously: 'It would be an interesting task for statistics to develop appropriate methods of accounting for disadvantages and damages that society has to suffer in a free market economy due to the principle of maximizing returns applied by private enterprise' (Kapp 1936: 42, fn.).

After arguing that decisions by private enterprises based on market values cause, and at the same time do not account for, social costs, Kapp proceeded to show why societal needs and interests *cannot* be expressed in the valuation of goods according to market prices. Here, Kapp built on Carl Menger's distinction between the substantive and the formal economy (Berger 2008),[3] arguing that societal needs and interests cannot find 'value-expression' in the exchange between isolated individuals (formal economy). Societal efficiency, thus, cannot be reached based on market price accounting. This constitutes the essence of what may be termed Kapp's countervailing 'impossibility thesis', directed against Mises' thesis. Kapp supported this argument by referring to the many 'corrections' that liberal-capitalist economies have to implement *ex post* via social policies to remedy losses. In a centrally planned economy, Kapp asserted, it would be possible to calculate possible damages *ex ante* and to consider these in economic decision-making.

Kapp also acknowledged Karl Polanyi's influence on his dissertation in a later letter:

> Dear Karl ... Did I ever mention that your early article in reply to Mises' thesis has been very helpful to me then [!] I did my dissertation on planning and foreign trade with Mises at the Postgraduate Institute of International Studies in Geneva in the early thirties. I thought you ought to know this and that it may please you.
>
> (Kapp to Polanyi, 18 October 1962)

Polanyi participated in the early stages of the debate on possible forms of socialism in Vienna in the 1920s. In his 1922 essay, 'Sozialistische Rechnungslegung' ('Socialist accounting'), he took on Mises' argument and outlined the traits of 'rationally' planned economic production and exchange that is guided by social and democratic decision-making (Cangiani 2006: 25; Berger 2008).

While the dissertation's argument was directed against Mises' thesis, Kapp directed his *Social Costs* (1950) also against Friedrich August von Hayek, who at the time was the leading figure in neoliberal projects, such as the Chicago School and the Mont Pelerin Society (Van Horn and Mirowski 2009). Kapp paid attention to Hayek's work since the 1930s and his dissertation – partially written at Hayek's workplace, the London School of Economics – already cited the latter's *Collectivist Economic Planning* (1935). The unpublished version of the introduction to 'Social costs' addressed itself to Mises' and Hayek's 'successful books' and their doctrine of liberalism (Kapp, unpubl. manus.), probably referring to Hayek's *Road to Serfdom* (1944) and Mises' *Bureaucracy* (1944):

> Social Costs and Social Returns: A Critical Analysis of the Social Performance of the Unplanned Market Economy – In harmony with the faith of 19th century liberalism traditional equilibrium economics states that the unregulated forces of supply and demand in an unplanned market economy tend to lead to an optimal allocation of scarce resources among competing ends and objectives. This doctrine continues to be regarded by many as an apparently scientific foundation for all arguments against positive intervention with the economic process in the capitalist economy; its strength is attested by the current success of the books by Hayek and Mises. Economic planning is still on the defensive and in many minds the presumption seems to be against purposive action in economic affairs despite all experience of depressions and other inefficiencies in the operation of the capitalist economy. This study offers a critique of the basic premises of 19th century economic liberalism by examining the social performance of the unplanned market economy in the light of several facts which are usually omitted and neglected in economic theory.... In the first place it attempts to indicate the limitations of all economic calculations in terms of private costs and private returns. To allocate economic resources merely in accordance with private costs and private returns defeats any endeavour to find a rational solution to the economic problem.
>
> (Kapp, unpubl. manus.)

This supports the thesis that Kapp was keenly aware of the revival of the doctrines of liberalism in the works of Mises and Hayek and considered them important enough to devote an entire book to their critique. The latter took on the basic premises of economic liberalism via a full-blown empirical investigation showing how entrepreneurial outlays fail to reflect important social costs of production and are no adequate measure of total costs. Kapp's argument on social costs thus emerged as an attack on Austrian liberalism à la Hayek and Mises, while being inspired by Austrian economists, such as Polanyi and the posthumous Menger (second edition of *Principles*), as well as Pigou.

The influence of American institutionalism: *ex ante* social controls vs. *ex post* Pigouvian taxes

Kapp explicitly traced the basic idea of *Social Costs* back to his dissertation, but also to the research of the National Resources Planning Board and John Maurice Clark's *Social Economics*.[4] The Kapp–Clark correspondence (Berger, 2012) evidences how Clark influenced Kapp's thinking. Kapp's copy of Allan G. Gruchy's *Modern Economic Thought: The American Contribution* (1947) shows intense underlining of the chapter on 'The social economics of John M. Clark', in particular, the concept of social value, new criteria for collective efficiency independent of price, Clark's social-liberal planning program and the democratization of the economy as a foundation of social economics. By changing the title of the second, enlarged and revised edition to *Social Costs of Business Enterprise* (1963) Kapp explicitly recognized that Thorstein B. Veblen's *Engineers and the Price System* (1921) and *The Theory of Business Enterprise* (1904) provided an analytical framework and demanded an economics that investigates the waste involved in the business-like control of industry.[5]

In the tradition of American Institutionalism, Kapp argued that social costs are to be subjected to democratic decision-making (social legislation) that would enable the majority interest to put an end to this problem. He directly attacked the argument that the elimination or more equal distribution of social costs – as well as the insistence on planning – are anti-growth and anti-change. In this way, Kapp raised the question of whether the lament about the eminent end of growth – said to result from the quest for security and protection against social costs – does not reflect a movement away from social and political democracy. According to Kapp, social costs are in opposition to one of the most fundamental tenets of our professed humanistic ideals, i.e., respect for the human personality and that the human being must not become a mere instrument for some 'cause', such as growth or efficiency (Kapp 1950: 18–22). In this view, the extent to which social costs are accounted for depends on the political structure of society, requiring environmental policy and institutional reforms to minimize them:

> [Social costs] are damages ... which under different institutional conditions could be avoided. For, obviously, if these costs were inevitable under any kind of institutional arrangement they would not really present a special theoretical problem ... to reveal their origin the study of social costs must always be an institutional analysis. Such an analysis raises inevitably the question of institutional reform and economic policy which may eliminate or minimize the social diseconomies under discussion.
>
> (Kapp 1963: 186)

> No democratic society can and will tolerate this subordination of the social system to the dictates of formal rationality. The universal reaction of society to the neglect of social costs ... has taken a variety of forms ... compelling private producers to internalize ... social costs.
>
> (ibid.: 202)

Kapp interpreted the growing recognition given to social costs as a shift in the balance of power from those groups responsible for damages to those groups who bear the

> brunt of social losses in the past and who now are using their growing political and economic power in an effort to protect themselves against undesirable consequences.... The political history of the last 150 years can be fully

understood only as a revolt of large masses of people (including business) against the shifting of part of the social costs of production to third persons or society.

(ibid.: 16)

Kapp concluded that in modern societies there are serious obstacles to rational behavior of consumers and entrepreneurs, not least because market prices fail to measure the relative importance and magnitude of various social costs and returns. He called for a revision of neoclassical price theory, questioning its philosophical foundations and formal value theory that is confined to alternatives measurable in terms of market values. Kapp called for a new science of economics that would include social costs and returns that differ in terms of their measurability from exchangeable commodities and constitute the category of social value. Elaborating on the question of social value, Kapp later demanded a kind of 'rational humanism', i.e., substantive criteria that are sought and found in the degree of satisfaction of human needs (Kapp 1967). In this theory, particular aspects of the quality of the environment such as clean air and water would be an end in itself via scientifically derived environmental norms that reflect basic human needs. Hence, human needs become operable as social minima, and fundamental requirements of human life and survival are integral parts of the constellation of goals of economic policy. Minimum standards in the fields of public health, medical care, education, housing, transportation and recreation based on empirical data can be determined with greater agreement than usually assumed. Kapp argued that the human being and basic human needs should be the primary values and criteria, from which secondary criteria, such as social minima, ecological maximum tolerance levels, socio-ecological indicators and social controls can be derived (Kapp 1974). Kapp used this argument also in a proposal for democratic planning of science and technology (Kapp 1975).

While his work derived a major impulse from Pigou's argument, Kapp later criticized that Pigou forced the problem of social costs into the conceptual framework of neoclassical economics, despite the fact that the latter was never designed to address non-market phenomena, such as pollution. Kapp also rejected Pigou's concepts of external costs and social costs, with social costs meaning 'total costs', i.e., the sum of private costs and external costs. Instead, Kapp reserved the term 'social costs' for all those negative consequences arising from unrestrained economic activity (public and private) that are shifted to third parties, future generations or society at large, and which do not appear in cost accounts of the responsible economic unit, thus avoiding responsibility. Kapp argued that Pigou's 'external costs' is a value-laden concept within the neoclassical pre-analytical vision of a rational (market)-system in which 'external costs' are external to the system – accidental side-effects of secondary importance. This plays down the pervasive nature of the problem and suggests that it is remediable with ad hoc, *ex post* measures of taxation. Kapp criticized that the latter are essentially conservative measures that do not change the mechanism of allocation and that constitute only a minor modification of the allegedly rational system. Yet, Kapp did not fail to notice that Pigou broadened his approach in the 1940s, starting to mention 'general disharmonies' arising in production and distribution and in connection with industrial fluctuations: '[We may be] confronted with evidence of the bankruptcy of capitalism and a prima facie case for extending the range of public ownership and public operation to industries in which they have not yet been invoked' (Pigou 1947: 43–45, in Kapp 1963: 38) While Pigou's solution to the problem was to some extent interventionist and his work highlighted some of the links between economics and ethics (Aslanbeigui and Medema 1998), Kapp pointed out the limitations of this neoclassical approach.

Neoliberal feedback à la Knight, Coase, Stigler, Calabresi, Buchanan and Beckerman

Recent research has characterized neoliberalism as a transdisciplinary and international thought collective with a long-term strategy to oppose what it described as collectivism or socialism. The term 'neoliberalism' emerged in the 1930s and the movement is considered to be a child of the Great Depression, with concerned liberals feeling the need to fight the evils of planning. The Chicago School and the Mont Pelerin Society were among its key organizations since 1947, with Hayek, Mises and Buchanan, but also Stigler, as leading members. Neoliberalism rose to hegemony by the 1980s, gaining acceptance even in nominally hostile environments, such as Social Democratic Parties and the Chinese ruling elite. Crucially, neoliberalism must not be confounded with neoclassical economics because Austrian and ordoliberal segments of neoliberalism were at odds with neoclassical economics. Yet, those versions of neoclassical economics compatible with the neoliberal policy preferences were accepted (Plehwe 2009; Mirowski 2009). While neoliberalism is not a clearly defined doctrine, some of its central tenets relevant to the discourse on social costs can be identified: (1) The market can always produce solutions for problems seemingly produced by the market in the first place; (2) the market always surpasses the state's ability as an information processor; (3) corporations can do no wrong, or at least they are not to be blamed if they do (Mirowski 2009).

In line with these tenets, the Chicago School spent the post-World War II years arguing 'for less government intervention, fewer wealth redistribution policies ... and an across the board promotion of more private enterprise' because this would promote a more efficient allocation of resources (Medema 1998: 210). The discourse on social costs was of interest to Chicago economists from the beginning and seems to have moved upward on the neoliberal agenda in the 1960s. Although Frank Knight was not part of what became the neoliberal project at the Chicago School, starting with Hayek (Van Horn and Mirowski 2009), he was the leading economist at the interwar Economics Department at Chicago, who convinced his students of the central importance of liberal values and competitive markets, which he favored over any other political process (Rutherford 2010). In 'Some fallacies in the interpretation of social costs' (Knight 1924), Knight attacked Pigou's interventionist taxation solution, favoring instead a market-based solution because under conditions of 'private ownership of the factors significant for production [...] the ideal situation which would be established by the imaginary tax will be brought about through the operation of ordinary economic motives' (ibid.: 164). Knight also published a book review of Kapp's *Social Costs* (Knight 1951: 233–234), calling it 'socialist propaganda' and lamenting that it 'does not mention freedom'. Also, Knight found a discussion of 'costs of eliminating costs' missing and that Kapp's use of the term 'waste' was problematic because waste can only be defined in reference to costs of conservation. Knight saw no practical use in criticizing the status quo if possible alternatives were not compared, and the worst defect was that the 'author is oblivious of the question as to the politico-economic organization requisite for carrying out such "reforms".... He does not say what are the alternatives and their costs' (Knight 1951: 234).

Knight was also the dissertation advisor of George Stigler, who later became a leading member of the mid-twentieth-century neoliberal Chicago School and Mont Pèlerin Society, promoting Knight's arguments (Knight 1924) on social costs in *Readings in Price Theory* in 1952 (Stigler and Boulding 1952). Ronald Coase admitted that Knight's ideas and terminology had greatly influenced his famous argument in *The Problem of Social Costs* (1960) (Coase 1983: 215; Medema 2010). It has been pointed out that Coase's political orientation was different from Pigou's – i.e., decidedly anti-interventionist – and that this clearly influenced his approach (Aslanbeigui and Medema 1998). Coase received a scholarship through the 'Free Market Study' funds of the neoliberal Chicago School, and can be considered as the second generation of neoliberals (Van Horn and Mirowski 2010). Coase critiqued Pigou's interventionist solution because it aimed at eliminating harmful effects via public intervention 'at all costs'. Coase's article contained a call for a close examination of alternative policy options, viewing both market and government solutions as imperfect, and the option of doing nothing at all about social costs (Medema 2010). It was Stigler who later shaped the 'Coase Theorem', i.e., a radicalized version of Coase's argument, to serve his neoliberal purposes in the discourse on social costs. In this, Stigler also referenced Knight's anti-Pigouvian 1924 article (Stigler 1966: 119).

Conversely, Stigler's silence on Kapp's and Clark's work on social and overhead costs in *Readings in Price Theory* (Stigler and Boulding 1952) can be interpreted as an 'ignore' strategy. Instead, Stigler chose to republish Knight's almost 30-year-old, anti-interventionist 'Fallacies' (1924) article. Kapp's *Social Costs* referred to Stigler's *New Welfare Economics*, arguing that the 'compensation principle' cannot effectively encompass the phenomenon of social costs due to the immeasurability of interpersonal utility comparisons and the impossibility of guaranteeing equal satisfaction after compensation (Stigler 1943, in Kapp 1950: 40). Kapp also noticed that Stigler had rejected the Marshallian notion of external economies as early as 1941 because it involved an 'abandonment of static analysis and serves only the purposes of historical analysis' (Stigler 1941:

68–76, in Kapp 1950: 40). Likewise, Stigler must have known Clark's famous work, which was awarded the Francis A. Walker medal by the American Economic Association in 1952 'given to that living American economist who … has made over the course of his life the most distinguished contribution to economics' (Shute 1997; Rutherford 2011). While recent research has elevated the role played by Stigler within the neoliberal political-economic agenda of the Chicago School (Nik-Khah 2010; 2011), more research is needed concerning Stigler's strategy to attain neoliberal hegemony in the discourse on social costs. Yet, this brief intellectual history clearly shows the emergence of an increasingly coherent intellectual effort to turn the discourse on social costs to the preferred anti-interventionist direction. This effort yielded its perhaps most prominent results in the field of law and economics, influencing the way judges think about social costs.

Stigler's 'Coase Theorem', together with Guido Calabresi's 'Some thoughts on risk distribution and the law of torts' (1961), became very influential in the New Law and Economics movement, which transformed the US field of law and economics (Medema 1998). Paraphrasing Knight's concerns about the costs of eliminating social costs,

> Calabresi acknowledged that Kapp was probably correct in projecting a vast web of unpaid social costs, but took the position that it would be 'too costly' for our society to determine those social costs (and even more 'costly' to attempt a redistributive remedy).
>
> (Gaskins 2007: 6–7)

According to Gaskins, the US legal movement had favored Kapp over Coase until the early 1960s because of the commonalities between American-led Legal Realists and American Institutionalists. The former were based on German pioneers of 'sociological jurisprudence'. Kapp's line of reasoning fit with this tradition mainly because he had absorbed the influence of American Institutionalism at Columbia. Franzini correctly pointed out that social and human rights, as opposed to property rights, lie at the heart of Kapp's approach (Franzini 2006).

James M. Buchanan, another leading member of the neoliberal thought collective, countered Kapp's thesis even more radically, arguing that intervention cannot possibly reduce externalities:

> Such improvements in the organisation of economic activity have, almost without exception, involved the placing of restrictions on the private behaviour of individuals through the implementation of some political action…. If this were not the case, it is difficult to see why … K. W. Kapp should have entitled his work 'The Social Costs of Private Enterprise'…. The primary criticism of theoretical welfare economics (and economists) that is advanced in this note is that its failure to include analyses of similar imperfections in realistic and attainable alternative solutions causes the analysis itself to take on implications for institutional change that are, at best, highly mis-leading…. In

what follows I shall try to show that, with consistent assumptions about human behaviour in both market and political institutions, any attempt to replace or to modify an existing market situation, admitted to be characterised by serious externalities, will produce solutions that embody externalities which are different but precisely analogous, to those previously existing.

(Buchanan 1962: 19)

Wilfred Beckerman, a leading neoliberal environmental economist, devoted an entire article to attacking Kapp's work, which was widely read and recognized in the emerging debate about increasing environmental degradation (Beckerman 1972; Franzini 2006).[6] Hayek praised Beckerman as a 'competent expert' who provided a 'devastating critique' of *The Limits to Growth* report (Hayek 1974). Beckerman's direct attack illustrates most prominently the growing self-confidence with which neoliberals promulgated their ideas in the context of the ensuing environmental discourse.

In conclusion, several major protagonists of the neoliberal thought collective developed their arguments in response to Kapp's challenge of (neo-)liberalism à la Hayek and Mises. Changing the social costs discourse was on the neoliberal agenda since the 1940s, with intellectual roots developing earlier, in the interwar period. The neoliberal argument redefined the discourse in crucial ways. First, it defined the goal no longer as the elimination of harmful effects but, instead, as either maximum efficiency, i.e., maximum value in terms of utility and exchange value or simply economic growth. Thus, social costs were no longer considered a fundamental threat to society that had to be eliminated at all costs, and it was even argued that social costs cannot be eliminated at all. In comparison, Kapp's *Social Costs* had explicitly rejected the idea that the pursuit of the higher end (maximum efficiency) justified harmful effects (compensated for until equivalency is reached at the margin between costs and benefits). Kapp had also argued that history provided ample evidence for the successful struggle against social costs.

Second, by shifting the discourse away from discussing the institutional causes of social costs, and toward market-based solutions for social costs, the neoliberal thought collective boldly turned the problem upside down and proscribed as the cure what Kapp had identified as the disease. The debate was shifted away from the limitations of market-based accounting and allocation decisions, toward an idealist vision of a private bargaining system that would not develop naturally but would have to be constructed.

Third, although this was not explicitly stated by neoliberals, the state would play an important role in enforcing and determining property rights so that bargaining could work its magic. This then became the double-truth in the neoliberal intellectual effort (Mirowski 2009), insinuating an efficient and 'free-market'-based solution, while obscuring the fact that the state played an even larger and more coercive role as an omnipresent guarantor and enforcer of the necessary preconditions. The neoliberal thought collective got away with eagerly pointing out inefficiencies and costs involved in Kapp's proposal for

social-democratic controls of the economy, while obscuring altogether the necessary costs of the neoliberal state.

Fourth, neoliberals did not provide an analysis of asymmetric economic
power relations and corresponding economic inequality, with which the problem
of social costs is imbued. This is squarely in line with the neoliberal tenet that
inequality is a precondition for a well-functioning economic system, while Kapp
pointed out the dangers of unequal distribution leading to a 'the poor sell cheap'
doctrine that would boil down to giving corporations full sovereignty to achieve
their aims, simply paying as little as they could get away with to anyone who
can make a legitimate social cost claim.

In sum, this is how the neoliberal thought collective completely reformulated
the problem of social costs, bearing similarities with their revision of the definition of monopoly (Van Horn 2009).

Responding to neoliberalism: Kapp's 'impossibility thesis' reformulated

As shown above, Kapp had used the concept of social cost originally to refute
Mises with the 'impossibility thesis' that markets do not and cannot express social
costs. His empirical study, *Social Costs*, supported this thesis, directly attacking
liberalism à la Hayek and Mises. As a consequence of the above-outlined neoliberal responses in the 1960s, Kapp found himself in a new position, having to
reformulate his 'impossibility thesis' into an argument why markets cannot solve
the problem of social costs. In 'Reply to Beckerman' (1971) Kapp first tried to
remind everyone that the debate was originally focused on the fact that markets
are the cause of social costs. He repeated his original argument that the maximization of net income by micro-economic units was likely to reduce the income of
other economic units and of society at large, questioning the efficiency of the
market as a mechanism of steering and coordinating the decisions of the various
micro-economic units. The main reason for this, he argued, was that the conventional measurements (accounting systems, standards, indicators) of the performance of the economy are unsatisfactory and misleading. Kapp then addressed
Beckerman, who proposed that the standard tools of economics and the logic and
criteria of choice (including the aggregation of numerous (environmental) dispa-
rate items in terms of money and willingness to pay) could be used as criteria for
evaluating things according to their equivalence at the margin, i.e., how much
money one would accept in order to be indifferent between having the previous
number of units of some 'good' and one unit less. Kapp argued that there are two
'impossibilities' that make this framework logically defective and operationally
ineffective, as noted in the subsections below.

Impossibility of expressing the absolute value of human life

Human health, life and death do not have exchange value per se. Original physical
needs, the inviolability of the individual and fundamental human requirements

must not be evaluated in terms of a desire for money because it falsifies the original need and the core of the problem of decision-making (Kapp 1971). Referring to Immanuel Kant, Kapp also argued that that which cannot be exchanged has no exchange value but intrinsic absolute value. Thus, human life and survival are not exchangeable commodities and their evaluation in terms of market prices is in conflict with reason and human conscience (Kapp 1974: 132). According to Kapp, it makes no sense to ask a person how much money he would accept if he died (e.g., due to pollution) in order to be as well off as if he was alive. 'Willingness-to-pay' (WTP) as a criterion of evaluating the quality of the environment has the insidious effect of reinterpreting original human needs and requirements into a desire for money and of evaluating the relative importance of such needs in terms of criteria which reflect the existing inequalities in the wage and income structure.

Kapp favored an empirical and pragmatic approach to value. The evaluative judgment must, according to Kapp, correspond to the subject matter as it affects human health and life. Monetary criteria (WTP, compensation principle, etc.) are inappropriate because they do not evaluate characteristics which define the quality of the environment and its negative impact on human health, well-being and survival. The issue is not whether WTP can be established but whether this is cognitively responsible. Kapp argued that monetary criteria are not cognitively responsible because these evaluative criteria are detached from the evaluative criteria outside of the 'economic' discourse, and thus are irresponsible because they are untrue to the empirical fact of the matter. Quantitative standards must be correlated in an appropriate way with the defining characteristics of the qualitative definitions.

Impossibility of expressing complex and cumulative causation and uncertainty

WTP is further undermined by the individual's inability to ascertain the full range of short- and long-term benefits of environmental improvements, or the full impact of environmental disruption upon his health and well-being. Environmental disruption is the result of a complex interaction between the economic system with physical and biological systems. Pollutants from different sources also act upon one another, and what counts is the total toxicological situation. Complex causation relationships in environmental disruption can become disproportionate effects per unit of additional pollutant. The effects are cumulative over time with possible time lags, and there can be considerable uncertainty about future effects. These effects are not transparent to the individual, meaning that the individual does not have the information or knowledge required to make a sound judgment. Asking the individual what he is willing to pay for the improvement of the quality of the environment or what amount of compensation he is willing to accept to tolerate current and higher levels of pollution is an inadequate, ineffective and highly problematic basis for evaluating the value of environmental goals (Kapp 1971).

Kapp predicted that forcing new facts of environmental disruption into the conceptual box designed for market exchanges served to downplay the significance of the phenomena of social costs, making them appear more harmless than they are, and as a pretext for endless delays, or for doing too little too late.

Conclusion

This rational reconstruction shows that the history of the concept of social costs is from the beginning intertwined with the planning debate and the neoliberal project, and that Kapp's arguments were part of the discourse early on. Since the 1930s Kapp targeted (neo-)liberal doctrines with his empirically grounded theory of social costs, arguing, on the one hand, the impossibility of market-based solutions to social costs and, on the other, the need for social controls of the economy. Evidence shows that key figures of the neoliberal thought collective attacked Kapp's work, shrewdly turning the social cost discourse toward a pro-market direction. As is typical of the social sciences, this debate was never settled in the sense that Kapp's theory was proven wrong and was thus rightfully forgotten. Rather, the disappearance of his arguments from economic discourse may be attributed to larger developments, such as overall decline of post-World War II institutional economics (Berger and Steppacher 2011), and the parallel success of the neoliberal project (Plehwe 2009). In the face of ever-greater social and environmental damages emanating from economic decision-making, reintroducing Kapp's theory could help to prevent the gradual encroachment of ideas.

Notes

1 This chapter was presented at the 2010 annual meeting of the Association for Social Economics at the Eastern Economics Association conference in Philadelphia. I am grateful for comments from Steve Medema, Edward Nik-Khah and two anonymous reviewers. All mistakes are my own.
2 'Wirtschaftlichkeit vom Standpunkt der Gesellschaft'.
3 Kapp builds on Menger's enlarged and revised second edition of *Principles of Economics*, published posthumously by his son.
4 Kapp had emigrated with his wife, Lore, to the United States in 1937, where he was initially affiliated with Columbia University, the workplace of John M. Clark.
5 Kapp also referred to Marx's way of viewing capitalism: 'No matter how economical capitalist production may be in other respects, it is utterly prodigal to human life.... Capitalism loses on one side for society what it gains on another for the individual capitalist' (Marx, *Capital III*,1909: 104, in Kapp 1970: 844).
6 Dieter Plehwe has identified Beckerman as part of the neoliberal thought collective; personal conversation 2010.

References

Aslanbeigui, N. and Medema, S.G. (1998) 'Beyond the dark clouds: Pigou and Coase on social costs', *History of Political Economy*, 30(4): 601–625.

Beckerman, W. (1972) 'Environmental policy and the challenge to economic theory', *Social Science Information*, 11(1): 7–15.

Berger, S. (2008) 'Karl Polanyi's and Karl William Kapp's substantive economics: important insights from the Kapp–Polanyi correspondence', *Review of Social Economy*, 66(3): 381–396.

Berger, S. (2009a) 'The normative matrix of social costs: linking Hayden's social fabric matrix and Kapp's theory of social costs', in Natarajan, T., Elsner, W. and Fullwiler, S.T. (eds.), *Institutional Analysis and Praxis*, New York: Springer.

Berger, S. (2009b) *The Foundations of Non-equilibrium Economics*, London: Routledge.

Berger, S. (2012) 'The Kapp–Clarke correspondance', mimeo.

Berger, S. and Steppacher, R. (eds.) (2011), *The Foundations of Institutional Economics: by Karl William Kapp*, London: Routledge.

Buchanan, J.M. (1962) 'Politics, policy and the Pigovian margins', *Economica*, 29(113): 17–28.

Calabresi, Guido (1961) 'Some thoughts on risk distribution and the law of torts', *Yale Law Journal*, 70(4): 499–553.

Cangiani, M. (2006) 'Freedom to plan', in Elsner, W., Frigato, P. and Ramazzotti, P. (eds.), *Social Costs and Public Action in Modern Capitalism: Essays Inspired by K. William Kapp's Theory of Social Costs*, London and New York: Routledge.

Coase, R. (1960) 'The problem of social costs', *Journal of Law and Economics*, 3: 1–44.

Coase, R. (1983) 'The fire of truth', *Journal of Law and Economics*, 26: 163.

Franzini, M. (2006) 'Social costs, social rights and the limits of free market capitalism: a re-reading of Kapp', in Elsner, W., Frigato, P. and Ramazzotti, P. (eds.), *Social Costs and Public Action in Modern Capitalism: Essays inspired by Karl William Kapp's Theory of Social Costs*, London and New York: Routledge.

Gaskins, R. (2007) 'Social insurance and the unpaid social costs of personal injury: a second look at K. William Kapp', Conference paper, 7th International Congress of ESEE, Leipzig.

Gruchy, A.G. (1947) *Modern Economic Thought: The American Contribution*, New York: A.M. Kelly.

Hayek, F.A. von (1935) *Collectivist Economic Planning*, London: G. Routledge and Sons Ltd.

Hayek, F.A. von (1944) *Road to Serfdom*, Chicago: University of Chicago Press.

Hayek, F.A. von (1974) 'Award ceremony speech for the Bank of Sweden Prize'.

Kapp, K.W. (1936) *Planwirtschaft und Aussenhandel*, Genf: Georg & Cie.

Kapp, K.W. (1950) *The Social Costs of Private Enterprise*, Cambridge, MA: Harvard University Press. (Second, enlarged and revised edition published as (1963) *The Social Costs of Business Enterprise*, republished in 1977 and 2000 by Spokesman.)

Kapp, K.W. (1963) 'Social costs and social benefits: a contribution to normative economics', in E. von Beckerath and H. Giersch (eds.), *Probleme der normativen Ökonomik und der wirtschaftspolitischen Beratung*, Berlin: Duncker & Humblot, pp. 183–210.

Kapp, K.W. (1967 [1985]) 'Economics and rational humanism', in Ullmann, J.E. and Preiswerk, R. (eds.), *The Humanization of the Social Sciences*, Lanham and London: University Press of America.

Kapp, K.W. (1970) 'Environmental disruption and social costs: a challenge to economics', *Kyklos* 23(4): 833–848.

Kapp, K.W. (1971 [2011]) 'Social costs, neo-classical economics, and environmental planning: a reply', Berger, S. and Steppacher, R. (eds.), *The Foundations of Institutional Economics: by K. William Kapp*, London and New York: Routledge.

110   S. Berger

Kapp, K.W. (1974 [2011]) 'Environmental indicators as indicators of social use value', published as 'Substantive vs. formal rationality', in Berger, S. and Steppacher, R. (eds.), *The Foundations of Institutional Economics: by K. William Kapp*, London and New York: Routledge.

Kapp, K.W. (1975) 'Staatliche Förderung umweltfreundlicher Technologien', *Kommission für wirtschaftlichen und sozialen Wandel 74*, Göttingen: Otto Schwarz. (Also published translated and abbreviated as 'Science and technology in the light of institutional analysis', in Berger, S. and Steppacher, R. (eds.) (2011) *The Foundations of Institutional Economics: by K. William Kapp*, London and New York: Routledge.

Kapp, K.W. (unpublished manuscript), 'Preface' to *The Social Costs of Private Enterprise*. (Probably written in the mid 1940s at New York University).

Knight, F.H. (1924 [1952]), 'Some fallacies in the interpretation of social costs', in Stigler, G.J. and Boulding, K.E. (eds.), *Readings in Price Theory*, Chicago: Homewood.

Knight, F.H. (1951) 'Review: the social costs of private enterprise', *Annals of the American Academy of Political and Social Science*, 273: 233–234.

Medema, S.G. (1998) 'Wandering the road from pluralism to Posner: the transformation of law and economics in the twentieth century', *History of Political Economy*, 30: 202–224.

Medema, S.G. (2010) 'Ronald Harry Coase', in Emmett, R.B. (ed.), *The Elgar Companion to the Chicago School of Economics*, Cheltenham: Edward Elgar.

Mirowski, P. (2009) 'Postface: defining neoliberalism', in Mirowski, P. and Plehwe, D. (eds.), *The Road from Mont Pèlerin: The Making of the Neoliberal Thought Collective*, Cambridge, MA and London: Harvard University Press.

Mises, L. von (1944) *Bureaucracy*, New Haven: Yale University Press.

Nik-Khah, E. (2010) 'George J. Stigler', in Emmett, R.B. (ed.), *The Elgar Companion to the Chicago School of Economics*, Cheltenham: Edward Elgar.

Nik-Khah, E. (2011) 'George Stigler, the Graduate School of Business, and the pillars of the Chicago School', in Van Horn, R., Mirowski, P. and Stapleford, T. (eds.). *Building Chicago Economics: New Perspectives on America's Most Powerful Economics Program*, Cambridge: Cambridge University Press.

Pigou, A.C. (1929) *The Economics of Welfare*, London: Macmillan.

Pigou, A.C. (1947) *Socialism vs. Capitalism*, London: Macmillan.

Plehwe, D. (2009) 'Introduction', in Mirowski, P. and Plehwe, D. (eds.), *The Road from Mont Pèlerin: The Making of the Neoliberal Thought Collective*, Cambridge, MA and London: Harvard University Press.

Rorty, R. (1984) 'The historiography of philosophy: four genres', in Rorty, R., Schneewind, J.B. and Skinner, Q. (eds.), *Philosophy in History*, Cambridge: Cambridge University Press.

Rutherford, M. (2010) 'Chicago economics and institutionalism', in Emmett, R.B. (ed.), *The Elgar Companion to the Chicago School of Economics*, Cheltenham: Edward Elgar.

Rutherford, M. (2011) *The Institutionalist Movement in American Economics, 1918–1947*, Cambridge: Cambridge University Press.

Shute, L. (1997) *John Maurice Clark: A Social Economics for the 21st Century*, London: Macmillan.

Stigler, G.J. (1941) *Production and Distribution Theories*, New York: Macmillan.

Stigler, G.J. (1943) 'The new welfare economics', *American Economic Review*, 33: 355–559.

Stigler, G.J. (1966) *The Theory of Price*, 3rd edition, London and New York: Macmillan.

Stigler, G.J. and Boulding, K.E. (eds.) (1952) *Readings in Price Theory*, Chicago: Richard D. Irwin.

Tool, M. (1978) 'Review: economics in institutional perspective, memorial essays in honor of K. William Kapp', *Journal of Economic Issues*, 12(4): 891–901.

Van Horn, R. (2009) 'Reinventing monopoly and the role of corporations: the roots of Chicago law and economics', in Mirowski, P. and Plehwe, D. (eds.), *The Road from Mont Pèlerin: The Making of the Neoliberal Thought Collective*, Cambridge, MA and London: Harvard University Press.

Van Horn, R. and Mirowski, P. (2009) 'The rise of the Chicago School of economics and the birth of neoliberalism', in Mirowski, P. and Plehwe, D. (eds.), *The Road from Mont Pèlerin: The Making of the Neoliberal Thought Collective*, Cambridge, MA and London: Harvard University Press.

Van Horn, R. and Mirowski, P. (2010) 'Neoliberalism and Chicago', in Emmett, R.B. (ed.), *The Elgar Companion to the Chicago School of Economics*, Cheltenham: Edward Elgar.

Veblen, T.B. (1904) *The Theory of Business Enterprise*, New York: Charles Scribner's Sons.

Veblen, T.B. (1921) *Engineers and the Price System*, New York: B.W. Huebsch.

Part II

Social costs of the present crises

6 From the crisis of distribution to the distribution of the costs of the crisis

The case of Europe

Özlem Onaran

Introduction

The aim of this chapter is to analyze the rise in inequality as a main cause of the global crisis and discuss how the crisis is further increasing the inequality at the expense of labor. The neoliberal policies and the deterioration in labor share have created a fertile ground to bury the seeds of a major global crisis together with the risky developments in the credit, housing and security markets. Beneath the financial aspects of the crisis lie the long-term contradictions of neoliberalism: a declining wage share, thus rising profit share, which generated a potential realization crisis; and shareholder value orientation as a consequence of the finance-dominated regime, which changed the relationship between profits and investments, which also undermined the long-term growth potential of the economies.

Debt-led consumption based on financial innovations in the banking sector, as in the case of the United States or Britain, or export-led growth as in the case of Germany, were the ways to postpone the solutions to these contradictions. Thus wage suppression was deeply connected to global imbalances. In the European context, the wage suppression strategy and current account surpluses of Germany in particular created imbalances within Europe in the form of current account deficits, public or private debt in the periphery of the Eurozone, in particular in Greece, Portugal, Spain and Ireland, or in Eastern Europe, in particular in Hungary, the Baltic States, Romania and Bulgaria. The crisis laid bare the historical divergences within Europe, and led to a European crisis and a new stage in the global crisis. The restrained policy framework, which is based on a strict inflation targeting, and which lacks a common fiscal policy, is the root of the problem, as it has failed to generate convergence within the EU in the first place. In countries of the periphery like Greece, where both public debt and budget deficit to GDP ratio is high and is coupled with a high current account deficit, the attack of the speculators asking dramatically higher yields has brought the country to the edge of a sovereign debt crisis in 2010. Indeed, before Greece, in 2009 Hungary, the Baltic States and Romania were under attack. It looked as if the euro saved Slovakia and Slovenia from the turbulences in the currency markets, but their problem will be a permanent loss of international competitiveness as is unfortunately illustrated by the problems of the periphery of the Eurozone. Initially, Eastern Europe was seen as the only problem zone in Europe. However, together with Greece, the attention of the speculators turned to the public debt and deficits in Portugal, Spain and Ireland, and then toward the core: Italy, Britain and Belgium. Now market pressures are threatening convergence and social cohesion both in the East and the West.

What we are going through is a crisis of distribution; and similarly the policy reactions to the crisis are part of a distributional struggle. Although the profits of this fragile growth regime were privatized, the losses and risks are now being socialized. The number of wealthy people (high net worth individuals) in the world has already returned to pre-banking crisis levels according to a report of Merrill Lynch and Capgemini. The governments agreeing to the cuts are avoiding taxing the beneficiaries of neoliberal policies and the main creators of the crisis. The public debt would not be there if it were not for the bank rescue packages, counter-cyclical fiscal stimuli and the loss of tax revenues during the crisis. Finally, the crisis would not have happened without the major pro-capital redistribution and financialization. Thus this is a crisis of distribution, and a reversal of inequality at the expense of labor is the only real solution, which in turn connects the demands for full employment and equality with an agenda for an alternative economic model.

The following section discusses the distributional background of the crisis. The subsequent section presents the effects of the former crises in the developing countries and in Japan on income distribution and unemployment. A discussion then follows on the crisis in the core and periphery of Western Europe and Eastern Europe. The final section concludes with policy implications.

The crisis of inequality

Since the 1980s, the world economy has been guided by neoliberal economic policies such as the dismantling of government regulations in financial markets, as well as goods and labor markets, and increased openness to trade, foreign direct investment and financial capital flows. These policies have reduced the role of macroeconomic policy interventions with the claim that free-market capitalism would increase efficiency and growth, and provide a fair distribution. The focus of macroeconomic policy has shifted away from full employment toward mere price stability. Neoliberalism tried to solve the crisis of the golden age of capitalism via a major attack on labor. The outcome was a secular deterioration in the labor share since the early 1980s. The increase in globalization, in particular the mobility of capital, and the stagnation in aggregate demand and rise in unemployment have been the central powers behind this pro-capital redistribution of income.

Here lie the two important long-term contradictions of neoliberalism. First, laissez-faire capitalism has generated higher profits for multinational firms, and especially for the financial sector. However, the high financial returns have replaced profits from real activity in many cases. As the finance-dominated regime rose, the investment behavior of the firms was significantly affected by the rising shareholder value orientation. Financial market-oriented remuneration schemes based on short-term profitability increased the orientation of management toward shareholders' objectives. The unregulated financial markets and the pressure of financial market investors have created a bias in favor of asset purchases as opposed to asset creation. At the same time most of the effort of macroeconomic policy-makers has been going to policies to retain the confidence of volatile financial markets. Markets have been deregulated mainly to support the interests of the rentier capitalists, who went on benefiting from investment subsidies, tax concessions and rescue operations during crises. The same process has limited the demands of workers. In a way, the loss in labor's share has prevented the profits in the real sector from being eroded by increased interest payments. Consequently, the relationship between profits and investment has changed; the investment–profit ratio shows a clear declining trend, thus higher profits do not automatically lead to higher investment. Thus in spite of higher profit rates, not only in the United States, but also in the major advanced capitalist economies (Germany, France and the United Kingdom), as well as some developing countries (e.g., Latin America, Turkey), economic growth rates have been well below their historical trends.

Second, from a macroeconomic perspective, the decline in the labor share has also been a problem for the micro-level beneficiaries of these policies. Profit can only be realized if there is sufficient effective demand for the goods and services. But the decline in the purchasing power of labor has a negative effect on consumption, given that the marginal propensity to consume out of profits as well as rentier income is lower than that out of wages. This affects investments negatively, which are already under the pressure of shareholder value orientation. The decline in the labor share has been the source of a *potential realization crisis* for the system – one of the major sources of crisis in capitalism according to Marxian economics. Thus neoliberalism only replaced the profit squeeze and over-accumulation crisis of the 1970s with the realization problem.

Exactly at this point the financial innovations seemed to have offered a short-term solution to the crisis of neoliberalism in the 1990s: debt-led consumption growth. It is important to note that without the unequal income distribution the debt-led growth model would not have been necessary or possible. Particularly in the United States, but also in the United Kingdom, Ireland or some continental European countries like the Netherlands, Denmark, Spain and Greece, as well as Eastern Europe, household debt increased dramatically in the last decade. The increase in housing credits and house prices fueled each other; then the increased housing wealth thanks to the housing bubble served as collateral for further credit, and fueled consumption. Financialization leads to a debt-led growth by fueling consumption in the short-term, but debt has to be serviced in the future. The debt channel is a redistribution of income from indebted low-income households to rentier households. Thus the positive effects of the debt-led growth are destined to be partially offset by the negative effects of redistribution on consumption. Because of high debt levels, the fragility of the economy to the possible shocks in the credit market also increases.

This debt-led consumption model created a current account deficit in the United States that exceeded 6 percent of the GDP. This deficit was financed by the surpluses of some other developed countries like Germany and Japan, developing countries like China and South Korea, and the oil-rich Middle Eastern countries. In Germany and Japan current account surpluses and the consequent capital outflows to the United States were made possible by wage moderation, which has suppressed domestic consumption and fueled exports. Similar imbalances took place within Europe between the surplus countries in the core and the periphery of Europe. Thus this is again an outcome of the crisis of distribution. On the side of the developing countries like China and South Korea, the experience of the Asian and Latin American crises stimulated a policy of accumulation of foreign reserves as a bail-out guarantee against the speculative capital outflows. Here the international dimension of inequality plays an important role: These countries, threatened by the free mobility and volatility of short-term international financial flows, invested their current account surpluses in US government bonds instead of stimulating their domestic development plans.

Over the fertile ground of inequalities grew the debt-led growth model, facilitated by the deregulation of the financial markets and the consequent innovations in mortgage-backed securities, collateralized debt obligations and credit default swaps. These innovations and the 'originate and distribute' model of banking have multiplied the amount of credit that the banks could extend given the limits of their capital. The premiums earned by the bankers, the commissions of the banks, the high CEO incomes thanks to high bank profits, and the commissions of the rating agencies all created a perverse mechanism of investments that led to short-termism and ignorance about the risks of this banking model.

Learning from the past: crisis, unemployment and distribution

This section analyzes the effects of some previous financial crises on the distribution of income, wages and unemployment. Past crisis experiences show that the episodes of crisis intensify the distributional struggle and the question on who will carry the burden of adjustment becomes part of the struggle. We will focus on the experiences of developing countries, as well as the Japanese slump of the 1990s as a developed country case. This comparison is important because it highlights the differences of the currency crises vs. domestic financial crises regarding the distributional consequences.[1] There are two important aspects related with this comparison: (1) While the currency crises of the developing countries come with inflationary effects, the issue in Japan's crisis was deflation; (2) the duration and the size of the shock – in most of the developing country crises, the recession is a very deep, but one-year-long phenomenon, whereas during the Japanese slump the initial shock to growth was moderate, but the recovery took more than a decade. As a consequence, the developing country crises lead to sharp declines in real wages, whereas the deflationary environment creates moderate real wage declines or even some minor increases, particularly in years of deflation. However, strikingly, the cumulative effect is in both cases a dramatic pro-capital redistribution. Needless to say, all these former crises of the neoliberal era were national or regional crises, and the effects of the global crisis will differ in terms of the global deflationary processes and demand deficiency, although with important lessons to be learned from Japan. The case of developing countries is, nevertheless, important, in particular for the case of Eastern Europe to evaluate the dangers that lie behind a currency crisis.

Developing countries

Despite former policy differences, many developing countries have experienced in the past similar outcomes as a consequence of financial crises that followed the liberalization of capital flows. The effects of the crises in the developing countries worked through four channels: (1) the decline in growth and thereby labor demand; (2) the increase in unemployment and thereby the decline in the bargaining power of workers; (3) inflationary shocks during currency crises; and (4) path-dependency effects, i.e., lagged effects. The outcome in the developing countries has been a radical deterioration in the real wage, and consequently wage share, which has persisted years after the crisis. Similarly, unemployment rates, which increased during the crises, did not return to pre-crisis levels for years after the crises.

We first focus on three developing countries – Mexico, Turkey and Korea – for which detailed data are available (Figure 6.1). Despite differences in economic policy and trends in income distribution, the crises following capital account liberalization have had very similar effects on the wage share in all three countries, leading to a sharp and long-lasting decline. In all three cases, the initial crisis year is always associated with a decline in the wage share, which by far exceeds the rate of decline in production. Capital account liberalization dates back to the late 1980s in Turkey and Mexico and the second half of the 1990s in Korea. Turkey was hit by crises in 1994 and 2001, Mexico in 1994–1995 and Korea in 1997–1998. During a crisis, employers push labor unions to accept dramatic wage cuts or compulsory unpaid leave to avoid job losses. The crisis also creates a hysteresis effect that destroys the bargaining power of labor for a long period afterwards. Diwan (2001) defines crises as episodes of distributional fights which leave 'distributional scars'. In all countries, a strong economic recovery took place the year after the crisis; however, the fall in the wage share usually continued for two or even three years. In Mexico, after the crisis in 1995, the wage share declined 27.7 percent as of 1996 compared to 1993, and indeed has still not returned to its pre-crisis level ten years after the crisis, based on the latest available data (for 2004). The post-2001 recession in Mexico has triggered a new declining trend in the wage share. In Turkey the cumulative decline in the wage share has been 24.8 percent and 30.2 percent following the 1994 and 2001 crises, with the decline continuing for two years (1994–1995) and six years

(2001–2006), respectively. Given the latest available data for 2006, the wage share is still not back to its pre-crisis level following the 2001 crisis. The wage share as of 2006 is even lower than its level in 1994. In Korea, the wage share has continued to decline for three years following the 1997 crisis, and was 21.6 percent lower in 1999 compared to 1996. Also in Korea the wage share has not returned back to its pre-crisis level ten years after the crisis. In that respect, crisis has brought Korea closer to the cases of Mexico and Turkey, reversing the increasing trend.

The major source of the decline in the wage share during the crisis year is the decline in the real wage. Real wages continued to decline for two more years after the crises in both Mexico and Turkey. Employment declined also in all crisis years. In both Mexico and Turkey during all crisis years the decline in the real wage is much higher than the change in employment. Thus wages adjust rather flexibly to changes in labor market conditions. In Korea the decline in employment also exceeded that in value added, leading to productivity increases. In Mexico both 1982 and 1995 were episodes of stagnant productivity (comparable declines in employment and value added), thus the decline in the wage share results solely from real wage declines. In the cases of crises of Turkey, both productivity and real wages decline, with the decline in the latter being significantly higher. The recovery that had started in 2004 in real wages was so weak compared to productivity increases that the wage share continued to decline during

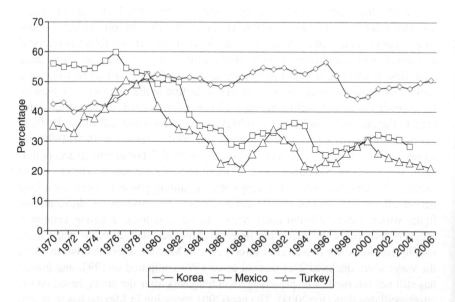

Figure 6.1 Wage share in manufacturing industry: Korea, Mexico, Turkey (source: share of labor compensation in value added, OECD STAN for Korea and Mexico, and Annual Survey of Employment, Payments, Production and Tendencies in Manufacturing Industry by the Turkey Institute of Statistics for Turkey).

the 2004–2008 recovery period as well. As of 2008 real wages were still 19.9 percent lower than in 2000.

Currency crises have strong implications for the wage share. Due to the import dependency of these countries, depreciation of the local currency has a pass-through effect on prices due to an increase in the price of the imported goods, which generates an important increase in overall input costs, and thus dramatic increases in inflation. The depreciation rates had reached up to 90.2 percent in Mexico in 1994; 169.5 percent and 96.0 percent in Turkey in 1994 and 2001, respectively; and 47.3 percent in Korea in 1998. Not only are these inflationary shocks unexpected, but also it is hard for the workers to ask for wage increases in line with inflation due to the magnitude of the shock. Depending on the balance of power relations, the firms try to compensate the increase in input costs by a decline in labor costs. The outcome is a radical deterioration in the real wage, and consequently wage share.

Onaran (2008; 2009) presents econometric evidence about the effect of the currency crises on the wage share in developing countries, estimating the percentage change in the wage share in manufacturing as a function of growth (current and lagged), nominal depreciation rate of the currency (current and lagged) and its own lag. To test whether there is a break in the cyclical behavior of labor's share during the crisis periods, the normal years vs. recession years are separated. During normal years the wage share is not pro-cyclical in most of the cases, but it is pro-cyclical during a recession in Argentina, Indonesia, Malaysia, Mexico and Turkey. Nominal depreciation has a negative significant effect on the wage share in six out of ten countries (Argentina, Chile, Indonesia, Korea, Mexico and Turkey).

Figure 6.2 shows the pre- and post-crisis trends in unemployment for selected developing countries, which have experienced a crisis in the post-1980s. During the crisis episodes the increases in unemployment go along with the decline in the wage share. Furthermore, as high unemployment rates suppress real wages, the decline in the share of wages contributes to the aggregate demand deficiency, making it worse for the recovery and job creation capacity of the economy; thus unemployment persists for a long time after the crisis. Overall, in six out of these ten countries (Indonesia, Korea, Thailand, Malaysia, Turkey and Brazil) unemployment rates are still higher than the pre-crisis levels.[2]

Japan

The wage share was declining since the late 1970s in Japan, and with the crisis the first stage was just a stagnation or slight decline in the wage share as can be seen in Figure 6.3. This is quite different from the emerging markets. A general property of the post-war Japanese economy, which related to the job security of core workers, played a role in this development: 'labor hoarding' during contractions and 'increasing returns to scale' during expansions (Uemura 2008). During the recession in the 1990s the real wage declined moderately (in 1992–1993, 1997–1999), but there were also slight recoveries in between (in 1994–1996), as

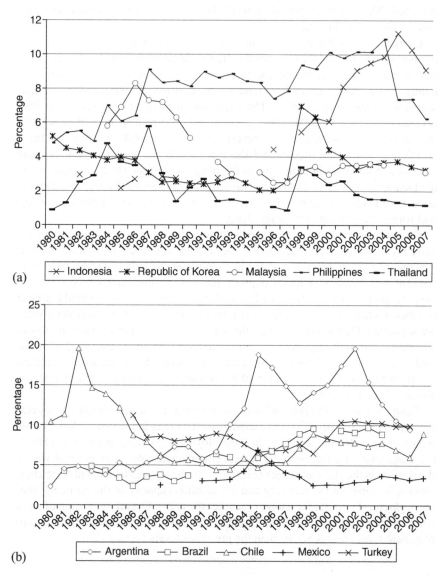

(a)   —×— Indonesia —*— Republic of Korea —○— Malaysia —■— Philippines —■— Thailand

(b)   —◇— Argentina —□— Brazil —△— Chile —+— Mexico —×— Turkey

Figure 6.2 Unemployment rate: (a) selected countries in Southeast Asia; (b) selected countries in Latin America and Turkey (source: ILO online database on the Key Indicators of the Labour Market (KILM)).

can be seen in Figure 6.4. The nominal wage increases, as well as the deflation of 1994–1996, contributed to this process. Nevertheless, except for 1994 and 1998 the difference between the wage and productivity changes was always negative (Figure 6.4), leading to a continuous decline in the wage share. Starting from 1998, we also observe nominal wage declines in the deflationary environment

Figure 6.3 Adjusted wage share, total economy, Japan (source: compensation per employee as percentage of GDP at factor cost per person employed, AMECO, online macro-economic database of the European Commission's Directorate General for Economic and Financial Affairs).

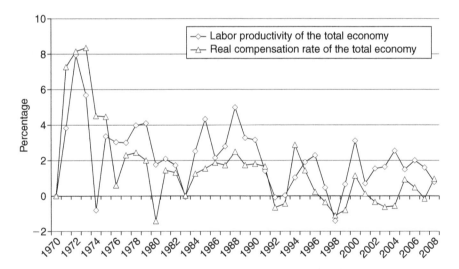

Figure 6.4 Labor productivity and real compensation rate, total economy, Japan, annual percentage change (source: *OECD Economic Outlook*, various years).

(1998–1999, 2002–2004, 2007), as well as wage freezes (2000, 2005–2006, 2008). The firing of many workers in the first half of the 2000s has been influential in this process. After the recession, the institutionalized wage coordination mechanism was also almost broken (ibid.). The employment system has also evolved in the

Japanese economy since the recession. As a measure against labor hoarding in large Japanese firms, the number of non-regular workers increased dramatically; there has also been a shift toward unstable service jobs (ibid.). All of these developments have led to a weakening in the bargaining position of unions and the suppression of nominal wage growth. Overall, the wage share decreased by 10.6 percent as of 2007 compared to 1998, and 8.9 percent compared to 1992. The

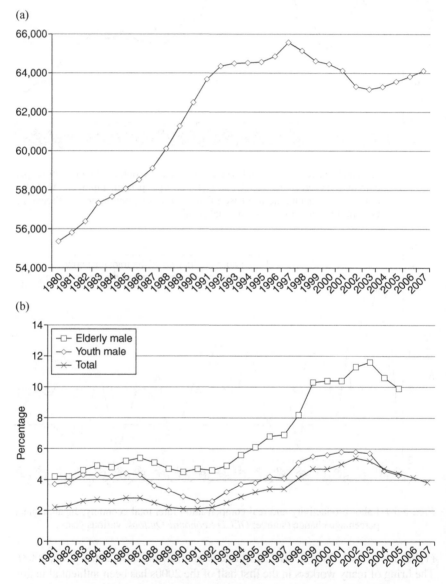

Figure 6.5 (a) Employment, Japan (in thousands); (b) unemployment rate, Japan (source: ILO online database on the Key Indicators of the Labour Market (KILM)).

decline in the wage share contributed to a decline in domestic demand, and exports became an important source of demand again in Japan, which also increased the pressure of international competition with the other Asian countries and the increasing number of foreign affiliates of Japanese multinational firms (ibid.).

In the meantime employment in the total economy first stagnated during 1992–1995 and, after a slight recovery, decreased in absolute terms during 1997–2003 (Figure 6.5a). The recovery since 2004 has, as of 2007, barely brought employment to 2001 levels. The decline in employment led to a strong and continuous increase in unemployment from a level of 2.1 percent in 1991 to 5.4 percent in 2002 (Figure 6.5b). Despite the recovery since 2004, unemployment as of 2007 is still higher than in 1997. Although the unemployment rate in Japan at its peak is still lower than in most other advanced countries, it is important to realize that drastic increases in unemployment can radically change the industrial relations and wage bargaining process in a persistent way. In the meantime, the unemployment rate of elderly males increased much more, but the most dramatic increase has been in male youth (aged 15–24) unemployment, increasing from 4.5 percent in 1990 to 11.6 percent in 2003 (Figure 6.5b). Long-term unemployment also increased from 0.3 percent in 1992 to 1.7 percent in 2003, with the incidence of unemployment (persons unemployed for a period of one year or more as a percentage of the total unemployed) increasing to 33.7 percent in 2004. These adverse developments in unemployment took place despite a strong decline in male as well as female labor force participation rates, which declined from 64.1 percent in 1992 to 59.6 percent in 2007. It is also worrying that the decline in the labor force participation rate is persistent despite the recovery in employment and unemployment. It can be argued that the discouraging effect of the crisis and the deterioration in the working conditions have had a permanent effect.

Core and periphery of Western Europe: from wage suppression to sovereign debt crisis

Although the recent crisis originated in the United States, it spread quickly to Europe due to the exposure of the European banks to the toxic assets, and the recession has been deeper in Europe. The difference in the depth of the crisis between the United States and Europe can be explained by the larger size of the fiscal stimulus plan as well as the faster reaction in the United States in terms of both monetary and fiscal policy compared to Europe.

There were also important divergences within the core of Europe as well as between the core and the periphery. In the core, Britain had a deep recession due to its dependence on the financial sector, over-extended banks and over-indebted private sector, and the housing bubble, so that GDP contracted by 6.2 percent between early 2008 and the third quarter of 2009. German and Italian GDP declined by 4.9 percent and 5.0 percent, respectively, in 2009, while French GDP contracted by just 2.6 percent in 2009. Germany did not have a household debt problem, but it is particularly suffering from the curse of its neo-mercantilist strategy of export-based growth via wage dumping, as export markets are shrinking. Contrary to Germany, in France a better developed system of automatic stabilizers, a larger state sector and a better position in terms of income inequality made the conditions of the crisis more moderate at the onset, since the weakening of demand was less important (Fitoussi and Saraceno 2010).

In the periphery of Europe, Ireland, with its disproportionately large banking sector and the bursting of its housing bubble, and Spain, with the collapse of the housing bubble and the consequent contraction in construction, have been in continuous recession in 2010. The contraction in Ireland's GDP in 2009 reached 7.5 percent. Most importantly, the imbalances between the core and periphery of Europe, and the limited fiscal capacity of the periphery to tame the crisis evolved into a sovereign debt crisis in Greece, followed by Portugal, Spain and Ireland at the end of 2009, with severe implications for growth in 2010. Greece has had a three-year recession prolonged into 2011.

At the root of the problem is the neoliberal model that turned the periphery of Europe to markets for the core countries without any prospect of catching up. The lack of a sufficiently large European budget and significant fiscal transfers targeting productive investments in the periphery led to persistent differentials in productivity. The Stability and Growth Pact, as well as EU competition regulations, limited the area for maneuver for the implementation of national industrial policies. In the absence of an industrial policy and productive investments to boost productivity, and unable to devalue, the strategy of competitiveness was based mainly on wage moderation and increased deregulation and precarization of the labor markets, which further eroded labor's bargaining power throughout the EU. Overall, labor's share in income declined sharply in that period (Figure 6.6). However, wage moderation did not save the periphery of the Eurozone, like Greece, Portugal, Ireland and Spain, since Germany was engaged in a much more aggressive wage and labor market policy.

In the periphery nominal labor costs have increased faster than in Germany due to a higher rate of inflation. This, however, does not mean that there was no wage moderation in these countries: during either the 1990s, 2000s or both periods productivity increases exceeded changes in real wages in all West European countries. In Germany as well as in Italy and Spain real wages even declined in the 2000s, with the gap being largest in Germany (Table 6.1). The gap between wages and productivity in Germany was due to real wage decline, and not necessarily high productivity. Indeed, the productivity increase in Germany has been quite modest; e.g., lower than in Britain, Ireland, Greece and Portugal in the period 1991–2007. The phenomenal competitive advantage of Germany was simply due to wage suppression rather than increasing productivity. The low investments despite high profit share explain the stagnant productivity and low rates of GDP growth in Germany. Most strikingly, the real wage decline in Germany in the 2000s went along with the worst employment performance in Western Europe (Table 6.1). Moreover, with significantly lower wages Eastern Europe was a much more attractive location if there were any investment motives in search for lower wages. The German case is also in

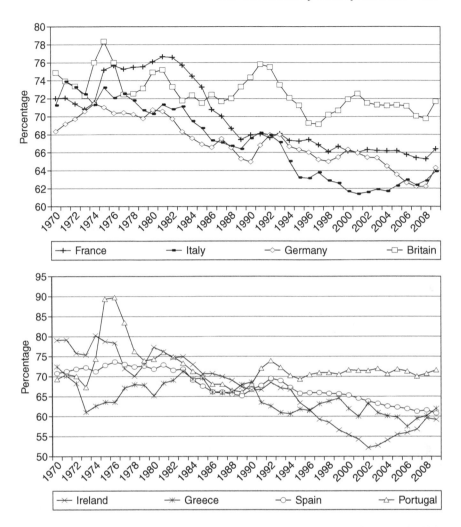

Figure 6.6 Adjusted wage share, selected Western EU member states (source: AMECO (Economic and Financial Affairs, Annual Macroeconomic Indicators online database).

Note
Compensation per employee as percentage of GDP at factor cost per person employed.

striking contrast to France, where real wage growth has more or less kept up with productivity. France did not have Germany's export boom, but domestic demand and employment growth have been much stronger.

With weak domestic demand due to low wages, exports were the main source of growth in Germany, but this has been detrimental for the exports of the peripheral countries due to both loss of competitiveness and the contraction of

Table 6.1 Average annual growth in GDP, employment, productivity, and real wage, 1991–2009, selected Western EU member states

	1991–2000				2000–2007			
	GDP	Employment	Productivity	Real wage	GDP	Employment	Productivity	Real wage
Britain	2.98	0.55	2.45	1.79	2.56	0.88	1.61	2.06
Germany	1.75	0.15	1.62	1.23	1.24	0.21	1.01	−0.46
France	2.09	0.56	1.39	1.00	1.83	0.77	1.03	1.19
Italy	1.60	−0.15	1.64	−0.50	1.14	1.38	−0.21	−0.01
Spain	2.83	1.92	1.00	0.39	3.42	3.86	0.09	−0.06
Greece	2.26	1.34	1.38	0.83	4.20	1.41	2.73	2.51
Ireland	7.69	4.01	3.41	1.81	5.53	3.22	2.20	2.21
Portugal	2.72	0.75	2.39	3.32	1.09	0.41	0.82	0.32

	2008				2009			
	GDP	Employment	Productivity	Real wage	GDP	Employment	Productivity	Real wage
Britain	0.55	0.76	0.32	−1.09	−4.65	−2.09	−2.76	1.53
Germany	0.97	1.39	−0.13	0.21	−4.90	−0.09	−4.97	0.17
France	0.32	1.39	−0.17	−0.33	−2.30	−0.45	−1.01	1.97
Italy	−1.04	0.83	−1.60	−0.34	−4.80	−0.91	−3.43	0.89
Spain	0.86	−0.48	1.26	2.55	−3.59	−6.77	3.22	3.77
Greece	2.01	1.10	1.91	1.69	−1.06	−1.19	−0.81	4.15
Ireland	−3.02	−0.51	−1.92	0.33	−7.47	−8.18	1.15	4.73
Portugal	−0.04	0.62	−0.41	0.36	−2.75	−2.40	−0.10	6.77

Source: OECD National Accounts, online database.

Notes

Employment is for the whole economy. Productivity is real GDP/employee. Real wage is labor compensation deflated by private consumption deflator, index 2000=100. Period averages are geometric averages.

domestic demand in Germany. Indeed, Germany is like the China of Europe, with a large current account surplus, high savings and low domestic demand. This neo-mercantilist policy has also been a model for some other countries like Austria and the Netherlands. In the countries of the periphery, consumption led by private debt has filled in the gap that low exports and high imports have created. Construction booms, real-estate bubbles and private debt have been a typical feature, particularly in Spain and Ireland. In Greece and, to a lesser extent, Portugal fiscal deficits also played a compensating role along with the debt of the households and corporations. This is the background of the sovereign debt crisis in the periphery, as it was unleashed in Greece in December 2009.

Following speculation about Greece's default and exit from the euro, the Eurozone governments' first decision came at the end of March 2010 after months of hesitation. Under pressure, the initially announced amount of €30 billion turned out to be the first part of a larger three-year bail-out package of €110 billion. The EU unveiled later in May a further surprise package of €500 billion to be supported by a €250 billion IMF facility to defend all Eurozone countries. The Eurozone governments are indeed protecting their own banks that are holding Greek bonds against a default; the bulk of the Greek bonds are held by German and French banks (*Economist*, 2010a).

The ECB's initial response was only to announce in March 2010 that it will continue to accept from the banks bonds with ratings as low as triple-B-minus as collateral; later it even accepted the Greek bonds after they were downgraded to Junk status. Finally, in May, under pressure from banks and the Commission, the ECB finally made a U-turn and launched a program of buying up the bonds of the peripheral Eurozone countries.

Germany, backed by the Netherlands, Austria and Finland, all current account surplus countries, initially resisted the €750 billion package. Weber, the Bundesbank president, did not hide his critique of the ECB's new decision. The package was pushed by France and the deficit countries like Spain, Italy and Portugal, and most importantly by the external intervention of the United States, with the fear of a second 'Lehman Brothers' turning point in the global economy. Interestingly, the information about Sarkozy's threat to leave the euro to stop Merkel's block was leaked to the press by the Spanish Prime Minister Zapatero's colleagues. Barroso, the head of the European Commission, also pushed for moving the monetary union in the direction of a fiscal union. Life for Germany's ruling elite is not easy: Merkel's party lost in a local state election amid the Greek crisis. Her liberal coalition partner (FDP) complains that transfers to imprudent Eurozone members have a higher priority than tax cuts. The social democrats (SPD) oppose that banks are again being bailed out. The German technocracy is expressing its fears about fiscal federalism and the euro turning into a French euro; the German media is spreading fears of inflation. Sarkozy, who for now seems to be the winner, is also not free of troubles. The IMF's eager involvement, which was supported by Germany, is improving Strauss-Kahn's profile, who may be considering a run against Sarkozy for the French presidency. Outside the Eurozone, Britain is also troubled: it is trying to stay out of the large defense scheme; however, this might be premature and ignorant about a future attack to the pound. Financial regulation is another issue that Britain tries to resist to protect the City of London.

The role model pointed out by the EU politicians for Greece is Ireland: Ireland has already slashed public sector wages between 5–15 percent, cut social welfare spending and other spending in order to decrease its budget deficit from 12.5 percent in 2009 to 10 percent in 2011 and 2.9 percent in 2014. These brutal spending cuts and the detrimental pro-cyclical fiscal policy in Ireland have been praised, since they have restored market confidence without aid from the EU. Portugal and Spain have also committed to austerity packages with higher tax on consumption and wage cuts.

Greece is now pushed to cut its budget deficit from 13.6 percent of GDP in 2009 to 3 percent in 2013 via dramatic cuts in spending, public sector wages and pensions, an increase in retirement age and tax hikes along with a fight against tax evasion. The bulk of the austerity measures will hurt the wage earners in the private as well as the public sector, as the wage cuts in the public sector play a signal role for bargaining. Cuts in public services will also increase the cost of living. However, there is a major inconsistency in this austerity plan: As the recession becomes deeper, tax revenues will become lower and despite severe cuts, the budget deficit might not improve as much as planned. The high interest rates are also increasing the problem of insolvency further. If the interest rate on public debt is higher than the growth rate, the stock of government debt will rise as a ratio to GDP unless the government runs a very high primary budget surplus (budget balance excluding interest payments). The estimates of the IMF indicate that if Greece reduces its budget deficit to 2.6 percent of GDP by 2014, its GDP will contract so much that its debt to GDP ratio will rise above 150 percent. Thus it is unclear how the austerity plan will rescue Greece from insolvency.

Outside the Eurozone, Britain is also aiming for cuts in the budget deficit. Although the deficit is one of the highest in the EU, with a ratio of 11.7 percent to GDP in 2009, the entire buzz about Britain's public debt is surprising when one considers that average maturity of the debt is 13.7 years, the interest rate is at historical lows and the ratio of debt to GDP is 68.6 percent. Moreover, part of the increase in the public debt to GDP ratio is because of a lower GDP in both actual and potential terms due to the decline in the productive capacity of the private sector. At the end of 2009 the recession turned into stagnation; public sector cuts at this stage will turn stagnation into a double-dip recession. Under these circumstances the talk about a fiscal crisis looks more like an excuse of the business lobbies to avoid tax increases to finance the budget deficit, and make the wage earners pay the costs of the crisis through cuts in income, jobs and social services, and to create a situation of 'national emergency' to smash the power of the trade unions in the public sector.

The speculators now worry that these measures are not a solution to the problems: first, they think that the default of Greece is inevitable given the popular resistance, the size of the debt and the recession. Second, in a schizoid way, they are also worried that austerity measures will deepen the recession in not only

Greece but many other rich countries, create a double dip in the global economy, decrease tax revenues and make it even harder to pay the debt back.

A long recession seems very likely without the support of strong fiscal stimuli. The uncertainty about the strength of the recovery is making new investments as well as hirings less likely. Decline in income and confidence, job losses and the pressure to pay back debt is restraining household consumption. Both investments and consumption will not return to normal even when the banks relax credit. The presumed positive effect of reduced budget deficits on private investments is based on the argument that lower government borrowing leads to lower interest rates and higher private investment and spending. Under the current conditions, where consumers and firms are trying to reduce their debt and interest rates are already low, this channel has no relevance.

The decision of the EU is assuming that the problem is a lack of fiscal discipline and repeats the old faith in strengthening the surveillance of budget deficits; it does not question the reasons behind the deficits; it ignores all the structural problems regarding divergence in productivity, imbalances in current accounts due to the 'beggar my neighbor' policies of Germany. The austerity packages throughout the EU are pushing the countries into a model of chronically low internal demand based on low wages. The deflationary consequences of wage cuts may turn the problem of debt to insolvency for private as well as the public sector. In the past in Germany low domestic demand was substituted by high demand for exports. But it is not possible to turn the whole Eurozone into a German model based on wage suppression and austerity, since without the deficits of the periphery the German export market will also stagnate. Particularly for the periphery of Europe, a contraction in domestic demand means prolonged recession.

Real wages have already declined in 2008 compared to 2007 in Britain, France and Italy. Ireland, Greece, Portugal and Spain have had severe real wage cuts in 2010 and 2011. Sharp and long-lasting increases in unemployment are likely to make the wage losses much stronger. The share of wages in GDP has already declined in 2009 in Spain and Ireland; the counter-cyclical increase in the wage share in other countries is rather a symptom of the productivity decreases. The case of Japan shows that during the initial phase of a deflationary crisis (or a long-lasting recession), labor's income share either stagnates or slightly increases, but as the recession and deflation persists, even nominal wage declines take place. The decline in the wages in Eastern Europe will add further international competitive pressures on wages in Western Europe.

Unemployment increased in 2009 by 1.9 percent in the Eurozone, and 2.3 percent in Britain. Particularly high increases took place in Ireland and Spain (6.0 and 6.7 percent, respectively) due to the collapse of the construction industry and the loss of temporary jobs. Unemployment is expected to increase further and display a significant persistence. The ILO (2010) estimates that employment rates will not return to the pre-crisis levels before 2014. In all countries working hours decreased more than employment, and there has been a rise in part-time employment. Some countries like France, Germany, Austria and the Netherlands have had short working-time arrangements, supported by government subsidies. However, the short working-time arrangements will eventually be terminated as the financial markets are increasing the pressure on governments to decrease public debt. The ILO (2010) estimates that five million additional jobs could be lost if these practices are discontinued. This may spread the problem of unemployment from lower-skilled temporary workers to higher-skilled workers. Moreover, firms might want to make use of the recession to rationalize a strategy of increasing productivity and start a new wave of firing or engage in hiring freezes long after the recovery. If firms increase the working hours and delay hiring, this would worsen the job chances of the unemployed and the young, first-time job-seekers. The crisis will then lead to an increase in long-term unemployment as well as in discouraged workers who drop out of the labor market. There are also structural problems of unemployment in sectors like the automotive and construction industries, where the crisis only uncovered the already existing bottlenecks. Recovery of the aggregate economy will not necessarily create jobs in these sectors.

Eastern Europe: forgotten fragilities

Eastern European New Member States (NMS) are being severely affected by the credit crash and capital outflows, and possible currency crises accompanying the banking crises, although the recent problems in the old periphery countries of Europe removed the focus on these countries as Europe's 'sub-prime'. Nine Eastern European economies in the EU have had a recession in 2009, Poland being the only exception (Table 6.2). Employment has declined and unemployment increased significantly in all countries, with the sharpest increases taking place in the Baltic States. Real wages have fallen in the Czech Republic, Hungary, the Baltic States and Romania. The austerity programs in Hungary, Romania and Latvia will further reinforce the pressures of the crisis. The wage share has already fallen in Latvia, Hungary, Poland and the Czech Republic in 2009 (Figure 6.7). Moreover, a long-lasting recession cannot be ruled out, which would certainly have negative effects on the real wage and labor share.

After the initial transition shock and a decade of restructuring, these countries will once again face the costs of integration to unregulated global markets. The hopes for soft landings were replaced by fears of hard landings in the fall of 2008. The fundamental problem of the region was an excessive dependency on foreign capital flows, and as a typical consequence of this a bust episode following the boom was an unavoidable outcome of capital flow reversals. Many authors, including myself, were pointing at these risks, and a bust did happen again (Onaran 2007; Becker 2007; Goldstein 2005). If it were not due to the global crisis, this could have been triggered through traditional channels of expectations regarding the sustainability of the over-valued exchange rate and high current account deficits.

The difference of this crisis compared to the former boom–bust cycles in the periphery is that it is a global and not a regional crisis. It has originated from the

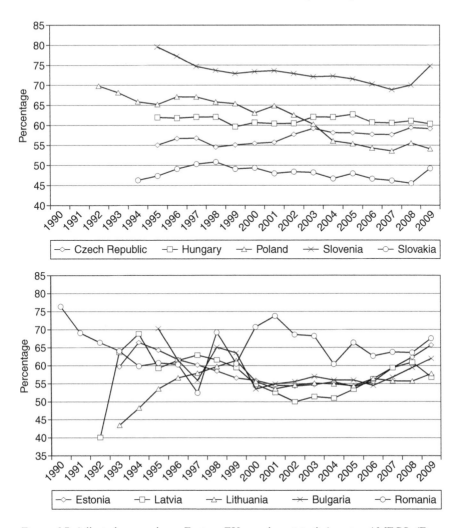

Figure 6.7 Adjusted wage share, Eastern EU member states* (source: AMECO (Economic and Financial Affairs, Annual Macroeconomic Indicators online database)).

Note
*Compensation per employee as percentage of GDP at factor cost per person employed.

core, but the consequences for the periphery of Europe are heavier. The credit crunch has a global dimension, which makes the usual capital inflows after the bust phase unlikely. The export markets have severely contracted, and depreciation, which is a usual outcome of boom–bust cycles, now only determines a negative balance-sheet effect, and no positive demand effect. The austerity packages in Western Europe further threaten recovery. The extent of debt-led growth,

Table 6.2 Average annual growth in GDP, employment, productivity, and real wages, 1989–2009 and sub-periods, Eastern EU member states

	1989*–1994				1994–2000				2000–2007			
	GDP	Employment	Productivity	Real wage	GDP	Employment	Productivity	Real wage	GDP	Employment	Productivity	Real wage
Czech Republic	−2.3	−2.0	—	−3.0	2.2	−0.8	3.2	3.2	4.5	0.8	3.8	4.7
Hungary	−3.2	−4.2	3.7	−1.9	3.3	0.5	2.1	−1.9	3.7	1.1	2.0	4.3
Poland	−1.6	−3.6	2.0	−3.5	5.7	−0.2	5.0	4.8	4.1	0.6	2.6	1.1
Slovenia	−2.3	−4.6	3.8	−6.0	4.3	−0.3	4.7	2.9	4.4	0.9	3.3	3.0
Slovakia	−2.4	—	12.6	−5.6	3.8	−0.6	4.8	5.3	6.2	1.0	5.9	3.3
Estonia	−1.6	−4.3	2.7	−17.3	6.0	−2.7	8.9	8.0	8.1	1.7	6.4	8.6
Latvia	−11.2	−5.1	19.0	8.2	4.3	−2.3	2.7	3.4	9.0	2.4	5.7	9.9
Lithuania	−11.5	−2.0	0.0	−19.8	4.5	−1.2	8.3	6.9	8.1	1.3	5.6	8.5
Bulgaria	−5.7	−5.8	8.5	−13.4	−0.2	0.0	0.0	−4.4	5.6	2.0	3.2	4.0
Romania	−4.6	−1.8	1.6	−6.7	0.1	−2.4	5.0	6.5	6.1	−0.8	5.5	9.3

	2008				2009			
	GDP	Employment	Productivity	Real wage	GDP	Employment	Productivity	Real wage
Czech Republic	2.5	1.2	1.1	1.3	-4.2	-1.2	-2.3	-1.1
Hungary	0.6	-1.3	1.6	0.9	-6.3	-3.6	-3.4	-4.5
Poland	5.0	3.8	0.5	3.8	1.7	0.4	1.0	1.0
Slovenia	3.5	2.8	0.5	1.5	-7.8	-2.2	-5.4	4.0
Slovakia	6.2	2.8	4.1	1.3	-4.7	-2.4	-0.5	3.6
Estonia	-3.6	0.2	-5.1	0.6	-14.1	-9.9	-4.2	-2.2
Latvia	-4.6	0.9	-6.2	-1.0	-18.0	-13.6	-3.7	-14.6
Lithuania	2.8	-0.5	0.7	2.9	-15.0	-6.9	-8.1	-11.5
Bulgaria	6.0	3.3	2.3	7.4	-5.0	-2.9	-0.9	6.9
Romania	7.3	-0.2	6.7	13.5	-7.1	-1.0	-6.1	-0.1

Source: own calculation based on AMECO (Economic and Financial affairs, Annual Macroeconomic Indicators online database); in case of the missing values for 1989–1991 growth rates of the variables in WIIW (The Vienna Institute for International Economic Studies), *Handbook of Statistics*, online database are used.

Notes

The starting date differs with respect to data availability. GDP data is only available in Estonia from 1993; the employment data starts in Slovakia in 1994, in Hungary in 1992 and in Estonia in 1990; the employee data starts in 1995 in the Czech Republic, in 1992 in Hungary and Latvia, in 1993 in Slovakia, Estonia and Lithuania, in 1990 in Romania; the wage data starts in Latvia in 1993 and in Estonia in 1990.

GDP is in 2000 prices in national currencies. Employment is for the whole economy. Productivity is real GDP/employee. Real wage is labor compensation deflated by the private consumption deflator, index 2000=100.

Period averages are geometric averages.

and household and private sector debt, most of all in foreign currency, is also increasing the risks more than the former crises.

The slow-down in global demand, the decline in FDI inflows, portfolio investment outflows, the contraction in remittances and the credit crash are affecting all the Eastern European countries, but the degree of accumulated imbalances, including current account deficits, exchange rate appreciation, housing market boom and foreign-currency denominated private debt, determine the differences in the depth of the effects among these countries. The Baltic States, Hungary, Romania and Bulgaria are more exposed than Poland, the Czech Republic, Slovenia and Slovakia. In Hungary the public sector and households, as well as firms, are indebted. But even Poland, the Czech Republic, Slovenia and Slovakia are suffering from the contagion effects, the slowdown in global demand and the decline in FDI inflows. Excessive dependence on export markets and a dangerous specialization in the automobile industry, as in the case of Slovakia in particular, but also in the Czech Republic and Slovenia, turn out to be major risks. Poland is experiencing only stagnation rather than a recession thanks to its more diversified market and large domestic economy with a lower trade volume as a ratio to GDP. Both Slovakia and Slovenia have escaped turbulences in the currency markets by adopting the euro; however, their problem will be a permanent loss of international competitiveness relative to their Eastern European competitors, whose currencies depreciate. To avoid speculation, Estonia is also willing to opt for the lesser evil – i.e., to adopt the euro.

The myth that these countries would not experience bottlenecks regarding the current account deficits thanks to FDI being a major source of finance of the deficit also proved to be wrong. It is true that FDI is still more robust than the other capital flows, but FDI inflows have also fallen significantly, reaching the level of 2001–2002 (Hunya 2009). Although the current account deficits are also falling because of lower imports, FDI is now financing a declining part of the deficits. Furthermore, FDI not only finances but also creates current account deficits via imported inputs as well as repatriation of profits.

The current global crisis has created no change in the policy stance regarding the European enlargement. The concerns of the EU for the NMS are shaped by the interests of the multinational enterprises (MNEs), in particular Western banks, and are limited to maintaining the stability of the currency rather than employment and income. The EU did not have the political will to create the institutions and tools for a unified counter-cyclical stimulus plan, but rather delegated the issue of the NMS to the IMF, albeit with some financial support to prevent a meltdown of the Western European MNEs in the region. Faced with the pressure of capital outflows, Hungary, Latvia and Romania have resorted to the IMF. As in the case of the former crises in the developing countries, during the 1990s and 2000s, IMF policies are again much more restrictive than what the IMF finds appropriate for the Western European countries. The credit line to Poland without conditionality is the only new tool the IMF has used. Otherwise Hungary, Romania and Latvia are having strongly pro-cyclical fiscal policy; fiscal discipline is still the norm, and cuts in public sector wages and pensions are part of the recipes. In the fixed exchange rate countries the prevention of devaluation was the major aim in order to protect the foreign banks, which had extended the majority of the loans in foreign currency. The governments of these countries were also not willing to push domestic firms and households, indebted in foreign currency, into bankruptcy through devaluation. Thus nominal devaluation was replaced by a brutal internal real devaluation via wage suppression. In Latvia, as of the fourth quarter of 2009, average salaries fell by 12.1 percent. Public sector wages were down by 23.7 percent compared to a year before; pensions have been cut by 10 percent. The government has forced through spending cuts and tax rises worth one-tenth of GDP (Ward 2010). The VAT rate increased from 18 percent to 21 percent. The cost of this internal devaluation has been a 25.0 percent loss of GDP in two years and 22.9 percent unemployment in 2009. Estonia and Lithuania also followed similar programs of cuts in public wages and a reduction in social benefits. Thus the current account imbalances are being corrected not through nominal but real devaluation and deep recession.

One difference during this crisis is that the IMF is now trying to bail-in the banks to maintain the level of credits in the countries that have an IMF financial program. The major difference compared to East Asia and Latin America was reliance on parent banks in the mature markets with a longer-term strategy of expansion in the region rather than market finance via foreign capital flows. The parent banks' loyalty to the region did not happen automatically though. For example, the Austrian government initially said that it would only support its troubled Erste Bank, which was over-exposed to risky loans in foreign currency in Eastern Europe, provided the money went to loans inside Austria, thus not to further expansion of loans in the East (*Economist*, 2010b). This approach would have led to each individual bank reducing its exposure by calling in loans and dumping assets, and a major currency crisis, which would have hurt the banks themselves as well. The small number of large, international players with a long-term investment in the region facilitated coordination, and the European Bank for Reconstruction and Development led the 'Vienna Initiative'. The ECB's liquidity provision to foreign banks in Eastern Europe encouraged them to keep financing their subsidiaries. IMF support helped the central banks of Eastern Europe to provide liquidity to foreign-owned banks as well as to the minority of domestic-owned banks. However, given the global crisis and the crunch in the wholesale credit markets, the ability of parent banks to maintain the credit booms in the region is exhausted, and even without further capital outflows, the region suffers from a deeper recession than in the West in the absence of capital inflows. Speculation on the Greek sovereign debt is creating particular liquidity restraints for Greek banks and their affiliates in Bulgaria and Romania; the funding problems of other European parent banks are also rising. Currency depreciation or the recession will lead to increases in non-performing loans and further affect the parent banks' approach to the Eastern affiliates.

Another difference in this crisis in the Eastern member states compared to the former crises in the developing countries was the moderate scale and pace of depreciation. In the countries with the floating exchange rate regime there has been some contagion even in countries like Poland, but not a total breakdown until now; the exchange rate only depreciated by 20–30 percent in Hungary, Poland and Romania, with some recovery afterwards, and the fixed pegs are still holding in the Baltic States and Bulgaria. The maintenance of the problematic pegs required rather large international rescue packages in comparison to the size of the economy. The Western European banks operating in the region, like the Swedish in the Baltic States and the Austrian in Bulgaria, and their home country governments have pressurized to avoid devaluation in fear of high non-performing loan rates, which would erode their profitability. The local governments also stand behind the pegs. However, preserving this over-valued, fixed exchange rate came at the cost of a very deep recession and wage deflation.

On the other hand the consequences of an unmanaged devaluation following a market-made currency crisis would also lead to very severe distributional effects, as was the case during the Asian or Latin American crises. The reason for this is the inflationary effects of high devaluation rates following a currency crisis, as discussed above. So far during the recent global crisis, not only the depreciation rate has been moderate, but also the pass-through effect to inflation has been restrained by the global deflationary environment and the falling commodity prices. However, any problem in the periphery in Eastern or Western Europe or other developing countries regarding speculative attacks to sovereign debt and capital outflows can easily trigger contagion effects and pressures on currencies in Eastern Europe again.

Capital controls on outflows or a managed devaluation are not even mentioned in the IMF or EU debates. The only recent revision has been a recent 'IMF Staff Position Note' about capital controls on inflows to moderate the effects on the exchange rate (Ostry *et al.* 2010); however, this does not help at the moment when the boom has already been followed by a bust.

An alternative economic policy framework for Europe

The existing wage suppression policies hurt all working people alike. Multinational bank and business lobbies are determining the policies of the governments and EU institutions by boycotting government bonds as a threat; thus the opposition also needs to be internationally organized. Uncovering this fact along with the idea of unequal distribution as the main cause of the crisis is an important step toward building a progressive alliance for an alternative Europe.

Such a radical transformation of the EU requires a major change in the institutions and policy framework that places regional and social cohesion at the core of policy and builds a bridge from the urgent demands of people for decent living standards and a sustainable environment to an alternative economic model.

Today, the most important obstacle to initiating any progressive economic policy in Europe is the speculation on public debt and the governments' commitment to satisfy the financiers. Public finance has to be unchained via debt default in both the periphery and the core. This has to be coordinated at the EU level as part of a broader public finance policy to make the responsible pay for the costs of the crisis and to reverse the origin of the crisis, i.e., pro-capital redistribution. This has to be complemented by a highly progressive system of taxes, coordinated at the EU level, not only on income but also on wealth, higher corporate tax rates, inheritance tax and tax on financial transactions. This would make the banks, the private investment funds and the high-wealth individuals pay the costs of the fiscal crisis.

Fiscal policy should completely abandon the Stability and Growth Pact, and public spending should aim at the multiple targets of full employment, ecological sustainability, equality and convergence via generating public employment in labor-intensive social services, as well as public investments in ecological maintenance and repair, renewable energy, public transport, insulation of the existing housing stock and building of zero-energy houses.

Monetary policy should be consistent with fiscal policy targets. The ECB should be turned into a real central bank with the ability to lend to member states. Higher public spending financed by monetary expansion does not pose a threat of inflation today given the recession, low demand and deflationary environment. However, it is important that monetary expansion serves the priorities of development, sustainability, full employment and equality.

While keeping the euro in the current Eurozone countries under the conditions outlined above is acceptable, in Eastern Europe, a direct transition from the pegged exchange rate to the euro as is planned in Estonia, or insistence on preserving the over-valued pegged exchange rate as in the case of Latvia, Lithuania and Bulgaria is ignoring the need for a major adjustment in the exchange rate. Devaluation pushed by market forces would be devastating, but this can be overcome with capital controls, debt restructuring and a managed devaluation with price controls. To avoid the negative effects of devaluation on indebted households and firms, the foreign currency denominated debt can be converted to local currency at the current exchange rate, and the burden of devaluation must be shifted to the private banks of the core countries. Similarly, to avoid the inflationary effect of devaluation, price controls could be introduced. For the future the conditions of the Maastricht Treaty for adopting the euro must be abolished and the process must be supported by policies of regional and social convergence.

At the incomes and labor market policy level there is need for a fundamental correction of the wages in both the periphery and the core to reflect the productivity gains of the past three decades fully. To facilitate convergence a minimum wage should be coordinated at the EU level. Fiscal policy and income policy should also be coordinated: Higher productivity growth in poorer countries of the EU will help to create some convergence in wages, but regional convergence should be supported by fiscal transfers and public investments to boost productivity in poorer regions. Furthermore, a European unemployment benefit system should be developed to redistribute from low to high unemployment regions. This requires a significant EU budget financed by EU-level progressive taxes.

To maintain full employment, a substantial shortening of working time, again coordinated at the EU level, in parallel with the historical growth of productivity, is also required. This is also an answer to the ecological crisis: If the use of environmental resources is to maintain a certain 'sustainable' level, economic growth, in the long term, has to be zero or low, i.e., equal to the growth rate of 'environmental productivity'. However, for such a regime to be socially desirable it has to guarantee a high level of employment and an equitable distribution of income; i.e., shorter working time and substantial redistribution via an increase in hourly wages and a decline in the profit share.

In cases of sectors that are under the threat of mass layoffs, like the automotive industry, nationalization of the firms and restructuring of these public firms should be considered, e.g., in the automotive industry a shift of focus toward the production of public transport vehicles, and a gradual transfer of labor toward new sectors.

The redesign of the financial sector needs to be contextualized within these priorities of macroeconomic policy. Financial regulations including capital controls are important but not enough. Finance is a crucial sector which cannot be left to the short-termism of the private profit motive. Finally, this crisis calls for a major shift in decision-making to facilitate economy-wide coordination of important decisions. This in turn requires public ownership and the participation and control of the stakeholders (the workers in the firms, consumers, regional representatives, etc.) in critical sectors of the society, such as banking, housing, energy, infrastructure, pension system, education and health.

Notes

1 Although in recent papers Claessens *et al.* (2008) and Eichengreen and Bordo (2001) compare different crises and their macroeconomic consequences, the differences regarding the distributional effects are not discussed in this literature.
2 Unemployment rates in the East Asian countries were hit by the crisis in 2008, in Turkey in 2001 and in Brazil in 1998–1999.

References

Becker, J. (2007) 'Dollarisation in Latin America and Euroisation in Eastern Europe: parallels and differences', in Becker, J. and Weissenbacher, R. (eds.), *Dollarisation, Euroisation and Financial Instability*, Marburg: Metropolis.
Claessens, S., Kose, A. and Terrones, M. (2008) 'What happens during recessions, crunches and busts?', IMF Working Paper, 08/274.
Diwan, I. (2001) 'Debt as sweat: labor, financial crises, and the globalization of capital', mimeo, World Bank.
Economist (2010a) 'Greece's sovereign debt crisis', 17 April: 66–68.
Economist (2010b) 'East European economies', 20 March: 41.
Eichengreen, B. and Bordo, M. (2001) *Crises Now and Then: What Lessons from the Last Era of Financial Globalization?* Conference in honor of Charles Goodhart, the Bank of England, 15–16 November.
Fitoussi, J.P. and Saraceno, F. (2010) 'Europe: how deep is a crisis? Policy responses and

structural factors behind diverging performances', *Journal of Globalization and Development*, 1(1): n.p.

Goldstein, M. (2005) 'What might the next emerging-market financial crisis look like?', Institute for International Economics, Working Paper 05-7.

Hunya, G. (2009) 'FDI in the CEECs under the impact of the global crisis: sharp declines', *The Vienna Institute for International Economic Studies Database on Foreign Direct Investment in Central, East and Southeast Europe*.

ILO (2010) *World of Work*, Geneva: ILO.

Onaran, Ö. (2007) 'International financial markets and fragility in the Eastern Europe: "can it happen' here?", in Becker, J. and Weissenbacher, R. (eds.), *Dollarization, Euroization and Financial Instability*, Marburg: Metropolis-Verlag.

Onaran, Ö. (2008) 'Life after crisis for labor and capital', in Yeldan, E., Kose, A. and Senses, F. (eds.), *Neoliberal Globalization as New Imperialism: Case Studies on Reconstruction of the Periphery*, New York: Nova Scientific Publishers.

Onaran, Ö. (2009) 'Wage share, globalization, and crisis: the case of manufacturing industry in Korea, Mexico, and Turkey', *International Review of Applied Economics*, 23(2): 113–134.

Ostry, J.D., Ghosh, A.R., Habermeier, K., Chamon, M., Qureshi, M.S., Reinhardt, D.B.S. (2010) 'Capital inflows: the role of controls', IMF Staff Position Note.

Uemura, H. (2008) 'Growth, distribution and institutional changes in the Japanese economy: faced by increasing international interdependence with Asian countries', presented at the Annual Conference of Evolutionary Political Economy, November, Rome.

Ward, A. (2010) 'Latvia hacker calls for fat cat revolt', *Financial Times*, 4 March.

7   The financial crisis viewed through the theory of social costs

L. Randall Wray

This chapter will look at the causes and consequences of the current global financial crisis, largely relying on the work of Hyman Minsky, although analyses by John Kenneth Galbraith and Thorstein Veblen of the causes of the 1930s collapse will be used to show similarities between the two crashes. K.W. Kapp's theory of social costs will be contrasted with the recently dominant efficient-markets hypothesis to provide the context for analyzing the functioning of financial institutions. It will be argued that rather than operating 'efficiently', the financial sector has been imposing huge costs on the economy – costs that no one can deny in the aftermath of the collapse of the economy.

Introduction

Mainstream economists have developed theories in which financial markets are 'efficient', pricing financial assets according to fundamental values. Indeed, if finance is efficient in the manner described by orthodoxy, it does not even matter. This is a logical extension of the neoclassical conclusion that markets efficiently allocate real resources to the financial sector. In the form of rational expectations it led to the conclusion that no individual or regulator could form a better idea of equilibrium values than the market. This led to Chairman Greenspan's famous excuse for not intervening into the serial bubbles that preceded the global financial crisis that began in 2007. And it was this theory that provided the intellectual underpinning of the behavior of market participants as well as regulators that led to the current crisis in financial markets.

Yet, it is clear that financial 'markets' did not 'efficiently' price assets. The continuing crisis makes it clear that 'finance' does matter. This is now recognized by virtually all observers. However, most policy-makers are simply focused on 'getting finance flowing' again – as if we just need to take a big plunger to a blocked financial toilet – and on ensuring that asset prices more correctly reflect fundamental values. No fundamental changes are required – we just need to 'make markets work'. This chapter will argue that the orthodox approach to finance is useless because the market metaphor is particularly inapplicable to finance. Ronald Coase argued that while free markets might be the most efficient form of economic organization, the majority of economic transactions take place outside the market, which calls into question the role of markets as the organizing structure of capitalism. Thus, following the example previously set by Keynesians and Institutionalists, even Coase leaves an opening for institutions, including the state, in formulating rules and providing regulation and supervision. These institutions will not arise endogenously out of market processes; they must be imposed on the market. One could go even further and argue that the market itself is an institution – created and regulated through human agency.

These objections are even more relevant to the sphere of finance. At the most basic level, banking is concerned with building a relationship that allows for careful underwriting (assessing creditworthiness) and for ensuring that payments are made as they come due. Long-term relations with customers increase the possibility of success by making future access to bank services contingent upon meeting current commitments. Further, within the bank itself, a culture is developed to provide and enforce rules of behavior. Relations among banks are also extra-market, with formal and informal agreements that are necessary for mutual protection. Banks are often forced to 'hang together, or all will be hung separately' because of the contagion effects of runs on their liabilities.

Further, social policy promoted the use of bank liabilities as the primary means of payment. This is not something that arose naturally out of markets. A well-functioning payments system requires par clearing – the United States' long and sordid history of non-par clearing by 'free' banks stands out as singularly unsuccessful. For that reason, par clearing was finally ensured with the Federal Reserve Act of 1913, which created a central bank for the United States whose original primary purpose was to ensure par clearing of bank demand deposits. However, there was a glitch in the system because the Fed's role was limited to lending to solvent banks against good assets. Hence, the payments system collapsed in the 1930s, when runs on banks returned as depositors rightly feared insolvent banks would never make good on their promises. For that reason, Congress created the Federal Deposit Insurance Corporation (FDIC) to 'insure' deposits (with similar guarantees on deposits at thrifts and some other types of institutions). This effectively eliminated runs on banks (although later runs returned on other types of bank liabilities, such as brokered certificates of deposit (CDs)).

The combination of access to the Fed as lender of last resort, par clearing and deposit insurance provided very cheap and stable sources of finance for banks. In addition, Regulation Q limited interest on deposits (set at zero for demand deposits) to keep interest costs down. Banks could charge fees to handle deposit accounts. All of this made it possible for banks to operate the payments system while shifting most costs to consumers and government. Further, because these bank liabilities are guaranteed, bad underwriting leads to socialization of losses as the FDIC makes the deposits good. Clearly, operation of the payments system has not been left to 'free markets'.

While it now seems natural for banks to run payments through nominally private banks, there was no reason to combine lending (predominately commercial lending) and the payments system in this manner. An alternative arrangement would have been to separate the two – with the government operating the payments system as a public good (for example, through a postal savings system) and banks focusing on underwriting loans while financing positions in assets by issuing a combination of short-term and long-term liabilities. If these were not the basis of the payments system, there would have been no reason for the bank liabilities to maintain par – nor even any reason for them to circulate. Bad underwriting would first hit equity holders and then would reduce the value of the liabilities. Losses would not be automatically socialized. There might then have been some discipline on banks to do good underwriting.

Of course, Glass-Steagall did segregate a portion of the financial sector from the payments system: Investment banks were allowed more free rein on the asset side of their balance-sheets, but they could not issue deposits. Their creditors could lose. Creditors were protected mostly by the Securities and Exchange Commission (SEC) – which provided regulations primarily on the 'product' or liability side. Investment banks (and other non-deposit-taking financial institutions) were largely free to buy and hold or trade any kinds of assets they deemed appropriate. They were required to 'mark to market' and to provide reports to creditors. Other than rather loose rules requiring them to ensure that the products they marketed were 'suitable' for those who purchased them, it was expected that 'markets' would discipline them. As we will see, that did not work even for the less protected institutions that did not have bank charters. And when the financial system collapsed, the remaining investment banks were handed charters so that they could access the payments system.

Over the past half century there has been a trend toward reducing relationship banking in favor of supposedly greater reliance on 'markets'. This is reflected in the rise of 'shadow banks' that are relatively unregulated, that in many cases are required to 'mark to market', and that have successfully eroded the bank share of the financial sector. It is also reflected in the changing behavior within banks, which largely adopted the 'originate to distribute' model that is superficially market-based. This shift was spurred by a combination of innovation (new practices that were not covered by regulations), competition from shadow banks with lower costs and deregulation (including erosion of and finally repeal of Glass Steagall). It also reflects the changing views on the efficacy of markets. However, the move to increase reliance on markets is more apparent than real. As we shall see, the new innovations such as asset-backed securities (ABS) actually increased institutional linkages even as they reduced the free-market competitive pressures imagined by orthodoxy. And the prices to which asset values are marked reflect neither 'fundamentals' nor 'markets' – rather, they result from proprietary models developed (mostly) in-house and thus reflect the culture and views of teams working within institutions.

At the same time, these trends reduced 'social efficiency' of the financial sector, if that is defined along Minskian lines. Minsky (1992a) always insisted that the role of finance is to promote the 'capital development of the economy', defined as broadly as possible. Minsky would agree with Institutionalists that the definition should include enhancing the social provisioning process, promotion of equality and democracy and expanding human capabilities. Instead, the financial sector has promoted several different kinds of inequality as it captured a greater proportion of social resources. It has also promoted boom and bust cycles, and proved to be incapable of supporting economic growth and job creation except through the promotion of serial financial bubbles. And, finally, it has imposed huge costs on the rest of society, even in the booms, but especially in the crises.

Indeed, the continuing attempts to rescue the financial sector (especially in the United States) have laid bare the tremendous social costs created by the way finance dominates the economy. If anything, the various bail-outs have actually strengthened the hands of the financial sector, increasing concentration in a small number of behemoth institutions that appear to control government policy. Meanwhile the 'real' economy suffers, as unemployment, poverty and homelessness rise, but policy-makers claim we cannot afford to deal with these problems. Their only hope is to gently prod Wall Street to lend more – in other words, to bury the rest of the economy under even more debt. The rescue of Wall Street displaces other fiscal policy that would lead to recovery.

What I am arguing is that the financial sector has not been operating like a neoclassical market. In spite of the rhetoric that deregulation improved efficiencies by replacing government rules with market discipline, markets have not and cannot discipline financial institutions. Rather, we reduced regulation and supervision by government that was supposed to direct finance to serve the public interest. This was replaced by self-supervision for private profit that generated huge social costs. Financial institutions do not even pursue 'market' interests (of shareholders, for example). Instead, they have been largely taken over by top management with personal enrichment as the goal.

Kapp's theory of social costs applied to the financial sector

Along with other Institutionalists, Kapp developed the notion that market competition does not lead to socially efficient allocations of resources. Instead, competition promotes pursuit of private profit in a manner that shifts costs to society. Kapp offered the following definition: 'The term social costs refers to all those harmful consequences and damages which third persons or the community sustain as a result of the productive process, and for which private entrepreneurs are not easily held accountable' (Kapp 1950: 14). This goes beyond the neoclassical use of the term 'externality', although the two concepts share the belief that costs are shifted. However, unlike neoclassical theory, Kapp saw this phenomenon as the normal result of competition in a pecuniary society (Swaney and Evers 1989). There is no tendency for a 'free-market' economy to generate an efficient allocation of resources. Leaving to the side the possibility that an economy really could operate as a 'free market', the allocation will not be efficient because much of the costs will be shifted to society while the benefits accrue to entrepreneurs.

Kapp's theory of social costs is particularly relevant to developing an understanding of the situation. Above we have discussed the policies that have led to the operation of the payments system by nominally private institutions. The costs of poor underwriting are shifted to society because we guarantee bank liabilities. In addition, poor underwriting means that bad loans were made. In some cases these loans enabled borrowers to command resources that were used in socially costly ways – for example, to finance partially completed but substandard or otherwise unwise real-estate developments that must be bulldozed. While market discipline is supposed to lead to good underwriting, for reasons explored further below, it did not.

The operation of the modern financial institution directly imposes other costs, such as predatory mortgages that strip homeowners of their equity. This is not an unintended consequence – it is the business model behind sub-prime and Alt-A mortgage lending. But there are many other social costs. When the homeowner loses her home to foreclosure, social costs are imposed on neighbors (depreciating property values), on local public services (caring for vacant property, as well as homeless people), on retailers and on the tax base. The foreclosure process itself increases these costs as mortgage servicers often have an incentive to prolong procedures until the total cost of foreclosure equals the expected sales price of the house – leaving no value for those holding the mortgage-backed securities (MBSs). Again, this is not an unintended consequence – it is profitable behavior (Wray 2008a).

There are also many aggregative effects arising from the extensive and often unknown linkages among financial institutions. For example, downgrading the credit of a monoline insurer generates downgrading of insured MBSs. Holders of MBSs often pledge them to obtain finance – when MBSs are downgraded collateral must be supplied (alternatively, a bigger 'haircut' is applied, meaning the holder obtains less finance against the pledged MBSs). The ratings of holders of MBSs are also downgraded. Effects continue through the system as payments on credit default swaps (CDSs – issued as a sort of 'insurance' on MBSs and other debts) are triggered, which inevitably impact counterparties and counter-counterparties. The layering of debts upon debts adds to the linkages. The ratio of debts to GDP has reached 500 percent – meaning that each dollar of income is pre-committed to servicing five dollars of debts, not just the mortgage but the securities, the collateralized debt obligations (CDOs, which re-securitize the MBSs) and the CDOs squared and cubed. To that we can add the rest of the derivatives, including swaps, which totaled between $60 trillion and $70 trillion globally at the time of the crash. Finance is layered, with complex and unknown linkages and commitments, and with huge but uncertain implications for the economy.

As another example, after the dot-com bubble collapsed, pension funds and other institutionally managed funds looked for possible investments that would not be correlated with stock prices. It was found that commodities prices had historically been uncorrelated. As a result, financial institutions like Goldman-Sachs, as well as researchers from the Pension Benefit Guarantee Corporation, pushed pensions to diversify into commodities. Since holding commodities is costly, money managers went into the commodities futures markets (buying futures contracts for 1–4 month delivery of commodities; the contracts would be 'rolled' on the delivery date). If commodity prices rose, the contracts would be sold at a profit (since they had locked-in a price). Huge flows of managed money poured into the commodities market, driving up futures prices. Since commodities spot prices are normally set by the closest futures price there was a vicious cycle: managed money drove up futures prices, which drove up spot prices, which caused more speculative fervor in commodities. Meanwhile, grain and oil prices were driven up, hurting consumers and leading to starvation around the world. In other words, speculative finance (mostly by pension funds, which accounted for 85 percent of the speculative money in futures contracts) created huge social costs (for details, see Wray 2008b). When commodities prices collapsed, that created other social costs for farmers and others who had invested based on the belief prices would remain high.

It is tempting to include the social costs of a 'misallocation' of credit by financial institutions – say, too much housing was built but not enough daycare centers (or too much investment in corn farming and not enough in wind farms). We must be careful, however. While it is true that resources required for construction are limited (at least at a point in time) so that the sector could have been fully employed in residential construction leaving insufficient resources to build daycare centers, finance itself is not a limited resource. We can have as much or as little of it as we want. Finance is really just a system of credits and debits, keystroke entries on computerized balance-sheets. It is conceivable that human resources employed in the financial sector could have been fully tapped-out handling mortgages so that no one was left to arrange finance for new daycare centers. That, however, is implausible. For years the 'best and the brightest' had been flowing into Wall Street and devoting their energies to innovations that increased the layering and leveraging precisely because there was excess capacity in the sector. As a result we got far more finance in the aggregate than we needed. To be sure, it was 'misallocated' in the sense that much of it was not contributing to Minsky's 'capital development of the economy'. But that was almost certainly because the rewards to individuals were biased toward the activities actually pursued.

In recent years an extreme form of market fundamentalism has been applied to the financial sector – the efficient-markets hypothesis. Asset prices should reflect 'fundamentals'. Indeed, financial markets are said to be so efficient that they do not matter. According to the Modigliani–Miller theorem, it does not matter how a firm finances its activities – own funds, debt or equity are equivalent. With efficient financial markets, resources get efficiently allocated.

There are a number of traditions that have attempted to reject the self-adjusting vision of the system. Keynes, of course, had doubted that vision at least since his essay on the end of laissez-faire. Others, including Veblen, Kapp and Minsky within the Institutionalist tradition, all share a similar framework of analysis that rejects the notion of an equilibrium-seeking system, and sees money and finance as the major source of problems with capitalist systems – the pecuniary interests dominate. Minsky called this a 'preanalytic vision' of the operation of the financial markets and their role in directing the evolution of the economic system. In contrast to the 'efficient-markets' approach, this preanalytic vision concerns decision-making in a system whose dynamics are not equilibrating – indeed, in which rational behavior by individuals leads to systemically irrational results. This goes beyond the acceptance of 'radical uncertainty', as in Shackle's approach or in the Austrian approach. Instead, as Minsky put it, 'agents in the model have a model of the model' but they know their models are wrong. Their behavior is based on a model they know to be incorrect and thus subject to revision; when their model changes, they change their behavior.

In Minsky's financial instability hypothesis uncertainty is the result of engaging in commitments to make future financial payments with financial receipts that are uncertain because they, too, will occur in the future. In turn, those future receipts will not be forthcoming unless at that future time there is a willingness to enter into additional financial commitments (since spending in the future will determine future receipts). Hence, what one does today depends on what one expects others to do today, as well as into the future. Since commitments made in the past may not be validated today, and those made today may not be validated tomorrow, movement of the system through time need not be toward equilibrium. Minsky argued instead that behavior will change, based on outcomes, in such a manner that instability will be created. For example, a 'run of good times' (in which expectations are at least met) will encourage more risk-taking, which increases financial leveraging that creates more risk. While many accounts of Minsky's work focus on the behavior of non-financial firms (as in the investment decision of a manufacturing firm), Minsky argued that behavior within financial institutions also evolves with innovations that stretch liquidity.

This provides an endogenous, rational explanation of the possible volatile behavior of asset prices, which is not self-equilibrating. Indeed, financial crises are usually the result of the impact of decisions taken within organized financial institutions – outside the market process – on the balance-sheet stability of financial institutions. The 'run of good times' leads to changes of the rules of thumb guiding practice within financial institutions, leading decision-makers to test the limits of acceptable practice. Minsky's theory explains the evolution of the balance-sheet positions of financial institutions and the impact on financial markets through financial layering. In particular, financial institutions find it rational to increase leverage, and rising leverage plays a crucial role in the financial instability hypothesis

Minsky's theory argues that the endogenous process of profit-seeking innovation will be not only a source of instability, but also make it difficult – nay, impossible – to design financial reform proposals that produce financial stability. The search for such regulations only makes sense within a theory of self-adjusting equilibrium – where 'getting prices right' is all that is necessary. In an evolutionary theory of innovation and instability the concept of stability and the regulations that would be required are completely different. It requires a completely different view of the operation of financial institutions.

We can think of this tendency for financial fragility to rise as a result of financial sector innovation (responding to profit opportunities) as a tendency to impose ever-greater costs on society. Some of these costs result directly from normal business procedure; we might call this taking advantage of customers (examples are explored below). But other, greater, social costs are created through the aggregative effects as bubbles are created and then as they burst. Literally trillions of dollars of wealth can be wiped out, leading to mass unemployment and deep and long recessions. In other words, it is not simply a shifting of costs, but creation of social costs as the by-product of profit-seeking behavior. And to a great extent, these social costs are not offset by any social benefits. It would be difficult to maintain that there was any social benefit from the creation of sub-prime hybrid adjustable rate mortgages (ARMs; with very low 'teaser' rates that would rise to very high levels after two or three years). As Swaney and Evers put it:

> Over time, then, social costs multiply not so much as the result of unfortunate, accidental side effects of economic activity, but more as the result of incentives *within* the economic system itself. In short, *social costs are predictable, endogenous outcomes*, as well as exogenous accidents.
>
> (Swaney and Evers 1989: 12)

These results are not due to mistakes, irrationality or mis-pricing – bursting of the real-estate bubble, mass foreclosures, rising homelessness and a long period of unemployment were the foreseeable outcome. We know that the traders within financial firms as well as raters within the big ratings agencies fully expected defaults to explode and the system to collapse. They simply believed they would be able to get out before that happened.

In the next two sections we will quickly review the transformation of the financial system as fragility rose; we then look at specific examples of the social costs that resulted from 'innovative' financial practices.

The transformation away from banking to money managers

Early last century, Hilferding identified a new stage of capitalism characterized by complex financial relations and domination of industry by finance (Hilferding 1910). He argued that the most characteristic feature of finance capitalism is rising concentration which, on the one hand, eliminates 'free competition' through the formation of cartels and trusts, and on the other, brings bank and industrial capital into an ever more intertwined relationship (ibid.: 21–22). Veblen, Keynes, Schumpeter and, later, Minsky also recognized a new stage of capitalism: For Keynes it represented the domination of speculation over enterprise, for Schumpeter it was the command over resources by innovators with access to finance, while Veblen distinguished between industrial and pecuniary pursuits.

By the 1870s, plant and equipment had become so expensive that external finance of investment became necessary. External finance, in turn, is a prior commitment of future gross profits. This creates the possibility of default and bankruptcy – the concerns of Minsky – while at the same time it opens the door for separation of ownership from control. From this Keynes derives the 'whirl-winds of optimism and pessimism' addressed in chapter 12 of his *General Theory* (attributed to the precariousness of valuing firms based on average opinion), while Veblen's analysis points to management's manipulation of the value of business capital. Schumpeter's view was obviously more benign, as his 'vision' of markets was much more orthodox, but he still recognized the central importance of finance in breaking out of a 'circular flow' – where money merely facilitates production and circulation of a given size – through finance of innova-tion that allows the circular flow to grow. With the rise of finance capitalism, access to external finance of positions in assets was necessary. This fundament-ally changed the nature of capitalism in a manner that made it much more unstable.

Veblen designated the early twentieth-century version of capitalism the 'credit economy', where it is not the goods market that dominates, for 'The capital market has taken the first place.... The capital market is the modern eco-nomic feature which makes and identifies the higher "credit economy" as such' (Veblen 1958: 75). By 'capital' Veblen means the 'capitalized presumptive earning capacity', 'comprised of usufruct of whatever credit extension the given business concern's industrial equipment and good-will will support' (ibid.: 65). This is contrasted to 'effective industrial capital', the aggregate of the material items engaged in industrial output. Goodwill can be collateralized and thereby increase divergence between values of industrial and business capital (ibid.: 70). When presumptive earning capacity rises, this is capitalized in credit and equity markets; thus, access to credit fuels capitalized values, which fuels more credit and further increases the discrepancy between industrial and business capital values in a nice virtuous cycle. The 'putative earning-capacity' is subject to fluc-tuation and manipulation because it

> is the outcome of many surmises with respect to prospective earnings and the like; and ... they proceed on an imperfect, largely conjectural, know-ledge of present earning-capacity and on the still more imperfectly known future course of the goods market and of corporate policy.
>
> (ibid.: 77)

Increasing the discrepancy between business and industrial capital is the prime motivation driving the 'business interest' of managers – 'not serviceability of the output, nor even vendibility of the output', but rather 'vendibility of corporate capital' (ibid.: 79). They are 'able to induce a discrepancy ... by expe-dients well known and approved for the purpose. Partial information, as well as misinformation, sagaciously given out at a critical juncture, will go far.... If they are shrewd business men, as they commonly are' (ibid.: 77–78). Recall Keynes' famous warning: 'The position is serious when enterprise becomes a bubble on a whirlpool of speculation. When the capital development of a country becomes a by-product of the activities of a casino, the job is likely to be ill-done' (Keynes 1964: 159). While Veblen agrees there is uncertainty and speculation involved, he emphasizes the likely success of pecuniary initiative in manipulating stock values, even denying that 'business interest' faces much uncertainty: 'The certainty of gain, though perhaps not the relative amount of it, seems rather more assured in the large-scale manipulation of vendible capital than in business management with a view to a vendible product' (Veblen 1958: 82). While manipulation does carry risk, it is 'not so much to the manipulators as such, as to the corporations ... [and to] the business men who are not immediately concerned in this traffic' (ibid.: 82–83).

As John Kenneth Galbraith (1954) makes clear, stocks could be manipulated by insiders – Wall Street's financial institutions – through a variety of 'pump and dump' schemes. Indeed, the 1929 crash resulted from excesses promoted by investment trust subsidiaries of Wall Street's banks. Since the famous firms like Goldman Sachs were partnerships, they did not issue stock; hence they put together investment trusts that would purport to hold valuable equities in other firms (often in other affiliates, which sometimes held no stocks other than those in Wall Street trusts) and then sell shares in these trusts to a gullible public. Effectively, trusts were an early form of mutual fund, with the 'mother' investment house investing a small amount of capital in their offspring, highly leveraged using other people's money. Goldman and others would then whip up a speculative fever in shares, reaping capital gains. However, trust investments amounted to little more than pyramid schemes (the worst kind of what Minsky called Ponzi finance) – there was very little in the way of real production or income associated with all this trading in paper. Indeed, as Galbraith showed, the 'real' economy was long past its peak – there were no 'fundamentals' to drive the Wall Street boom. Inevitably, it collapsed and a 'debt deflation' began as everyone tried to sell out of their positions in stocks – causing prices to collapse. Spending on the 'real economy' suffered and we were off to the Great Depression.

For some decades after World War II, 'finance capital' played an uncommonly small role. Memories of the Great Depression generated reluctance to borrow. Unions pressed for, and obtained, rising compensation – allowing rising living standards financed mostly out of income. In any case, the government guaranteed mortgages and student loans (both at relatively low interest rates) – so most of the household debt was safe, anyway. Jimmy Stewart's small thrifts and banks (burned during the Depression) adopted prudent lending practices. The Glass Steagall Act separated investment banks from commercial banks, and various New Deal reforms protected market share for the heavily regulated portions of the financial sector. Military Keynesianism provided demand for the output of industry, often at guaranteed marked-up pricing. Low debt, high wages, high consumption and big government promoted stability.

The 1960s and 1970s saw the development of an array of financial institution liabilities circumventing New Deal constraints as finance responded to profit opportunities. After the disastrous Volcker experiment in monetarism (1979–1982), the pace of innovation accelerated as many new financial practices were adopted to protect institutions from interest-rate risk. These included securitization of mortgages, derivatives to hedge interest-rate (and exchange-rate) risk and many types of 'off-balance-sheet' operations (helping to evade reserve and capital restraints). Favorable tax treatment of interest encouraged leveraged buy-outs to substitute debt for equity (with the take-over financed by debt that would be serviced by the target's future income flows). Another major transformation occurred in the 1990s with innovations that increased access to credit and changed attitudes of firms and households about prudent levels of debt. Now consumption led the way as the economy finally returned to 1960s-like performance. Robust growth returned, now fueled by private deficit spending, not by growth of government spending and private income. All of this led to what Minsky called money manager capitalism.[1]

While many point to the demise of Glass Steagall separation of banking by function as a key mistake leading to the crisis, the problem really was the demise of underwriting. In other words, the problem and solution is not really related to functional separation but rather to erosion of underwriting standards that is inevitable over a run of good times, when a trader mentality triumphs. If a bank believes it can offload toxic assets before values are questioned, its incentive to do proper underwriting is reduced. And if asset prices are generally rising on trend, the bank will be induced to share in the gains by taking positions in the assets. This is why the current calls by some for a return to Glass Steagall separation, or to force banks to 'put skin in the game' by holding some fraction of the toxic waste they produce are both wrong-headed.

Minsky argued that the convergence of the various types of banks within the umbrella bank holding company and within shadow banks was fueled by growth of money manager capitalism. It was also encouraged by the expansion of the government safety net, as Minsky remarked: 'a proliferation of government endorsements of private obligations' (Minsky 1992b: 39). Indeed, it is impossible to tell the story of the current crisis without reference to the implicit guarantee given by the Treasury to the mortgage market through its government-sponsored enterprises (GSEs; Fannie and Freddie), through the student loan market (Sallie) and even through the 'Greenspan Put' and the Bernanke 'Great Moderation' – that gave the impression to markets that the government would never let markets fail. In the aftermath of the crisis, the government's guarantee of liabilities went far beyond FDIC-insured deposits to cover larger denomination deposits as well as money market funds, and the Fed extended lender-of-last-resort facilities to virtually all financial institutions (with bail-outs also going to automotive companies, and so on). This really was a foregone conclusion once Glass Steagall was gutted and investment banking, commercial banking and all manner of financial services were consolidated in a single financial 'big box' superstore with explicit government guarantees over a portion of the liabilities. It was always clear that if problems developed somewhere in a highly integrated system, the Treasury and Fed would be on the hook to rescue the shadow banks, too.

By the 1990s the big investment banks were still partnerships so they found it impossible to directly benefit from a run-up of the stock market, similar to the situation in 1929. An investment bank could earn fees by arranging initial public offerings for start-ups, and it could trade stocks for others or for its own account. This offered the opportunity to exploit inside information, or to manipulate the timing of trades, or to push the dogs onto clients. But in the euphoric irrational exuberance of the late 1990s that looked like chump change. How could an investment bank's management get a bigger share of the action?

In 1999 the largest partnerships went public to enjoy the advantages of stock issue in a boom. Top management was rewarded with stocks – leading to the same pump-and-dump incentives that drove the 1929 boom. To be sure, traders like Robert Rubin (who would become Treasury secretary) had already come to dominate firms like Goldman. Traders necessarily take a short view – you are only as good as your last trade. More importantly, traders take a zero-sum view of deals: there will be a winner and a loser, with the investment bank pocketing fees for bringing the two sides together. Better yet, the investment bank would take one of the two sides – the winning side, of course – and pocket the fees and collect the winnings. Why would anyone voluntarily become the client, knowing that the deal was ultimately zero-sum and that the investment bank would have the winning hand? No doubt there were some clients with an outsized view of their own competence or luck; but most customers were wrongly swayed by the investment bank's good reputation. But from the perspective of hired management, the purpose of a good reputation is to exploit it for personal gain – what William Black (2005) calls control fraud.

Before this transformation, trading profits were a small part of investment bank revenues – for example, before it went public, only 28 percent of Goldman's revenues came from trading and investing activities. That is now about 80 percent of revenue. While many think of Goldman and JP Morgan (the remaining investment banks since the demise of Lehman, Bear and Merrill, which all folded or were absorbed) as banks, they are really more like huge hedge funds, albeit very special ones that now hold bank charters, granted during the crisis when investment banks were having trouble refinancing positions in assets – giving them access to the Fed's discount window and to FDIC insurance. That, in turn, lets them obtain funding at near-zero interest rates. Indeed, in 2009 Goldman spent only a little over $5 billion to borrow, versus $26 billion in interest expenses in 2008 – a $21 billion subsidy thanks to its access to cheap, government-insured deposits. The two remaining investment banks were also widely believed to be 'backstopped' by the government – under no circumstances would they be allowed to fail – keeping stock prices up. However, after the SEC began to investigate some of Goldman's practices, that belief was thrown into doubt, causing share prices to plummet.

In some ways things were even worse than they had been in 1929 because the investment banks had gone public – issuing equities directly into the portfolios of households and indirectly to households through the portfolios of managed money. It was thus not a simple matter of having Goldman or Citibank jettison one of its unwanted trust offspring – problems with the stock or other liabilities of the behemoth financial institutions would rattle Wall Street and threaten the solvency of pension funds and other invested funds. This finally became clear to the authorities after the problems with Bear and Lehman. The layering and link-ages among firms – made opaque by over-the-counter derivatives such as CDSs – made it impossible to let them fail one by one, as failure of one would bring down the whole house of cards. The problem we now face is that total financial liabilities in the United States amount to about five times GDP (versus 300 percent in 1929) – so every dollar of income must service five dollars of debt. That is an average leverage ratio of five times income. That is one (scary) way to measure leverage, for as Minsky (1992b) and Mayer (2010) argue, this is, histor-ically, the important measure for bank profitability – which ultimately must be linked to repayment of principle and interest out of income flows.

Another measure, of course, is the ratio of debt to assets. This became increas-ingly important during the real-estate boom, when mortgage brokers would find finance for 100 percent or more of the value of a mortgage, on the expectation that real-estate prices would rise. That is a trader's, not a banker's, perspective because it relies on either sale of the asset or refinancing. While a traditional banker might feel safe with a capital leverage ratio of 12 or 20 – with careful underwriting to ensure that the borrower would be able to make payments – for a mortgage origi-nator or securitizer who has no plans to hold the mortgage, what matters is the ability to place the security. Many considerations then come into play, including prospective asset price appreciation, credit ratings, monoline and CDS 'insurance' and 'overcollateralization' (markets for the lower tranches of securities).

We need not go deeply into the details of these complex instruments. What is important is that income flows take a back seat in such arrangements, and accept-able capital leverage ratios are much higher. For money managers, capital lever-age ratios are 30, and reach up to several hundred. But even these large numbers hide the reality that risk exposures can be very much higher because many com-mitments are not reported on balance-sheets. There are unknown and essentially unquantifiable risks entailed in counterparties – for example, in supposedly hedged CDSs in which one sells 'insurance' on suspected toxic waste and then offsets risks by buying 'insurance' that is only as good as the counterparty. Because balance-sheets are linked in highly complex and uncertain ways, failure of one counterparty can spread failures throughout the system. And all of these financial instruments ultimately rest on the shoulders of some homeowner trying to service her mortgage out of income flows – on average with $5 of debts and only $1 of income to service them. As Minsky argued, 'National income and its distribution is the "rock" upon which the capitalist financial structure rests' (Minsky 1992b: part III, 2). Unfortunately, that rock is holding up a huge finan-cial structure, and the trend toward concentration of income and wealth at the top makes it ever more difficult to support the weight of the debt.

Banking on crisis? The rise (and end) of 'casino' capitalism

In the modern era, it is not enough to put together Ponzi pyramid schemes or to sell trash to gullible customers. While investment banking today is often compared to a casino, that is not really fair. A casino is heavily regulated and while probabilities favor the house, gamblers can win 48 percent of the time. When a firm approaches an investment bank to arrange for finance, the modern investment bank immediately puts together two teams. The first team arranges finance on the most favorable terms for their bank that they can manage to push onto their client. The second team puts together bets that the client will not be able to service its debt. Legally, even brokers do not currently have a fiduciary responsibility to take their client's best interests into account when selling them assets. Magnetar, a hedge fund, actually sought the very worst tranches of MBSs, almost single-handedly propping up the market for toxic waste that it could put into CDOs sold on to 'investors' (I use that term loosely because these were suckers to the nth degree). It then bought credit default insurance (from, of course, AIG) to bet on failure. By 1998, 96 percent of the CDO deals arranged by Magnetar were in default – as close to a sure bet as financial markets will ever find. In other words, the financial institution often bets against households, firms and governments – and loads the dice against them – with the bank winning when its customers fail.

In a case recently prosecuted by the SEC, Goldman created synthetic CDOs that placed bets on toxic MBSs (Goldman agreed to pay a fine of $550 million, without admitting guilt, although it did admit to a 'mistake'). A synthetic CDO does not actually hold any mortgage securities – it is simply a pure bet on a bunch of MBSs. The purchaser is betting that those MBSs will not go bad, but there is an embedded CDS that allows the other side to bet that the MBSs will fall in value, in which case the CDS 'insurance' pays off. Note that the underlying mortgages do not need to go into default or even fall into delinquency. To make sure that those who 'short' the CDO (those holding the CDS) get paid sooner rather than later, all that is required is a downgrade by credit-rating agencies. The trick, then, is to find a bunch of MBSs that appear to be over-rated and place a bet they will be downgraded. The propensity of credit raters to give high ratings to junk assets is well-known, indeed assured by paying them to do so. Since the underlying junk is actually, well, junk, downgrades are also assured. Betting against the worst junk you can find is a good deal – if you can find a buyer to take the bet.

The theory behind shorting is that it lets you hedge risky assets in your portfolio, and it aids in price discovery. The first requires that you've actually got the asset you are shorting, the second relies on the belief in the efficacy of markets. In truth, these markets are highly manipulated by insiders, subject to speculative fever and mostly over-the-counter. That means that initial prices are set by sellers. Even in the case of MBSs – that actually have mortgages as collateral – buyers usually do not have access to essential data on the loans that will provide income flows. Once we get to tranches of MBSs, to CDOs, squared and cubed, and on to synthetic CDOs we have leveraged and layered those underlying mortgages to such a degree that it is pure fantasy to believe that markets can efficiently price them. Indeed, that was the reason for credit ratings, monoline insurance and CDSs. CDSs that allow bets on synthetics that are themselves bets on MBSs held by others serve no social purpose – they are neither hedges nor price-discovery mechanisms.

The most famous shorter of MBSs is John Paulson, who approached Goldman to see if the firm could create some toxic synthetic CDOs that he could bet against. Of course, that would require that Goldman could find clients willing to buy junk CDOs. According to the SEC, Goldman let Paulson increase the probability of success by allowing him to suggest particularly risky securities to include in the CDOs. Goldman arranged 25 such deals, named Abacus, totaling about $11 billion. Out of 500 CDOs analyzed by UBS, only two did worse than Goldman's Abacus. Just how toxic were these CDOs? Only five months after creating one of these Abacus CDOs, the ratings of 84 percent of the underlying mortgages had been downgraded. By betting against them, Goldman and Paulson won – Paulson pocketed $1 billion on the Abacus deals; he made a total of $5.7 billion shorting mortgage-based instruments in a span of two years. This is not genius work – an extraordinarily high percent of CDOs that are designed to fail will fail.

Goldman never told investors that the firm was creating these CDOs specifically to meet the demands of Paulson for an instrument to allow him to bet against them. The truly surprising thing is that Goldman's customers actually met with Paulson as the deals were assembled – but Goldman never informed them that Paulson was the shorter of the CDOs they were buying! While Goldman admitted it should have provided more information to buyers, its defense was that (1) these clients were big boys; and (2) Goldman also lost money on the deals because it held a lot of the Abacus CDOs. In other words, Goldman not only withheld crucial information, but it is also sufficiently incompetent to buy CDOs that it let Paulson put together with the explicit purpose of betting on failure. That is exploitation of reputation by Goldman's management – Black's control fraud: top management enriches itself at the expense of the firm.

In the AIG bail-out by the government, $12.9 billion was passed-through to Goldman because AIG provided the CDSs that allowed Goldman and Paulson to short Abacus CDOs. So AIG was also duped, as was Uncle Sam. I would not take Goldman's claim that it lost money on these deals too seriously. When Hank Paulson ran Goldman, it was bullish on real estate; through 2006 it was accumulating MBSs and CDOs – including early Abacus CDOs. It then slowly dawned on Goldman that it was horribly exposed to what was turning out to be toxic waste. At that point it started shorting the market, including the Abacus CDOs it held and was still creating. Thus, while it might be true that Goldman could not completely hedge its positions so that it got caught holding junk, that was not for lack of trying to push risks onto its clients. The market crashed before Goldman found a sufficient supply of buyers to allow it to short everything it held.

Previously, Goldman helped Greece to hide its government debt, and then bet against the debt – another fairly certain bet since debt ratings would likely fall if the hidden debt was discovered. Goldman took on US states as clients (including California, New Jersey and nine other states), earning fees for placing their debts, and then encouraged other clients to bet against state debt – using its knowledge of the precariousness of state finances to market the instruments that facilitated the shorts.

To be fair, Goldman is not alone – all of this appears to be common business procedure. In early spring 2010 a court-appointed investigator issued his report on the failure of Lehman. Lehman engaged in a variety of 'actionable' practices (potentially prosecutable as crimes). Interestingly, it hid debt using practices similar to those employed by Goldman to hide Greek debt. The investigator also showed how the prices by Lehman on its assets were set – and subject to rather arbitrary procedures that could result in widely varying values. But most importantly, the top management as well as Lehman's accounting firm (Ernst&Young) signed off on what the investigator said was 'materially misleading' accounting. That is a go-to-jail crime if proved. The question is why would a top accounting firm, as well as Lehman's CEO, Richard Fuld, risk prison in the post-Enron era (similar accounting fraud brought down Enron's accounting firm, and resulted in Sarbanes–Oxley legislation that requires a company's CEO to sign off on company accounts)? There are two possible answers. First, it is possible that such behavior is so widespread that no accounting firm could retain top clients without agreeing to overlook it. Second, these practices may be so pervasive and enforcement and prosecution thought to be so lax that CEOs and accounting firms have no fear. I think that both answers are correct.

In the latest revelations, JP Morgan Chase suckered the Denver public school system into an exotic $750 million transaction that has gone horribly wrong. In the spring of 2008, struggling with an under-funded pension system and the need to refinance some loans, it issued floating rate debt with a complicated derivative. Effectively, when rates rose, that derivative locked the school system into a high fixed rate. Morgan had put a huge 'greenmail' clause into the deal – they are locked into a 30-year contract with a termination fee of $81 million. That, of course, is on top of the high fees Morgan had charged up-front because of the complexity of the deal. To add insult to injury, the whole fiasco began because the pension fund was short $400 million, and subsequent losses due to bad performance of its portfolio since 2008 wiped out almost $800 million – so even with the financing arranged by Morgan the pension fund is back in the hole where it began, but the school district is levered with costly debt that it cannot afford but probably cannot afford to refinance on better terms because of the termination penalties. This experience is repeated all across America – the Service Employees International Union estimates that over the past two years state and local governments have paid $28 billion in termination fees to get out of bad deals sold to them by Wall Street (Morgenson 2010).

Conclusion

I believe all of these examples demonstrate the points made above about social costs while demonstrating the fallacy of the efficient-markets hypothesis. First, the financial sector is not operated as a 'market' – at least one as conceived by neoclassical economics. Second, it does not seek equilibrium; rather, it evolves toward fragility. Third, competition among financial institutions does not promote the public interest; rather, it creates costs and shifts them to society. Fourth, management of financial institutions have increasingly adopted practices that enrich themselves – control fraud – not only at the expense of customers but also at the expense of the reputation of the firms. In other words, the shifting of costs is in part onto the firms themselves – many of which did not survive the crisis (and many more will fail).

It is hoped that the current crisis will lead to a transformation of the economics discipline, similar to the creation of Keynesian economics during the Great Depression. This one, however, should pay more attention to the role that institutions play in organizing the economy while at the same time placing more emphasis on social costs and on orienting financial institutions to serve the public purpose. The idea that private pursuit of profit is sufficient to guide financial institutions to further the capital development of the economy has been discredited. Indeed, since there is nothing that is 'scarce' about finance, this area is the most ill-suited to the application of neoclassical theory based on the notion of scarcity. By its very nature, banking needs to be based on relationships, not on the sort of one-off exchanges imagined by orthodoxy.

Finally, Kapp's theory of social costs provides a strong rebuff to the orthodox belief that redirecting finance so that it is more 'market oriented' will improve its 'efficiency' – in fact, trying to inject more 'market' into financial institutions greatly increased social costs.

Note

1 Minsky defined it as follows

> Capitalism in the United States is now in a new stage, money manager capitalism, in which the proximate owners of a vast proportion of financial instruments are mutual and pension funds. The total return on the portfolio is the only criteria used for judging the performance of the managers of these funds, which translates into an emphasis upon the bottom line in the management of business organizations.
>
> (Minsky 1996: 1)

References

Black, W.K. (2005) *The Best Way to Rob a Bank is to Own One: How Corporate Executives and Politicians Looted the S&L Industry*, Austin: University of Texas Press.

Galbraith, J.K. (1954 [2009]) *The Great Crash 1929*, New York: Houghton Mifflin.

Hilferding, R. (1910 [1981]) *Finance Capital: A Study of the Latest Phase of Capitalist Development*, London: Routledge and Kegan Paul.

Kapp, K.W. (1950 [1971]) *The Social Costs of Private Enterprise*, New York: Schocken Books.

Keynes, J.M. (1964) *The General Theory of Employment, Interest, and Money*, New York and London: Harcourt Brace Jovanovich.

Mayer, M. (2010) 'The spectre of banking', *One-Pager*, 3, 20 May, Levy Economics Institute.

Minsky, H.P. (1992a) 'The capital development of the economy and the structure of financial institutions', Levy Working Paper No. 72.

Minsky, H.P. (1992b) 'Reconstituting the financial structure: the United States' 13 May, Manuscript in Minsky Archives at Levy Institute.

Minsky, H.P. (1996) 'Uncertainty and the institutional structure of capitalist economies', Levy Working Paper No. 155.

Morgenson, G. (2010) 'Exotic deals put Denver schools deeper in debt', *New York Times*, 5 August. Available at: www.nytimes.com/2010/08/06/business/06denver.html.

Swaney, J. and Evers, M.A. (1989) 'The social cost concepts of K. William Kapp and Karl Polanyi', *Journal of Economic Issues*, 23(1): 7–33.

Veblen, T. (1958) *The Theory of Business Enterprise*, New York: A Mentor Book, The New American Library of World Literature, Inc.

Wray, L. Randall (2008a) 'Financial markets meltdown: what can we learn from Minsky?' Levy Public Policy Brief No. 94.

Wray, L. Randall (2008b) 'The commodities market bubble: money manager capitalism and the financialization of commodities', Levy Public Policy Brief No. 96.

8 In charge of themselves

The social costs of workfare policies in Europe

Roberto Rizza

Introduction

Old institutionalists have long recognized that labor is a fixed cost from a social efficiency perspective (Clark 1957; Commons and Andrews 1967). Protective labor legislation has been institutionalized in most capitalist countries in order to induce business enterprises to pay a larger portion of the actual cost of the human factor of production than they would be prepared to pay in its absence. Hence, institutional economists argue the necessity of protective labor legislation, as well as the use of administrative controls and legal sanctions, in order to provide substantial measures to reduce the adverse consequences upon workers induced by a variety of interdependent conditions: unemployment, precarious employment and unsafe or unhealthy working conditions.

The basic assumption underlying this institutionalist analysis of the labor factor is that actual cost is determined by the institutional structure of production. Thus, the 'cost' of labor reflects the socially sanctioned production costs of the human resource.

Institutionalists maintain that a large portion of the effective cost of labor can be shifted by private businesses to workers or society as a whole. These avoidable costs are defined as the social costs of labor.

In recent years these thorough-minded assumptions have been replaced by more simplistic theorizations that treat labor as a commodity like any other. As Clark and Kapp have shown, the impossibility of treating the human factor of production as a saleable commodity – since the abolition of slavery – implies that labor deserves a specific analytic treatment. It runs the risk of being in a less favorable condition than non-human inputs – i.e., tangible assets such as machines or livestock – in the allocation choices taken by businesses (Kapp 1963).

The commodification of labor in recent theorizations puts into focus the so-called 'rigidities' affecting the competitive working of the labor market: From this point of view, unemployment and unstable employment occur because the labor market cannot operate as it should. Unemployment has thereby increasingly been tackled by resorting to supply-side schemes and by recurring to flexible labor market arrangements. More specifically, on the one hand, by liberalizing the labor market in order to encourage occupational growth through forms of temporary and fixed-term employment contracts with reduced welfare protection in comparison to full-time and open-ended contracts. And on the other side, by adopting activation policies in order to deploy the full potential of the labor market. Consequently, welfare must be reshaped, and benefits linked to the condition that recipients are ready to accept any job opportunities when these become available. As we will see later and according to a supply-side approach, in many European countries activation policies have been transformed into 'workfare' devices, emphasizing the obligation to take a job even if it is under-paid and without career prospects (Salais 2004).

Under these assumptions, a conceptual change can be seen in relation to the Keynesian/institutionalist point of view that addresses the social damage and social costs induced by the market mechanism, with protective measures directed at indi-viduals and families. By contrast, the new insight proposed by supply-side schemes and the workfare approach sees protective labor legislation as an intolera-ble cost in terms of economic efficiency. Subsidies are considered a trap and not a solution. The only way to face unemployment is through activation policies by placing the actor who is directly involved at the core of the solution. According to this individualistic approach job-seekers must take the responsibility for their con-dition of unemployment and find a way out of it (Valkenburg and van Berkel 2007): 'In other words, there is a subversion of the problem: intervention with regard to the object (unemployment) is turned into action aimed at the subject (the unemployed person)' (Crespo Suàrez and Serrano Pascual 2007: 109).

The impact of these public policies and the social costs stemming from them, such as growing economic and social inequalities in many countries, are evident. Several problematic issues in this regard should be noted:

- forced labor market flexibility has led to strong cleavages and to a further segmentation of the labor market;
- insecure occupational careers affect a growing number of persons, espe-cially adult workers with low qualification levels, young people and women;
- non-standard employment relations often fail to function as a springboard to a successful career and in most cases act as a trap (Scherer 2004);
- activation policies frequently create 'secondary labor markets' (low wage plus subsidies) characterized by marginality with no interaction with primary labor markets.

This chapter will examine both labor market deregulation and the growth of temporary employment by comparing the different European countries and stressing the consequences on occupational stratification and the increase of pro-longed job insecurity. The current economic crisis and its consequences in terms of social costs, especially for temporary workers, will then be focused upon. The second part of this chapter will focus on activation policies through a com-parison of European countries. In particular, we will see that many countries characterized by specific welfare regimes (Esping Andersen 1990; 1999) have restricted the eligibility to the protection system to those actively seeking a job, tightening up sanctions and obligations and thus promoting the growth of a secondary, low-wage labor market. From this point of view, the introduction of activation programs is itself part of the development of insecure, non-standard and low-wage employment (van Berkel and Moller 2004).

The effect is a growing gap between those who can be activated and can achieve positive results in terms of employability, and those who cannot because they are not endowed with the required educational and professional skills. Consequently, public policies tend to charge each individual with his successes and failures without taking into consideration the social support to individuality, such as social rights and welfare resources (Castel 2003). As Crespo Suàrez and Serrano Pascual argue (2007: 109),

> instead of providing the political condition for exerting the social rights to which they are entitled as citizens, policies of this kind are transformed into therapeutic policies, on behalf of a clinical state, focused on 'curing' the motivation and attitudes of jobseekers in order to achieve their compliance with their duty as citizens: to be in charge of themselves.

All things considered, temporary employment and activation policies, especially those influenced by a workfare approach, while inducing growing social costs tend to obscure the social costs provoked by business enterprises and the market mechanism.

Labor market deregulation and growing occupational insecurity

Mainstream economic literature has interpreted the low employment level in Europe as the result of excessive labor market regulation and overly generous benefits for the unemployed. Thus, policy guidelines have aimed at increasing flexibility on the one side, while reducing welfare supports on the other. This approach, essentially focused on the supply-side, assumes that policies directed at increasing flexible work automatically induce a higher demand and therefore a higher economic growth.

Starting from this point of view and aiming at adapting the occupational system to market instability and to growing international competition, over the past 20 years a considerable number of OECD countries have undertaken policies of liberalization of labor market legislation that have provoked a growth of temporary employment.

The theory of flexibility is based on some fundamental assumptions: To cope with international competition, enterprises must reduce direct and indirect labor costs in close connection with market trends. Therefore, labor market deregulation and the reduction of employment protection can encourage occupational growth, since a lower Employment Protection Legislation index and a higher job turnover rate would encourage the competitiveness of the national economic system.[1] In this way, enterprises should be able to recruit on fixed-term contracts instead of reverting to overtime work or intensive work plans.

However, analysis undermines the theoretical and empirical force of the labor market deregulation paradigm and the necessity to dismantle employment protection legislation, showing that in order to cope with international competition, as well as with market instability and demand volatility, it is fairer and economically more efficient to rely on the skills and participation of workers (Gallie *et al.* 1998; Gallie and Paugam 2000) – goals that can hardly be achieved with a temporary and low-cost workforce.

Another controversial aspect is the hypothesis that labor market deregulation and the growth of fixed-term contracts are the main roads to reducing unemployment. Indeed, juridical or contractual norms have limited effects on the general level of unemployment. On the contrary, the connection is between the rigidity/flexibility of the labor market and the dynamics, length and composition of occupation and unemployment (Berger and Dore 1996; Crouch and Streeck 1997; Esping Andersen 1999; Esping Andersen and Regini 2000)

Despite these doubts, the deregulation of the labor market and the growth of fixed-term contracts with limited welfare protection, in comparison to full-time and open-ended contracts, have considerably influenced the public policies of many European countries. In particular, initiatives undertaken in recent years that have introduced flexible work arrangements for accessing the labor market have mainly addressed the young and women.

The effect has been, with differing intensity in different national contexts, an increase in temporary employment. In 2008 temporary employment as a share of the entire workforce in the European Union (25 countries) was 14.2 percent, varying from 5.4 percent in the United Kingdom[2] to 29.3 percent in Spain.

Several factors help explain this national variation. A significant factor is the sector dynamics (Figure 8.1). Some sectors, such as agriculture, tourism and construction, feature a pronounced seasonal nature and often the marked temporariness of employment is linked to organizational and productivity requirements. As a consequence, the breadth and trend of temporary work are influenced by the weight that such sectors bring to the individual national contexts.

Nonetheless, the most prominent changes involve the manufacturing and service sectors. The first of these has experienced a replacement effect: The number of employees with open-ended contracts is falling everywhere, while there is a rise in temporary employment. The service sector has seen a noticeable increase in temporary employment, ranging from a minimum of 6.3 percent in the United Kingdom to 30.1 percent in Spain, with Italy, France and Germany standing between 13 percent and 15 percent.

From the standpoint of individuals, the dynamics differ depending on gender. Part-time employment features a prevalent female presence (Table 8.1).

In many countries women are low-wage earners, too (Table 8.2).

With regard to temporary jobs, the gender comparison is varied: In Germany and Austria women and men are more or less equally involved in temporary work, while in Finland, Spain and Italy the differences are marked.

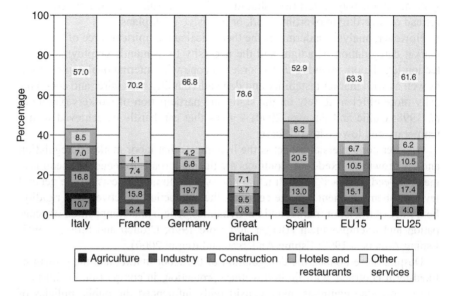

Figure 8.1 Temporary employment by sector in the EU, 2006 (source: Eurostat Labour Force Survey 2007).

Table 8.1 Part-time employment and gender (%), 2008

	Women	Men	Total
Greece	9.8	2.5	5.4
Portugal	13.9	4.1	8.6
Finland	17.8	7.9	12.7
Spain	22.6	4.0	11.8
Italy	27.8	4.8	14.1
France	29.3	5.6	16.7
Ireland	31.9	7.1	18.1
Denmark	36.0	13.1	23.9
Luxemburg	38.2	2.7	17.9
Belgium	40.8	7.5	22.4
Sweden	40.9	11.9	25.7
United Kingdom	41.0	9.8	24.2
Austria	41.1	6.9	22.6
Germany	44.9	8.4	25.2
Netherlands	75.2	22.8	46.8

Source: Eurostat Labour Force Survey 2009, part-time employment rate, age group 15–64.

Note

The total column represents the total percentage of all workers that are part-time workers. The gender columns represent the total percentage of all workers of that gender that are part-time workers.

Table 8.2 Low-wage earners in selected countries by gender (%), 2006

	Women	Men
EU-27	23.1	13.5
EA-16	20.1	11.7
Belgium	12.8	4.8
Bulgaria	27.7	26.5
Czech Republic	26.1	9.5
Denmark	11.6	4.7
Germany	28.0	15.9
Estonia	28.7	11.7
Ireland	28.7	15.6
EL	23.2	12.4
Spain	22.6	11.2
France	10.6	7.7
Italy	16.2	11.5
Cyprus	33.4	11.0
Latvia	32.3	29.2
Lithuania	30.1	25.0
Luxemburg	24.6	11.9
Hungary	22.3	24.5
Malta	13.3	10.1
Netherlands	25.0	10.5
Austria	28.7	9.2
Poland	26.3	18.3
Portugal	26.6	14.5
Romania	27.8	25.7
Slovenia	21.3	12.1
Slovakia	25.0	10.8
Finland	8.8	3.3
Sweden	14.9	7.6
United Kingdom	30.6	15.6
Norway	8.8	4.9

Source: Bosch and Weinkopf 2008.

Age difference is very pronounced. The growth and spread of temporary employment is in fact distinctly evident in the young, to the extent that it constitutes the main channel for entering the labor market in almost all European countries: four out of ten European workers aged 15–24 were employed under fixed-term arrangements in 2008 (Table 8.3).

Policies that have deregulated the labor market and have promoted a growth in fixed-term work contracts addressed primarily to young people – the so-called outsiders of the labor market – have had a large effect. In France, for example, liberalization of fixed-term contracts (*contrats a durée déterminée*) fueled a significant turnover in young workers, without, however, cutting unemployment (Cahuc and Kramarz 2004). In Spain, where fixed-term work relations have been considered as the main channel for joining the labor market for some time now, new measures have been introduced with the intent of reducing the number of

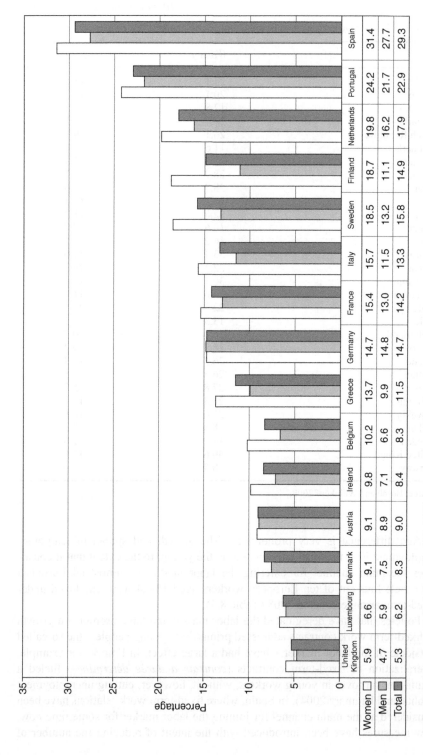

	United Kingdom	Luxembourg	Denmark	Austria	Ireland	Belgium	Greece	Germany	France	Italy	Sweden	Finland	Netherlands	Portugal	Spain
Women	5.9	6.6	9.1	9.1	9.8	10.2	13.7	14.7	15.4	15.7	18.5	18.7	19.8	24.2	31.4
Men	4.7	5.9	7.5	8.9	7.1	6.6	9.9	14.8	13.0	11.5	13.2	11.1	16.2	21.7	27.7
Total	5.3	6.2	8.3	9.0	8.4	8.3	11.5	14.7	14.2	13.3	15.8	14.9	17.9	22.9	29.3

Figure 8.2 Temporary jobs by gender (%), 2008 (source: Eurostat Labour Force Survey 2009).

Table 8.3 Temporary employment in selected European countries (%)

	15–24 years			25–49 years			50–64 years		
	1993	2000	2008	1993	2000	2008	1993	2000	2008
Italy	15.3	26.2	40.9	4.8	9.1	12.0	3.6	5.5	6.2
France	39.4	55.0	50.8	8.0	12.7	11.4	3.9	5.6	5.7
Germany	36.9	52.4	56.2	6.3	8.0	9.3	4.0	4.5	4.3
Great Britain	9.9	13.1	12.9	5.0	5.4	4.3	4.5	5.5	4.3
Spain	73.9	68.9	64.9	27.9	29.3	31.9	12.8	14.1	15.6
EU-15	29.3	39.5	41.4	8.0	11.0	12.2	4.8	6.0	6.1

Source: Eurostat Labour Force Survey 2009, part-time employment rate, age group 15–64.

fixed-term workers because of the increasingly precarious nature of work careers. Nonetheless, these measures do not appear to be particularly successful, and the increase in youth unemployment in the past year (38 percent) caused by the economic crisis is evidence of this.

In Germany, where the inclusion of young workers in the labor market is less problematic due to the effectiveness of the German apprenticeship system, the growth of temporary work is concentrated primarily in the east. However, this factor does not improve employment performance in that area, nor does it reduce the unemployment rate. Furthermore, the difficulties in the changeover from temporary to permanent occupation are very noticeable, particularly among poorly qualified young people. Also, these rising labor market risks are not equally distributed among young people: East Germans and young migrants, for instance, face higher risks of a long phase of job search and unemployment. These risks are still clearly linked to education and occupational classes. Finally, education and class have become increasingly important: The highest and the lowest qualified groups differ ever more in the duration of job search as well as in their unemployment risk. Accordingly, it is possible to observe a relative hardening of inequality structures in Germany in an era of increasing demand for worker flexibility (Buchholz and Kurz 2008).

In Italy, two legislative changes introduced between 1997 and 2003 with the intention of liberalizing fixed-term employment (the extension of fixed-term jobs for training purposes and the introduction of *ad interim* work) have led to an increase of young employees with contracts of limited duration. As a result, nearly half of the new workforce is recruited on fixed-term contracts (Cimaglia *et al.* 2009). In this respect some research findings appear useful (Bertolini 2002; Rizza 2003; Fullin 2004; Barbieri and Scherer 2005; Salmieri 2006; Berton *et al.* 2009; Palidda 2009): liberalization of the work market and the growth of temporary employment has had a selective and partial effect; linked with entry into the work market it has particularly affected young people and their first experience of work. The result has been an increase in precarious careers for young people caused by weak social protection for temporary contracts together with the high probability of alternating periods in occupation (fixed-time contracts) and unemployment (without welfare benefits). The economic crisis made the weakness of this situation more evident. The first to be penalized by the crisis were the temporary workers who did not have their contracts renewed. The result was a growth in youth unemployment in Italy – 30 percent at the beginning of 2011.

Many social costs may be observed as a result of the deregulation of employment contracts as discussed above. The social damage caused by the contextual, 'new' cost-shifting opportunities that become available to business operators can be seen in the growing number of young people who are faced with the risks inherent in work insecurity and potential instability throughout their working lives. From this viewpoint the risks linked to business allocation and investment decisions have moved from the entrepreneur to the human factor of production and a group of associated issues.

First and foremost, the rise in temporary employment has not cut unemployment, particularly among young people. On the contrary, with the current economic recession, it is primarily temporary workers – and therefore young people – who become unemployed, since their work contracts are in many cases not renewed.

Second, discrimination affecting the very young has increased, given that temporary employment also implies a significant reduction in employment protection legislation and welfare benefits. This situation forces these workers to find alternative jobs as soon as possible, without allowing them to choose selectively from the opportunities available to them. Moreover, the growth of intermittent careers with recurrent periods of unemployment and loss of income will have serious consequences on pension schemes, especially for the young.

Third, temporary work has, over time, grown to increasingly involve adults in the 25–49 age group, a period when people generally face fundamental decisions regarding living alone or with a partner, marriage and having children. A prolonged condition of unstable work has strong repercussions on these choices. As Scherer (2004: 10) points out: 'The undertaking of long-term commitments like marriage or parenthood requires some stability in the life circumstances and a secure economic basis.' From this viewpoint the social costs determined by business activity consist of the inability of individuals to plan their lives and of a reduced freedom of choice. As a consequence the demographic structure of industrialized societies reflects a growing elderly and inactive population and a drop in the number of young people of working age. The result is an already visible cut in the welfare benefits in many countries and particularly in the reduction of future pensions due to the lack of financial cover. Many workers therefore risk, particularly if they are in precarious work (on fixed term or temporary contracts), falling into poverty once they leave the labor market.

A further topic is the role played by temporary employment in the labor market and the career paths of those joining the labor market through fixed-term contracts. The question is whether temporary work acts as a stepping stone or as a dead-end. Empirical analysis shows that in Germany workers with poor education and low training levels are the most penalized – they can expect long periods of unemployment and entrapment in permanent, insecure jobs (Huber *et al.* 2009).

In France and Spain the probability of temporary work acting as a bridge to stable employment is very rare (Guell and Petrolongo 2007), while in Italy those joining the labor market for the first time through fixed-term contracts run a greater risk of being trapped in the same position compared to those workers starting their employment career on a open-ended contract (Barbieri and Scherer 2005).

As a confirmation of this it appears that a large number of workers on temporary contracts have lost their jobs during the current economic crisis. As a research report by the European Trade Union Institute remarks,

> temporary employment has therefore fallen steeply since the onset of the crisis. In the second quarter of 2009 it accounted for 13.4 percent of all employment, a figure quite close to the 2004 level. Youth and prime-age workers were, on average, more affected by unemployment in the immediate wake of the crisis than were older workers – a fact that may be due to the higher propensity among younger workers to be employed on fixed-term contracts but which is also attributable in part to dismissal rules ('last in – first out').
>
> (ETUI 2010: 38)

Furthermore, older workers who become unemployed are often transferred, relatively quickly, to early retirement measures or practical equivalents and are thus no longer counted as unemployed. However,

> the extent to which young people have been affected by the current economic crisis is likely to be under-estimated by the unemployment data, insofar as young people who lose their jobs, or who face problems in finding a first job, frequently decide to continue their education, which means they do not appear in unemployment statistics.
>
> (ibid.: 42)

In conclusion, we can argue, referring to European and international comparisons, that the percentage of temporary occupations within total employment have grown since the beginning of the twenty-first century. In addition, temporary employment is over-proportionally exercised by young workers and taken up, for the most part, as a matter of necessity rather than choice, in the absence of permanent jobs. These kind of contracts much more frequently lead to spells of unemployment and can entail adverse effects, especially on unemployment insurance benefit receipts.

In other words, it is clear that a larger portion of the private business costs of production is falling upon the human factor of production and the community as a whole than in the previously prevailing, contractually more rigid, post-war Fordist labor legislation framework. These shifted costs become visible in terms of the increasingly precarious nature of work careers, strong cleavages and further segmentation of the labor force, growing wage inequalities and increasing poverty (in 2009, 15.5 percent of the Germans, 19.5 percent of the Spanish,

12.9 percent of the French, 18.4 percent of the Italians and 17.3 percent of the British were at risk of poverty after social transfers).

It should be added that, 'work which is precarious in employment terms is likely to be physically precarious as well' (Dorman 2000: 4) (see also Frigato 2006: 185–188), given that precarious jobs imply multi-risk trajectories and working times that render obsolete the conventionally predisposed exposure levels in work environments.

From the analysis proposed so far it emerges that especially adult workers with low qualification levels and young people are the losers of the 'flexibilization era' and are the most affected by the current economic crises.

The activation paradigm: aporias and risks

Besides the deregulation of the labor market, there is a second trend connected with the idea whereby unemployment occurs because the labor market cannot operate as it should and it places the unemployed person at the core of problem resolution. This new insight turns to supply-side schemes and considers protective labor legislation as an intolerable cost in terms of economic efficiency. The only way to deploy all the potential of a self-regulated labor market is therefore to introduce active labor market policies, because subsidies are considered a trap and not a solution. Welfare has to be reshaped and benefits linked to the condition that recipients are ready to accept job opportunities when they become available.

From this point of view activation policies catch important elements of the neoliberal discourse and the shift 'from policies based on solidarity and equality, to ideas about equality of opportunities and pressure on the weakest parts of the population to take responsibility for their own life' (van Berkel and Moller 2002: 60).

Such an approach is strongly influenced by the force of concepts like human capital and employability, providing a consensual basis for ideas and interpretations of economic and social phenomena, which have underpinned the formulation of devices gauged on the activation policies paradigm (ibid.; Gallie 2004; Bonvin and Favarque 2003; Borghi 2006; Barbier 2008). The underlying idea is that of encouraging an increase in individual know-how and skills – what is commonly defined as human capital (Becker 1964) – for the purposes of growing employability, or to actively seek, find and keep a job. By consequence, this solicits a change in the social protection systems, from passive – particularly from the standpoint of its relationship with the labor market and economic growth – to active, thus fostering a rise in the employment rate. The trend is that of switching from 'protective' to 'productive' social spending, activating people for swift (re)inclusion in the labor market.

Frequently this involves a shift of policies away from an emphasis on progressive redistribution and away from security of income for public benefit recipients, toward greater emphasis on work incentives and measures to bring people into employment: 'Social policies are no longer geared to guarantee citizenship rights but to provide incentives and devise situations in which "work pays"' (Crespo Suàrez and Serrano Pascual 2007: 116).

In terms of policy devices, besides the liberalization of market norms to enhance fixed-term employment (as seen in the previous paragraph), a close link has been identified between social protection and participation in the labor market, where access to financial benefits and subsidies is restricted to a commitment to actively seek work, as under the 'work first' principle.

Different interventions follow this direction: re-inclusion in the labor market of those entitled to financial subsidies, from whom great readiness toward activation is in turn required. Then, employment services are strengthened in order to increase the probability of finding a job. Attention is also given to the development of life-long training, with the aim of sustaining individual employability. In addition, tax credits are introduced, as are income supplements for low wages, with the intention of making work profitable in comparison to welfare dependency (as under the 'make work pay' principle), while incentives are offered to companies recruiting from specific categories of disadvantaged persons. Lastly, the creation of jobs in the public sector, or subsidized labor, is encouraged.

Such measures imply a reorganization of social and labor policies, but also a transformation of the values and aims of the welfare state. They provide grounds for the affirmation of a full-blown paradigm shift at an international level,[3] one embodied precisely in activation policies and in a link between social protection, labor market policies and fiscal policies. A new vision of social justice is offered and this moves away from aims of equality and income security toward goals pursuing the rise of the occupational rate in competitive economic contexts. Thus a new paradigm emerges and a re-conceptualization of the work–welfare relationship is established. According to this new perspective, public policies should structure their interventions by changing priorities: from the struggle against unemployment to encouraging employability; from social protection to activation policies so that workers may quickly rejoin the labor market; from the fight against poverty and inequality to inclusion (in the labor market). In other words, from welfare to workfare.

The condition for asserting such an interpretation is the altered notion of risk socialization. While risk was seen as an external factor to the subject and outside of his control (unemployment, injury, illness, etc.), in the modern welfare system social risks are internalized and their handling depends on the individual's aptitude; or rather, risk resides in the individual's inability or difficulty in being activated. In the former model, fiscal and social protection systems were directed at society and had redistributive aims; in the latter they are conceived as a set of incentives and disincentives focusing on the individual's active behavior with a disciplinary intent (Crespo Suàrez and Serrano Pascual 2007).

It follows that activation is engaged mainly with the individual's readiness to be employed, which, from such a perspective, constitutes the essential condition for enjoying the social rights of citizenship.

The assertion of concepts such as activation and employability is therefore the effect of an ever more pronounced 'labor-oriented' slant to the welfare state, which sets the increase in employment rates as the key criterion in assessing national performance. Such an orientation – also widely shared by the European Employment

Strategy (Barbier 2008) – has exercised unquestionable pressure on the redefining of the concept of employment itself, which is reduced to paid labor for a few hours per week, with low social protection benefits (Salais 2006). It may even be stated that the tightening up of obligations and sanctions and the introduction of activation programs, combined with the fostering of a low-wage labor market area, has contributed to the growth of insecure and temporary employment with limited social protection, as examined in the previous paragraph.

Nonetheless, although most trends follow this track, individual governments have pursued different activation policies. It is useful, from this standpoint, to look briefly at the experience of a few European countries with different welfare regimes.

A symbol of the liberal regime (Esping Andersen 1990; 1999), the United Kingdom, has firmly adopted an approach that considers the market as the main factor of social integration. Benefits are means-tested and play a residual role; labor and social policies are directed at disadvantaged people. Employment becomes, in such a scenario, the most effective protection device to deal with a person's own needs. Several implications arise from this: first and foremost, lack of participation in the labor market brings with it stigmatizing effects; second, unemployment is not considered as a situation connected with the (mal)functioning of the economy, but rather as the result of an opportunistic decision taken by welfare recipients who find it convenient to take advantage of social security; lastly, the response in policy terms is not so much collective solidarity as the condition that recipients are ready to accept job opportunities when these become available.

This approach was dominant during the Conservative governments of the 1980s and the barycentre of social and labor polities was underpinned by a tight structure of conditioning, with the goal of reducing social spending and passive benefits.

When New Labour came to power such an approach did not change. Public policies followed two main paths: first, 'in-work benefits' and tax credits were introduced in order to make low wages preferable to welfare support. Second, the structure of benefits for the unemployed was changed by setting out tighter eligibility criteria, with more restrictive conditions for service access. In line with an orthodox view of workfare, the conditions introduced for entitlement to subsidies forced unemployed people to accept any job offer under the 'work first' imperative. In this sense it is possible to identify a shifting logic from a 'welfare to work' approach (that of supporting subjects during their path toward work) to a 'work for welfare' one, which establishes 'work instead of benefit' in place of 'work for benefit' policies.

The emergence of a rise in the working poor – spurred, nevertheless, by these same policies – forced the New Labour government to intervene on three fronts:

1   an increase in minimum wages;
2   greater investment in improving human capital and training; and
3   a restructuring of labor policies, particularly the active ones, by reorganizing employment services (job centers).

These adjustment measures, following the 'third way' logic, however, did not bring into discussion an individualistic interpretation of unemployment based on supply-side schemes.

Another well-known national experience is the Danish one, which is described internationally as a paradigmatic case of harmonization between labor market flexibilization and a universalistic welfare regime. This approach has been described using the term flexicurity (Madsen 2004; Wilthagen and Tros 2004) which is a benchmark for welfare policies within the European Union. Broadly summarized, this is a strategy that attempts to synchronically and intentionally increase the flexibility of the labor market while strengthening social security and employability among the weakest groups, both within and outside the labor market (ibid.). However, as has been observed, the universalistic structure of the Danish welfare state and the unconditional entitlement to rights and income benefits have nonetheless been moderated over time in favor of an approach that finds its cornerstones in the so-called 'active line' (*aktivering*) and in the centrality of work as the main factor of social inclusion (Jörgensen 2002). From this standpoint, in recent years there has been a shift from a universalistic, inclusive and unconditional model toward an activating paradigm that places 'work first' as its fundamental goal. This trend is symbolized, for instance, by the 2003 labor market reform named 'more people at work'. This introduced, among other things, the conditions that the unemployed should increase their active job-seeking and their readiness to move. Thus, Denmark has revised a previously very generous unemployment insurance system and implemented stricter eligibility rules and shorter duration of benefits (Johansson and Hviden 2007). The government has phased out the generous leave arrangements while the policy-makers are discussing how to dismantle early retirement benefit (ibid.). As elsewhere in Europe, recipients of social assistance were considered as at least partly to blame for their lack of sufficient income (van Oorschot 2006). They were identified as less responsible, less capable or less competent than other citizens in terms of finding and keeping regular paid work, and therefore in need of strict discipline and control. As Lodemal argues (2004: 202),

> in some cases programs are presented to social assistance recipients as a new offer, and the compulsory character is only revealed when this is not accepted. Because economic necessity often makes clients unable to reject the 'offer' of participation, it is perhaps best described as a 'throffer', combining offer and threats in one package.

A third national example worthy of attention and referring to a different welfare regime compared to those of Great Britain (liberal) and Denmark (universalistic) is Germany. This country, which is characterized by a Bismarckian welfare regime, has experienced a season of change in public policies heavily influenced by the idea of activation and by the tendency to privilege supply-side approaches.

We are in fact referring to the so-called Hartz reforms regarding several policy fields: the first involves the reorganization of employment services; the second concerns the reordering of unemployment benefits; the third refers to the attempt to boost the employment rate in particular.

As regards the reorganization of employment services, it has been established that the local job centers are obliged to reach quantitative and measurable targets. At the end of the process job-seekers are divided up into four types:

1   Marktkunden (market clients): job-seekers with the greatest chance of immediately finding a job;
2   Beratungskunden Aktivieren (clients for counseling and activation in job-seeking): those who require activation and consultancy;
3   Beratungskunden Fördern (clients to support): those needing careful supervision and encouragement to adopt active behavior; and
4   Betreuungskunden (clients requiring closer supervision): those with the poorest chances of inclusion in the labor market.

On the basis of this classification, active labor policies have been redrawn, especially in terms of the target population. Referring to training policies, for example, only those adults with a minimum 70 percent chance of joining the labor market are admitted. As a consequence, job centers embark on relations only with those training bodies respecting this standard. On the contrary, policies regarding the creation of jobs by the public body target those people who are difficult to find jobs for, and involve low-qualified workers and low-quality work activities.

As far as unemployment benefit is concerned, the fourth act of the Hartz reform (Hartz IV) has radically changed the system. First and foremost, the unemployment subsidy calculated on the size of the last salary received before redundancy or dismissal – now named unemployment benefit I (Arbeitslosengeld I) – is limited to a maximum of 12 months for all; 18 months for people over 55; and 24 months for those over 58 years of age. Once this period is finished, the unemployed pass over to the Arbeitslosengeld II program (unemployment benefit II), which combines the previous unemployment assistance (Arbeitslosenhilfe) and social assistance (Sozialhilfe) services in a single body. This system is gauged on means testing. The quantity of financial support provided is set at the level of the previous social assistance and is thus unrelated to the last salary received. This aspect constitutes the most significant discontinuity with the past, since the jobless persons who received a high salary before redundancy or dismissal now see their benefits drastically reduced to €345 per month for residents in West Germany and €331 for those in East Germany.

The third element in the Hartz reform is the intervention aiming to increase the employment rate in the secondary labor market area. The goal is to 'make work pay', and encourages work participation in low-qualified and low-wage jobs. The main intervention is the introduction of the so-called 'mini jobs', intended to facilitate finding a low-wage job and involving a reduction in the national insurance contributions for workers whose wages are lower than or equal to €400 per month. Instead, jobs with salaries ranging from €400 to €800 per month are called 'midi jobs'. These also involve a reduction of the average levels of national insurance contributions, with percentages equal to zero in the case of wages just over €400 and gradually climbing to the standard contribution level when the entire sum stands at about €800 per month.

Other labor market deregulation measures are the new norms regarding temporary jobs introduced for the purpose of encouraging its expansion. The Hartz reform has abolished the previous restrictions on the maximum number of renewals possible when stipulating a fixed-term contract, and it has also legalized temporary work in the construction sector. Another deregulation measure involves the simplification of dismissal procedures and their coverage: as of 1 January 2004, not only companies with fewer than five employees, but also those with up to ten, are exempt from applying the law regarding individual dismissal (Kündigungsschutzgesetz of 1951) and the norms regarding collective negotiations, which set out precise restrictions and require a well-grounded reason for the termination of a work relationship.

Lastly, still in reference to the goal of increasing job opportunities, besides the reduction in the quantity and duration of unemployment benefit mentioned above, two substantial changes have been introduced. First, and parallel to the setting up of the Arebeitslosengeld II program, the definition of acceptable employment has altered.

In the case of the long-term unemployed, job-seekers are obliged to accept a job without considering its salary level, provided this respects the legal standards. The law specifically states that a low professional status is no longer valid grounds for rejecting a job, which was possible prior to the Hartz reform. It also adds that the salary may be inferior to local standards or to union or social agreements and it specifies that, with the exception of certain circumstances, people must also be ready to accept jobs far from their place of residence.

A second new aspect in the Hartz reform is the tightening up of the sanctioning apparatus for those refusing a job opportunity. Traditionally the public labor services in Germany sanctioned the unemployed relatively little and the reason lay in the presence of an inflexible apparatus that involved the complete denial of benefits for the entire duration of 12 weeks. Now sanction modulation is admissible and may be set at three or six weeks, up to a maximum of 12.

Such aspects regarding the growing conditional nature of unemployment-support provision – that is increasingly linked to the willingness to accept any job and that makes activation policies essentially of a workfare type – are now widespread. Italy also, characterized by a conservative and family-oriented welfare regime (Esping Andersen 1990; Ferrera 1996; Mingione 1997), in 2004 changed the requisites for the access to unemployment benefits, introducing a pro-business approach (Marocco 2007; Liso 2008). More specifically, eligibility to unemployment benefit should be refused when:

- job-seekers refuse to be activated in a project for rejoining the labor market;
- the unemployed refuse to be activated through a training course or fail to attend it regularly; or

• job-seekers do not accept a job offer in a salary bracket that is a maximum of 20 percent lower than that of their previous employment.

From the brief illustration of these national cases, a clear trend seems to emerge: that of the previously mentioned 'labor-oriented' slant to the welfare state. To different degrees and depending on the country concerned, readiness to take part in the labor market becomes an essential condition for receiving social support. And this occurs both in the case of the adoption of a moderate 'welfare to work' approach – striving to provide welfare support to people as they move toward work – as well as in the case of the so-called 'work for welfare' approach, which prescribes the complete replacement of income support with paid work in its most radical version. In this scenario we may talk about 'work instead of benefit' policies rather than 'work for benefit' policies (Lodemal and Trickey 2001).

As already remarked, the problem is that, within such a framework, work is reduced to paid employment of a few hours per week with a low level of social protection entitlement. As a consequence, in many European countries social and economic inequalities are growing (Table 8.4) and the introduction of activation programs reducing social protection and encouraging the expansion of a low-wage labor market area with high levels of temporary and insecure work contracts does not provide protection against this phenomenon; on the contrary, it encourages it.

From this standpoint, as Crespo Suàrez and Serrano Pascual argue (2007: 120): 'The problem of unemployment becomes a problem of individual activation: it is people who have to be helped, motivated and activated so that they will avoid the 'snares' into which they might otherwise fall.' Also on the basis of these last considerations a prevalence of an individualistic approach to unemployment and the growing instability of work careers seems evident to us.

Policies of activation that insist on the conditionality of support-interventions, that are linked to the individual accepting any type of job regardless of its quality, are transforming the different welfare regimes into what Blank (2010) has called *work conditioned public support states*. In this situation – as well as in that examined already with regard to the deregulation of the labor market – the public policies of income support, by individualizing the interventions, make responsibility for events such as unemployment and temporary work careers move from enterprises to individuals. In this respect we can talk of individualization of social costs, given that the greater part of the actual costs of the business management of production falls upon the individual worker, who can aspire to a minimum level of social protection only in so far as he is capable of activating himself and finding a job as soon as possible. With a paradoxical effect though,

> since many benefits are tied to work, employers function as key gatekeepers of social entitlements. In this system the work contract with private employers is used as the basis of social protection, and this also means that the loss

Table 8.4 Inequality trends in selected advanced countries

	Inequality change between the mid-1970s and the mid-1980s	Inequality change between the mid-1980s and the mid-1990s	Inequality change between the mid-1990s and the mid-2000s	Inequality change between the mid-1990s and the mid-2000s*
Sweden	−	+	+ +	0.234
Finland	−	+	+ +	0.269
France	−	+	0	0.270
Netherlands	0	+ +	−	0.271
Belgium	0	+	−	0.271
Germany	−	+	+ +	0.298
Australia	0	+	−	0.301
Canada	−	+	+ +	0.317
Ireland	−	+ +	+	0.328
United Kingdom	+ +	+ +	−	0.335
Italy	− −	+ +	+	0.352

Source: OECD 2008.

Notes
* The Gini coefficient is a measure of the inequality of a distribution, a value of 0 expressing total equality and a value of 1 maximum inequality.

of a job is punished twice, because not only earnings from work, but also social rights are forgone.

(Alber 2010: 114)

Conclusions

In this discussion I have tried to highlight how social costs generated by an ideology of market absolutism tend to be shifted onto workers and onto society as a whole. The deregulation of labor market rules by way of temporary and fixed-term jobs with reduced welfare protections, as well as the introduction of activation policies restricting benefits to the condition that recipients are ready to accept job opportunities when these become available, have placed vulnerable people and the unemployed at the core of the problem resolution, by individualizing social risks and by placing the costs of business activity on individual workers.

As we have seen, the social costs caused by the growing commodification of laborers in contemporary capitalistic welfare regimes have given rise to the growth of temporary employment. Unstable employment tends to affect primarily young people, women and poorly qualified workers, accentuating labor market segmentation and prolonging the entrapment of certain groups in precarious life-courses (low wages, poor health and safety at work, low levels of work quality, inadequate social protection, postponement of family formation and parenthood, etc.).

With regard to activation policies, cuts in welfare benefits, the restriction of eligibility to social protection, and the reduction in the duration of benefits have given rise to a growing polarization between those who are able and those who are less able to be activated, making welfare dependency a stigma and something to be ashamed of. As van Berkel and Moller (2004: 238) state regarding this point: 'Target groups of social policies are objects rather than subjects of these policies. They have to conform to top-down and uniformly defined notions of good citizenship and will be sanctioned if they do not.'

But the situation generated is a paradoxical one: slotted within an era of precarious employment and the weakening of social protection, self-sufficiency becomes a particularly impelling principle just when the social supports to individuality – the rights, resources and collective regulations that have fueled that self-sufficiency – are brought into question. In other words, for a long time the social costs incurred by business enterprises (market failures, occupational crises, structural unemployment, unsafe and unhealthy working conditions, etc.) were considered as structural and unavoidable elements of the capitalistic system of production. Business enterprises were considered responsible for protecting the well-being of their employees, guaranteeing secure employment and contributing to the funding of institutions of social protection. At present, however, the legal obligations placed on companies to protect their employees have been substantially weakened. Risks and social costs induced by market mechanisms now fall on single individuals who are finding it increasingly difficult to respond to a labor market that is creating growing instability. What has been lost today is the awareness that individual emancipation and self-realization were gained by the majority within a framework of collective security traceable back to the *statute* of work and embedded in entitlements and rights.

Nowadays, work-conditioned public support, along with policies to encourage occupational inclusion, tend to discriminate those people with fewer resources and little to offer in terms of mobility and adaptability, dropping the social cost of capitalist development on those whose only option is to adapt to a situation they did not create.[4] The consequence is the institutionalization of a prescriptively unavoidable social expectation that induces workers to mold themselves as 'enterprisers promoting themselves': they are no longer persuaded to take part in the capital accumulation process through incentives and external constraints, but invited to shape their motivations to the company's business interests, in a generic readiness to recognize any change of their work position as the result of an individual choice (Sennett 1998). As Hartmann and Honneth argue (2006: 45):

> The most important criterion for describing the new capitalism is no longer the ability to efficiently fulfill hierarchically determined parameters within a large enterprise; it is the readiness to self-responsibly bring one's own abilities and emotional resources to bear in the service of individualized projects. In this way, the worker becomes an 'entreployee' or himself an entrepreneur; he is in a sense self-motivated.

Individual self-sufficiency and self-realization thus tend to be conceived not so much as a possibility or a right, but as a 'demand' and a necessity, and the metaphors describing work (adaptability, flexibility, mobility and employability) end up becoming a productive strength of the capitalist economy. And so it comes about that the social costs stemming from market mechanisms are no longer accountable to business enterprises but to the (wrong) choices of individuals and their inability to navigate a turbulent labor market.

This process has ultimately led to the adoption of measures that have given up social protection in exchange for a supposedly higher independence of workers. But as Crespo Suàrez and Serrano Pascual argue (2007: 121), it is the object of the dependence that has changed

> The social protection systems, which were developed as a condition of the autonomy of the worker in the face of asymmetrical relationships that characterized the market, are cast into disrepute because they encourage individual dependence and irresponsibility. Autonomy is to be promoted in this way, but it is an autonomy vis-à-vis institutions, one achieved at the cost of increasing 'dependence' on the market and its laws. As such, it is a question less of fighting dependence than of transforming the object of the dependence.

Notes

1 The EPL index represents a standardized measure provided by the OECD that approximates the degree of employment protection on three different dimensions: the strictness of employment protection for regular employment; the strictness of regulations for temporary employment; and the regulations governing collective dismissals.
2 The lower level of temporary employment in the United Kingdom can largely be accounted for by the fact that low regulation of the labor market and low levels of employment protection provide employers with the flexibility to hire or fire workers as required. Mainly for this reason temporary jobs are not resorted to.
3 Within the European Union, employability was one of the four cornerstones of the European Employment Strategy (EES). This strategy was reformulated in 2003 to include three new simplified objectives: full employment; better labor quality and higher productivity; greater cohesion and inclusion.
4 We refer, for instance, to those women charged with the care of others and for this reason unable to accept employment far from their homes or who have difficulty in attending retraining courses since the hours are incompatible with their *working* duties performed within the home.

References

Alber, J. (2010) 'What the European and American welfare states have in common and where they differ: facts and fiction in comparison of the European social model and United States', *Journal of European Social Policy*, 20: 102–125.
Barbier, J.C. (2008) *La longue marche vers l'Europe sociale*, Paris: Presses universitaires de France.
Barbieri, J.C. and Scherer, S. (2005) 'Le conseguenze sociali della flessibilizzazione del lavoro in Italia', *Stato e mercato*, 2: 291–322.
Becker, G.S. (1964) *Human Capital: A Theoretical and Empirical Analysis, with Special Reference to Education*, New York: National Bureau of Economic Research.
Berger, S. and Dore, R. (eds.) (1996) *National Diversity and Global Capitalism*, Ithaca, NY: Cornell University Press.
Bertolini, S. (2002) *Il lavoro atipico e le sue strategie*, Torino: Stampatori Libreria.
Berton, F., Richiardi, M. and Sacchi, S. (2009) *Flex-insecurity*, Bologna: Il Mulino.
Blank, R.M. (2010) 'The new American model of work-conditioned public support', in Alber, J. and Gilber, N. (eds.), *United in Diversity? Comparing Social Models in Europe and America*, Oxford: Oxford University Press.
Bonvin, J.M. and Farvaque, N. (2003) 'Employability and capability: the role of the local agencies in implementing social policies', paper presented at the 3rd Conference on the Capability Approach, Pavia, September.
Borghi, V. (2006) 'Do we know where we are going? Active policies and individualization in the Italian context', in Van Berkel, R. and Valkenburg, B. (eds.), *Making it Personal*, Bristol: Policy Press.
Bosch, G. and Weinkopf, C. (eds.) (2008) *Low-wage Work in Germany*, New York: Russell Sage Foundation.
Buchholz, S. and Kurz, K. (2008) 'A new mobility regime in Germany? Young people's labour market entry and phase of establishment since the mid-1980s', in Blossfeld, H.P., Buchholz, S., Bukodi, E. and Kurz, K. (eds.), *Young Workers, Globalization and the Labour Market: Comparing Early Working Life in Eleven Countries*, Northampton, MA: Edward Elgar.

Cahuc, P. and Kramarz, F. (2004) *De la précarité à la mobilité: vers un sécurité sociale professionnelle*, Paris: Rapport au Ministre de l'Emploi.

Castel, R. (2003) *L'insécurité sociale: Qu'est-ce qu'ètre protegè?*, Paris: Editions du Seuil.

Cimaglia, M.C., Corbisiero, F. and Rizza, R. (2009) *Tra imprese e lavoratori: Una ricerca sul lavoro non standard in Italia*, Milano: Bruno Mondadori.

Clark, J.M. (1957) *Economic Institutions and Human Welfare*, New York: Alfred A. Knopf.

Commons, J.R. and Andrews, J.B. (1967) *Principles of Labour Legislation*, New York: Kelley.

Crespo Suàrez, E. and Serrano Pascual, A. (2007) 'Political production of individualized subjects in the paradoxical discourse of the EU institutions', in Valkenburg, B. and van Berkel, R. (eds.), *Making it Personal*, Bristol: The Policy Press.

Crouch, C. and Streeck, W. (eds.) (1997) *Political Economy of Modern Capitalism: Mapping Convergence and Diversity*, London: Sage.

Dormann, P. (2000) 'The economics of safety, health and well-being at work: an overview', *Focus Programme on Safe Work*, Geneva: ILO, The Evergreen State College.

Esping Andersen, G. (1990) *The Three Worlds of Welfare Capitalism*, Cambridge: Polity Press.

Esping Andersen, G. (1999) *Social Foundations of Postindustrial Economies*, Oxford: Oxford University Press.

Esping Andersen, G. and Regini, M. (2000) *Why Deregulate Labour Markets?*, Oxford: Oxford University Press.

ETUI (2010) *Benchmarking Working Europe*, Brussels: ETUI.

Ferrera, M. (1996) 'Il modello sud-europeo di welfare state', *Rivista italiana di scienza politica*, 1: 85–110.

Frigato, P. (2006) 'Social costs and human health: Kapp's approach and its growing relevance today', in Elsner, W., Frigato, P. and Ramazzotti, P. (eds.), *Social Costs and Public Action in Modern Capitalism*, Routledge: London and New York.

Fullin, G. (2004) *Vivere l'instabilità del lavoro*, Bologna: Il Mulino.

Gallie, D. (ed.) (2004) *Resisting Marginalization: Unemployment Experience and Social Policy in the European Union*, Oxford: Oxford University Press.

Gallie, D. and Paugam, S. (eds.) (2000) *Welfare Regimes and the Experience of Unemployment in Europe*, Oxford: Oxford University Press.

Gallie, D., White, M., Cheng, Y. and Tomlinson, M. (1998) *Restructuring the Employment Relationship*, Oxford: Oxford University Press.

Guell, M. and Petrolongo, B. (2007) 'How binding are legal limits? Transitions from temporary to permanent work in Spain', *Labour Economics*, 14: 153–183.

Hartmann, M. and Honneth, A. (2006) 'Paradoxes of capitalism', *Constellations*, 13: 41–56.

Huber, M., Lechner, M., Wunsch, C. and Walter, T. (2009) 'Do German welfare-to-work programmes reduce welfare and increase work?', IZA Discussion Paper No. 4090.

Johansson, H. and Hviden, B. (2007) 'Re-activating the Nordic welfare states: do we find a distinct model?', *International Journal of Sociology and Social Policy*, 27: 334–346.

Jorgensen, H. (2002) *Consensus, Cooperation and Conflict: The Policy Making Process in Denmark*, Cheltenham: Edward Elgar.

Kapp, K.W. (1963) *The Social Costs of Private Enterprise*, Nottingham: Russell Press.

Liso, F. (2008) 'Gli ammortizzatori sociali', in Guerzoni, L. (ed.), *La riforma del welfare*, Bologna: Il Mulino.

Lodemel, I. (2004) 'The development of workfare within social activation policies', in Gallie, D. (ed.), *Resisting Marginalization: Unemployment Experience and Social Policy in the European Union*, Oxford: Oxford University Press.

Lodemel, I. and Trickey, H. (eds.) (2001) *An Offer you Can't Refuse: Workfare in International Perspective*, Bristol: The Policy Press.

Madsen, P.K. (2004) 'The Danish model of flexicurity', *Transfer*, 10: 187–207.

Marocco, M. (2007) 'Ammortizzatori sociali: L'ordinamento italiano tra condizionalità crescente e polverizzazione della governance', *La Rivista delle Politiche Sociali*, 2: 213–230.

Mingione, E. (1997) *Sociologia della vita economica*, Roma: Carocci.

OECD (2008) *Growing Unequal? Income Distribution and Poverty in OECD Countries*, Paris: OECD.

Palidda, R. (ed.) (2009) *Vite flessibili*, Milano: Angeli.

Rizza, R. (2003) *Il lavoro mobile*, Roma: Carocci.

Salais, R. (2004) 'Incorporating the capability approach into social and employment policies', in Salais, R. and Villeneuve, R. (eds.), *Europe and the Politics of Capabilities*, Cambridge: Cambridge University Press.

Salais, R. (2006) 'On the correct (and incorrect) use of indicators in public action', *Comparative Labour Law & Policy Journal*, 27: 237–256.

Salmieri, L. (2006) *Coppie flessibili*, Bologna: Il Mulino.

Scherer, S. (2004) 'Stepping stones or traps? The consequences of labour market entry positions on future careers in West Germany, Great Britain and Italy', *Work, Employment and Society*, 18: 369–394.

Sennet, R. (1998) *The Corrosion of Character*, New York: W.W. Norton.

Valkenburg, B. and van Berkel, R. (2007) *Making it Personal*, Bristol: The Policy Press.

van Berkel, R. and Moller, I. (2002) *Active Social Policies in the EU: Inclusion Through Participation?*, Bristol: The Policy Press.

van Berkel, R. and Moller, I. (2004) 'The experience of activation policies', in Gallie, D. (ed.) (2004) *Resisting Marginalization: Unemployment Experience and Social Policy in the European Union*, Oxford: Oxford University Press.

van Oorschot, W. (2006) 'Making the difference in social Europe: deservingness perceptions among citizens of European welfare states', *Journal of European Social Policy*, 16: 23–42.

Wilthagen, T. and Tros, F. (2004) 'The concept of flexicurity: a new approach to regulating employment and labour market', *Transfer*, 10: 166–186.

9 The social costs of water commodification in developing countries

Manuel Couret Branco and
Pedro Damião Henriques

Introduction

The problem of social costs came to light chiefly associated with the idea of negative externalities in Arthur Pigou's *Economics of Welfare*, first published in 1920 (Pigou 1932). In Pigou's understanding a social cost was the outcome of accidentally rendering disservices to other persons besides those directly involved in a transaction. In the presence of negative externalities the social cost of economic activity is not covered by the private cost; in other words, market prices do not reflect real costs, which may lead to over-consumption of a product or resource. In these circumstances the free play of self-interest may induce an inefficient distribution of resources, and Pigou's aim was precisely to find a way for the state to improve upon markets' natural tendencies (Coase 1960), which means internalizing social costs.

Harmful effects of private activities were taken as a side-effect of the economic process and considered primarily with the purpose of correcting inefficiencies affecting economic transactions, not of unveiling unfair shifting of costs onto other individuals or society at large. William Kapp, in his seminal work *The Social Costs of Private Enterprise*, first published in 1950, provided a different insight to social costs. In his mind, contrary to what had been considered before, social costs were not a mere side-effect of private activity, but an intrinsic element of profit-maximizing behavior by firms (Kapp 1978) which, in addition, could not be internalized in real life. In Kapp's understanding the essence of social costs was precisely the fact that they fall upon third persons and imply the sacrifice of human well-being.

According to William Kapp, in order to be recognized as social costs, harmful effects and inefficiencies must have two characteristics. It must be possible to avoid them and they must be part of the course of productive activities and be shifted to third persons or the community at large (Kapp 1969). Additionally, because social costs are rooted on the minimization of the private costs of production they take on a third characteristic, which is the redistribution of income. Indeed, as Kapp declares, by shifting part of the costs of production to third persons or to the community at large, producers are able to appropriate a larger share of the natural product than they would otherwise be able to do (Kapp 1969).

The purpose of this chapter is to examine the social costs generated by the activity of collecting and distributing water, most especially in developing countries. In as much as water can be technically considered a private good, its supply, either by aiming at minimizing costs in the case of public provision or maximizing profit in the case of private distribution, engenders social costs. However, the critical issue here will not be private activity per se as generally in social costs literature, but commodification of the resource. In business jargon, commodification is usually interpreted as the transformation of goods and services into commodities; in other words, into goods or services fully or partially fungible. In this sense water, as the great majority of natural resources, has always been considered a commodity. Indeed, in theory there is no qualitative differentiation in the product provided by the various suppliers in the market, drinking water being roughly the same in Buenos Aires or Tokyo.

The commodification we wish to address here, however, is of a different category. Our understanding of the concept is closer to that of political economy, where commodification means above all a process within which economic value is assigned to something not previously considered in economic terms. As a commodity water has, therefore, a price, and is collected and distributed in order to meet a viable demand. This commodification of the resource can also be characterized by the marketization of the state – in other words, by the growing tendency of the state to behave like a market-oriented firm. It is this process that is at the origin of the majority of the social costs generated in the water sector, regardless of the resource being privately or publicly collected and distributed, as we will see.

If one wants to improve the livelihood of the populations in the developing world, water supply is on the front line of the services that should be provided in the next decades. Indeed, the lack of water hampers development by constraining food production, health conditions and industrial development. Water scarcity, in both its quantitative and qualitative manifestations is, therefore, not only emerging as a major development challenge for many countries, but also as an ecological challenge. Some 2 percent of the earth's visible blue landscape is freshwater, the rest being salt water, and only about half of the freshwater is available for use by human beings. Furthermore, since 1950, as world population doubled, water use tripled.

It is, therefore, crucial to examine social costs in the light of both the development and the ecological crisis. On the one hand, the socio-economic crisis puts pressure on public finances to cut back infrastructural investment and pushes governments toward marketization, either by adopting the behavior of market-oriented firms or by privatizing water collection and distribution. The ecological crisis, on the other hand, restrains human well-being by demanding that the rate of water consumption does not exceed the natural recharge rate, forcing the developing world to contemplate the possibility of a water-restrained development path.

We shall start examining the social costs of water collection and distribution by describing the process through which water is transformed into a commodity.

Second, we will identify some of the harmful effects induced by the commodification of water and the criteria that takes us into considering them as social costs. More specifically, we will examine social costs generated by both water use and water exclusion and, despite the fact that these costs are generated regardless of water being privately of publicly managed, we shall insist on the fact that water privatization entails a larger amount and variety of social costs.

The commodification of water

Until the second half of the twentieth century, because of the relatively weak demographic pressure put on available resources by demand, the consumption of water by an individual did not significantly reduce the amount of water available to others. Water was taken as a free good – in other words, as a good available for consumption according to the principle of first-come first-served (Bontems and Rotillon 1998). However, since then the fast pace of economic and demographic growth boosted water consumption in order to meet all kinds of demands and implied that water management had to be thought of within a framework of scarcity, which in turn implied changes in the way water was classified as a good.

Economics commonly divides goods into two main categories, public and private, according to particular combinations of rivalry and exclusion in their consumption. In economics, a public good is a good that is non-rivalrous and non-excludable. This means that the consumption of this good by one individual does not reduce the amount of the good left for the consumption of other individuals, and that no individual can effectively be excluded from consuming that good. Take the example of a glass of Port wine. If one individual drinks it, that particular glass ceases to be available for the consumption of other individuals. It is also possible to prevent an individual from consuming the glass of Port wine if he or she is not willing to pay for it. In this case it is that rivalry and exclusion which makes our glass of Port wine a private good. On the contrary, breathing air, for example, does not significantly reduce the amount of air available to others, nor can people be excluded from breathing it. That is why air, unlike the glass of Port wine, is a public good.

However, when economics states that individuals cannot be excluded from breathing air, it is not stating a moral imperative, it is not indeed referring to the fact that an individual prevented from breathing air will die; it is just saying that individuals cannot be prevented from breathing air because it is technically impossible to exclude from consumption individuals who are not willing to pay. In other words, it is openly pointing out that no individual can make a living out of selling air to breathe, because there is plenty of free air available. Consequently, air cannot be commodified on our planet.

In reality, however, it is very hard to make all goods fall exclusively into these two categories. Indeed, based on the combinations of exclusion and rivalry one can determine two other categories of goods. There are goods that are rivalrous but non-excludable and goods that are excludable but non-rivalrous. Goods that fall into the first group are called common-pool goods, and goods that fall into the second group toll or club goods. In the first case it is impossible or very hard to stop people from consuming these goods, but the consumption of one individual limits the consumption of another individual.

Fish in the ocean, for instance, is often given as an example of a common-pool good. One can freely fish in the ocean but the stock is limited and therefore excessive fishing by one individual can prevent another individual from fishing. In the other group, consumption of one individual does not affect the ability of another individual to consume in his or her turn, but it is possible to exclude individuals from consumption if they are not willing to pay. An often used example is cable television. By watching a particular show, an individual does not limit the ability of another individual to watch the same or another show, but if an individual does not pay for cable, service is cut. Now, what does this tell us about the classification of water as a good?

From a strictly technical point of view, classifying water is not an easy task. Sustainable consumption of water in nature, drinking it out of a river or a lake, does not imply rivalry nor does it provoke exclusion, and therefore in these circumstances water must be considered a public good. This public character of water seems to have been already suggested by Adam Smith in the eighteenth century, when he declared that 'nothing is more useful than water: but it will purchase scarce any thing; scarce any thing can be had in exchange for it' (Smith 1776: n.p.). The absence of exchange value, in other words the impossibility of reaching a market price, is indeed another interpretation of a public good. Non-rivalry and non-exclusion are reinforced by the fact that there are no property rights on water in its first state – that is to say, natural. But this does not mean that there should be no rules for its distribution besides that of first-come first-served. Freshwater may not be unlimited on the planet, especially if pollution and over-consumption continue at the current pace.

For this reason it should be more realistic to include water among common-pool goods, where unsustainability of consumption has been identified in the absence of strict distributive rules. Garrett Hardin, in his famous article on the tragedy of the commons, shows how the inexistence of property rights along with the absence of distributive rules can lead to an unsustainable use of a resource (Hardin 1968), and therefore, in the case of water, to eventually depriving every individual of a good that is essential to life. Preservation and supply of common-pool goods are, consequently, a collective responsibility, and thus demand the presence of a public authority. The *Tribunal de Las Águas* in Valencia, Spain, is an institution that is more than 1,000 years old and still meets every week to allocate the use of the regional water distribution network for agriculture, demonstrating, once again, the longevity of water's public character.

Nevertheless, the form in which water appears before consumers today does not have much to do with the classification suggested above. Indeed, the great majority of the world's population has access to water by the intermediation of infrastructures such as plumbing and other forms of collection and distribution. Contrary to water, strictly speaking, however, these infrastructures can be privately appropriated, which means that exclusion and rivalry can be simultaneously introduced in the process of supplying water. Indeed, one can be excluded from consuming water because one only has access to the water tap if one is willing to pay, and there can be rivalry because one particular water tap may only serve one particular home and cannot be used without its owner's permission. In modern times, therefore, water could, technically speaking, be considered a private good like any other, making it possible for water to be commodified.

This commodification of water means that, regardless of water being privately or publicly supplied, a price can be attached to it and, therefore, the possibility of a market of some sort can be considered. Consequently, both exclusion and rivalry are allowed. As a result, part of the population can be technically deprived of access to a resource that is essential to human survival. In the case of private distribution of water, the market is not obliged to reach every individual as, according to its logic, its only purpose is to satisfy viable demand, as it is the case for any other private good. In satisfying viable demand the main issue is ability to pay, or purchasing power. What matters for markets is that agents are satisfied; in other words, that sellers are able to sell the amounts they wish at market prices and that buyers are able to buy what they intend at the same market prices. The fact that some agents are not able to buy what they wish, or need, at market prices on account of an excessively tightened budget constraint is of almost no concern to private corporations.

In the case of insufficient public distribution of water this same issue must be viewed in a slightly different manner, though. Indeed, the purpose of the state is not to satisfy viable demand, as for markets, but to meet citizens' requests. This means that individual purchasing power and willingness to pay do not play the same part as with private goods supplied by markets. Nevertheless, availability of means, a twin concept of purchasing power, is crucial. Despite the fact that public goods generally do not have a price reflecting their market value, means are, indeed, needed for supplying them as they do have a cost. The main difference of public provision relative to private, here, is that means are needed on the supply side rather than on the demand side, at least in a direct form. That is why taxation is fundamental to the production of public goods that are exclusive to the state.

But if markets lack incentives to supply public goods, the state can supply both public and private goods. Indeed, water can be publicly distributed as a private good, allowing the state to charge consumers for it; consequently pricing becomes a critical policy issue. Means can also be needed on the demand side, therefore. In Africa, for example, water users have not been paying – and probably will not have conditions to pay in the future – the true costs of supplying water. Indeed, only a small proportion of the cost of transferring, treating and disposing of water has been supported by users, the remaining cost having been subsidized. Despite this fact, many water users do not even have the ability to pay these subsidized prices, hence the exclusion.

If people are deprived of access to public or private goods supplied by the state this means that either the state does not have the necessary means to produce them or that it has chosen not to. In the first case, exclusion is mainly a development issue because the state may be unable to supply part of the goods and services needed by the population as a result of unavailability of means. In the second case, on the contrary, it is mainly a social and political issue because it means that lack of access is not inevitable. While exclusion and inequality in the distribution of many private goods do not forcibly imply harmful effects and inefficiencies which could shape a social cost, with water, as we will see in the next section, they do so, since water is essential to human life and water deprivation is not inevitable in the world today.

The social costs of water exclusion

If one agrees with a simple general economic principle, vaguely suggested by one of Murphy's popular laws, stating that if exclusion is possible then exclusion will take place, then it should not come as a surprise that access to water is far from being guaranteed to everybody, most especially in developing countries, and that, amidst those communities which benefit from this access, water is also far from being distributed equitably, once again regardless of water being publicly or privately distributed. As a matter of fact, with the exception of extremely water-scarce environments, deprivation is the logical consequence of the exclusion possibility inherent in the commodification of water.

The World Health Organization (WHO) believes that more than one billion people are deprived of basic access to water (WHO 2000: 1). In Africa, for example, of the estimated 800 million people living on the continent, 300 million live in a water-scarce environment, mostly in northern and southern regions. On average, 64 percent of the African population has access to a safe water supply. However, about two-thirds of the African population live in rural areas where water supply coverage is the poorest, covering about 50 percent of the population only. In urban areas an estimated 86 percent of the population has access to safe water. However, these areas face two main problems: many urban centers have declining water distribution systems due to inadequate, ageing and overloaded networks; and peri-urban dwellers live in slums and are poor, and a large proportion lack reasonable access to safe water (2003 IYFW 2008).

Besides the fact that depriving an individual from access to water may constitute a violation of a human right (see Branco and Henriques 2010) which, alone, can be considered a harmful effect on society, there are other important consequences and characteristics of this exclusion that encompass social costs. First of all, water deprivation resulting from resource commodification can be avoided; second, costs of this deprivation are shifted to third persons or society at large; and, finally, it raises issues of income redistribution. However, it is obvious that these harmful effects do not arise from producing, but from refusing to produce. Therefore, we should probably consider them social opportunity costs rather than strict social costs (see Kapp 1983: 9). Despite this conceptual difference, both types of costs share the same essence and, thus, can be dealt with similarly.

Once more with the probable exception of an environment suffering from extreme water scarcity, as far as the satisfaction of basic needs is concerned one could fairly safely state that it is relatively easy and cheap to provide access to water to everybody, which means that harmful effects associated with exclusion from access to water are clearly avoidable. Pedro Arrojo, a leading scholar in issues concerning the ethics of water use, awarded with the Goldman Environmental Prize in 2003, declares that providing water for people's basic needs is within reach of every national economy (Arrojo 2006: 109). Depending on technology, universal access to drinking water and sanitation in the developing world would cost $20–30 billion (UNDP 2006: 42).

Furthermore, universal coverage is cheaper than exclusion and inequality in access for society as whole. Research carried out for the 2006 *Human Development Report* by the WHO suggests that the direct and indirect costs of keeping the current deficit of safe water provision in developing countries represents nine times the cost of providing universal coverage. The overall loss due to lack of water and sanitation is about $170 billion, or 2.6 percent of developing countries' GDP. For sub-Saharan Africa these figures are even more significant. Losses there represent 5 percent of GDP, a figure that exceeded total flows of aid and debt relief in 2003 (UNDP 2006: 42). The economic return in saved time, increased productivity and reduced health costs for each $1 invested in achieving the Millennium Development Goal target of merely halving the proportion of people without access to water and sanitation by 2015 is $8 (UNDP 2006: 58).

What kind of costs are we talking about? Not only are there direct costs like those generated by diseases connected to both shortage and poor quality of water, but also indirect costs such as poverty related to poor health. These costs arise from the avoidable exclusion allowed by the commodification of water and end up being shifted to other persons or the community as a whole, which is the second characteristic of a social cost, as recognized above.

The United Nations estimates that about 2.3 billion people suffer from diseases connected to water, both its shortage and poor quality (UN 1997: 39). In Africa, about three million people die annually as a result of water-related diseases (UNEP 2002). Almost half of Africa's population, for example, suffers from one of the six major water-related diseases. Every day, 650 people die from diarrhea, for example, mainly children under five years of age. As a matter of fact, many of these diseases, such as schistosomiasis or cholera, seem to have become an African specialty, with 82.8 percent and 78 percent, respectively, of world cases occurring in Africa. Malaria, for example, is the leading cause of disease in young children and represents 10 percent of the overall disease burden, contributing to slowing down economic growth of African countries by 1.3 percent per year (2003 IYFW 2008; WWF 2002). According to the WHO, the burden of water-related diseases, measured by conventional global health indicators, accounts for 60 million disability-adjusted life years lost each year, or 4 percent of the global total (Hutton and Haller 2004).

Children are the most affected by both direct and indirect costs. Medical costs directly related to poor health can be easily deduced from the figures above, but indirect costs, although harder to account and with longer-term effects, are as much a burden as these. Poor health reduces benefits from education, for example, by weakening cognitive potential and fostering absenteeism. Indeed, tests point to adverse effects on memory, problem-solving skills and attention spans (Kremer and Miguel 1999). Water-related diseases cost 443 million school days each year, which is equivalent to an entire school year for all seven-year-old children in Ethiopia (UNDP 2006: 45). Furthermore, children who suffer repeatedly from infectious diseases and diarrhea are likely to be shorter in adulthood. Research has shown a correlation between adult height and income (Strauss and Thomas 1998), strengthening the arguments that support the connection between poor health and lower income. Therefore, one may deduce that reduced earning power and poverty in adulthood are among the consequences of being excluded from access to safe water. Despite children being clearly the most affected, whole countries pay the cost of lower productivity and diminished human capital, as was thoughtfully stressed by the 2006 *Human Development Report* (UNDP 2006: 45).

This loss of opportunities, and subsequent diminished income perspectives, also raises redistribution issues, suggesting yet another form of social cost. In Africa, women and children spend eight or more hours per day collecting water; they travel 10–15 km, on average, carrying up to 15 liters per trip (Conteh 2006). As one can easily deduce, time spent collecting water strongly interferes with attending school, girls being particularly affected. In Tanzania, for instance, school attendance levels are 12 percent higher for girls in homes 15 minutes or less from a water source than in homes an hour or more away (Government of Tanzania 2002). If one considers the days of school and the opportunities lost by girls due to the time spent in water collection, the insufficient water coverage decisively contributes to poverty striking women in adult age.

In addition, girls, especially after puberty, are also more likely to drop out of school because of inadequate sanitation facilities. Indeed, because of concerns about security and privacy, girls are often withdrawn by their families from schools which do not offer adequate and separate toilets for girls. UNICEF estimates that about half of the girls in sub-Saharan Africa who drop out of school do so because of poor water and sanitation (UNICEF and IRC International Water and Sanitation Centre 2005). As a result of opportunities lost by women, the gender development index in Africa is 0.513, meaning that women on the continent benefit from 20 percent less well-being than men (UNDP 2006). Disparities in education related to water and sanitation induce other social costs. In adulthood, less-educated girls tend to have larger, unhealthier families and their children are less likely to receive an education than children of more educated mothers (UNDP 2006: 47), which can generate a negative process of cumulative causation.

Moreover, redistribution does not operate only through income losses. Indeed, poor people not only pay a high price for the safe water they do not get, but they also pay more than the rich for the little water they manage to get. It seems that, in developing countries, price is inversely related to ability to pay – the poorer you are, the more you pay (UNDP 2006: 51). The *Human Development Report* notes that households living in slums frequently pay 5–10 times more for water than wealthier households in the same developing-world cities (UNDP 2006: 10). In Manila, for example, about four million of its residents get water re-sold through kiosks, pushcart vendors or tanker deliveries, which in turn usually purchase in bulk from the water utility. Their average monthly water bills are $10–20, contrasting very sharply with the average of only $3–6 for households directly connected to the utility, which in addition consume five times more water (McIntosh 2003).

This discrimination is essentially due to the fact that many poor households do not have access to public distribution of water. Indeed, formal water providers operating municipal networks usually supply water at the cheapest price. Households directly connected to the network get access to that water through a tap at home. Poor households without a connection, on the contrary, have to pay higher prices because water passes through several intermediaries. There are two main reasons for poorer households to be excluded from a connection to the network. First, the prohibition of connecting people living in informal settlements in the absence of formal property rights and, second, the high capital costs (UNDP 2006: 52). However, no matter how high the capital cost of universal connection may be, it is still dramatically lower than the social cost of not providing it, as we have stated earlier. This apparent irrationality can be explained by the fact that capital costs are concentrated on one or few agents, whereas social costs are scattered among the population.

The social costs of water use

Until this stage we have mainly devoted our attention to those social costs generated by the exclusion outcome of commodified water. These social costs are, indeed, very significant and undoubtedly constitute our major concern. However, they are not the only ones. Indeed, if there are many individuals excluded from water consumption in developing countries, the truth is that a great majority of them has some access to water. Despite the fact that this access narrows the impact of the harmful effects of water exclusion, the occurrence of consumption does not eliminate the possibility of social costs. To a greater or lesser extent almost all water uses by human beings produce social costs in the form of environmental degradation, diminished availability of natural resources and reduced present and future water supplies, all leading to unsustainable ways of life and thus to a decline in human well-being. The main direct water consumption by human beings is for satisfying basic and luxury human needs, agricultural irrigation to produce food and raw materials and industrial purposes to produce commodities. Indirectly, natural ecosystems have water consumptive uses to produce biomass, later on used by humans for different purposes, and alongside natural ecosystems contribute to the water cycle, which plays a crucial role in water supply.

The social costs of water consumption in the industrial sector, most especially as far as pollution is concerned, have already been well documented in the literature (Tientenberg and Lewis 2008; Hussen 2000; Pearce and Turner 1990). William Kapp himself dedicated a chapter to this subject, entitled 'The social costs of water pollution' in his book *The Social Costs of Business Enterprise*. In it Kapp declares that contamination and pollution directly reduce the limited supply of clean water and are an integral part of the problem of conservation, management and development of water resources (Kapp 1978: 75).

Agriculture, most especially irrigated agriculture, interferes on many occasions with the use of water. Not only does it affect the quantity of water available, because it competes with other activities for the use of water, but it may also affect its quality. Agriculture, particularly intensive irrigated and non-irrigated agriculture, is an important source of pollution of water resources, principally of ground-water sources, rivers, lakes and dams. Agricultural pollution occurs when water containing chemicals leaches through the soil and off the soil into the different water supply sources. Because agricultural pollutants are diverse and the source of agricultural pollution is difficult to identify with accuracy and efficiency, such pollutants are called non-point pollutants (Tietenberg and Lewis 2008; Seitz *et al.* 1994). The main difference between social costs generated by industrial and agricultural consumption of water concerns the fact that the source of social costs in pollution by industry can easily be identified, whereas with non-point pollutants in agriculture, additional effort and thus costs are necessary to measure them and identify their source.

Although human consumption does not use water as an intermediate good to produce other goods, human consumption, particularly for hygiene and sanitation purposes, is a major source of water pollution and therefore of social costs. These social costs are worth mentioning considering the steadily increasing demand of water for human consumption in the developing world. Pollution, and ultimately exhaustion, of freshwater resources also result from an improper treatment of sewage in most urban and industrial areas of this part of the world. Moreover, the 2006 *Human Development Report* alerts us to the fact that in the developing world tackling the problem of water supply has to be made in parallel with solutions for human and industrial sewage (UNDP 2006).

Harmful effects of water use encompassing social costs can also be detected in many other domains of economic and social life. When agricultural systems and irrigation techniques are inappropriate, for example, water used in irrigated agriculture leads to water logging and soil salinity (Small and Carruthers 1991). As reported by Kapp, most especially in canal irrigation in Asia (1969), this problem generates lower yields and higher land preparation costs, which can ultimately lead to abandoning land and to seriously threatening human well-being. A similar problem of salinization can occur in irrigation agriculture, mainly in arid zones, when soils attached to irrigation systems have improper drainage capacity, leading to the accumulation of soluble salts.

Furthermore, in surface-water irrigation systems, the risk of human infection by water-related diseases increases substantially, mainly by malaria and schistosomiasis, generating significant social costs both for the individuals benefiting from the irrigation scheme and for others living in the vicinity. The above arguments led Small and Carruthers (1991) to consider drainage and health protection as merit goods – goods which should be promoted by government to a level higher than what markets or individuals probably would, since consumers may not fully appreciate or realize their potential benefits.

As far as irrigation from ground-water sources is concerned, social costs may arise when the rate of water consumption from the well exceeds the natural recharge rate. In this situation water reserves are depleted and the water table falls, causing wells to run dry, requiring deeper wells to be sunk in order to reach water (Upton 1996). In this case the excessive consumption of some clearly shifts costs to third persons. The costs of depletion of water reserves due to the additional costs required by the necessity of sinking deeper wells and pumping deeper water are non-negligible social costs incurred by current and future generations. In addition, if farmers are excluded from sinking deeper wells due to insufficient means, unequal water distribution may occur, resulting in the end in income redistribution and, thus, in further social costs.

Additional redistribution effects arise in irrigated agriculture. In irrigation systems where water rights are allocated according to land rights and where the size of landholdings is very unequal, the benefits of irrigation water will also be unequally distributed. The largest holdings would, therefore, grab a larger share of water, thus increasing the income gap between poor (small) and rich (large) farmers. Through this process rich farmers are able to appropriate a larger share of the agricultural product than they would otherwise be able to do, so leading to the production of a social cost in the shape of a redistribution effect.

The social costs of water privatization

Despite the fact that many of these social costs are generated regardless of water being publicly or privately distributed, as we have already pointed out, in the developing countries they usually rise with privatization. In this section we will examine social costs specifically produced by privatization from two points of view. First, privatization exacerbates exclusion from access to water and, second, privatization is responsible for different forms of inefficiency that clearly represent shifting costs to third persons and reducing human well-being.

Since the 1980s privatization has been considered the panacea for all that was wrong with the economies in many developing countries. The most important factors behind this surge were the conditionalities attached to IMF, IFC and World Bank loans and debt-relief programs. Privatization was also a central component of donor-funded aid programs financed by development agencies of the developed countries. Water privatization in Africa, for example, took different forms: fee contract on a fee for service basis; management contract; lease agreement; concession; build–operate–transfer agreement; and divestiture. The first three forms of privatization are short-term and do not involve responsibility for capital investment (Conteh 2006). French multinational companies have dominated this process (Bayliss and Hall 2000).

The arguments in favor of water privatization were: to enhance operational efficiency, economic growth and development of the water sector; the inability of public utilities to raise capital investment; and to provide fiscal benefits. There is little practical evidence that privatization does in fact result in increased efficiency, economic growth and development; private firms are interested in profit not in social objectives; and the end-users are unable to pay the tariffs required by private companies. Indeed, if in Senegal, for example, privatization outcomes can be described as mixed, meaning that household connections to water services have consistently risen, although many of the poorer households remain unconnected because of costs (Conteh 2006: 36), in South Africa privatization has proven to be a poor alternative to public distribution. In Bhofolo, for example, a black township in the Eastern Cape province, water prices increased by 300 percent for township residents in 1995, and in 1996 increased again by 100 percent (Conteh 2006: 37). These high tariffs, and also connection fees, meant that many households could not afford water, being either disconnected from water services or unable to get connected to the water supply system (Conteh 2006: 38). The same global phenomenon occurred in many other townships such as Mlungusi and Nelspruit.

In Manila, in the Philippines, Maynilad Water Services, a private company controlled by the multinational corporation Suez-Ondeo, which held Manila's west zone concession, raised tariffs by as much as 400 percent between 1997 and 2003. Manila Water Company, owned by the Ayala Corporation, the east zone concessionaire, in turn raised water tariffs by 700 percent in the same period (Netto 2005). Considering the purchasing power of the average citizen of the Philippines and the fact that for the same period prices in general rose 36.9 percent in the country (WDID 2008), it should not be difficult to predict that the privatization of water distribution resulted in a considerable part of Manila's population being excluded from access to water. As a matter of fact, unlike Manila Water, Maynilad was since returned to public management by Manila's Metropolitan Water and Sewerage System as a result of public protest motivated by unmet concession agreement targets in terms of coverage, pricing, service obligations, non-revenue water and water quality (Montemayor 2005).

In some of the poorer neighborhoods of La Paz, Bolivia, the same multinational company Suez-Lyonnaise des Eaux (Lyonnaise des Eaux and Ondéo are both subsidiary firms of Suez Environnement), through its local subsidiary, Aguas del Illimani, raised water tariffs by 600 percent in 2004, whereas the inflation rate was 4.5 percent (WDID 2008), and the objective of connecting 15,000 households to the water distribution system was cut down to zero (Chavez 2005: 11). As a result of the pressure exerted by more than 600 district associations, the government eventually revoked the concession contract with Aguas del Illimani (Chavez 2005: 11) just as happened with the American-based Bechtel in April 2000 in Cochabamba following dramatic water tariff increases and expropriation of community water systems (Gómez and Terhorst 2005).

Private companies supplying water in developed countries have inherited a heavy infrastructure paid for by past public investments, supplying universal coverage to an average high-income market. In developing countries, on the other hand, limited and frequently damaged infrastructure, low levels of connection and high levels of poverty increase the tensions between business profitability and the supply of water at a fair price to all. In Buenos Aires, Argentina, for example, the water concession holder managed to expand the connections to the supply system, but at a slower pace than agreed in the concession contract because progress was slower in the poorer areas of the city. In Jakarta, Indonesia three-quarters of the new connections concerned medium- and high-income households or private and public institutions (UNDP 2006: 93). As a matter of fact, according to Pedro Arrojo (2006), multinational companies, which got hold of the majority of the privatized concessions in the world, may be interested in water distribution management but not in infrastructural investment.

Lets us now examine the social costs of privatization from the point of view of inefficiency. The privatization of water supply presupposes the creation of a market for water in which price is the main mechanism for regulating supply and demand and profit the main factor in attracting companies to enter and remain in the market. Privatization of water supply gives rise to several types of social costs because competitive markets are inappropriate to fully account for the many dimensions that have to be considered in the supply and demand of a good so singular as water.

Let us illustrate this inappropriateness by describing the effects of private and social water pricing on a simplified competitive market model that excludes market structure and fixed costs. Considering only private costs (S_p) and benefits (D_p), private market price and quantity are set respectively at P_p and Q_p, as shown in Figure 9.1. On the supply side, harmful effects of water provision can be detected through the external costs resulting from pollution by human, industrial and agricultural use and from over-exploitation of water, especially non-renewable ground-water sources. If all these costs were to be accounted, the private supply curve S_p would shift upwards to S_s and a new equilibrium would be found at P_{S1} and Q_{S1}. The differences between the private price P_p and the

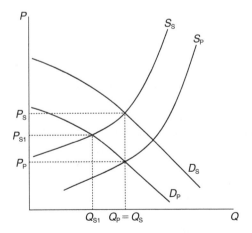

Figure 9.1 Private and social water pricing.

price P_{S1} and the private quantity Q_P and the quantity Q_{S1} represent the social costs generated by the inability of the market to account for all costs concerning water. If all costs were considered, water prices would be higher and quantities consumed lower. In other words, ignoring the negative externalities of water consumption leads to low prices and excessive consumption.

The price of water obtained in a competitive market not only does not account for all costs but it is also based on the direct use value of water, leaving out indirect and non-use values, such as the important ecological, option and bequest values. The ecological value concerns the important supporting and regulating services water provides in natural and semi-natural ecosystems which are essential for human survival, while option and bequest values regard the insurance to provide the resource for possible future use by present or next generations, respectively. If these values were to be taken into account, the private demand curve should shift toward D_P. The disregard for total economic water value by competitive markets implies a private demand curve (D_P) below the social demand curve (D_S), causing the private price for water to stand clearly below the social price for water.

If putative market equilibrium were to consider simultaneously both society's demand (D_S) and supply (S_S), a higher price for water should then be charged. The social price should, therefore, be set at P_S, while changes in the quantities consumed and supplied would depend on the relative shifts of social demand and supply. Assuming that the magnitude of the relative changes in society's demand (D_S) and supply (S_S) is equivalent, this would lead users to consume a quantity Q_S, equal to Q_P. In this special case, social costs are represented only by the difference between prices P_S and P_P. If the magnitude of external costs (S_S) is higher than the magnitude of indirect and non-use water values (D_S), social costs are also represented by a reduction in the quantity consumed. However, if the magnitude of external costs is lower than the magnitude of indirect and non-use water values, the price rise is compensated by an increase in the quantities consumed. The gap between private and social prices and quantities represents the social cost generated by a private water market, these costs being shifted to society at large and to future generations.

Additionally, if the price of water does not reflect society's total costs and benefits, high-income individuals may be driven to consume socially unacceptable levels of water, giving rise to over-consumption and, therefore, to social costs. These over-consumption social costs arise when excessive consumption from some individuals implies not only the possibility of resource depletion in the long run, but also less water available for the consumption of others in the immediate term. Over-consumption social costs are higher in those regions in which scarcity is an important issue, whereas social costs of deprivation are most significant whenever access to water represents a significant proportion of personal income, or in those regions in which cheap alternative water sources to market supply are unavailable.

As far as water for irrigation is concerned, Frank Ellis (1992) and Martin Upton (1996) state that, from an economic point of view, water for irrigation represents a classic example of market failure demanding state or community involvement because of, on the one hand, the inability and difficulty to define private ownership on rights to water as a resource and, on the other hand, the production of negative externalities caused by farmers' individual behaviors. Furthermore, some goods and services necessary to supply irrigation water clearly have a public nature, such as dams and canals, and therefore there is a risk of under-provision and thereby of a shortfall in terms of human well-being.

In most rural communities, rights to water, and in particular rights to water for irrigation, have a customary nature and cultural and religious significance. Furthermore, they are connected with land property rights, the essence of water as a common-pool good thus being reinforced. As demonstrated below, the best solution for the allocation of available supplies of a common-pool good among individuals, communities and activities, that affects both efficiency of production and equity of social justice, cannot rely upon the free market (Upton 1996).

The allocation of water between alternative uses if made by the market has important social costs. Water can be used by people for different purposes, from human consumption to production activities such as transportation, industry, agriculture and fishing, as well as cultural, recreational, leisure, conservation and environmental activities. Taking into consideration the diversity of uses and the indispensability of water to satisfy basic human needs, the question is how to rank the different types of water demand in a scarce environment.

Given its crucial role to human survival, it is perfectly admissible that society sets up priorities. In this context, when water supplies are not enough to satisfy all uses, it seems quite consensual that priority should be given to direct human consumption over other uses such as leisure. As a matter of fact, this priority should be kept even when the alternative use is land irrigation, despite the fact that in many parts of the planet, mainly in developing countries, the lack of access to irrigation water can lead to the production of social costs resulting from insufficient food.

Now, supporting water allocation between alternative uses on laws of economic efficiency can produce inefficient social allocation, especially when the arbitrage is between human consumption and agricultural or industrial uses. A competitive market allocates water between different alternative uses in accordance with the laws of private economic efficiency. These so-called laws only consider the direct use value of human consumption and the exchange value of goods produced when water is used as an input, and exclude the social use value of water. As Kapp (1974) states, social use value is the value which is socially – i.e., politically – appraised and determined. Therefore, market mediation can generate the same social costs that were seen earlier in the section on water exclusion, because private economic efficiency is substantially different from social economic efficiency.

In the same line of reasoning, by ignoring or excluding natural ecosystems from accessing minimum ecological flows, for instance – which are crucial to produce public goods such as nutrient cycling, waste assimilation and primary production – market mediation imposes a social cost in the shape of a loss in the flow of goods and services produced by nature. Furthermore, religious, ritual and symbolic values assigned by peoples and communities to water negatively interfere with their willingness to pay for it. In this instance, by pricing water while ignoring these values, the market generates important social costs for those people and communities for whom water is much more than a commodity.

The inappropriateness of the market to manage common-pool goods such as water generates yet another form of social cost. Water being an exhaustible resource over a given period of time, its use can only be renewable if the extraction rate is lower than, or equal to, the recharge rate. However, no market mechanism can prevent the total amount of individual consumption resulting from the maximization of individual utility or profit from exceeding the recharge rate. In such circumstances it is difficult to conciliate individual and social interests, since unsustainable water consumption leads to social costs and sustainability implies extraction rates to be lower, or at least not higher, than recharge rates. Using game theory, for example, namely the prisoner's dilemma, in order to optimize water management, one concludes that the best outcome for each individual user is to act selfishly while the other user acts cooperatively, and the worst outcome is to act cooperatively while the other user acts selfishly. On the other hand, the best outcome for society and resource conservation, which produces less social costs, is reached when there is cooperation among the several users of the resource. This cooperation is only possible in the presence of a strong public or community engagement. This outcome, if used in the arbitrage between the different alternative uses or in the allocation between users, may maximize social welfare, but demands for a mediation that is beyond the competitive market mechanism.

Finally, for technological reasons, water supply is considered a natural monopoly in the sense that if competition is allowed between companies in order to get hold of a concession, the consumer cannot choose his or her supplier as he or she can, for instance, with cable TV. If one is dissatisfied with one's cable TV supplier, one can change. On the contrary, one cannot change on an individual basis one's water supplier. As a classical market failure, monopoly produces harmful effects very similar to social costs. Indeed, under monopoly firms have the ability to determine the terms on which individuals shall have access to a good or service, which means that they can sell it at higher prices than would result from perfect competition. In this process firms do not really shift costs to third persons, but end up obtaining abnormal profits at the expense of their customers and, therefore, grab a larger share of global income than they would otherwise, exactly like in a typical social cost situation.

The issues raised above clearly show that for mainstream market theories and practices, the variables accounted, such as prices, cost, benefits and profits, are based on direct exchange value. This value is clearly insufficient to accommodate all the non-saleable characteristics that water has, such as to be a natural element essential to human life, as well as to the vast majority of other living species, or, in Kapp's words, the social use value of water. Furthermore, mainstream market theories and practices and their traditional economic indicators are unable to measure and explain all the economic and social changes, and above all, fail to satisfy basic human needs and requirements (see Kapp 1974).

Conclusion

In this chapter we believe to have revealed the major social costs that are generated today by the activity of collecting and distributing water in developing countries. Although to a greater or lesser extent almost all water uses by human beings produce harmful effects that affect human well-being, the most important issue concerns the social costs generated by the exclusion from access to water. Despite the fact that social costs emerge regardless of water being privately or publicly collected and distributed, we also believe that this chapter has shown that privatization of the water sector exacerbates these same social costs. At the origin of this production of social costs lies the commodification of water – in other words, the process through which water is transformed into a good that is bought and sold. From this conclusion it follows that reducing or avoiding social costs and, thereby, improving human well-being, can only be achieved by decommodifying water.

Decommodifying water implies first of all recognizing the fundamentally public character of water collection and distribution. However, if public intervention is a necessary condition to decommodify water, it is not sufficient. Indeed, many examples have been given in this chapter of a public production of social costs. Decommodifying water involves much more than just simply changing the nature of its provider; it implies changing the very nature of water as a good. That is precisely what lies behind the claim for the recognition of the human right to water. As a human right, water, or any other good needed to exercise rights, must not be treated as a commodity, even if in any other occasion it can be (see Branco and Henriques 2010; Branco 2009). In this sense decommodifying water falls within a human rights approach to development, according to which human rights are simultaneously the means and the ends of development.

This does not mean that some market mechanisms, such as prices and, therefore, private actors should forcibly be excluded from this process. Indeed, because in reducing the social costs of water collection and distribution the decisive element concerns changing the nature of water as a good and not forcibly the nature of its provider, some sort of private activity, although inevitably strictly regulated, could be accepted. By stating in its General Comment on the human right to water that people should have the means to access water, the United Nations Committee on Economic, Social and Cultural Rights has clearly stressed that the key issue here is not so much the identity of the provider as the entitlement of the consumer, and agreed to the fact that it is acceptable for water to have a price (UN 2002: 6). A price system can, therefore, be used to avoid the social costs generated by both over-consumption and exclusion, within a human-right-to-water frame. In South Africa, for example, the government used its regulatory powers to require all municipalities to provide a basic minimum of 25 liters free of charge to each household and established stepped tariffs to provide a cross-subsidy from high-volume users to low-volume users (UNDP 2006: 64).

However, using a price mechanism in such a fashion implies valuing water in a way that reflects collective purposes rather than putative market equilibriums. In this sense, communities and society are the only entities fully enabled to account for all of water's values and to gradually incorporate them in decision-making processes concerning water collection and allocation. In order to overcome the conflicts that emerge when common-pool resources are shared, for instance, society can promote the participation of the engaged users in the decision-making process about resource allocation. With respect to user participation and resource valuation, group valuation proposed by social and political theory has gained increasing attention recently. This valuation method is based on the principles of deliberative democracy and assumes that public decision-making should result from an open public debate rather than from the aggregation of separately measured individual preferences (see De Groot 2006).

As a matter of fact, participation is one of the key concepts for reducing social costs in the water sector. Comparative studies show that it is not so much the divide between public and private that matters in achieving social and environmental efficiency in collecting and distributing water, but the divide between accountable and unaccountable systems (UNDP 2006). Consequently, the 2006 *Human Development Report* stresses the need to create governance systems that make governments and other water providers accountable for achieving the goals set under national policies (UNDP 2006: 97). This seems to be in contrast with William Kapp and the old institutionalists, for whom social costs are first of all the result of private enterprise. It may be useful to remember that *The Social Costs of Private Enterprise* was the first title of Kapp's *The Social Costs of Business Enterprise*. But in the same way that Kapp altered his title, we believe that it is the business rather than the private character of the enterprise that raises the accountability issue. There are many institutions besides the state that could probably meet the accountability demand, but not the purely free market. Indeed, if the state, for example, is both elected and known, the market, on the contrary, is by definition independent and anonymous, and therefore unaccountable to the community.

References

2003 IYFW (2008) *A Look at Water Resources in Africa*. Available at: www.wateryear2003.org (accessed 10 March 2009).

Arrojo, P. (2006) *El Reto Ético da la Nueva Cultura del Água: Funciones, Valores y Derechos en Juego*, Barcelona: Ediciones Paidós.

Bayliss, K. and Hall, D. (2000) 'Privatisation of water and energy in Africa', PSIRU, University of Greenwich, London.

Bontems, P. and Rotillon, G. (1998) *Économie de l'environnement*, Paris: Editions La Découverte.

Branco, M. (2009) *Economics versus Human Rights*, London: Routledge.

Branco, M. and Henriques, P. (2010) 'The political economy of the human right to water', *Review of Radical Political Economics*, 42(2): 142–155.

Chavez, W. (2005) 'Effervescence Populaire en Bolivie', *Le Monde Diplomatique*, March.

Coase, R.H. (1960) 'The problem of social cost', *Journal of Law and Economics* 3: 1–44.

Conteh, S. (2006) 'Inhibiting 'progressive realization'? The effect of privatization on the right to water in Senegal and South Africa', LLM Dissertation, Faculty of Law, Centre for Human Rights, University of Pretoria.

De Groot, R.S. (2006) 'Function analysis and valuation as a tool to assess land use conflicts in planning for sustainable, multi-functional landscapes', *Landscape and Urban Planning*, 75: 175–186.

Ellis, F. (1992) *Agricultural Policies in Developing Countries*, Cambridge: Cambridge University Press.

Gómez, L.S. and Terhorst, P. (2005) 'Cochambamba, Bolivia: public–collective partnership after the water war', in Balanyá, B., Brennan, B., Hoedeman, O., Kishimoto, S. and Terhorst, P. (eds.), *Reclaiming Public Water Achievements, Struggles and Visions from Around the World*, Amsterdam: TNI/CEO.

Government of Tanzania (2002) *Poverty and Human Development Report*, Dar es Salaam: Poverty Monitoring Service.

Hardin, G. (1968) 'The tragedy of the commons', *Science* 162: 1243–1248.

Hussen, A. (2000) *Principles of Environmental Economics*, London: Routledge.

Hutton, G. and Haller, L. (2004) 'Evaluation of the costs and benefits of water and sanitation improvements at the global level', World Health Organization.

Kapp, K.W. (1969) 'On the nature and significance of social costs', *Kyklos* 22(2): 334–347.

Kapp, K.W. (1974) 'Environmental indicators as indicators of social use value, in environmental policies and development planning', in *Contemporary China and Other Essays*, Paris/The Hague: Mouton.

Kapp, K.W. (1978) *The Social Costs of Business Enterprise*, Nottingham: Spokesman.

Kapp, K.W. (ed.) (1983) *Social Costs, Economic Development and Environmental Disruption*, Lanham: Rowman & Littlefield Publishers.

Kremer, M. and Miguel, T. (1999) 'The educational impact of de-worming in Kenya', Northeast Universities Development Conference, 8–9 October, Harvard University.

McIntosh, A.C. (2003) 'Asian water supplies. reaching the urban poor', Asian Development Bank and International Water Association, Manila.

Montemayor, C.A. (2005) 'Possibilities for public water in Manila', in Balanyá, B., Brennan, B., Hoedeman, O., Kishimoto, S. and Terhorst, P. (eds.), *Reclaiming Public Water: Achievements, Struggles and Visions from Around the World*, Amsterdam: TNI/CEO.

Netto, A. (2005) 'Private sector still running after water rights', *Asia Times Online*, 26 March, available at: www.atimes.com/atimes/Asian_Economy/GC26Dk01.html (accessed 11 March 2008).

Pearce, D. and Turner, K. (1990) *Economics of Natural Resources and the Environment*, Baltimore: Johns Hopkins University Press.

Pigou, A.C. (1932) *The Economics of Welfare*, 4th edition, London: Macmillan. Available at: www.econlib.org/library/NPDBooks/Pigou/pgEWCover.html (accessed 5 July 2011).

Seitz, W.D., Nelson, G. and Halcrow, H. (1994) *Economics of Resources, Agriculture and Food*, New York: McGraw-Hill.

Small, L.E. and Carruthers, I. (1991) *Farmer-financed Irrigation: The Economics of Reform*, Cambridge: Cambridge University Press.

Smith, A. (1776) *An Inquiry into the Nature and Causes of the Wealth of Nations.* Available at: http://socserv2.socsci.mcmaster.ca/~econ/ugcm/3113/smith/wealth/wealbk01 (accessed 12 April 2008).

Strauss, J. and Thomas, D. (1998) 'Health, nutrition, and economic development', *Journal of Economic Literature*, 36(2): 766–817.

Tietenberg, T. and Lewis, L. (2008) *Environmental & Natural Resource Economics*, 8th edition, Upper Saddle River: Prentice Hall.

UN (1997) *Comprehensive Assessment of the Freshwater Resources of the World*, New York: Commission on Sustainable Development.

UN (2002) 'Substantive issues arising in the implementation of the International Covenant on Economic, Social and Cultural Rights: general comment No. 15', Committee on Economic, Social and Cultural Rights, 19–29 November. Available at: www.unhchr.ch/html/menu2/6/gc15.doc (accessed 5 May 2008).

UNDP (2006) *Human Development Report: Beyond Scarcity – Power, Poverty and the Global Water Crisis.* Available at: http://hdr.undp.org/hdr2006/pdfs (accessed 9 May 2011).

UNEP (2002) 'The state of the environment and policy retrospective: 1972–2002', in *Global Environmental Outlook.* Available at: www.unep.org. (accessed 10 March 2009).

UNICEF (United Nations Children's Fund) and IRC International Water and Sanitation Centre (2005) 'Water, sanitation and hygiene education for schools: roundtable proceedings and framework for action', Roundtable Meeting, 24–26 January, Oxford.

Upton, M. (1996) *The Economics of Tropical Farming Systems*, Cambridge: Cambridge University Press.

WDID (2008) *World Development Indicators Database: Facts and Statistics.* Available at: www.nationmaster.com. (accessed 8 February 2009).

WHO (2000) *The Global Water Supply and Sanitation Assessment 2000*, Geneva: WHO.

WWF (2002) *The Facts on Water in Africa.* Available at: www.panda.org/livingwaters (accessed 8 February 2009).

10 The social costs of private elderly care

*Remi Maier-Rigaud, Michael Sauer and
Frank Schulz-Nieswandt*[1]

The process of civilization is characterized by an increasing collectivization of various risks (Swaan 1988). The rise of welfare states covering many life-threatening risks to humankind has been the most visible outcome of this evolution. In Germany the introduction of the social long-term care insurance in 1995/1996 was the last major milestone of the Bismarckian welfare state, covering the risk of elderly care within the framework of social insurance. Beyond this long-term trend of risk-collectivization, a short-term trend of risk-privatization has evolved in parallel since the 1980s, putting welfare states under pressure.[2] Both trends have influenced the way the care risk has been addressed in institutional terms in Germany. Given this more recent second trend, as well as the reform pressures stemming from demographic ageing combined with severe economic difficulties, it is obvious that private sector actors have become a relevant player in the respective welfare mix in the policy field of elderly care. The contemporary financial and economic crisis poses an important challenge to welfare states, which have to find practical solutions to the most pressing problems in an environment of public budget retrenchment. Obviously the recent economic downturn has negatively influenced labor markets, which are key determinants for financing public social insurance via compulsory contributions from wages. In terms of decreased employment and wage growth rates, the financial base of social insurances is weakened, thus leading to further reform pressure within the system. Although welfare spending – in particular, unemployment benefits – performs the important macroeconomic function of an automatic stabilizer in phases of economic downturn, it is important to free additional resources by means of reducing social costs and thereby enabling social spending that is even more needed in times of crisis. Against this background, and through Kapp's theory of social costs, the policy field of elderly care is examined for the empirical case of Germany. The proposal of increased coordination to improve the quality of out-patient elderly care indicates an avenue for public policy that makes better use of various existing resources (e.g., family, third sector).

The chapter proceeds as following: The first section explains Kapp's social cost concept. It emphasizes that cost-shifting takes a variety of forms and is an inherent feature of market economies. Still, the definition of social costs depends necessarily on political and institutional choices. The second section explores a specific type of costs, namely the social costs associated with insufficient integration of actors in a policy field. Based on Kapp's normative concept of basic human needs and social choice as political avenues for limiting social costs, a social policy intervention that would reduce social costs by meritorization of the coordination effort within a sector is put forth. The third section applies the theoretical framework to out-patient elderly care in Germany with the aim of analyzing privatization trends and associated social costs in this sector. Based on the understanding of private actors' roles in the institutional setting of care policies in Germany and against the background of major challenges and reform necessities in the policy field, the empirical analysis elaborates disadvantageous effects resulting from private care providers' decision-making, concentrating on the lack of cooperation and integration among service providers. Based on these findings, conclusions are drawn suggesting a governance configuration of private–public elderly care that would foster cooperation between private actors in the framework of a meritorization of the coordination between care stakeholders. It supports the idea of local authorities performing the role of a moderator and developing as a hub for varying interests of care stakeholders.

Kapp's conceptualization of social costs and cost-shifting

Social costs

Kapp defines social costs as covering 'all direct and indirect losses suffered by third persons or the general public as a result of private economic activities' (Kapp 1971: 13). His broad concept of social costs engulfs a variety of losses. First, it includes deteriorating effects on human health and the natural environment, but includes also less tangible effects, such as economic activities that adversely affect esthetic values of third parties. Second, it covers everything from losses felt by a single person to losses for society. Third, these costs can be direct and immediately felt, or they can be creeping, long-term effects, only felt slowly. A typical example of creeping social costs are environmental damages that become visible only after sustained cumulative activities of private enterprises.[3] Kapp provides an open concept based on the ubiquity of the various forms of social costs going beyond a defined set of cost types. This 'substantial methodological umbrella' (Swaney and Evers 1989: 10) enables the analysis of social costs, defined as all costs that remain unaccounted for under given institutional settings (including the economic and socio-political system). Hence, social costs are located where a divergence between private or public costs, on the one hand, and actual total costs, on the other, are observed (Kapp 1969: 337). The fact that social costs are strongly dependent upon the given institutional setting underlines the importance of taking a critical institutionalist perspective. To this end, Kapp conceived 'social opportunity costs' (Kapp 1969: 338; 1971: 14). If the inefficiencies associated with social costs in a given institutional setting were remedied, then resources would be freed for alternative ends, which Kapp describes as social opportunity costs or social costs of missed opportunities (Kapp 1971: 14; 1956: 524).

Cost-shifting

A core element of the social costs concept is cost-shifting, which transforms private or public costs into social costs.[4] This is because the harmful consequences of private enterprise are social costs only in so far as 'private entrepreneurs are not easily held accountable' (Kapp 1971: 14) for these damages. The competitive environment of a market economy gives rise to incentives for private enterprises to shift costs to third parties or society. Thus, social costs are not exogenous to the economic system, but 'predictable, endogenous outcomes' (Swaney and Evers 1989: 12). Hence, private enterprises are pressured by systemic forces to engage in cost-shifting in order to secure their survival. The market economy therefore coordinates individual decisions inefficiently, because it fails to account for social costs in their price system (Kapp 1970: 843–844; 1969: 334).[5] Still, the problem of cost-shifting is not simply about incorporating certain cost categories into the system of relative market prices. An important element leading to cost-shifting, and transcending the neoclassical approach, is the unequal power between economic units that allows for this type of behavior. More generally, cost-shifting results from market and non-market interdependencies between units exhibiting unequal power (Kapp 1969: 335). A particular type of social costs that Kapp developed in view of his analysis of the transportation sector is the social costs resulting from 'insufficient integration'. This means that a lack of coordination allows actors or actor groups to shift costs to third parties. Thus, insufficient integration as used in the subsequent sections is to be understood as leaving room for abuse of their position in terms of cost-shifting.

Social and political definition of social costs

Social costs, much more than externalities, defined as inter-personal interdependencies of utility functions in the theoretical framework of Paretian economics, are results of political processes. But there is a deeper grammar of social construction. What is a private risk? What are risks of public interest? What about the distribution of private and public responsibilities relating to social risks? There are binary cultural codes constructing a deeper grammar of privatization and public relevance of social risks in the lifespan. The cultural codes are influenced by social change in historical time. Therefore, there are political debates and social struggles concerning the definitional power generating the hegemony in such discourses (Mühlenkamp and Schulz-Nieswandt 2008).

The relative importance of different social costs is to be determined by society through democratic processes subject to political and social discourses. This forms the institutionalist core of Kapp's theory of social costs (Heidenreich 1998). Social costs are subject to 'social evaluation and social value' (Kapp

1971: 256). This requires opening up the narrow focus of economics for insights from philosophy, political science and further social sciences[6] in order to 'pass even beyond the abstractions and formal solutions of modern welfare economics' (Kapp 1971: 261). Beyond merely identifying social costs, democratic society has a legitimate interest in finding remedies so that private enterprises account for social costs in their decision-making. The political history of the nineteenth and twentieth centuries has seen a growth in democratic governance, which resulted in a struggle of the masses in order to reduce the cost-shifting (Kapp 1971: 16–17). Hence, the level of cost-shifting present in society reflects the level of undemocratic governance structures.

For public preferences to translate into social choice and ultimately public policies that remedy social costs, Kapp emphasized the importance of public-opinion polls and similar enquiry tools.[7] At first, this seems a rather technocratic exercise, but Kapp (1971: 259–261) opposed simplistic total welfare concepts because he was realistic about democratic processes being influenced by power struggles of pressure groups and, above all, conflicts between individual and social preferences. Kapp identifies that pressure groups and vested interests 'distort and abuse the legitimate struggle for a more equal distribution of social costs to the detriment of society' (Kapp 1971: 17). Therefore, it becomes clear that cost-shifting and the concept of social costs are not merely economic concepts, but concepts of broad political economy. They lead to the problem of social choice and social economy, which require a comprehensive political approach to economic science.

The social costs of insufficient integration

Coordination failures

In *The Social Costs of Private Enterprise* Kapp analyzed several sectors of the economy where significant social costs arise as a systemic product of economic activity. The mixed public–private transportation sector (Kapp 1971: 197–206) exhibits many peculiarities, in particular its social character, where the value of each road depends on further roads (and other transportation means) connected to it, but also on many other factors.[8] With respect to the transportation sector in the United States, Kapp described how land, water and air transportation all work separately from each other, with different public authorities being responsible for transportation policies. Kapp identified a lack of overall coordination at the national and international level:

> It is easy to see that this need for an integrated transport system is not confined to the national plan; there exists at the same time a genuine need for an international integration and coordination of such national transport facilities as railroads, canals, shipping and, most important of all, airports and planes.
>
> (Kapp 1971: 199)

The efficiency of the transportation sector depends essentially on the coordination of its parts. If coordination is missing, efforts and infrastructure are duplicated, causing substantial social costs, i.e., shifting costs on the consumers and third parties in general. The social costs of 'insufficient integration' (Kapp 1971: 201) are pervasive in the case of transportation, as described by Kapp:

> The most noticeable evidence of diseconomies resulting from the absence of an over-all plan in the promotion of transport facilities and from their insufficient integration is to be found in the existence of costly and unnecessary competition between different transport agencies and, concomitantly, the great duplication of transport facilities.
>
> (Kapp 1971: 201)

Kapp concludes that coordination between the plans created for the distinct areas of different transportation means would be required.

Remarkably, Kapp perceives common ownership or a 'nationalization of the transport industry' as the ultimate solution for the sector (Kapp 1971: 206). This conclusion is not shared. To the contrary, welfare-enhancing effects of competition are also feasible in the transportation sector. However, it is important to identify in a breakdown of the sector and its entities the areas where competition or alternative steering mechanisms are warranted. Even if business enterprise and market competition are the institutional arrangements at the very origin of social costs, it should be noted that the focus here is on social costs of insufficient integration. This category of social costs is more nuanced vis-à-vis the merits of the market mechanism. 'Insufficient integration' is diagnosed when a sector lacks public policy, which may well include an improved steering of private competition. It stands far from an overall rejection of the principles of market economies one might think a social costs perspective warrants. Therefore, reference to Kapp's study of the transportation sector is made solely in order to identify similar problem structures in other sectors without prejudice to his regulatory conclusions which appear to be unbalanced nowadays.

The transportation sector provides a good illustration of the costs associated with insufficient integration. The example of this sector is of general interest, because insufficient integration and cooperation between different actors within one sector is the outcome of a social dilemma structure, relevant to several sectors including out-patient care for the elderly. The findings could equally be applied to other sectors of the welfare state, e.g., to health or child care or in general to all social services characterized by a public–private actor constellation.[9] For instance, in the prisoner's dilemma, individual rationality warrants a dominant strategy that keeps the actors locked into Pareto-inferior outcomes. From an evolutionary perspective, this social dilemma can be solved through agents that learn the advantages of cooperation as described in Axelrod's seminal *The Evolution of Co-operation* (1984). However, Elsner (2001: 69–71) has observed that the more individualistic the assumed culture, the more time-consuming and unstable the process of cooperation learning becomes. Hence, coordination failures and insufficient integration can lead to repeated social costs with no self-regulated solutions available in the short and medium term. As will be analyzed in greater detail below, out-patient care for the elderly in Germany is a sector in which insufficient integration is apparent but difficult to overcome. One of the main reasons is that the actors requiring coordination have various professional and non-professional backgrounds and operate according to the different logics guiding private, public, third sector and family care arrangements.

Merit wants and social choices: strengthening cooperative capacities

In order to sustain and accelerate cooperation in a sector, Elsner (2001: 69–71; 2005: 38–40) suggests a public policy intervention, based on social decision-making and leading to a meritorization[10] of the good in question. In order to reach these social choices and policies, Kapp would probably suggest refining traditional democratic processes with public-opinion polls. This could be an option, but the idea of meritorization suggests an alternative approach. The delegation of choices concerning a policy field, where fine-grained steering requires a high level of expertise and knowledge, could be a rational and efficient policy choice of individuals in a representative democracy (Mackscheidt 1984: 588). It would disburden the individual, freeing some of his capacities for other activities or more fundamental policy choices, which he would prefer to decide more directly. The public policy intervention would be aiming to change the interactive process between agents in order to provide a superior quantity or quality of the merit good (Elsner 2001: 71).[11]

To this end, the public policy intervention requires specification. First, the 'specific characteristics of the goods he wants the private agents to produce by means of coordination and cooperation' (Elsner 2001: 75) have to be identified. Second, such behavior has to be promoted by instruments changing the incentive structure and/or instruments increasing the frequency of interaction between private actors, because increasing the probability of meeting again fosters cooperation (Elsner 2001: 71). Ultimately, insufficient integration raises the problem of narrow optimization by private enterprises, which necessitates regulatory intervention in order to avoid social costs. Such a regulation entails, but is not limited to, creating an environment that fosters competition between private actors on quality, service and prices. Beyond this type of regulation typical of a social market economy, public coordination is required in order to ensure that the benefits and services consumers receive from different sides are complementary and interlocking. Social choice has to guide public policy in its intervention in order to ensure that they also meet merit wants. Short-term-oriented individual economic rationality is at the origin of social costs in the sector for out-patient care for the elderly. Private business motives need to be better channeled and embedded in order to meet basic human needs. Coordination and integration are the proposed avenues for a public policy intervention that would aim at minimizing social costs. In this respect, the insight of 'insufficient integration' (Kapp 1971: 201) that Kapp formulated for the transport sector can be transposed to the regulatory challenges found today in the provision of private elderly care in Germany.

The social costs of private care in Germany

Institutional setting: private actors' role

With the introduction of social long-term care insurance (SLTCI) along pay-as-you-go principles in 1995/1996 the last milestone in Bismarckian welfare state development in Germany was set. Through the establishment of this fifth pillar of social insurance in Germany, the risk of care dependency has evolved as an independent theme for social policy, as well as for social legislation – a new social risk (Bonoli 2006). This reform initiated the trend of collectivization and de-privatization of the care dependency risk (Schulz-Nieswandt 2006a), but at the same time a significant private sector for the provision of services in the sector of long-term care benefits was established.

The specific set of welfare-mixture describes the different players offering care services. Long-term care facilities are run under the auspices of private and/ or public actors. Private care proceeds mainly within the family but also within kinship and/or neighborhood arrangements. Additionally, professional private enterprises offer long-term care services following the logic of the market economy, with economic profit as the dominant stimulation. Public care has to be separated into direct allocation of services by public authorities and funding of public institutions or services on the one hand, and the support of individuals through cash or in-kind benefits on the other (Lampert and Althammer 2007: 340–346). A *third sector* for the provision of care services can be further identified as the intermediate sector, such as the non-statutory welfare services (e.g., the German Red Cross or Caritas, the welfare association of the Catholic Church in Germany). This third sector has to be grasped as an open and polymorphic area, located between state, market and family (Schulz-Nieswandt 2008a: 323). Due to the sector's flexible specification between the informal logic of networks and the formal logic of organizations, as well as between common welfare and profit orientation, the delineations between the segments must be regarded as dynamic. Figure 10.1 summarizes the morphology of the long-term care sector.

According to the long-term care statistics published by the Federal Statistical Office (Statistisches Bundesamt Deutschland 2008), in 2007 2.25 million people were in need of long-term care in the sense of the Social Security Code (SGB) No. XI, §14. A further breakdown shows that out of the 1.54 million people in need of long-term care and covered by out-patient care, 1.03 million are cared for solely by relatives, whereas one-third (504,000) relies in addition on professional ambulant providers. Furthermore, 709,000 people benefit from in-patient care. Table 10.1 illustrates the relevance of professional private actors within the long-term care sector.

Between 1999 and 2007 in the field of out-patient care, ambulant public and private non-for-profit providers lost market shares in favor of private professional providers, which underlines the growing relevance of the latter.[12]

In contrast to the statutory health insurance in Germany, providing comprehensive benefits according to what is medically appropriate, the SLTCI follows

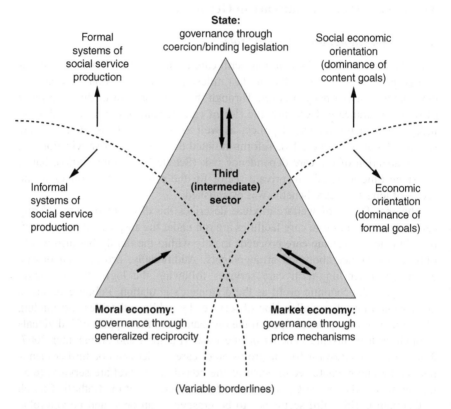

Figure 10.1 Morphology of the long-term care sector.

the logic of basic security and subsidiarity. This means that, depending on the need of care, benefits provided through the SLTCI do not provide a full-cost model and are thus merely additional to private expenses.[13] Full costs are covered neither for in- nor out-patient care. Only in the case of need defined by the German Social Code No. XII in combination with a means test, can the so-called residual costs – costs which exceed the benefits from the SLTCI – be covered by social welfare. Benefits include cash benefits (care allowance) and/or allowances in kind. The statutory long-term care insurance funds are required to enter into contracts with all care providers which fulfill the standards set by law. The sector does not have any demand planning such as in the health care sector. Instead, one objective is to establish intense competition among care providers, encouraging people in need of care to freely choose a provider. Framework agreements are contracted at the federal level, regulating modalities, substance and scope of care services, which are then equal for all providers (SGB XI §75 (1)). Despite the objective to establish a competition regime, the scope of services and the contribution rate are equal for all statutory long-term care insurance funds. The mechanism of competition predominately operates on the market for

Table 10.1 The role of professional private actors within the long-term care sector

	In-patient care	Out-patient care	
	2007	1999	2007
Number of elderly care providers			
Private professional providers	4,322	5,504	6,903
Private non-for profit providers (non-statutory welfare)	6,072	5,103	4,435
Public providers	635	213	191
Patients cared for by elderly care providers			
Private professional providers	–	147,804	228,988
Private non-for profit providers (non-statutory welfare)	–	259,648	265,296
Public providers	–	7,837	9,948
Employed workforce by elderly care providers			
Private professional providers	–	65,159	113,431
Private non-for profit providers (non-statutory welfare)	–	115,147	118,926
public providers	–	3,476	3,805

Source: Bundesrepublik Deutschland 2010; Statistisches Bundesamt Deutschland 2008.

service delivery, e.g., via the quality of service delivery (Gerlinger and Röber 2009: 73). The remuneration of the care services relates to performance (SGB XI §82 (1)) and is stipulated prospectively, usually for one or two years in advance. Therefore, real costs, which are realized for the service delivery, might exceed the costs stipulated beforehand. The remuneration entitles the service provider to fulfill the service guarantee under the premise of profitability. But as most of the characteristics of the respective services are strictly defined[14] – e.g., the format and schedule of services – achieving profitability must follow the logic of delivering qualitative services while minimizing the deployed resources (Gerlinger and Röber 2009: 79). The described dependencies are summarized in Figure 10.2.

Major challenges and reform necessities

The argument in view of the necessity to introduce new forms in the provision of long-term care services, which will be described below, is three-fold: (1) demographic development; (2) societal changes; and (3) an expected change in the health status of the elderly following the demographic change.

1 *Demographic change*: Depending on maternity, mortality and migration rates, the demography in Germany is changing in the sense of a double ageing process: In absolute terms the people are getting older and in relative terms the share of old people is increasing (Schulz-Nieswandt 2006b: 160). Average life expectancy at birth is supposed to increase by 7–10 years

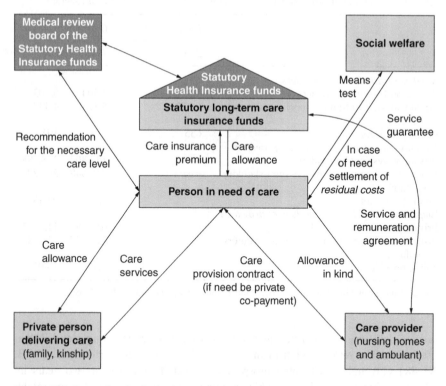

Figure 10.2 Dependencies in the long-term care sector.

within the next 50 years. Moreover, the share of people older than 80 years might triple to 12 percent, the ratio of people 65 years and older to people at working age might increase from 34 percent in 2008 to 67 percent in 2060 (Statistisches Bundesamt Deutschland 2009). This development, which has been known about for the last 30 years, has led to a shrinking population. Depending on different assumptions, scenarios can be calculated for the future population trend, forecasting a reduction of 5–17 million people in Germany until 2060.

2   *Societal changes*: The capacity of families to deliver care is limited and has increasingly come under pressure due to the various challenges typical of modern life-cycles. Although whether a traditional, one-dimensional family role model has existed breadth-wise has to be questioned, changes in terms of flexibilization in the way of life, marriage and divorce, individualization and mobilization, etc. are evident. In this sense questions concerning work–life balance are only the peak of the discussion.

3   *Health status changes*: The prevalence of morbidity and care dependency exponentially increases with age; the susceptibility to chronic diseases generally increases as well, although the risk depends on a number of individual

and environmental factors. Especially the number of people suffering from dementia will increase tremendously within the next decades. Estimations expect a doubling of the numbers, reaching up to 2.8 million people in 2050 (Lützau-Hohlbein 2004: 126; Hallauer 2002: 16). The demographic change will definitely result in an increased prevalence of morbidity and care dependency, though the scope of this development is unclear. Different scenarios exist in the literature: The *compression thesis* (Fries 1980) is based on the assumption that the period during which people are in need of care will not be longer in the future, but compressed, more likely and more severe at the end of the lifespan. The *medicalization* thesis (Gruenberg 1977; Verbrugge 1984) describes a different scenario, assuming that the morbidity period increases disproportionately to the gain in age, thereby contributing to an even higher care dependency in the future.

Ceteris paribus, two major effects will result from these three conditions. First, the number of people in need of long-term care will increase; and second, the availability of family care will diminish. Geiger (2009: 10) estimates that the number of people in need of long-term care in 2050 will be more than four million. For the same period Blinkert and Klie (2004) calculate a reduction of the informal care potential of around 30 percent. Already today the trend of increased demand for institutionalized long-term care is obvious. Thus the share of in-patient care has grown from 28 percent in 1997 to 33 percent in 2008.

The described new dimensions of care dependency risks and the erosion of informal aid networks require changes within care structures, especially targeting out-patient care. New resources have to be unlocked and existing resources utilized more effectively. Future modes of provision have to improve the situation of people in need of care while utilizing the capacities of professional and informal providers of long-term care. Bound by budgetary restrictions, much of the effort has to be spent on the involvement of informal care, targeting a well-balanced welfare mix. Hence the proposal for more coordination put forward here ties in nicely with the requirements of austerity measures in times of financial and economic crisis because it makes better use of various existing resources (e.g., family, third sector). The aim must be the integration of medical, care and social service landscapes and resources, finding a path toward ideal living and housing forms, targeting the person as the focal point and supporting modes of integration, networking and cooperation between different authorities, providers and professions (Weidner *et al.* 2010: 13–14, 79; Schulz-Nieswandt 2006a: 81). These complex challenges require a certain level of governance. As will be further outlined in the next section, private professional elderly care providers do not tend to foster necessary forms of cooperation and integration of their own volition. Thus disadvantageous effects result from private care providers' decision-making, which can be identified as social costs.

214 R. Maier-Rigaud et al.

Private actors' decision-making creating social costs

With the introduction of the SLTCI in 1995/1996 a market for long-term care services was created and opened for private market actors. Pursuant to the colloquial use of the word 'social' in the sense of solidarity and humanity, Pantenburg (1996: 88) describes social services as primarily personal services in the cases of an individual in need of help, which enable the person to conduct as far as possible an autonomous life. Providing social services poses a complex challenge for professional private actors.[15] On the one hand, long-term care services have to be provided in line with the principles of a free-market economy. On the other hand, the respective actors have to consider the needs of their customers, which are not only of economic but of emotional nature as well. In contrast to rationally acting private enterprises, public and charitable actors are attributed with a socio-economic rationality,[16] that, according to Siegler (1997), not only targets efficient and effective criteria but moreover political and cultural rationality as well. A dichotomy of professional private actors only oriented toward economic principles, and public or charitable actors only oriented toward socio-economic and emotional principles would be overly simplistic, however. Of course, professional private action is not solely guided through economic criteria. Instead, thoughtful caring is provided with respect to ethical principles.[17] However, due to the market logic, economic interests must be at the core of service provision. Professional long-term private care providers are bound by economic interests, preventing comprehensive collective needs from being considered while providing social services. In the case of permanent absence of economic success, private care service providers must downsize their activities and capacities or even quit operating. Dreßke (2001) distinguishes two kinds of motivations for private out-patient elderly care suppliers: substantial motivation, which draws on the self-conception of the caretaker and occupational ethics; and formal motivation, which aims at profitability and economic rationality. When considering the regulatory framework of the elderly care policy-field in the sense of limiting factors, it is evident that the formal motivation dominates the substantial motivation. Within a Tayloristic and schematic operational procedure there is hardly room for empathy and emotions. Such an interpretation can be traced back to what has been mentioned earlier, namely that systemic forces are pressuring private enterprises and individuals acting in the name of these enterprises to follow economic rationality. Hence, the inherent self-conception and occupational ethics of individual caretakers are consequently eclipsed. In this context the problem of narrow optimization again arises, consequently causing social costs. In order to interlock additional informal actors, which are supposed to amend the services provided by the professional market actors, especially given the emotional aspects in the process, coordination is necessary. The market has severe difficulties providing empathic services, particularly within the framework of existing financial restrictions. In the market of professional ambulant elderly care, which is largely determined – and thus restricted – by the demand generated via the SLTCI, professional private care providers have to calculate prices for services. Necessary services, which are not indicated via the price mechanism, are not or only insufficiently offered and thus produce a deficit of professional authenticity (Dreßke 2001: 83).[18] Moreover, informal caretakers, other professions, competitors or other stakeholders providing potential substitutes and/or complements are usually not involved. Here, it is formal inherent economic necessities that form the reference points rather than ethical motivation, such as satisfaction of patients. Hence, the interaction of professional and non-professional actors providing long-term care services is of crucial importance and requires governance. Parallel to the transportation sector, described above, the efficiency of out-patient long-term care essentially depends on the coordination of its various actors. However, in contrast to the transportation sector, duplication is an existing problem, but not the driving problem. The main problem is how to interlock the services of actors following different logics and motivations, especially in the light of the complexity of respective services. In this respect, Kapp's notion of 'insufficient integration' (Kapp 1971: 201) is not only pervasive in the case of transportation, but also in the case of long-term care.

Moreover, the concept of social costs includes the scarce efficiency of production factors, so-called social costs of missed opportunities (Kapp 1956: 524). Falling back on this understanding of social costs we will further specify our argument that private actors, while following their narrow objectives, cause social costs, especially as they might see only limited advantage in cooperation. Thus we argue in terms of a positive correlation between cooperation and the efficient employment of production factors.

The German Social Security Code (SGB) No. XI, concerning the SLTCI, states in §3 that social long-term care insurance shall preferentially support domestic care in order to improve the chances that people in need of care stay within their habitual living environment as long as possible. The market of private ambulant care services, established in the aftermath of the introduction of the SLTCI, supports this principle of home care primacy. But realizing care services at home substantially depends on the interaction of professional and informal services. Thus various questions regarding the growing importance of private professional long-term care services emerge. Ambulant services are heavily reliant on the cooperation and support of family members, self-help organizations or civic involvement. This co-production of formal and informal resources aims at the 'crowding-in' of different resources: the objective must be to interlock both forms of resources, professional and informal. Relying solely on the market for private ambulant care services causes social costs such as an increased risk of stationary care (Weidner *et al.* 2010: 39), thereby eroding the principle of home care primacy.

In particular, these problems relate to the principle of utility maximization, which does not fully fit into the care system due to the central significance of care relations (Thiele 2004: 1). The concept of *homo economicus* within conventional economics does not correspond to the requirements of empathy and sentimentality within the care system. More striking for the analyses conducted here is that interdisciplinarity does not play a role in standard economics (Thiele 2004: 176–177) and is therefore not reflected within professional elderly care providers' decision-making. This specific economic configuration for decision-making of professional private elderly care providers is opposed to the necessity of cooperation and networking and thus causes social costs. Economic interests do not correspond to the demanding concepts interlocking different levels and instances of care. As explained above, professional ambulant care services are provided under the premise of profit maximization. The guiding principle must be: minimize input as the *formalized*[19] output is given. This is not an outcome-oriented logic and highly relevant aspects such as investing in life quality, subjective self-contentment, optimization of provision, humane conditions to overcome care dependency and/or handicaps, as well as successful handling of irreversible chronic diseases, are therefore missing (Weidner *et al.* 2010: 41).

Another aspect limiting the interest of professional private care providers in cooperation is the existence of substitution effects. According to Dreßke (2001) a certain level of informal support is accepted and even demanded by professional providers as long as informal efforts do not substitute professional care. In this sense professionalism and de-professionalism – sustaining as far as possible the habitual normality – can constitute rivaling logics.

What has been outlined so far is that social costs in the sense of Kapp are induced mainly by the growing diffusion of market arrangements. In our analysis we have stressed the complexity and multidimensional governance structure of care service provision. While market actors in out-patient care primarily follow specific motivations mainly attributed to a one-dimensional economic rationality, services provided clearly lack a more comprehensive orientation toward collective needs. For example, social and cultural needs of the people in need of care are rather marginally considered by private business actors but largely covered by other actors, mostly those of the moral economy, foremost the family. In this respect, the motivation of private business actors to cooperate with informal actors is limited. Informal actors might even be considered competitors for the provision of care services. Following this argument we have highlighted the problems of narrow optimization, missed opportunities and substitution effects, all inducing social costs. Public coordination is necessary to ensure that the benefits and services consumers receive from different sides are complementary and interlocking. Such a public policy intervention might then lead to a meritorization of long-term care services.

Suggestions for an optional governance structure

Drawing on Elsner (2001), crucial questions to be answered in the context of public coordination concern the specification of public policy intervention and the instruments increasing the frequency of interaction between private actors. Both questions will be addressed within the following section.

As outlined above, in the future the number of elderly in need of long-term care, as well as complex needs concerning long-term care, will increase while at the same time the capacity of primary social nets will diminish. Thus respective services of general interest have to be realized comprehensively and sector-wide, and cost-effectiveness has to be understood as an economic and socio-political structural task. At the heart of the quest for optional governance structure stands a concerted balance and systematic interlinkage of organized professionalism and self-organized participation. Relevant questions include: How to develop forms of communication and cooperation between the actors? How to establish networks of currently loose structures and processes? Which are the specific incentives as well as stimulations to include more civil commitment? The principles of interaction, cooperation and networking are opposed to the economic principle of competition. Decision-making on the basis of economic rationality causes social costs such as the above-described missed opportunities, narrow optimization, coordination failures and substitution effects, all resulting in insufficient integration. From this analysis we derive our call for a governing body within the system in order to approach the reform necessities in the sector. It needs to be stressed that governance must not be understood in the sense of planning, but rather in the sense of steering and coordinating.

Due to manifold interests and governance aspects, the question of where to install the gate-keeper and navigator functions are unsolved to date. In line with Weidner *et al.* (2010) it is argued that such governance competencies shall be concentrated at the level of municipalities. Considering the mix of resources and actors, the objective for the municipality must be to support integration and cooperation between different professions, sectors, institutions and services as well as take account of the resources of the respective patients and their networks. Of course, this network-networking proves to be a tremendous challenge for organizational development. Besides other fruitful proposals (such as district-management, case-management, etc.), long-term care supporting-points and regional care-conferences, in particular, play a key role for answering the question of how the network can be designed to meet the needs of the people within municipalities.

Care supporting points: Supporting points offer information, consultation and evaluation of personal care needs, case-management and cooperation with services and further institutions. Under the coordination of health and long-term care insurances, capacities and services originating from different agencies such as long-term care insurances, communal assistance to the elderly and social benefits authorities are bundled under one umbrella. All services concerning elderly care shall be locally available from the supporting points, including the involvement of informal and voluntary capacities, aiming at a modern interface management. Since 2008, 16 pilot projects have been subject to the scientific evaluation conducted by the Kuratorium Deutsche Altenhilfe. First, preliminary insights from this evaluation suggest that care supporting points are an incremental piece of broader care- and case-management approaches aiming at a reduction of uncoordinated service delivery, an improvement of prevention and rehabilitation, and a better locally based management of services (Kuratorium Deutsche Altenhilfe 2009). The German Association of Cities and Towns (Deutscher Städtetag

2008) advocates that the coordination of care supporting points should be in the hand of municipalities in order to reduce possible redundant structures and to provide experiences and services beyond the pure care services.

Care conferences: The tasks of care conferences lie in planning, securing and developing the structure of care services' supply, considering the civic commitment and cooperative networks at local level. Care conferences might work as a place of communication and decision initiation, e.g., in view of provision of residential environments, designed according to the requirements of elderly persons such as barrier-free environments, access to local public transport, shopping and leisure facilities. Communal actors might use the care conference to motivate not only original care actors but also other stakeholders (retailers, house-building companies, etc.) to meet face-to-face. More focused conferences including fewer actors – the ones at the core of long-term care – might also be suitable as conferences dealing with individual cases and thus improving the neutrality of competition as, e.g., information asymmetry among competitors can be reduced to a level playing field.

The role of municipalities: Municipalities are actors predestined to take over the key function for tasks such as initiating, monitoring, supporting and networking the communicative and governance processes for inventions concerning long-term care and assistance with the residential environment of elderly people. The governing principle must be moderation, integrating all relevant actors. Instead of establishing centralist structures, the object is to provide infrastructure, communication and platforms for dialogue, as well as to remove barriers between actors in order to create space and tolerance for new answers, targeting the challenges. One of the critical factors of success will be how far municipalities are able to activate, integrate and sustain the informal care potential. Moreover, only few problems are seen in terms of legitimacy and confidence building, as the municipalities are generally not regarded as competitors. Neutrality and absence of economic self-interests support the acceptance of communal actors.

Care supporting points, care conferences and more generally an enhanced role for municipalities to play in governance are three examples significantly improving coordination among providers and thus consequently reducing the social costs generated by professional private care providers.

Conclusions

In Germany the social risk of care dependency is characterized by two trends: the long-term trend of risk collectivization associated with the introduction of social long-term care insurance in 1995/1996; and a short-term trend of risk privatization related to the increased relevance of private professional providers of long-term care services. At the same time three challenges – demographic change, societal changes and health status changes – are increasingly affecting the way in which the risk of care dependency has been and will be addressed in institutional terms. Against this background and through the lens of Kapp's theory of social costs the risks which originate from the provision of long-term care services delivered by actors who follow the economic logic of markets have been analyzed.

In the first section, the idea that cost-shifting takes a variety of forms and is inherent to market economies was emphasized. Political and institutional choices still matter in limiting the scope of social costs. In particular, this holds for the social costs of insufficient integration or coordination among actors in a policy field such as elderly care. Based on Kapp's thinking, a social policy intervention that would reduce social costs by meritorization of the coordination effort within a sector is advocated (second section). In the third section these various social costs according to Kapp, such as costs in terms of missed opportunities, narrow optimization, coordination failures and substitution effects, were identified for the sector of private professional long-term care services. Furthermore, the need for public responsibilities (Schulz-Nieswandt and Mann 2010) in the re-designing of governance structures that take into account the advantages of care supporting points and care conferences has been emphasized. A key role in the management of this type of coordination effort has to be played by the munici-palities. In a nutshell, we argue in favor of a modern type of meritorization in the field of long-term care services in Germany. It implies the institutionalization of a certain level of coordination, thereby minimizing the long-term and social-cost-intensive learning of cooperative solutions.

The essential changes are embedded in the political process, defining the situ-ation and constructing relevant aspects and features concerning the problem of social costs in the framework of risk privatization and privatization of the long-term care system. Policy developments depend on various determinants. One crucial factor is the dependency of policy changes on the struggle about ideas. For several years social policy processes have exhibited an emerging trend toward a new mental order relating the role of private and public responsibilities (Berner 2008). The social acceptance of welfare states' public role depends on cultural patterns of interpretation (Schulz-Nieswandt and Maier-Rigaud 2008) regarding the nature of social risks in the lifespan of people.

Are the results from the analysis of the long-term care sector in Germany transferable to other policy fields or other countries? The findings presented here might be useful as starting points for equal or similar analysis in other social policy fields such as child care, health care or even labor market services. All examples share the attribute of private business actors' involvement, and more-over the services provided within these policy fields are rather complex, two characteristics that make these policy fields open to our approach. Such analyses would then have to elaborate, e.g., the specific motives of actors, which might differ from those treated here. Other sectors that are not directly linked to the welfare state such as public transportation or power supply might be well worth consideration for further analyses. The possibilities for policy transfers or policy learning in the international context in this special case seem to be difficult. In order to identify possible subjects for policy transfer, the classic approach of *The Three Worlds of Welfare Capitalism* by Gøsta Esping-Andersen (1990) is only of limited value as we expect inconsistent results in the policy field of long-term care compared to the classic study of welfare state comparison. Analyses targeting specific policy fields seem to be more promising. For the case of care regimes Bettio and Plantenga (2004) have shown that only Austria can be considered to follow strategies for elderly care comparable to those in Germany. In a nutshell, a transfer of the analysis conducted here to other countries which exhibit long-term care sectors dissimilar to the German one is possible, but this approach must then strictly account for the peculiarities of the respective countries.

Notes

1 The authors thank Wolfram Elsner and Pietro Frigato for their comments on an earlier version of this chapter and Alexandra Patin for her linguistic review of the text.
2 These strong pressures for privatization and deregulation need to be scrutinized closely, taking into account the peculiarities of each sector (Nelson 2005: 2). This pressure, with which welfare states have to cope after their *trente glorieuses*, has so far not generally led to a race to the bottom.
3 For example, Kapp is concerned with the interaction between waste products and the environment causing additional harm, including 'delayed cumulative consequences on human health' (Kapp 1970: 836).
4 Kapp was fully aware that social costs can also arise from the activities of public authorities (Kapp 1969: 334).
5 Here Kapp's ideas come close to traditional externality theory, which calls for an internalization of external costs. However, Kapp repeatedly and relentlessly unveiled the limitations of the externality concept of neoclassical welfare economics in the tradition of Marshall and Pigou, mainly due to its focus on individual autonomy, instead of social choice (Kapp 1971: 37–41; 1970: 840–845). Kapp also refuted the narrow focus on technological externalities and, by contrast, included negative pecuniary effects in his social cost concept (Kapp 1969: 338–339). According to Kapp, neoclassical economists developed the concept of externalities because the problem of social costs was overwhelmingly pertinent and challenged their theories. In this situation they incorporated the limited externality concept in order to protect their traditional general equilibrium analyses (Kapp 1969: 334–335).
6 Kapp (1946) strongly supported an interdisciplinary approach to economics, where students of economics would benefit from a general education integrating social sciences such as history, political science, cultural anthropology and sociology in order to provide the students with an 'understanding of the mutual interdependence among the various aspects of life that have become the subject matter of the different social sciences' (Kapp 1946: 379). In this respect there are striking parallels to the works of Alexander Rüstow, who emphasized the necessity to embed and limit the scope of markets as well as to overcome the self-imposed blindness of economists for sociological and institutionalist insights (Maier-Rigaud and Maier-Rigaud 2009: 71–74).
7 Ultimately, Kapp was convinced that it could be identified objectively what is 'essential for human life and survival' (Kapp 1969: 336), thereby providing a social value basis on which social choices could rely.
8 This phenomenon is known in standard economics as network externality.
9 Further examples are private employment services, private rescue services, etc. The existence of social costs due to problems of insufficient integration and cooperation is particularly pressing in the case of more complex welfare services, such as long-term care.
10 Meritorization is understood here to be a rational delegation of decisions to democratically elected public policy actors. This definition contrasts with the interpretation of

meritorization as preference correction by a paternalistic state. Originally, Musgrave defined 'merit wants' as a case where 'public policy aims at interference with individual preferences and consumer sovereignty' (Musgrave 1956/1957: 341). Wants that are to some extent satisfied by market supply are defined as merit wants if public policy fosters their provision, e.g., through subsidies, thereby making them public (Musgrave 1969: 14–17). For an overview of the broad literature on merit goods see Ver Eecke (1998), who argues that frequently a single good incorporates aspects of private, public or merit goods (Ver Eecke 1998: 146).

11 Kapp was aware of Musgrave's merit wants concept (but in the sense of correcting 'false' preferences), as documented by one of his book reviews, in which he discusses the suggestion of the author to use Musgrave's concept for the control of social costs associated with air pollution (Kapp 1969: 344).

12 In out-patient care, public and private non-for-profit providers have lost absolutely in terms of care providers between 1999 and 2007. During the same period they have also lost some of their relative weight within the sector in terms of the number of patients and employees (see Table 10.1).

13 Depending on the need of care's scope, the Social Security Code (SGB) No. XI §15 distinguishes three different care levels: level 1: substantial need of care; level 2: high need of care; and level 3: severe need of care. The medical review board of the statutory health insurance funds decides about the classification, depending on the degree to which people are (or are not) able to fulfill habitual and constantly recurring everyday life activities. Cash benefits and allowances in kind vary, depending on the care level, from €225 (cash benefits in level 1) to €1,825 monthly (maximum allowances in kind for stationary care in level 3). A special care level 0 has been introduced to consider the increased prevalence of dementia, as people suffering from this disease are not immediately classified under care level 1. The maximum allowance from this level amounts to €2,400 per year.

14 Almost 80 percent of services provided by professional out-patient care providers is due to individual arrangements between the provider and the SLTCI fund. The system to calculate the specific remuneration is based on the so-called *service module system*. Specific services (e.g., personal hygiene, ingestion, etc.) are reimbursed through a lump-sum agreement, which mainly considers an average for the expenditure of time. The amount and the form of compensation, as well as the specification of services, varies considerably between federal states (Gerlinger and Röber 2009: 83–88).

15 Of course, the complexity of social services has to be considered as well when dealing with private non-for-profit organizations and public providers, which are not the subject of interest here.

16 For empirical literature regarding the different motivational patterns, see Schulz-Nieswandt (2008b).

17 Public and non-for-profit organizations are, however, increasingly the subject of economic criteria, not least due to the influence of EU regulations in this field (Schulz-Nieswandt and Sauer 2010).

18 The range of services considered as necessary is derived from the Social Security Code. The term of care dependency is defined under Social Security Code (SGB) No. XI §14 (1) and encloses mainly somatic attributes. Thus, the scope of services mainly encloses activities related to daily life performance. In particular the growing number of people suffering from dementia (in general people suffering from cognitive or mental disturbances) are only marginally covered by this classification. For the present the related discussion around a new, extended term of care dependency has culminated in the suggestion to further account for social and cultural aspects in view of daily living skills, such as mobility, cognitive abilities, social contacts, extramural activities, etc. (BMG 2009).

19 'Formalized' refers to the system of remuneration of services described above.

References

Axelrod, R. (1984) *The Evolution of Co-operation*, London: Basic Books.

Berner, F. (2008) *Der hybride Sozialstaat: Die Neuordnung von öffentlich und privat in der sozialen Sicherung*, Frankfurt am Main and New York: Campus.

Bettio, F. and Plantenga, J. (2004) 'Comparing care regimes in Europe', *Feminist Economics*, 10(1): 85–113.

Blinkert, B. and Klie, Th. (2004) 'Gesellschaftlicher Wandel und demographische Veränderungen als Herausforderungen für die Sicherstellung der Versorgung von pflegerischen Menschen', *Sozialer Fortschritt*, 53(11–12): 319–325.

BMG (Bundesministerium für Gesundheit) (2009) 'Bericht des Beirats zur Überprüfung des Pflegebedürftigkeitsbegriffs'. Available at: www.bmg.bund.de/SharedDocs/Downloads/DE/Pflege/Bericht__zum__Pflegebed_C3_BCrftigkeitsbegriff,templateId=raw,property=publicationFile.pdf/Bericht_zum_Pflegebed%C3%BCrftigkeitsbegriff.pdf (accessed 5 July 2010).

Bonoli, G. (2006) 'The politics of new social risks', in Armingeon, K. and Bonoli, G. (eds.), *The Politics of Post-Industrial Welfare States: Adapting Post-War Social Policies to New Social Risks*, London: Routledge, 3–26.

Bundesrepublik Deutschland (2010) 'Das Informationssystem der Gesundheitsberichterstattung des Bundes'. Available at: www.gbe-bund.de/gbe10/pkg_isgbe5.prc_isgbe?p_uid=gast&p_aid=20456387&p_sprache=D (accessed 17 March 2010).

Deutscher Städtetag (2008) 'Deutscher Städtetag kritisiert Koalitionskompromiss zur Pflege. Pflegestützpunkte nicht in die Hand der Pflegekassen geben- sondern in die Verantwortung der Städte'. Available at: www.staedtetag.de/imperia/md/content/verffentlichungen/mitteilungen/2008/2.pdf (accessed 22 March 2010).

Dreßke, St. (2001) 'Kooperation und Aushandlungen in der ambulanten Pflege', *Zeitschrift für Gesundheitswissenschaft*, 9(1): 68–84.

Elsner, W. (2001) 'Interactive economic policy: toward a cooperative policy approach for a negotiated economy', *Journal of Economic Issues*, 35(1): 61–83.

Elsner, W. (2005) 'Real-world economics today: the new complexity, co-ordination and policy', *Review of Social Economy*, 63(1): 19–53.

Esping-Andersen, G. (1990) *The Three Worlds of Welfare Capitalism*, Cambridge: Princeton University Press.

Fries, J.F. (1980) 'Aging, natural death, and the compression of morbidity', *The New England Journal of Medicine*, 303(3): 130–135.

Geiger, M. (2009) *Pflege in einer alternden Gesellschaft: Projekt – Perspektiven auf den demografischen Wandel*, Saarbrücken: ISO-Institut.

Gerlinger, T. and Röber, M. (2009) *Die Pflegeversicherung*, Bern: Huber.

Gruenberg, E.M. (1977) 'The failure of success', *The Milbank Memorial Fund Quarterly: Health and Society*, 55(1): 3–24.

Hallauer, J.F. (2002) 'Epidemiologie für Deutschland mit Prognose', in Hallauer, J.F. and Kurz, A. (eds.), *Weißbuch Demenz: Versorgungssituation relevanter Demenzerkrankungen in Deutschland*, Stuttgart and New York: Georg Thieme, 15–18.

Heidenreich, R. (1998) 'Economics and institutions: the socioeconomic approach of K. William Kapp', *Journal of Economic Issues*, 32(4): 965–984.

Kapp, K.W. (1946) 'Teaching of economics: a new approach', *Southern Economic Journal*, 12(4): 376–383.

Kapp, K.W. (1956) 'Sozialkosten', in Beckrath, E. v., Brinkmann, C., Gutenberg, E., Haberler, G., Jecht, H., Jöhr, W.A., Lütge, F., Prdöhl, A., Schaeder, R., Schmidt-Rimpler,

W., Weber, W. and Wiese, L. v. (eds.), *Handwörterbuch der Sozialwissenschaften: Zugleich Neuauflage des Handwörterbuch der Staatswissenschaften*, Göttingen: Gustav Fischer, pp. 524–527.

Kapp, K.W. (1969) 'On the nature and significance of social costs', *Kyklos*, 22(2): 334–347.

Kapp, K.W. (1970) 'Environmental disruption and social costs: a challenge to economics', *Kyklos*, 23(4): 833–848.

Kapp, K.W. (1971 [1950]) *The Social Costs of Private Enterprise*, New York: Schocken Books.

Kuratorium Deutsche Altenhilfe (2009) 'Werkstatt Pflegestützpunkte. Aktueller Stand der Entwicklung von Pflegestützpunkten in Deutschland und Empfehlungen zur Implementierung und zum Betrieb von Pflegestützpunkten'. Available at: www.werkstatt-pflegestuetzpunkte.de/tl_files/werkstatt_pflegestuetzpunkte/PDF%20Dateien/2.%20 Zwischenbericht.pdf (accessed 15 April 2010).

Lampert, H. and Althammer, J. (2007) *Lehrbuch der Sozialpolitik*, 8., revised and updated edition, Berlin: Springer.

Lützau-Hohlbein, A. (2004) 'Ambulante Pflege: Aus Sicht der Angehörigen – Zusammenarbeit in Angehörigen', in Hasseler, M. and Meyer, M. (eds.), *Ambulante Pflege: Neue Wege und Konzepte für die Zukunft*, Hannover: Schlütersche, 126–132.

Mackscheidt, K. (1984) 'Meritorische Güter: Musgraves Idee und deren Konsequenzen', *WISU*, 84(12): 585–589.

Maier-Rigaud, F. Ph. and Maier-Rigaud, R. (2009) 'Rüstows Konzept der Sozialen Marktwirtschaft: Sozial und wettbewerbspolitische Dimensionen einer überwirtschaftlichen Ordnung', in Aßländer, M.S. and Ulrich, P. (eds.), *60 Jahre Soziale Marktwirtschaft. Illusionen und Reinterpretationen einer ordnungspolitischen Integrationsformel*, Bern: Haupt, 69–94.

Mühlenkamp, H. and Schulz-Nieswandt, F. (2008) 'Öffentlicher Auftrag und Public Corporate Governance', in Schaefer, C. and Theuvsen, L. (eds.), *Public Corporate Governance: Bestandsaufnahme und Perspektiven – Zeitschrift für öffentliche und gemeinwirtschaftliche Unternehmen.* Suppl. 36. Baden-Baden: Nomos, 26–44.

Musgrave, R.A. (1956/1957) 'A multiple theory of budget determination', *Finanzarchiv*, 17(3): 333–343.

Musgrave, R.A. (1969) *Finanztheorie*, 2nd edition, Tübingen: Mohr.

Nelson, R.R. (2005) 'Introduction', in Nelson, R.R. (ed.), *The Limits of Market Organization*, New York: Russell Sage Foundation, 1–24.

Pantenburg, St. (1996) *Marketingstrategien freigemeinnütziger Unternehmen im Altenhilfesektor*, Baden-Baden: MWV.

Schulz-Nieswandt, F. (2006a) *Sorgearbeit, Geschlechterordnung und Altenpflegeregime in Europa*, Berlin: LIT.

Schulz-Nieswandt, F. (2006b) *Sozialpolitik und Alter*, Stuttgart: Kohlhammer.

Schulz-Nieswandt, F. (2008a) 'Zur Morphologie des Dritten Sektors im Gefüge zwischen Staat, Markt und Familie: Ein Diskussionsbeitrag zur CIRIEC-Studie "Die Sozialwirtschaft in der Europäischen Union"', *Zeitschrift für öffentliche und gemeinwirtschaftliche Unternehmen*, 31(3): 323–336.

Schulz-Nieswandt, F. (2008b) 'Zur Einführung: Ein Corporate Governance Kodex für das öffentliche Wirtschaften?', in GÖW (ed.), *Corporate Governance in der öffentlichen Wirtschaft*, Berlin, 7–18.

Schulz-Nieswandt, F. and Maier-Rigaud, R. (2008) Review of Elsner *et al.* (eds.), *Social Costs and Public Action in Modern Capitalism: Essays Inspired by Karl William*

Kapp's Theory of Social Costs', *Zeitschrift für öffentliche und gemeinwirtschaftliche Unternehmen/Journal for Public and Nonprofit Services*, 31(2): 238–241.

Schulz-Nieswandt, F. and Mann, K. (2010) 'Das doppelte Ideologem: Inhouse ohne Defizite oder privat? Öffentliche (kommunale) Krankenhäuser als Akteure der Daseinsvorsorge im Kontext des europäischen Rechts und das nationale Privatisierungs-Dispositiv', in Kurscheid, C. (ed.), *Die zukünftige Rolle öffentlicher Krankenhäuser im Gesundheitswesen, Zeitschrift für öffentliche und gemeinwirtschaftliche Unternehmen*, suppl. 38, Baden-Baden: Nomos, 120–129.

Schulz-Nieswandt, F. and Sauer, M. (2010) 'Social and health services in the EU: an analytical sketch', in Chobanov, G., Plöhn, J. and Schellhass, H. (eds.), *Policies of Economic and Social Development in Europe*. Frankfurt am Main: Peter Lang, 181–192.

Siegler, B.F. (1997) *Ökonomik Sozialer Arbeit*, Freiburg im Breisgau: Lambertus.

Statistisches Bundesamt Deutschland (2008) 'Pflegestatistik 2007: Pflege im Rahmen der Pflegeversicherung Deutschlandergebnisse'. Available at: https://www-ec.destatis.de/csp/shop/sfg/bpm.html.cms.cBroker.cls?cmspath=struktur,vollanzeige.csp&ID=1023269 (accessed 17 March 2010).

Statistisches Bundesamt Deutschland (2009) '12. koordinierte Bevölkerungsvorausberechnung'. Available at www.destatis.de/jetspeed/portal/cms/Sites/destatis/Internet/DE/Navigation/Statistiken/Bevoelkerung/VorausberechnungBevoelkerung/VorausberechnungBevoelkerung.psml (accessed 18 March 2010).

Swaan, A. de (1988) *In Care of the State: Health Care, Education and Welfare in Europe and the USA in the Modern Era*, Oxford: Oxford University Press.

Swaney, J.A. and Evers, M.A. (1989) 'The social cost concepts of K. William Kapp and Karl Polanyi', *Journal of Economic Issues*, 23(1): 7–33.

Thiele, G. (2004) *Ökonomik des Pflegesystems*, Heidelberg: Economica.

Ver Eecke, W. (1998) 'The concept of a 'merit good': the ethical dimension in economic theory and the history of economic thought or the transformation of economics into socio-economics', *Journal of Socio-Economics*, 27(1): 133–153.

Verbrugge, L.M. (1984) 'Longer life but worsening health? Trends in health and mortality of middle-aged and older persons', *The Milbank Memorial Fund Quarterly: Health and Society*, 62(2): 475–519.

Weidner, F., Isfort, M., Brandenburg, H., Kohlen, H., Adam-Paffrath, R., Schulz-Nieswandt, F. and Kurscheid, C. (2010) *Pflege und Unterstützung im Wohnumfeld: Innovationen für Menschen mit Pflegebedüftigkeit und Behinderung*, Hannover: Schlütersche.

11 Business bias as usual

The case of electromagnetic pollution[1]

Angelo Gino Levis, Valerio Gennaro and Spiridione Garbisa

Introduction: protecting human health or protecting business? How to identify the *business bias*

About 50 years ago, Lorenzo Tomatis anticipated – with bitterness, but also with the clarity and optimism that distinguish the competent researcher – that 'the world of research consists of a few dozen people who really matter, a small group of trusted workers, a significant number of uninformed (guilty and non guilty) ones, and a cohort of unscrupulous profiteers, true violators' (Tomatis 1965: 139). It is not easy to identify the honest researchers, picking them out from among the violators and profiteers, whose main aims are promoting career and business. It is much simpler to actually carry out good research and identify any studies that are flawed or biased. This is, of course, a true researcher's main goal.

Indeed, best practice in both environmental and occupational epidemiology has been well established for years (Hernberg 1981). However, the correct use of these methods is not routinely applied, a failure regrettably borne out by numerous studies on exposed workers (e.g., in oil refineries, petrochemical or steel plants), military personnel (e.g., exposure to depleted uranium) and people living in areas suffering from pollution (e.g., due to the presence of industrial plants and urban traffic congestion). Moreover, the findings of studies carried out with the benefit of corporate funding often conclude that a population exposed to some occupational or environmental risk factor, or to treatment with this or that drug, is healthier than the control population (though only until truly independent studies are carried out, these often uncovering very different results). An article published quite recently highlighted this common failure, and proposed how it might be corrected, pointing out 15 errors and biases, and so enabling epidemiologists to avoid the most serious diagnostic error that can be made: reporting a sick population as healthy (Gennaro and Tomatis 2005).[2]

This serious under-estimation of the epidemiological risk of disease can be produced in good or bad faith. The latter – termed *business bias* in occupational and environmental epidemiology – can be understood as an intentional study bias, specifically set up to prioritize both economic and career-related ambitions over scientific research, whose legitimate goal should be the minimization of avoidable health damage. In later studies there is mounting evidence concerning how what is considered *health-oriented research* could in fact turn into *business-* or *funds-oriented research* (Egilman and Bohme 2005; Bailar 2006; Michaels 2008; Pearce 2008; Oreskes and Convay 2010). Today there are 25 points in place of the earlier 15 points, and it is increasingly clear that the business bias issue has become a new risk factor for the health of populations (Gennaro *et al.* 2009). Inconsistencies, contradictions and omissions can easily be identified by carefully reading all the sections of a scientific article. Furthermore, there is a clearly notice-able, tell-tale inconsistency in the contrast between the reassuring tone of the con-clusion of a study (the part that is always read) and the alarm evident in other sections (those often disregarded: materials, methods and results).

Interest conflicts and exposure limits to non-ionizing electromagnetic fields

Discussion on the need to minimize exposure to electromagnetic fields (EMF) (frequency range: 0–300 GHz) has for over half a century been split between two irreconcilable positions. On the one hand, a 'conservative' stance rooted in the definition of exposure limits fixed since the mid-1950s on the assumption that the only effects of EMF dangerous to human health are the acute effects result-ing from the passage of electric current or overheating (stimulation of muscles and peripheral nerves, shocks, burns, heating of surface tissues). Simple avoid-ance of these effects would ensure the safeness of exposure to EMF.[3] This posi-tion was agreed upon at the end of the 1990s by a group of scientists which was self-constituted under the International Commission for Non-Ionizing Radiation Protection (ICNIRP). Working with so-called 'ghosts' (dummies reproducing the human shape and biochemical constitution of human tissue), this group iden-tified the EMF values at which a significant thermal effect is registered, and introduced reductions of 10–50 times for workers and the general population, respectively.[4] The ICNIRP set a single exposure limit to protect from acute and thermal effects: For the general population this limit is 100 microTesla (μT) for magnetic fields (MF) produced by the EMF at low frequencies (0–100 KHz), in particular at 50–60 Hz (ELF, extremely low frequencies: e.g., power lines), and 27–61 Volts/meter (V/m) – depending on the frequency – for electric fields pro-duced by the EMF at high–very high frequencies (100–300 GHz; radiofrequen-cies or RF; e.g., radio/TV and mobile telephony emissions). For workers, the 'safe limits' are 500 μT for ELF/EMF and 137 V/m for RF/EMF,[5] respectively. For the ICNIRP, the acute effects with thermal origin are the only EMF effects harmful to human health that have specifically been determined, while other effects – in particular long-term effects and biological effects of non-thermal origin – are inadequately documented or give contradictory results, for which reason they have been excluded from consideration when setting exposure limits. The position and limits defined by the ICNIRP have been accepted by the prin-cipal organizations overseeing health care, including the WHO, as well as by many national scientific committees and the European Commission (EC).[6]

On the other hand, a large part of the scientific community – especially where there is no constraint from funding by manufacturers or managers/operators of the technologies concerned – maintains a 'cautionary' position based on application of the Precautionary Principle and the necessity to minimize EMF exposures. This position is justified by both epidemiological and experimental data. The former data – documented after exposure of human subjects to EMF so weak as to be able to exclude any significant heating – show immediate and long-term health effects including tumors and cancers, while the latter data reveal biological effects on *in vitro* systems, animals and human volunteers, indicating molecular, cellular and functional mechanisms supporting a biological plausibility (see Box 11.1). The cautionary limits suggested for the population are lower by about two orders of magnitude than those set by the ICNIRP: 0.1–0.2 µT (rather than 100) for ELF/EMF and 0.5–0.6 V/m (rather than 27–61) for RF/EMF.[7]

Box 11.1 Non-thermal biological effects of EMF supporting the plausibility of a possible carcinogenic action of these radiations*

1 Alteration of the synthesis of the hormone melatonin, involved in the deactivation of peroxide radicals, which produce DNA damage triggering carcinogenesis;
2 stimulation of Fenton's reaction, with consequent increase in damage due to free radicals on biological macromolecules;
3 modification of the permeability of the cell membrane and consequent alteration of the flow of biologically important ions, in particular calcium;
4 modification of the brain's electrical activity and of the permeability of the hemato-encephalic membrane, with consequent damage to the cerebral neurons and alteration of the functioning of the cerebral neuroreceptors and neurotransmitters;
5 alteration of the functioning of the immune system;
6 inhibition of apoptosis (programmed cell death);
7 expression of heat shock proteins;
8 genetic and epigenetic effects;
9 synergistic interactions with other carcinogens (ionizing radiation, polycyclic aromatic hydrocarbons, benzene derivatives).

* See all the articles published in *Pathophysiology*, 16 (2009): 67–250, and in *European Journal of Oncology Library*, 5 (2010): 1–403)

Residential and occupational exposure to ELF/EMF

Childhood leukemias, tumors in adults, neurodegenerative disorders and acute diseases

IARC's monograph no. 80 on this topic is based on dozens of increasingly sophisticated studies, plus two 'pooled analyses' (IARC 2002). The first of these two includes nine carefully conducted studies and shows a statistically significant doubling of the risk of contracting childhood leukemia through exposure at home to power lines, in the presence of MF equal to or greater than 0.4 µT, relative to those exposed to less than 0.1 µT (OR=2.00; 95 percent CI=1.24–3.13) (Ahlbom *et al.* 2000).[8] The second pooled analysis covers 15 studies and shows a statistically significant increase in the same type of risk for exposures above 0.3 µT (OR=1.7; 95 percent CI=1.2–2.3) (Greenland *et al.* 2000). According to IARC, the association between childhood leukemia and high levels of magnetic fields is not likely to be due to chance, but it could be affected by distortions. In particular, a distortion of the selection could explain part of the association. However, it is highly unlikely that the distortion due to unknown confounding factors can explain the entire effect observed. In addition, if the relationship observed was a result of a causal link, the risk associated with the exposure might be higher than that reported. In fact, a number of studies have shown statistically significant increases in risk of childhood leukemia exceeding those cited above, even at MF values lower than 0.3–0.4 µT (Table 11.1). The fraction of the infant population exposed at home to leukemogenic MF levels (0.3–0.4 µT) could range between 1 and 4 percent, but these MF levels represent just one average of values produced during the year by the voltage arising from power lines, and today it is still not known whether average or maximum values of MF should be correlated with the incidence of childhood leukemias. Consequently, in view of the fact (see Table 11.1) that increase in risk often far exceeds a simple doubling (up to 5–6 times) and is found even at low MF levels (up to 0.1 µT) – and noting that much higher MF peaks are common (3–5 µT, and in some cases over 10 µT) – this fraction could be very much higher. Furthermore, it is possible that children living close to power lines and who are exposed to MF of intensities of the order of those mentioned above are subject to an increased risk of contracting other types of cancer. Finally, a number of studies indicate that children exposed in the home to MF produced by power lines suffer from restricted growth and shorter lifespan, and have raised risk of developing some form of cancer in adult life (Fadel *et al.* 2006; Foliart *et al.* 2006; Svendsen *et al.* 2007).

Various authors have also noted statistically significant increases in various types of tumor in adults with residential and occupational exposures (Table 11.2). Much common office equipment (computers, photocopiers, fax machines, video-display units) causes simultaneous exposure to ELF/EMF and RF/EMF, and evaluation of the contribution from these various EM sources shows the need to minimize exposure to this equipment to avoid harmful health effects from using them (Seyhan *et al.* 2010).

In adults, occupational or residential exposure to ELF/EMF may also raise incidence of spontaneous abortion (Lee *et al.* 2002; Li *et al.* 2002) and cause alterations of electrical brain activity and of the muscular, cardiocirculatory, hormonal and immune systems, of the cutaneous tissue, as well as neurological disturbances (of the attention, memory, visual-motor coordination and of mental health: depression and risk of suicide). Furthermore, epidemiological data

Table 11.1 Childhood leukemias in residential exposures to ELF/EMF

Authors	Reference	Year	OR	95% CI	x^1
Wertheimer and Leeper	American Journal of Epidemiology, 109: 273–284	1979	3.0	1.1–8.1	>0.30
Savitz et al.	American Journal of Epidemiology, 128: 21–38	1988	3.8	1.2–11.7	>0.30
London et al.	American Journal of Epidemiology, 134: 923–937	1991	2.2	1.1–4.3	>0.15
Olsen et al.	British Medical Journal, 307: 891–895	1993	5.6	1.6–19.0	>0.40
Feychting and Ahlbom	American Journal of Epidemiology, 138: 467–481	1993	3.8	1.4–9.3	>0.30
Coghill et al.	European Journal of Cancer Prevention, 5: 153–158	1996	4.7	1.2–27.8	>0.20
Michaelis et al.	Epidemiology, 9: 92–94	1997	3.8	1.2–11.9	>0.20
Linet et al.	New England Journal of Medicine, 337: 1–7	1997	3.3	1.2–9.4	>0.40
Li et al.	Journal of Occupational and Environmental Medicine, 40: 144–147	1998	2.7	1.1–5.6	<100 m
UKKCS[2]	Lancet, 354: 1925–1931	1999	2.4	1.2–5.1	>0.1–0.2
Green et al.	Cancer Causes Control, 10: 233–243	1999	4.5	1.3–15.9	>0.14
Green et al.	International Journal of Cancer, 82: 161–170	1999	3.5	1.1–10.5	>0.15
Bianchi et al.	Tumori, 86: 195–198	2000	3.5	1.1–9.7	>0.10
Schuz et al.	International Journal of Cancer, 91: 728–735	2001	3.2	1.3–7.8	>0.20
Schuz et al.	International Journal of Cancer, 91: 728–735	2001	5.5	1.2–27.0	>0.40
Draper et al.	British Journal of Medicine, 330: 1290–1293	2005	1.7	1.1–2.5	<200 m
Draper et al.	British Journal of Medicine, 330: 1290–1293	2005	1.2	1.02–1.5	200–600 m
Kabuto et al.	International Journal of Cancer, 119: 643–650	2006	4.7	1.2–19.0	>0.40

Note
1 For exposures in µT or for distance in meters from the power lines;
2 UK Childhood Cancer Study Investigators.

Table 11.2 Tumors in adults in occupational and residential exposures to ELF/EMF

Authors	Reference	Year	Condition, sex	Tumors	OR (95% CI)
Floderus et al.	Cancer Causes and Control, 5: 189–194	1994	Railway workers ♂	Leukemia, brain tumors	4.3 (1.6–11.8)
Floderus et al.	Cancer Causes and Control, 5: 189–194	1994	Train drivers ♂	Breast tumors	4.9 (1.6–15.7)
Tynes et al.	Cancer Causes and Control, 7: 197–204	1996	Electricity network workers ♂	Breast tumors	1.5 (1.1–2.0)
Coogan et al.	Epidemiology, 7: 459–464	1996	Electricity workers ♀	Breast tumors	1.8 (1.1–3.1)
Milham	American Journal of Industrial Medicine, 30: 702–704	1996	Environmental exposure♂,♀	Leukemia and other tumors	3.9 (1.6–8.0)
Rodvall et al.	European Journal of Epidemiology, 14: 563–569	1998	Electricity workers ♂	Gliomas	1.9 (0.8–5.0)
Pollan et al.	American Journal of Public Health, 89: 875–881	1999	Electronic programmers ♀	Breast tumors	1.8 (1.2–2.7)
Pollan et al.	American Journal of Public Health, 89: 875–881	1999	Telegraph line operators ♀	Breast tumors	1.5 (1.1–2.0)
Pollan et al.	American Journal of Public Health, 89: 875–881	1999	Telephone line operators ♀	Breast tumors	1.3 (1.1–1.5)
Pollan et al.	American Journal of Public Health, 89: 875–881	1999	Various ELF occupations ♀	Breast tumors	from 1.3 to 1.7 (s.s.)
Villeneuve et al.	Occupational and Environmental Medicine, 57: 249–257	2000	Electricity workers ♂	Non-Hodgkin lymphoma	3.6 (1.3–9.8)
van Wijngaarden	Occupational and Environmental Medicine, 57: 258–263	2001	Electricity workers ♂	Brain tumors	1.7 (1.0–3.0)
Bethwaite et al.	Cancer Causes and Control, 12: 683–689	2001	Electrical welders ♂	Leukemia	2.8 (1.2–6.8)
Villeneuve et al.	Journal of Epidemiology, 31: 210–217	2002	Electrical welders >0.6 μT ♂	Glioblastomas	5.4 (1.2–24.8)
Hakansson et al.	Occupational and Environmental Medicine, 59: 481–486	2002	Electrical welders ♀	Renal tumors, leukemia	1.4 (1.0–2.0)

Hakansson et al.	Occupational and Environmental Medicine, 59: 481–486	2002	Electrical welders ♀	Gliomas	3.0 (1.1–8.6)
Tynes et al.	Occupational and Environmental Medicine, 60: 343–347	2003	Residents exposed to >0.2 µT♂, ♀	Skin melanomas	1.9 (1.2–2.8)
Charles et al.	American Journal of Epidemiology, 157: 683–691	2003	Electricity workers ♂	Prostate tumors	1.6 (1.1–2.4)
Weiderpass et al.	Journal of Occupational and Environmental Health, 45: 305–315	2003	Electricity workers ♀	Gastrointestinal tumors	1.5 (1.1–2.0)
Weiderpass et al.	Journal of Occupational and Environmental Health, 45: 305–315	2003	Electricity workers ♀	Pancreatic tumors	1.8 (1.2–2.8)
Fazzo et al.	Epidemilogia & Prevenzione, 29: 243–252	2005	Residential ELF exposure ♂, ♀	Peritoneal tumors, digestive system	2.2 (1.2–4.3)
Fazzo et al.	Epidemilogia & Prevenzione, 29: 243–252	2005	Residential ELF exposure ♂,♀	Leukemia	4.5 (1.1–17.9)
Lowenthal et al.	International Medicine Journal, 37: 614–619	2007	Residential ELF exposure ♂, ♀	Lymphomas and myelomas	3.2 (1.3–8.3)
Fazzo et al.	Journal of Occupational and Environmental Health, 15: 133–142	2009	Residential ELF exposure ♂, ♀	Pancreatic tumors, leukemia	8.2 (3.1–21.8)

Notes

Negative data are given in over 50 articles published since 1998, all funded by the major electricity companies (National Grid Corporation UK, Electric Power Research Institute USA and other electricity companies), or by private bodies with interests in the development of technologies that use ELF/EMF. A few of these articles were signed by Leeka Kheifets and John Swanson, who participated in the IARC ELF/EMF monograph working group and did not declare their conflict of interests in spite of being employees of two of the world's largest electric utilities (see footnote 9).

Most of the data refer to exposures with MF values of 1–5 µT.

indicate a statistically significant increase in risk in certain cases, of neuro-degenerative diseases (Bortkiewicz *et al.* 2006): lateral amyotrophic sclerosis (Hakansson *et al.* 2003), Parkinson's disease (WHO 2007) and Alzheimer's disease (Huss *et al.* 2009), in subjects with occupational exposure to ELF/EMF. The increase in risk is found at magnetic field levels comparable with those present in some residential situations (0.2–5.0 μT).

Finally, a number of types of tumor, pre-neoplastic effects and synergistic interactions with chemical and physical carcinogens have been observed in rodents irradiated with ELF/EMF in the laboratory, at MF levels corresponding to those in man – bearing in mind the different conditions of exposure and life-time – to 0.3 μT in residential exposure to power lines (Zapponi and Marcello 2004).

A number of mechanisms of biological action have also been identified that could explain the induction of short- and long-term effects of the ELF/EMF, possibly in association with predisposition through genetic factors (Box 11.1).

Criticism of the positions held by IARC, ICNIRP, the EC and WHO

The IARC monograph concludes by stating that (IARC 2002): (1) there is limited evidence in man of carcinogenicity of ELF/EMF in reference to child-hood leukemia; (2) there is insufficient evidence of other forms of cancer in man and, in general, in experimental animals. For these reasons, ELF/EMF are con-sidered 'possible carcinogenic agents for man' (Group 2B). In view of the above epidemiological and experimental data – most already available in 2001 – the conclusions of IARC cannot be justified except in the light of the new IARC 'trends' described by Tomatis, founder and scientific director of IARC (1969–1993) (Tomatis 2002), and by J. Huff, editor of IARC monographs (1977–1979) (Huff 2002).[9]

The classification of ELF/EMF (Group 2B) determined by the IARC working group in 2001 is still upheld today by the WHO/EC/ICNIRP and other interna-tional and national organizations.[10]

The innovative position of the Italian civil magistracy

The limits put forward by the international agencies and even those set by law should not be the only points of reference in the controversy on the possible damage to human health deriving from exposure to ELF/EMF. This was estab-lished by Sentence 9893/2000 of the Italian Supreme Court (*Corte di Cassazi-one*), which established that the regular judge had full power, including for determination of the danger to health on the basis of scientific knowledge acquired at the time of the ruling. This is a principle that has frequently been emphasized in the sentences of various court cases: Milan 43678/2003; Potenza 195/2003; Modena 1430/2004; Como 1490/2005; Venice 441/2008; Criminal Court (*Cassazione Penale*) 33285/2008. These hearings established that: (1) the constitutional right to health is understood in the broadest sense, including the right to live in an environment that is healthy and that should also be protected preventively – that is, where there is the presence of merely a danger of falling ill or contracting a disease. This protection, to be effective, cannot in fact be subordinate to a state of illness or disease arising. (2) The harm, in the form of risk, should be prevented and compensated for, even if it is not known who will be struck, nor when, but it is instead known that when it does strike it will be too late, in the sense that a harmful event that could have been avoided has instead arisen. (3) Observation of the limits set by the regulations in force does not make exposures to ELF/EMF in themselves legal and compatible with the protection of the right to health. Instead, account should be taken of the constitutional relevance of the right to health (Article 32 of the Italian Constitution) and of the consequent level of protection, necessarily prevailing over freedom of enterprise, provided for by Article 41 of the Constitution, stating that: 'Private economic endeavor is free but may not be carried out in conflict with social utility or in any way that compromises safety, freedom or human dignity' and that: 'The law determines the programs and appropriate controls in such a way that public and private activity can be directed toward and coordinated for social goals'. (4) The scale of values set out by the Constitution should also include the Precautionary Principle, as provided for by Article 174 of the EU Treaty, which should be considered part of the national regulations. (5) In cases of doubt as to the level of risk, the Precautionary Principle requires the adoption of the most conservative arrangement consistent with minimizing risk, where necessary opting for 'zero risk'. (6) Where a number of epidemiological studies have shown a significant increase in risk, the emissions should be considered dangerous, even though the mechanisms of action are still not known. Here, in fact, the causality link can only be determined in terms of probability.[11]

Mobile phones and head tumors: a representative case

The worldwide spread of the use of mobile phones (MPs: analog and digital cellulars, and cordless) has heightened concerns about possible adverse effects, especially head tumors. According to the International Telecommunications Union, the number of mobile phone subscriptions has reached five billion (mid-2010), with over half of all users thought to be children and young adults. There are no data for cordless users, but a figure of two billion is a reasonable assumption. Given these figures, even an established modest increase (20–30 percent) in tumor risk for MP users would result in significant social and health costs and individual suffering, while higher risks could give rise to a health crisis of dramatic proportions. While most technologies carry risks, these should be assessed accurately and responsibly.

Whether or not there is a relationship between MP use and head tumor risk is still a matter of debate. On the one hand there are researchers who recognize the validity of positive results – such as those by Hardell, who has documented a statistically significant increase (100 percent) of head tumors (brain gliomas and acoustic nerve neuromas) in people exposed to MPs for a long overall time

234 A.G. Levis et al.

(more than ten years) – and who are requesting application of the Precautionary Principle, especially for children who face decades of exposure (Hardell and Carlberg 2009; Hardell *et al.* 2011). On the other hand there are researchers who form their own conclusions, largely reassuring, on the basis of the results of the Interphone project, which involved research groups from 13 countries (Interphone Study Group 2010). It is therefore vital to understand the weight of the conflict between Hardell's positive results and those from other studies considered reassuring in their failure to find any increased risk of head tumors in MP users. Progress requires a critical analysis of the methodological elements necessary for an impartial evaluation of contradictory results (Box 11.2).

Box 11.2 Main methodological elements that should be considered to ensure the reliability of epidemiological studies on the relationship between MP use and increased risk of head tumors

1   The compatibility of latency and/or exposure time since first use of MPs with the progression time of the examined tumors;
2   the inclusion among the exposed of all users of MPs, cordless included;
3   the laterality of the head tumor localization relative to the habitual laterality of MP use;
4   the percentage of actually exposed subjects, based on the frequency and duration of the MP use;
5   the number of subjects selected (cases and controls), and the percentage of their participation in the study;
6   the distribution of the relative risk values (OR) above and under 1, and the probability that such distribution might be casual;
7   the full and correct selection and citation of data included in the meta-analyses.

The pooled analyses of epidemiological case-control studies by Hardell produced positive results indicating a cause–effect relationship (Hardell and Carlberg 2009; Hardell *et al.* 2011): exposures for or latencies from at least ten years to MPs increase by up to 100 percent the risk of tumors on the same side of the head preferred for phone use (ipsilateral tumors) – which is the only side significantly irradiated – with statistical significance for brain gliomas and acoustic neuromas. On the contrary, studies published under the Interphone project produced 'negative' results and are characterized by a substantial under-estimation of the risk of tumors (Interphone Study Group). The data published a year ago by Interphone included the risk of malignant (gliomas) and benign (meningiomas) brain tumors in people using only cell phones (not cordless), and have been widely publicized as reassuring by the authors as well as by the organizations that promoted and funded the study (IARC and EU 70 percent, the cell phone companies 30 percent), by the main agencies responsible for protecting human health and by more than 100 newspapers that have made headlines around the world. This, despite the article being accompanied by a 'commentary' with a very telling title: 'Call me on my mobile phone ... or better not?' – a look at the Interphone study results' (Saracci and Samet 2010). This commentary pointed out some major defects of the Interphone protocol and results that would have substantially 'diluted' risk estimates. In this context we consider even more important the editorial by E. Cardis – former coordinator of the Interphone project – and S. Sadetzki. The latter headed the Israeli Interphone team and his own studies – showing large increases in parotid tumor risk in regular and long-time cell phone users (Sadetzki *et al.* 2008) – were presented in September 2009 to the US Senate (Havas 2010). This editorial has a rather eloquent title: 'Indications of possible brain-tumor risk in mobile phone studies: should we be concerned?' (Cardis and Sadetzki 2011). Furthermore, the highly risk-assertive response of the two editorial authors was not based on new experimental data, but instead on a critical review of the results of the Interphone study (2010), to which they themselves contributed. It seems to us that such a stance represents a milestone in the quest for truth.[12] Additional factors contributing to 'dilution' of risk estimates, not reported by Cardis and Sadetzki in their editorial, are pointed out in our recent article (Levis *et al.* 2012a).[13]

Cardis and Sadetzki did not limit themselves to criticism, but reported that the Interphone data obtained using the essential factors for identifying a carcinogenic effect due to cell phone exposure – significant time use, continuity of use or latency of at least ten years and ipsilateral tumor detection – showed a statistically significant rise of up to 100 percent glioma risk in five studies – and the same is observed for acoustic neuromas (two studies) and parotid gland tumors (one study). As they stated: 'The overall balance of the above-mentioned arguments suggests the existence of a possible association' between cell phone use and increase in brain tumor risk.[14]

There are therefore many biases and flaws in the non-blind Interphone protocol, giving rise to a systematic under-estimate of the risk, whereas the double-blind protocol by Hardell producing positive results is without apparent errors, the results indicating a cause–effect relationship supported by biological plausibility (Box 11.3).

Box 11.3 Methodology errors in the Interphone negative studies on tumor risk from MP use, based on non-blind protocol. Reliability of positive Hardell studies on tumor risk from MP use, based on 'double-blind' protocol

1   *Interphone: inadequate assessment of the 'regular use of cell phones'* defined as 'at least 1 phone call/week, for at least 6 months': 2–5 minutes/day, often for less than five years. *Hardell: MP use is significant:* from over 16 to over 32 min/day for at least ten years.

2   *Interphone: inadequate exposure or latency time* in relation to the time required for diagnosing the tumors concerned: less than 5 percent of cases have latency time of at least ten years. *Hardell: 18 percent of cases were exposed for or from 10–15 years.*

3   *Interphone: fails to include cordless users,* even though they are exposed. *Hardell includes them.*

4   **Interphone:** *fails to include people younger than 30,* although they are exposed. **Hardell** *includes them.*

5   **Interphone:** *fails to include people living in rural areas,* although this group has high exposure. **Hardell** *includes them.*

6   **Interphone**: *fails to include subjects who had died or were too weak* to respond to the interview carried out during post-operatory convalescence. **Hardell** *includes them.*

7   **Interphone**: *fails to distinguish tumor laterality in relation to laterality of MP use.* **Hardell**: *tumor laterality is always considered in relation to laterality of MP use.*

8   **Interphone**: *fails to consider other types of malignant and benign head tumor, except for astrocytomas, neuromas, meningiomas and salivary gland tumors.* **Hardell**: *other types of head tumor are considered separately.*

9, 10 **Interphone:** *participation and selection bias.* The participation of the controls is reduced to 60 per cent, at times less than 40 per cent, with prevalence of the exposed. **Hardell:** exposed and non-exposed controls participate in equal proportion and in high percentage (nearly 90 percent). *There is no selection or participation bias.*

11   **Interphone:** *delayed interviews*: the controls are interviewed at a later stage than the cases (up to more than nine months). Also for this reason, given the rapid spread of MPs, the control group contains more exposed than the case group. **Hardell**: *case and control interviews are both conducted with no delay.*

12   **Interphone:** *data collection bias.* As it is impossible to collect responses from hospitalized cases that are frail, the information is collected from a relative (up to 40 percent of cases) with consequent data uncertainty. **Hardell**: the data are always provided by the subject concerned. *There is no collection bias.*

13   **Interphone:** *attribution bias in laterality of MP use.* The patient, interviewed face-to-face when still in a confused state during the post-operatory period, may report the most recent laterality of use which, owing to the disturbances brought about by the tumor, may not actually be the side habitually used before the development of the tumor. **Hardell**: the data are double-blind collected through questionnaires sent to the homes of the cases on their dismissal from hospital, when they are recovering. *There is no attribution bias.*

14   **Interphone:** *documentation bias.* In the bibliography cited to support the Interphone findings as reassuring, negative studies are widely reported and discussed; instead the positive studies of Hardell group are regularly ignored, under-evaluated or even selectively chosen. **Hardell**: negative Interphone studies are always cited and criticized, and their significant data are included in the meta-analyses. *There is no documentation bias.*

15   **Interphone:** *funding bias*: the findings from Interphone, which is co-funded by the cell phone companies, are publicized as fully reassuring – even though these at times include positive data indicative of increased carcinogenic risk, e.g., for only ipsilateral tumors, or only in the subgroup exposed for ten or more years, or only in residents in rural areas (one study). **Hardell:** all studies are funded by public bodies. *There is no funding bias.*

The discrepancy between the positive data of Hardell and the negative data from Interphone is also highlighted by other authors, who performed a meta-analysis of 24 case-control studies (Myung *et al.* 2009). These authors observed a statistically significant positive association between MP use and increased head cancer risk in ten studies using blinding ('high-quality studies', including seven studies by Hardell, just one by Interphone, and two by other groups), whereas a negative association (i.e., an apparent 'protective effect') was observed in 14 studies not using blinding ('low-quality studies', including 12 by Interphone, two by other groups, and one by Hardell). Elements in the method used to evaluate the 'quality' of the studies were: (1) blind or non-blind protocol; (2) presence or absence of participation and selection bias of cases and controls; (3) relevant or marginal MP exposures; (4) adequate or inadequate latency or overall time of MP use; (5) scrutiny of tumor laterality; (6) funding by independent sources or by cell phone companies. The authors reach the following conclusion: 'We feel the need to mention the funding sources for each research group because it is possible that these may have influenced the respective study designs and results'.[15]

Statistical relationships between positive or negative results and public or private funding in studies on EMF effects

Notes have already been made of the degree of conflicts of interests commonly found among researchers, scientific consultants and international organizations, and the ensuing consequences this situation has for the spread of distorted information, favoring the interests of the funding industries. According to Tomatis, the method used was 'the careful and systematic production of results, both experimental and epidemiological, whose sole purpose is to raise the background noise, increasing confusion and thereby making correct assessment of risk more difficult' (Tomatis 2007), and 'the best way to halt, or at least delay, a decision of public health issues is … to inject doubts about the validity of data that are uncomfortably positive' (Tomatis 2008: 39).[16] Conflicts of interests are particularly widespread in research on the effects of EMF. In fact, Hardell reports the following data (Hardell *et al.* 2006): (1) in 2001, out of 1,386 articles, 16 percent were funded privately; (2) by 2004 the number of articles funded privately had increased to 33 percent; (3) in 2004, 25 percent of articles published in two of the world's leading biomedical journals were signed by one or more authors with conflicts of interests. According to Hardell, these data are an underestimate owing to the accepted and now widespread custom in many journals not to indicate – or to indicate only partially – the sources of funding for the work carried out. This state of affairs means that information produced by independent research on the environmental and health risks of EMF has almost no influence.

In an interview published in July 2007 by the Association 'Liberterre', G. Carlo, author of the book *Cell Phones: Invisible Hazards in the Wireless Age*, stated that: (1) while perfectly aware of the health risks inherent in exposure to EMF, industry does not alter the present situation unless there is a drastic intervention from governments and national and international agencies responsible for protection of health; (2) the 'pollution' of scientific information due to funding given by industry to researchers, agencies and governments themselves has today reached unimaginable proportions – at least 50 percent of studies on the effects of EMF are funded by sector industries; (3) many scientists funded by these industries have stated that the results of their research, where unfavorable to the interests of the commissioner of the work, have been modified by this latter or deleted in full; (4) the likelihood of finding a no-effect result is six times higher in studies funded by the industry companies than in those funded by public bodies; (5) industry also controls the dissemination of scientific information about the effects of EMF, so also influencing the way the public perceives the dangers connected with the technologies in question.

One significant item of data has been published by Huss *et al.* (2007), who selected particularly important articles about the biological and health effects of MPs. If 1 is the average probability of statistically significant results in work funded by public bodies ($p < 0.05$), the probability of at least one positive result in those funded by the cell phone companies is almost zero (OR=0.11; 95 percent CI=0.02–0.78); that is just one positive result out of 10. The probability for studies with mixed funding sources falls in an intermediate position (OR=0.56; 95 percent CI=0.07–3.80), and even studies not citing any source of funding – increasingly common as a result of the permissive approach of too many editors – are affected by some influencing (OR=0.76; 95 percent CI=0.12–4.70). Huss *et al.* (2007) concludes by recommending that 'the interpretation of the results from existing and future studies of the health effects of RF radiation should take sponsorship into account'.

A critical review of studies on the biological and health effects of RF/EMF found that, out of 1,056 articles published in peer-reviewed journals, 44 percent reported negative results (no effect), with 93 percent being funded either by private bodies or by non-specified sources. Instead, 56 percent of the articles reviewed reported some kind of biological effect or harm to health, with 95 percent funded by public bodies (Levis *et al.* 2012b). As shown in Figure 11.1, there is massive intervention by the private funders in expensive testing and testing that is long and difficult to perform, such as experimental carcinogenesis on animals, genotoxicity testing which is predictive of possible carcinogenesis effects and epidemiological studies on head tumors in MP users, which is one of today's most controversial debates involving a possible relevant risk for human health. The intervention of private funders is instead lower in less costly tests, such as short-term testing of biological effects in *in vitro* systems and in animals, epidemiological studies of tumors in small numbers of occupationally or residentially exposed subjects and testing on electro sensitivity, which tends to use simple and quick tests on volunteers or statistical sampling on populations of limited size. Even so, there is a constant vast prevalence of negative results in studies funded by private bodies, and of positive results in those funded by public bodies, just as there is a constant, almost-zero probability that this difference is due to chance (Fisher test: p-value<0.0001–0.0004).

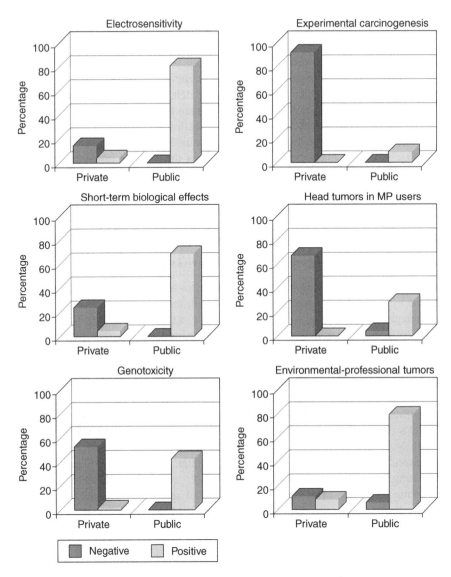

Figure 11.1 Relative percentage of results from all studies on health effects of RF/EMF of the individual topics, relative to the source of funding (public or private).

Epidemiological studies aimed at defending industrial interests: the case of EMF

Funding for EU programs on EMF effects

The EU programs on the effects of EMF (besides Interphone, these include Guard, CEMFEC, RAMP 2001, Perform A, EMF-NET, Reflex, Cefalo,

Cosmos), as the EU itself recognizes (European Commission 2005), are all co-funded by the mobile telephony industries. In fact, as that document explains:

> With strong public resistance to the siting of mobile antennae masts, the mobile telecommunications industry is naturally very concerned. The roll-out of new mobile technologies has been delayed and the wider take-up of beneficial new mobile services is slower than expected. The industry is well aware of the problems of risk communication and public perceptions and therefore contributes funds to research into the health effects of RF-EMF that is guided by the research priorities of the WHO's international EMF Project's research priorities. Industry funding contributions to national and EU research projects is provided in such a way as to ensure complete scientific independence. Worldwide, industry funding for EMF health effects is comparable to public funding.

The quality of reassuring opinions on health risks due to EMF

All the major national and international agencies and commissions are compromised by conflicts of interests and, as a result, make reference only to studies with negative results, that is, that are reassuring, so confirming the complete inability of mobile telephony radiation to induce head tumors, disregarding, dismissing or even manipulating the results of Hardell's work and even those – despite their indication of increased cancer risk – reported in some of the Interphone studies (see the above section on 'Mobile phones and head tumors').[17]

Among the mobile telephony companies, a major role is played by the Mobile Manufacturers Forum (MMF), which co-funds the Interphone Project and the WHO's EMF Project, as well as other international and national EMF programs. MMF is an umbrella body for the 12 main mobile telephony industries (Alcatel, Ericsson, Mitsubishi Electric, Motorola, Nokia, Panasonic, Philips, Sagem, Samsung, Siemens, Sony Ericsson and TCL and Alcatel Mobile Phones). Working alongside MMF in terms of financial support provided to the Interphone Project and other EU projects is the GSM Association, another strong lobby of the mobile telephony industries. And linked to these two is the 'Wi-Fi Alliance', which brings together the many industries involved in the uptake of new technologies and wireless services: there are 309 listed on the website www.wi-fi.org/our_members.php.[18]

Even some international science journals are involved in conflicts of interests

A number of scientific journals are compromised by conflicts of interests leading to manipulation of data on EMF effects: for example, supplement 6 *Bioelectromagnetics* from 2003, one of the leading journals in the sector, was commissioned by the 'Radiofrequency Committee' of the Institute of Electrical and Electronic Engineers to justify maintenance of the exposure limits set by

ICNIRP. The supplement contains seven monographs, all funded by the US Air Force and Navy, and written by their employees, who maintain that RF is harmless. The monographs cover all possible effects (mutagenesis, teratogenesis, *in vitro* transformation, carcinogenesis, effects on the nervous, endocrine, immunological systems, etc.). *Radiation Research*, another major journal in the field, published 21 articles between 1997 and 2006 on the genotoxic effects of RF: 17 of these (81 percent) described negative results, and all were funded by the mobile telephony operators (Motorola: ten articles) or the US Air Force (seven articles). In 1991 J. Moulder became editor of *Radiation Research* and was promoted to senior editor in 2000: all the while he acted as consultant to the electricity and mobile telephony industries (Electric Power Research Institute and Federation of the Electronics Industry, respectively), despite at the same time being a member of the UK's Independent Expert Group on Mobile Phones. In 2001 Vijayalaxmi joined the *Radiation Research* editorial committee, funded by the US Air Force and by Motorola, for whom he published seven articles in this journal, reporting negative results for the genotoxicity of RF.

These actions allow the international scientific agencies to postpone indefinitely any review of their opinions on the presumed harmlessness of EMF. Every 3–4 years, through one of the scientific journals funded by the operators of the technologies concerned, researchers employed or funded by these private companies are given the task of reviewing the effects of EMF. Through careful choice of negative studies and particular interpretation of some of the positive work, a fully reassuring picture is produced. The following year the international agencies call on a group of scientists apparently above suspicion (Ahlbom, Feychting, Repacholi, Kheifets, van Deventer, Vecchia, etc.) to obtain – using the reviews produced as described – the support necessary to confirm their reassuring conclusions.

Recent precautionary positions on health risks of EMF exposures

Alongside the strongly cautionary stance regarding the risks due to EMF exposure put forward by D. Gee, 'project manager of the emerging programs' of the EEA (set out in his chapter in the *BioInitiative Report* on the applications of the Precautionary Principle (Gee 2009)), an appeal was made in September 2007 and reiterated in January 2008 by the EEA's Executive Director, J. McGlade, calling for EU governments to lower the EMF exposure limits, especially for Wi-Fi emission, mobile telephony and their radio-base stations. In McGlade's words,

> There are many examples of the failure to use the Precautionary Principle in the past, which have resulted in serious and often irreversible damage to health and environments. Appropriate, precautionary and proportionate actions taken now to avoid plausible and potentially serious threats to health

from EMF are likely to be seen as prudent and wise from future perspectives. We must remember that precaution is one of the principles of EU environmental policy.

McGlade is convinced that:

> Over the last two years the epidemiological evidence of possible cancer risk amongst the 10 year plus mobile phone user group, has got stronger. It is now also supported by preliminary scientific reports on the damaging effect to cells of RF and ELF EMF exposures. This is a cause for concern, given the widespread and generally rising exposure of the public to RF from mobile phone technology.... For example, the French part of the WHO coordinated International Interphone study reported that the risk of head tumors is particularly evident in those mobile phone users who have had RF exposures at and above 460 hours per year for over 15 years. This evidence is supported by several other epidemiological studies carried out in Sweden, UK, Germany, and Israel, all of which find some evidence of increased risks of head tumors in the 10 year plus exposure groups.

Furthermore, she underlines that:

> The evidence, though necessarily limited at this point in time, is sufficient for health authorities to consider advising the reduction of RF exposures, where feasible. I note that such advice was issued by the German Federal Office for Radiation Protection (July 2007), and the French Ministry of Health (January 2008). It would also be prudent to reconsider the adequacy of the ICNIRP guidelines on exposure limits of 1998 to protect public health, especially of vulnerable groups.

Even stronger positions supporting the need for a cautionary approach to EMF exposure and more critical of the failure of the ICNIRP, WHO and EC to act are set out in two important documents, again from the EEA: one article by Gee (2009) and one report by the EEA (2007/2008) from 2008. These two documents re-examine the history of the errors made in science and by public health in tackling the problems arising in the past by 15 chemical and physical agents found to be harmful to human health, and underline what these 'past lessons' can teach in terms of prevention of risks from EMF, in particular RF (mobile telephony). Furthermore, they also provide vital keys for a proper understanding of the status of knowledge and criteria for assessing the risks to human health from EMF exposure, and for drawing up the consequent, pressing cautionary measures.

On 19 December 2008, the Commission on the Environment, Public Health and Food Safety of the European Parliament (EP) announced a 'Preliminary report on preoccupations concerning the effects on human health of electromagnetic fields' (www.next-up.org). Among other statements, the report:

1 'reiterates its demand to the Council to update its recommendation 1999/519/CE in favor of more stringent exposure limits for all devices that emit electromagnetic radiation in the frequencies between 0.1 MHz and 300 GHz, taking into account the best available technology on the market';

2 'asks the Commission to find a way to accelerate the enactment of the directive 2004/40/CE and thus to ensure that workers are protected effectively from EMFs';

3 'draws attention to the appeal for prudence made by the coordinator of the Interphone study, E. Cardis, who, on the basis of current knowledge, recommends that children should not make unreasonable use of a mobile phone and should preferably use a landline phone';

4 'suggests also to the Commission, prompted by concern for political and budgetary efficiency, a re-routing of the Community funding devoted to the study of EMFs towards a far-reaching campaign to educate young Europeans in the best ways to use a mobile phone, such as using a 'hands-free' kit, making only short calls and using a phone in the areas where the reception is good';

5 'proposes an addition to the mandate of the European group for Ethics in Science and New Technologies: the task of evaluating scientific integrity in order to help the Commission forestall possible situations of risk, conflicts of interests or even the frauds which tend to arise in a context of heightened competition among researchers';[19]

6 'condemns certain marketing campaigns by the phone operators, which are particularly strident in the year-end holiday period, such as the sale of mobile phones designed exclusively for children, or the "free minutes" deals aimed at adolescents';

7 'proposes that the Union includes in its policy regarding the quality of indoor air the study of wireless devices used in the home, such as Wi-Fi for internet access and cordless phones, which have multiplied these last few years in public places and in homes, exposing people to continuous microwave emission';

8 'calls on the Council and the Commission, in coordination with member States and the Committee for the Regions, to work towards putting in place a single standard in order to minimize the exposure of those living nearby if there is an extension to the network of high-voltage power lines';

9 'is very struck by the fact that the insurance companies tend to exclude cover for risks linked with EM fields from their policies of public liability, which means evidently that European insurers are already acting on the principle of precaution';[20]

10 'charges the President to transmit the present resolution to the Council, to the Commission, to the governments and parliaments of member States, to the Committee for the Regions and to the WHO'.

The Commission also states that:

This is the approach chosen by the EEA which in September 2007 courageously advised the public authorities of the 27 member States to take measures to provide better protection for the public, measures that are appropriate and in proportion in order to avoid serious dangers in the future. This represents a significant move forward on this issue, a call for action that contrasts with the *status quo* favored by the WHO. In fact the WHO seems to want to play for time, offering us an appointment in 2015 for a full estimate of the impact of electromagnetic radiation of human beings.

On 4 September 2009 the EP approved in plenary session and with wide majority the text proposed by the Commission noted above (www.europarl. europa.eu/sides/getDoc.do?type=TA&reference=P6-TA-2009-0216&language=IT&ring=A6-2009-0089), and at the same time issued a press release that, bearing the logos of the then-imminent European elections (www. elezioni2009.eu-1/3), assumed the sense of a real and proper program for the future parliamentary mandate.

In May 2011 a draft resolution adopted unanimously by the Committee on the Environment, Agriculture and Local and Regional Affairs of the EP riveted that:

1   'as regards standards or threshold values for emissions of electromagnetic fields of all types and frequencies, the Assembly recommends that the ALARA or "as low as reasonably achievable" principle is applied, covering both the so-called thermal effects and the athermic or biological effects of electromagnetic emissions or radiation. Moreover, the Precautionary Principle should be applicable when scientific evaluation does not allow the risk to be determined with sufficient certainty, especially given the context of growing exposure of the population, including particularly vulnerable groups such as young people and children, which could lead to extremely high human and economic costs of inaction if early warnings are neglected';

2   'the Assembly regrets that, despite calls for the respect of the Precautionary Principle and, despite all the recommendations, declarations and a number of statutory and legislative advances, there is still a lack of reaction to known or emerging environmental and health risks and virtually systematic delays in adopting and implementing effective preventive measures. Waiting for high levels of scientific and clinical proof before taking action to prevent well-known risks can lead to very high health and economic costs, as was the case with asbestos, leaded petrol and tobacco';

3   'moreover, the Assembly notes that the problem of electromagnetic fields or waves and the potential consequences for the environment and health has clear parallels with other current issues, such as the licensing of medication, chemicals, pesticides, heavy metals or genetically modified organisms. It therefore highlights that the issue of independence and credibility of scientific expertise is crucial to accomplish a transparent and balanced assessment of potential negative impacts on the environment and human health';

4   'in light of the above considerations, the Assembly recommends that the member states of the Council of Europe: a) take all reasonable measures to reduce exposure to electromagnetic fields, especially to radio frequencies

from mobile phones, and particularly the exposure to children and young people who seem to be most at risk from head tumors; b) reconsider the scientific basis for the present electromagnetic fields exposure standards set by the ICNIRP, which have serious limitations, and apply Precautionary and ALARA Principles, covering both thermal effects and the athermic or biological effects of electromagnetic emissions or radiation; c) put in place information and awareness-raising campaigns on the risks of potentially harmful long-term biological effects on the environment and on human health, especially targeting children, teenagers and young people of reproductive age; d) pay particular attention to "electrosensitive" persons suffering from a syndrome of intolerance to electromagnetic fields and introduce special measures to protect them, including the creation of wave-free areas not covered by the wireless network; e) in order to reduce costs, save energy, and protect the environment and human health, step up research on new types of antennas and mobile phone and DECT-type devices, and encourage research to develop telecommunication based on other technologies which are just as efficient but have less negative effects on the environment and health';

5   'concerning the private use of mobile phones, DECT phones, Wi-Fi, WLAN and WiMAX for computers and other wireless devices such as baby phones: a) set preventive thresholds for levels of long-term exposure to microwaves in all indoor areas, in accordance with the Precautionary Principle, not exceeding 0.6 V/m, and in the medium term to reduce it to 0.2 V/m; b) undertake appropriate risk-assessment procedures for all new types of device prior to licensing; c) introduce clear labeling indicating the presence of microwaves or electromagnetic fields, the transmitting power or the specific absorption rate (SAR) of the device and any health risks connected with its use; d) raise awareness on potential health risks of DECT-type wireless telephones, baby monitors and other domestic appliances which emit continuous pulse waves, if all electrical equipment is left permanently on standby, and recommend the use of wired, fixed telephones at home or, failing that, models which do not permanently emit pulse waves';

6   'concerning the protection of children: a) develop within different ministries (education, environment and health) targeted information campaigns aimed at teachers, parents and children to alert them to the specific risks of early, ill-considered and prolonged use of mobiles and other devices emitting microwaves; b) ban all mobile phones, DECT phones or Wi-Fi or WLAN systems from classrooms and schools, as advocated by some regional authorities, medical associations and civil society organizations';

7   'concerning the planning of electric power lines and relay antenna base stations: a) introduce town planning measures to keep high-voltage power lines and other electric installations at a safe distance from dwellings; b) apply strict safety standards for sound electric systems in new dwellings; c) reduce threshold values for relay antennas in accordance with the ALARA principle and install systems for comprehensive and continuous monitoring of

all antennas; d) determine the sites of any new GSM, UMTS, Wi-Fi or WiMAX antennas not solely according to the operators' interests but in consultation with local and regional government officials, local residents and associations of concerned citizens';

8   'concerning risk assessment and precautions: a) make risk assessment more prevention oriented; b) improve risk-assessment standards and quality by creating a standard risk scale, making the indication of the risk level mandatory, commissioning several risk hypotheses and considering compatibility with real life conditions; c) pay heed to and protect "early warning" scientists; d) formulate a human rights oriented definition of the Precautionary and ALARA Principles; e) increase public funding of independent research, *inter alia* through grants from industry and taxation of products which are the subject of public research studies to evaluate health risks; f) create independent commissions for the allocation of public funds; g) make the transparency of lobby groups mandatory; h) promote pluralist and contradictory debates between all stakeholders, including civil society (Aarhus Convention)'.

This resolution is accompanied by a 'memorandum' underlining that:

1   'with regard to the frequently inconclusive if not contradictory findings of scientific research and studies on the possible risks of products, medicines or, in this case, electromagnetic fields, a number of comparative studies do seem to suggest a fairly strong correlation between the origin of their funding – private or public – and the findings of risk assessments, a manifestly unacceptable situation pointing to conflicts of interest which undermine the integrity, the genuine independence and the objectivity of scientific research';

2   'accordingly, in this field and in others, one should call for genuine independence on the part of the expert appraisal agencies and for independent, multidisciplinary and properly balanced expert input. There must no longer be situations where whistle-blowers are discriminated against and renowned scientists with critical opinions are excluded when experts are selected to sit on expert committees or no longer receive funding for their research';

3   'it seems obvious that the prime considerations for societies dependent on electricity, mobile telephony and telecommunication are the economic and financial parameters, hence profits and market shares. Understandably, in this context more stringent regulations and threshold values which ostensibly inhibit their business dealings are viewed with disfavor and forcefully resisted – as could be seen from the irritated and sometimes emotional statements of a representative of French mobile telephony at our committee's hearing for contrastive expert opinion';

4   'serious scientific and medical studies revealing biological effects of a pathological nature have existed since the 1930s concerning radio frequencies and microwaves from radar installations and harmful effects of protracted

exposure to the low or very low frequency electromagnetic fields of electrical transmission lines or computer screens were observed already in the late 1970s'.

And this resolution concludes that:

1 'after analyzing the scientific studies available to date, and also following the hearings for expert opinions organized in the context of this Committee there is sufficient evidence of potentially harmful effects of electromagnetic fields on fauna, flora and human health to react and to guard against potentially serious environmental and health hazards';

2 'that was moreover already the case in 1999 and 2009 when the European Parliament overwhelmingly passed resolutions upholding the Precautionary Principle and efficient preventive actions vis-à-vis the harmful effects of electromagnetic fields, in particular by substantially lowering the exposure thresholds for workers and the general public according to the ALARA Principle, by restoring genuine independence of research in that field, and through a policy of enhanced information and transparency towards the anxious populations';

3 'lastly, the Assembly could endorse the analyses and warnings issued first in September 2007, then in September 2009, by the European Environment Agency (EEA) concerning the health hazards of electromagnetic fields, mobile telephony and not least mobile phones. According to the EEA, there are sufficient signs or levels of scientific evidence of harmful biological effects to invoke the application of the Precautionary Principle and of effective, urgent preventive measures'.

The above text was adopted on 27 May 2011 by the EP Standing Committee, acting on behalf of the EP Council (http://assembly.coe.int/Documents/Adopted-Text/ta11/eRES1815.htm). This EP Resolution no. 1815 modified only the above point 6b, adopting a less stringent recommendation, that is: 'For children in general, and particularly in schools and classrooms, give preference to wired internet connections, and strictly regulate the use of mobile phones by school-children on school premises.'

How to promote protection against the health effects of exposure to EMF

In view of the considerable volume of experimental data demonstrating the biological and health effects of EMF, plus possible mechanisms of action, the position held today by the WHO, EC, ICNIRP, IARC and other major national and international agencies appears unsustainable and without justification – this stance draws from guidelines drawn up at the end of the 1990s and is based on theoretical assumptions from over 50 years ago. In fact, for defining the exposure limits these guidelines are based on: (1) health effects alone, thus ignoring the biological data that underpin them and help explain the mechanisms by which they arise; (2) only effects that have been unequivocally demonstrated and accepted by the whole scientific community, quite overlooking the Precautionary Principle; (3) thermal effects alone, while non-thermal effects, in particular effects at low intensity, are now well documented; (4) short-term effects alone, disregarding long-term effect data found in the literature, in particular genetic and carcinogenic effects.

This position – also shared by the main bodies concerned with protection of human health, is a priori rigid, refutes historical evidence, declines scientific challenge and appears to be influenced not by prudence but by conservation of clearly identifiable financial interests. Data in the scientific literature in fact clearly justify an urgent revision of national laws on EM pollution, in particular in terms of the principle of minimization through the preventive planning and programming by the regions and municipalities as regards development of EMF-emitting installations, along with information campaigns and participation of the citizen.

Quantifying the long-term risks is difficult for residential exposure to ELF/ EMF because this requires conclusive data on the body of the population exposed and on the values of the magnetic fields present. As regards mobile telephony, our examination of the literature data leads us to conclude that even today the risk of head tumors resulting from MP use is very high (Levis *et al.* 2011, 2012a). Lloyd-Morgan (2009), while under-estimating by 50 percent the number of cell phone users, without considering the risk for cordless users and assuming a minimum latency time of 30 years, calculates 'there would be about 1,900 cell phone-induced brain tumors out of about 50,000 brain tumors diagnosed in 2004, increasing to about 380,000 cell phone-induced brain tumors within 2019 in the USA alone', which would require 'an increase in health costs of an annual US\$9.5 billion and the need for a 7-fold increase in number of neurosurgeons'. An estimate of the incidence of head tumors must begin with the correct number of cell phone users (five billion subscriptions worldwide at mid-2010), should also consider the risk to cordless users and assume at least a doubling of the incidence of head tumors and of acoustic neuromas as documented by Hardell already after a latency of at least 10–15 years, which gives about 750,000 new cases worldwide even today.

As if this were not enough, a number of factors raise our concern still further: the latency of head tumors induced by MPs can exceed 30 years; risk is higher in those starting MP use when young and who have not yet accumulated ten years of latency; there is a continued rise in MP use by young people, attracted to new facilities from the MP companies (photography, listening to music, videophony, internet); the data by Hardell on the increase in risk of other types of malign and benign head tumor – besides brain gliomas, astrocytomas, acoustic neuromas and parotid gland tumors – are for the main part today only indicative. Therefore, there is no doubt that today we are dealing with just the tip of an iceberg, and will have to wait one or two decades before its real dimensions come to light. But it is clear that a significant increase in tumor risk is already established, so that the use of MPs could lead to a health crisis of dramatic proportions (Lloyd Morgan *et al.* 2009).

While recognizing that mobile telephony is an extraordinary technology of inestimable value, responsible science must raise awareness of the risks involved.[21]

As also expressed by the EEA and the EP, we thus conclude that there is sufficient epidemiological evidence to warrant application of the Precautionary Principle aimed at:

- setting exposure limits that are precautionary;
- limiting the spread of wireless technology in schools and highly frequented places (libraries, offices, hospital wards);
- providing accurate information about the risks from exposure to MPs, with low-cost voluntary options ('prudent avoidance') based on caution in the use of MPs and other devices emitting MFs. A ten-point list of simple personal actions designed to substantially reduce exposure to cell phone radiation was produced by Viennese Medical Officers in 2006, adopted in the same year by the French Agency on Radiofrequencies (www.sante_radiofrequences.org), and by several international scientific committees (see note 7 and a document signed by 20 scientists: www.devradavis.com);
- awareness-raising in schools through a campaign on the use of the various wireless transmission technologies;
- discouraging the use of MPs by minors under 14 years;
- epidemiological monitoring of the possible harmful effects produced by residential and occupational ELF and RF/EMF exposures.

Given the results and considerations set out in the section on 'Mobile phones and head tumors', it is small wonder that a number of scientists have maintained that 'the long-term use of cell phones was leading to brain tumors and was more dangerous to health than smoking cigarettes' (Pawl 2008: 445), and that 'MPs could kill far more people than smoking or asbestos' (the reader is referred to Khurana – an Australian neurosurgeon who collaborated with Hardell in the meta-analyses showing increased risk of head tumors in MP users – interviewed by G. Lean for *The Independent*, 30 March 2008).

In conclusion, it is perfectly clear that an *ex ante* evaluation of the overall impacts of today's technological innovations is not only compatible with the Precautionary Principle, but actually necessary, as also borne out – as we saw above – both in some of the Italian magistracy's statements and in the recommendations of the EP and of the EEA. This evaluation is particularly vital in the case of exposure to EMF, given the state of advancement of scientific knowledge about their possible/probable harmful effects on human health. In fact, the Precautionary Principle was designed to justify actions to protect the public and the environment even in the absence of any significant knowledge, so it could be used to justify exposure reductions to EMF despite the amount of – seemingly but almost never ad-hoc produced – conflicting evidence of risks.

Should any doubt still remain, it is worth recalling the consequences of the four main scenarios facing us with EMF, especially with RF from mobile phones, underlined by Gee (2009):

> The first is similar to the case studies where much avoidable harm was not prevented. The second is where precautionary actions to reduce MF exposure prevent much potential harm, whilst stimulating more sustainable innovation in the production and use of MP technologies and energy systems. The third is where such precautionary actions to reduce exposures are taken but turn out to have been unnecessary, needlessly costly, and worrisome. The fourth is that no action is taken to reduce exposure and no convincing harm emerges from EMF exposure. We do not know which scenario will unfold, but we do know that a choice over current and future EMF exposures must be made now, if the costs of possibly being wrong are to be minimized. The choice is ours. Shakespeare might have described our dilemma thus: to know or not to know, to act or not to act?

The tragedy is that the unfolding story of EMF looks set to become another case of history repeating itself – following in the tracks of ionizing radiation, asbestos, tobacco smoke and many other now-demonstrated human carcinogens where evidence of harm was officially recognized only a score or even more years after the initial warnings. In view of the evidence we already have, this time we can act early, rather than giving cause for future generations once again to regret our inaction – it is our duty and responsibility as scientists, in particular to our offspring!

Conclusions

Disguising or playing down the evidence of harm to health is not simple to do; in fact, this deception is often easy to detect. The malpractice uses a few elements that can be found almost systematically in the formal studies of many corporations and government agencies. These often show an exposed population to be at lower incidence and/or mortality risk for all diseases than the control population (at least for the few times the results are actually examined). But how is this paradoxical conclusion possible? Authors usually try to argue that exposure does not induce adverse health effects, the '*healthy worker effect*'[22] being produced unintentionally. Once the source(s) of the biases in scientific studies on public health have been identified, attempts can be made to determine whether these limitations and errors are structurally inevitable, accidental or intentional. It is possible, however, that financial motives are a driver in certain research areas, for example industrial chemicals, asbestos, vinyl chloride, beryllium, alcohol, cigarette smoke, diagnostics, some pharmaceuticals, and as we see here, electromagnetic fields.

A recent communication laid the groundwork for an initial, systematic identification of the criteria needed for a fast, transparent and standard assessment of intentional deception through the integrated evaluation of three elements: the *quantity* of errors (or biases), the *direction* of these errors/biases and the *size* of the incorrect estimates present in each epidemiological study (Gennaro and Ricci 2010). We believe that evaluation of these three elements can enable the detection of the deliberate manipulation and deviation of public health scientific studies in favor of economic and career interests. Systematic bias detection may also help counter the skepticism and mistrust surrounding most epidemiological research, and enable all but sound, socially useful, evidence-based epidemiological research to be filtered out.

Business biases as collective risks are very common. There is mounting evidence to show that cartels are very influential in the assessment of the overall effects of most scientific/technical innovations. This state of affairs matters in reality. Indeed, in many countries over the past two decades (data for Italy are available only up to 2008) the reported trend of improvement in healthy life expectancy – for many years showing an increased number of disease-free years of life (over six months) – came to an abrupt halt and reversed (Eurostat 2011). Is it possible to postulate causes of the situation described in this chapter other than the *business bias*?

Appendix: abbreviations

CI	confidence index
EC	European Commission
EEA	European Environment Agency
ELF	extremely low frequencies
EMF	electromagnetic fields
EP	European Parliament
EU	European Union
Ghz	gigahertz
Hz	hertz
IARC	International Agency for Research on Cancer
ICNIRP	International Commission for Non-Ionizing Radiation Protection
Khz	kilohertz
μT	microTesla
MF	magnetic field
MMF	Mobile Manufacturers Forum
MPs	mobile phones
OR	odds ratio
RF	radiofrequencies
SCENIHR	Scientific Committee on Emerging and Newly Identified Health Risk (EC)
UN	United Nations
V/m	Volts/meter
WHO	World Health Organization

Acknowledgments

Financial support was provided by the University of Padua, Italy. The authors wish to thank Dr. Susan Biggin for precious suggestions and language/editorial input in preparation of the manuscript. Special thanks are due to Laura Masiero, Pietro Frigato and Simona Gennaro for their valuable suggestions.

Notes

1 *Conflict of interests*: the authors declare they do not have any conflict of interest.
2 There are rather well-established methods used to confuse epidemiological results and compromise their consequences. The most common biases identified are: (1) inadequate design of the epidemiological study; (2) lack of a standardized protocol; (3) incorrect reference population – wrong selection, combination and dilution of both cases and controls, e.g., inclusion of cases among the controls; (4) failure to choose the subjects most exposed and most sensitive; (5) a priori decision to study only a few and rare selected diseases, e.g., a few rare risk factors; (6) over-short follow-up for tumors with long-term latencies; (7) only high risks (OR > 2) are taken into account, despite the relevance of even lower risks when exposure concerns a high number of subjects; (8) undervaluation of the synergistic role of multiple risk factors (simply because law limits are respected for each single factor); (9) the epidemiological study is considered only from a simple statistical point of view; (10) experimental data supporting the plausibility of harmful biological effects are systematically ignored; (11) flawed multicenter results are given too much weight, overlooking the much more significant results produced by just one research center; (12) constant reference is made to unreliable results in order to bolster the interests of private corporations; (13) even when funding from industry is actually reported, conflicts of interests are often not declared; (14) Precautionary and Prevention Principles are both ignored; (15) there is preference to protect the economic status quo rather than public health.
3 Documents published since 1953 by the American Conference of Government and Industrial Hygienists (ACGIH), and by the Conferences of American Military Bodies held since 1957 by the Air Research and Development Command, USA. The ACGIH is neither a public body nor a government organization, but an industry-based private association of hygienists, despite the misleading name (Casson 2007: 23). The ACGIH's role in underlining the inadequate exposure limits for protecting human health – totally ignoring experimental and epidemiological evidence – has been widely reported. The ACGIH has very close ties with private industry and, of the over 600 threshold values set by the ACGIH, at least 100 are based exclusively on the opinion of industry experts, without any experimental support (Davis 2008: 357). As regards the interests of the American military bodies in the development of RF, we can note the report by the Naval Studies Board, Division of Engineering and Physical Sciences (2002: 2–13). In this report, the section on 'Directed-energy non lethal weapons' states that:

> The first RF non-lethal weapons are based on a biophysical susceptibility known empirically for decades. The heating action of RF signals is well understood and can be the basis for several additional directed-energy weapons. Leap-ahead non-lethal weapons technologies will probably be based on more subtle human–RF interactions in which the signal information within the RF exposure causes an effect other than simply heating: for example, stun, seizure, startle and decreased spontaneous activity.

This admission by the Naval Studies Board confirms that:

1) some of these non-thermal effects can be weaponized with bioeffects that are incontrovertibly adverse to health; 2) there has been knowledge for decades about the susceptibility of human beings to non-thermal levels of RF exposure; 3) the concept that RF interacts with humans based on the RF information content (signal information) rather than heating, so it can occur at subtle energy levels, not at high levels associated with tissue heating, is well established; 4) a dedicated scientific research effort is promising enough for continued federal funding.

(Sage *et al.* 2007: §4, 11–12)

The magazine *Nexus* (no. 69, August–September 2007: 'EM Arms and Human Rights'; www.nexusitalia.com) shows that the American military–industrial–intelligence complex has an arsenal of EM arms for use in today's battlefields and against the citizen as a means of social control, in contravention of the convention on human rights. During the 1950s and 1960s the CIA began seeking methods for influencing cognition, emotions and human behavior. This research included the wireless use of EM energy defined as 'informatic war' and 'non-lethal arms'. New technological capabilities have been developed under projects financed through slush funding over recent decades: these technologies bring about the ability to influence the human emotions, disturb thought and inflict severe pain through the manipulation of EM fields. The EM spectrum has provided a range of new weapons that have already been adopted in both private and military arenas, for example millimeter waves, pulsed energy projectiles (PEPs) and other high-power EM arms. PEPs represent a type of weapon used to paralyze a victim with pain: the expansion of the plasma acts on the nerve cells and the long-term effects are still quite unknown. The direct acoustic device 'voice-to-skull' is a non-lethal EM weapon that produces highly disturbing noises within the cranium. This technology has been tested by businesses including McDonald's and Wal-Mart to direct advertising messages into the consumer's head. The power of the US Defense Department (UDD) is hard to believe: in May 2006 the Air Force provided a total of $24 million in contracts for 'research and development' (R&D) on EMF to Northrop Grumman, Voss Scientific, Lockheed Martin, Electro-Magnetic Applications and other private companies. Already in 1996 the UDD had recognized a key element in wars of the future in R&D on EM radiation. The development of non-lethal weapons has also been taken up by the universities, with millions of dollars being set aside for grants and research doctorates: the Pennsylvania State University hosts the Institute for Non-Lethal Defense Technologies, the New Jersey University of Medicine and Dentistry hosts the Institute for Stress and Motivated Behavior, the University of New Hampshire hosts the Center for Non-Lethal Technological Innovation, while many military schools fund courses on the technology of non-lethal weapons.

4 ICNIRP (1996). Overview of research papers limited to the biological and health effects of RF/EMF with negative results, funded mainly by managers or operators of the technologies concerned. The few papers showing positive results cited – of the many found in the literature – were labeled as 'inadequate number of repetitions', 'not significant' or 'carried out under conditions of sizable thermal increase', even though these criticisms were quite invalid.

5 ICNIRP (1998). Overview regarding all EMF frequencies (0–300 GHz), carried out using the same criteria as above. At the time, the ICNIRP members with conflicts of interests included: M. Repacholi, president until 1996; M. Grandolfo, vice-president until 1996; M. Hietanen, vice-president from 1996; R. Matthes, scientific secretary; R. Saunders, P. Vecchia and E. Vogel, 'external experts'. At a later date, P. Vecchia became president of ICNIRP, M. Hietanen became vice-president and M. Repacholi became emeritus president.

6 ICNIRP: in 1974 the self-appointed working group of the International Radiation Protection Association (IRPA) set up a sub-group on Non-Ionizing Radiation (NIR). At

the Paris conference of 1977 IRPA and NIR then formed the International Non-Ionizing Radiation Committee (INIRC). In the following years, IRPA, INIRC and the WHO collaborated on developing the guideline criteria for protection of human health from EMF. Finally, at the Montreal conference of 1982, IRPA and INIRC formed ICNIRP. Since 1996 (see note 4) this body has adopted the proposal – already drawn up earlier by the WHO and IRPA – of considering only the acute effects of a thermal nature when defining the limit values of exposure to EMF, and since that date these values have remained unchanged in all subsequent revisions made by ICNIRP (1998, note 5; Ahlbom *et al.* 2004: see note 16). The particular attention given to ICNIRP by authoritative international bodies results from the close ties this body has established with the WHO (M. Repacholi was for many years president then emeritus president of ICNIRP and, at the same time, head of the WHO's EMF Project), and with the EC (see the following note).

European Commission: despite the unanimous view expressed by the EP on the basis of a report from one of its scientific committees, in conflict with adoption of the guidelines and limits proposed by ICNIRP, the EC on 12 July 1999 adopted recommendation 519/EC, which accepted in full the ICNIRP/WHO proposals. The following years saw an ever-increasing strengthening of the links between ICNIRP, the WHO and EC (through SCENIHR, the EC's scientific commission on EMF), expanding to increasing numbers of national commissions (see note below and notes 16 and 17), and also tighter relationships even with operators of the technologies using EMF, in particular MMF (see note 18). A well-documented criticism of the conflicts of interests compromising the initiatives of the ICNIRP–WHO–EC consortium – listing cases where the founding principles of these bodies are flouted – was published by D. Maisch (2006). Anyway, ICNIRP remains a private and fully autonomous body, and as sanctions cannot be applied to this association – as was recognized by the UN Secretary-General when responding to one of the many cases brought by associations, private citizens and groups of scientists – since intervening to alter the static positions of ICNIRP was not possible precisely because of its body's private nature. Instead, there are the cautionary positions held by other 'independent' committees, medical associations and even the EEA and EP, to protect human health from the short-term biological effects and the long-term effects (certainly not thermal in nature) of EMF – these positions are highly critical of the 'monopoly' formed by ICNIRP, the WHO, EC and their countless 'ramifications' (see note 7 and the main text).

WHO: the reader is referred to the 'fact sheets' published since 1998 regarding the 'EMF Project' launched by the WHO and co-funded by the electricity network operators and the mobile telephony companies. Leading the project until 2006 was M. Repacholi, also emeritus president of the ICNIRP, member of various national scientific committees and consultant to various electricity and mobile telephony companies, as he himself has admitted to the Australian Senate and in a number of interviews. In 2006 E. van Deventer took over the position. See: Valberg *et al.* (2007), review funded by the National Institute of Environmental Health Sciences and by the WHO, despite Valberg having a senior role in a private energy company for which Repacholi himself often acted as consultant (Gradient Corporation USA).

National scientific committees: the reader is referred to the reports of the Royal Society of Canada (Krewski *et al.* 2001; the Independent Expert Group on Mobile Phones (IEGMP 2000); the 'Zmirou Report' (2001); the reports of the UK National Radiological Protection Board (NRPB 2004) and the most recent reports (Swedish Radiation Protection Authority 2006; SCENIHR/EC 2007; Health Council of the Netherlands 2007; Mobile Telecommunications and Health Research Programme 2007). All set out almost only the negative data, while the few positive results quoted, among the many that exist, are considered 'inadequate' or 'inadequate number of repetitions' or sometimes are even partially processed to make them appear 'not significant'. Furthermore, many of the members of these committees have clear conflicts of interests even though they declare that the funding received from the companies with interests in the area concerned does not represent any conflict of interests.

7 From 1997 positions of caution have been presented at conferences putting forward the need to minimize exposure, with drastic reduction in the limits adopted by ICNIRP/WHO/EC: for example, Rockville ('Physical characteristics and possible biological effects of microwaves applied in wireless communication' 1997); Vienna ('Possible biological and health effects of electromagnetic fields' 1998); Salzburg ('International conference on cell tower siting' 2000: www.land-sbg.gu.at/celltower); Stockholm ('Workshop on electrosensitivity' 2001: www.Feb.se/NEWS/Program10927.pdf) In addition, the 'STOA Report' by Hyland (2001); the 'independent' International Commission for the Electro-Magnetic Safety (ICEMS) funded in Venice 2002; the influential *BioInitiative Report* 2007 (see note 3), noted by bodies including the EEA and the EP; and the extremely cautionary position of the Russian National Committee on Non-Ionizing Radiation Protection 2008. Many strongly 'cautionary' appeals have also been published by doctors from various countries: Freiburg 2002; Helsinki 2005; Brussels 2007, Holland 2009. In particular there is the well-known 'Appeal from the Viennese Doctors' 2007, with an attached 'vademecum' for voluntarily limiting the risk from EMF exposure, plus a review of initiatives of various European governments (France, Austria, Germany, Great Britain, Spain, Luxembourg) for minimizing the dissemination of new wireless technologies (Wi-Fi, WiMAX) and for reducing exposure limits to RF.

8 OR ('odds ratio'): the relationship between the number of sick (cases) in exposed and non-exposed subjects. The OR is calculated on the basis of the ratio: exposed cases/non-exposed cases × non-exposed controls (non-sick subjects)/exposed controls. A 95 percent CI (confidence interval): probability interval at 95 percent of OR. When OR is above 1 and 95 percent CI does not include 1 (i.e., the whole 95 percent CI interval lies above 1) means that in the exposed there is a statistically significant increase at 95 percent probability of falling ill. In the specific case, the values indicate that there is 95 percent probability that the risk of falling ill from leukemia (OR) in children who lived exposed to $0.4\,\mu T$ lies between 1.3 and 3.1 relative to that (OR=1) of children who live exposed to below $0.1\,\mu T$, and that the most probable increase in risk is a doubling (OR=2.0).

9 IARC is an international scientific organization which operates under the sponsorship of the WHO. Tomatis and Huff warn that from 1994 IARC has witnessed a complete overhaul of the criteria for evaluating carcinogenicity, with a wholesale devaluation of the criteria underpinning identification of carcinogenic factors: (1) the criteria for evaluating the carcinogenicity of an agent, based on study of the mechanisms of action (biological effects, in particular genotoxic) are no longer applied; (2) the evidence of carcinogenicity deriving from animal experimentation is undervalued; (3) possible confounding factors of the scientific criteria aimed at primary prevention of carcinogens in the workplace or at home are highlighted out of all proportion; (4) consequently, epidemiological data are hardly ever conclusive; (5) there is a higher percentage (from less than 10 percent in the 1970s to over 30 percent in the 1990s) of experts predisposed to favor the industrial interests, who are being invited by IARC into the working groups (see, for instance, note 16). It follows that, according to Tomatis and Huff, the IARC monographs have lost the authority and independence they original had. This criticism can easily be leveled at the ELF/EMF monograph: in fact, the IARC working group involved in the preparation of the IARC ELF/EMF monograph (2002) included M. Repacholi, president of ICNIRP and coordinator of the WHO's EMF Project, funded by electricity network and mobile cell phone companies (see note 6: ICNIRP and WHO); L. Kheifets, employee of Electric Power Research Institute (EPRI), a private body which enjoys all US electricity company research funding; J. Juutilainen, C. Blackman, D. McCormick, C. Porter, M. Mevissen, J. Schuz – all participating also in the IARC 2011 RF/EMF panel (see note 16) –

and R.D. Saunders and B. Veyret, all members of various national committees, but all with conflicts of interests; and also representatives of major electricity companies: J. Swanson (National Grid Company, UK); W.H. Bailey (Exponent, United States); V. del Pizzo (CA EMF Program, USA).

10 A very important example, in view of the authority of the source, is report no. 238 of June 2007 ('Environmental health criteria 238: extremely low frequency fields'), sponsored by the WHO, ICNIRP and the World Labor Organization. The report, signed by the new head of the WHO's EMF Project, E. van Deventer, was actually put together in October 2005 by a working group whose members included scientists with conflicts of interests (M. Repacholi, L. Kheifets, A. Ahlbom, C. Johansen, J. Juutilainen, R. Matthes, E. Van Rongen, P. Vecchia). Furthermore, it was prepared – in clear conflict with WHO and ICNIRP principles – in the presence and with the contribution of 'observers' from electricity companies of the United States (APRI), United Kingdom (National Grid Transco), Canada (Hydro-Quèbec), France (EDF Gaz), Japan (Japan NUS Co.) and Brazil (Electric Energy Research Center). The report notes that there is no justification whatsoever for application of the Precautionary Principle to ELF/EMF: there is a lack of clear evidence of either long-term effects (even childhood leukemias) or acute non-thermal effects. Consequently, a single limit is applied of 100 µT to give protection from 'clearly documented' effects, i.e., only short-term biological thermal effects!

11 It is beyond the scope of this chapter to give an overview of the workings of the magistracy of other countries. It might be useful to offer a comparison limited to the very contrasting positions of the Italian magistracy and that of the United States: reference is made to the paper by Prof. E. Al Mureden (2010). In the United States it is an absolutely unbroken rule that any manufacturer not observing the norms is responsible, while manufacturers who do observe them are never responsible. For this reason, there can never be compensation for damage arising despite full observance of the norm – including exposure limits set by law. Health protection is assured in the United States through the judgment of administrative agencies, who have been conferred powers to draw up rules and regulations. In fact, the Food and Drugs Administration (FDA) has the role both of assessing risks, costs and benefits associated with the commercialization of goods and technologies (risk management), including those products using and emitting EMF (risk assessment), and also of drawing up the regulations designed to protect users' health. The 'technical regulations' approved by the FDA at once are the absolute reference point for justifying any sanctions imposed by the FDA itself, and also give legal backing to the decisions whereby the civil judge demands the employer or insurance body to pay compensation commensurate with the level of resulting invalidity and, when appropriate, also punitive damages. However, even considering the problem of compensation, reference must necessarily be made to the prescriptions of the FDA, since otherwise application of the norms regarding civil liability would prove misguided. Concerning atmospheric pollution, too, American environmental legislation has almost always chosen to grant wide discretionary powers to the Environmental Protection Agency (EPA) for setting pollution safety levels. The EPA is required to set the national standards of environment quality at levels 'appropriate for protecting public health' – the wording here is vague, which in practice means that the EPA has broad discretionary powers in setting air-quality control levels. However, a decision of the American Appeal Court has pointed out two areas to clarify: (1) what criteria the EPA should adhere to in setting air-quality control levels; and (2) (of greater resonance) what are the best ways of monitoring the EPA's discretionary powers. In the case brought by the American Trucking Association Inc. versus United States EPA (1999 Westlaw 300618), the Court maintained that the EPA did not base its decisions on any clearly set out principles when considering the principles in terms of criteria used for setting quality levels, and that there should be clear guidelines for monitoring the EPA's powers. According to the

Court, a well-founded reasoning must be provided either by the statute drawn up by Congress, or by the EPA itself. Since the statute is set out in general terms ('appropriate for protecting public health'), the Court's view is that the EPA is best positioned to give this reasoning. This decision deserves close examination, because it highlights an important aspect of environmental law, i.e., how wide does the law allow the discretionary powers of public agencies such as the EPA to be? In fact, American law has for a long time (since 1930) accepted the principle that Congress can authorize the public agencies – through a rather generalized legislation – to take responsibility for specific issues.

The Italian legal system – as clearly seen from the cases noted above – takes the extreme opposite position: once an activity has been classified as 'dangerous', there is a tendency for the absolutory proof to be considered as never obtained, and the employer or body responsible for monitoring of harmful technologies can only try to demonstrate that all suitable means of preventing the harm have been adopted. Instead, the performer of the dangerous activity has to attempt to undermine 'upstream' the categorization as dangerous, or else demonstrate that the case in question is coincidental – this is because once a technology is included among those labeled as harmful, the responsibility for it becomes an automatic consequence of demonstration of the harm caused (see also note 14, in the reference to the sentence regarding the damage (tumor) caused by radiation emitted by MPs).

12 The editorial of Cardis and Sadetzki (2011) leaves little doubt about the relevance of their criticisms, which we documented in Levis *et al.* (2012a). Within the 17 Interphone studies: (1) less than 5 percent of total cases had completed at least ten years of latency or continued cell phone use, which means that over 95 percent had a totally inadequate exposure time – since in most of the tumors examined the latency is high (10–30 years), this is a factor giving rise to 'dilution' of risk. The percentage of cases or controls exposed for at least ten years within the 17 Interphone studies is 0 percent in four studies, less than 5 percent in four studies, less than 10 percent in five studies, not even given in one study; Hardell documents 18 percent of cases with exposure to MPs of at least ten years. (2) The failure to identify the ipsilateral tumors, arising on the side of the head habitually used for calls, mainly in the temporal lobe which is exposed to 97–99 percent of the radiation emitted during phone use, with consequent further 'dilution' of risk due to the detection of tumors on the whole brain mass, for the most part not exposed to radiation – within the 17 Interphone studies only 2 percent of total cases of ipsilateral tumors were actually exposed for at least ten years; Hardell reports 16 percent of his total cases with ipsilateral tumors, some of which involved exposure for an overall total time or latency of 15 years. (3) The Interphone protocol defines 'exposed' subjects as having used a cell phone 'at least once a week for at least six months' (which means almost never!). Therefore, even if a risk exists, it is 'diluted' because of the dominance, in the sample examined, of subjects exposed too little or not at all: the average daily use of cell phones in subjects considered 'exposed' by Interphone is just 2–5 minutes per day, often for less than five years. These data obviously are barely significant relative to today's intensive use of cell phones, especially by those who use them for work purposes; in Hardell's studies, MP use is reported to be over 1,000 hours for 194 cases and over 2,000 hours for 85 cases, so that the average daily use of MPs ranges from over 16 to just over 32 minutes per day for at least ten years. (4) In the Interphone studies, participation in the epidemiological study of cases or controls is low: less than 50 percent in three studies, less than 60 percent in five studies, less than 70 percent in five studies; in Hardell's studies, participation is always very high (85–90 percent) for both cases and controls. (5) The reduced participation in the study by the non-mobile users initially selected – in particular, controls who are not affected by tumors, naturally less interested in the aims of the research than regular users, especially cases affected by tumors – represents a further factor of 'dilution' of risk

estimates (see note 8). This 'selection bias' is recognized by the Interphone authors themselves, but in their view it does not cause reduction in risk estimated by more than 10 percent, which is true for the overall Interphone data, but in some studies this bias alone can result in a more significant reduction in risk assessment; more than 15 percent in two studies, more than 25 percent in three studies, and even more than 30 percent in two studies; in Hardell's studies the percentage participation is basically equivalent for the exposed and non-exposed cases and controls.

13 (1) The Interphone protocol considers cordless phone users as not exposed, while it is documented that the radiation emitted by cordless can even exceed the intensity of a cell phone, so much so that Hardell records significant increases in the risk of meningiomas and acoustic nerve neuromas also in people using only cordless. (2) The Interphone study fails to consider other types of malignant and benign head tumor, except gliomas, meningiomas, neuromas and parotid gland tumors; in Hardell's studies, increased risks in MP users also involve other types of head tumor, which are considered separately. (3) The risk values of head tumors in three of the Interphone studies even fall off with increased duration of exposure to cell phones and/or latency time; in Hardell's studies, the trend for risk as a function of time of MP use is statistically significant and the combined use of various types of MP raises the risk of developing head tumors. (4) In the Interphone study the combination of these factors leads to strong under-estimation of the risk, showing that the majority of risk values are below 1, often statistically significant: in the 17 Interphone studies, out of 1,084 risk values different from 1, 76 percent are below 1 and only 24 percent are above 1. The prevalence of OR values below 1 is extremely unusual in most of these studies: 100 percent in one study, more than 90 percent in two studies, more than 80 percent in five studies, more than 70 percent in three studies, and the probability of this asymmetric distribution of risk values – which seems to indicate a protective effect – being chance is very low in six of these studies, while in another six studies, as in the overall data, is practically zero; in Hardell's studies, over 90 percent of the risk values are above 1, of which 41 percent are statistically significant, and the probability of this asymmetric distribution – indicating a carcinogenic effect of MP use – being due to chance is almost zero.

14 The association is found and well documented in 2007 by the Italian Association of Medical Oncologists, with specific reference to Hardell's data, emphasized in his monograph *Guidelines for Brain Tumors* (www.aiom.it), which established 'a doubling of the risk of brain gliomas and acoustic neuromas among long-term (at least 10 years) users of cellular and cordless phones', recommending 'caution in the use of mobile phones'. Recently, even a judgment (614/2009) of the Appeal Court, Labor Section of Brescia, Italy recognized for the first time the association between MP use and increased risk of head tumors. The case was a neurinoma of the trigeminal nerve on the left side of the head in a subject having been exposed for more than ten years and more than 15,000 hours on analog and digital cellular and cordless phones. This subject was involved professionally in customer services for his employer; he was right-handed and, during MP calls, used his right hand for making notes and the left hand for holding the MPs. As a result, this tumor was ipsilateral as are most of those Hardell identified. This case therefore concerned a personal situation where the experts – including one of us (Angelo Gino Levis) – evaluated the pathology as a probable consequence of a causal link, even if weak, to the subject's exposure to MPs. This carried weight in the decision of the Court, which recognized that there was a link of causality, or at least of a contributing cause, in the sense that exposure in the workplace to wireless radiation from MPs contributed to the malignant pathology. This led in turn to the recognition of and compensation for the suffering of a physical impairment, which in the present case was evaluated at 80 percent. There are two particularly interesting aspects of this sentence: (1) until 2008, non-ionizing EMF was included in the 'tables of professional diseases' and for any employment involving

possibility of exposure this covered an indemnity of unlimited duration for appearance of tumors. Certification of tumor and demonstration of there having been exposure to EMF radiation during work would therefore have been sufficient for the Istituto Nazionale per l'Assistenza sugli Infortuni Lavorativi (INAIL, national body aiding workplace incident sufferers) – or the labor tribunal in the case of a legal hearing – to confirm payment of compensation. Through decree of 9 April 2008 of the Italian Ministry of Labor and Social Welfare, non-ionizing EMF were removed from the tables of workplace diseases. However, through a deliberation of the Italian Constitutional Court (no. 179 of 18 February 1988), welfare care was extended to include pathologies that, while omitted from the tables, were traceable to exposure in the workplace; here though, the worker has responsibility for demonstrating the cause–effect relationship. The person involved in fact has to show with reasonable certainty that the pathology has arisen through workplace exposure, and that there is therefore a high probability that the pathology in question has a workplace origin – *Cassazione Penale* (penal instance) no. 11087 of 15 May 2007. The case cited here is the first in which a Labor Court has recognized this causal link for workplace exposure to EMF, despite this being omitted from the tables of workplace illnesses/diseases. (2) The literature gives wide documentation of increased risk of acoustic neuromas in long-term users of MPs (see above), while there is complete absence of cases showing correlation between exposure to MPs and increase in tumors of other cranial nerves, in particular the trigeminal. In this case, recognition of workplace disease is based on the fact, documented by consultants, that the acoustic nerve and the trigeminal nerve both originate in the same well-defined, limited area of the endocranial volume, clearly irradiated during the use of MPs. Instead, attempts have failed in the United States to have manufacturers held responsible in cases where cell phones caused tumors because of a lack of convincing demonstration of the existence of a causal link between the harm caused and the use of the cell phone (see Motorola *v.* Ward, 1996, and for a more updated overview see Capriotti 2002). In a more recent case (Murray *v.* Motorola, 2009), it is clearly stated that the cell phone conformity to the technical standards for commercialization, set by the FDA in accordance with the Federal Communications Commission, categorically excludes the possibility of recognizing such products as defective, thus refusing to recognize the responsibility of the manufacturer in the case that this is harmful to the user's health (including where the harm is severe).

15 The Hardell group was always supported only by grants from public bodies, whereas the Interphone-related studies received funding through the Quality of Life and Management of Living Resources program of the EU and the International Union Against Cancer, but the latter received funding for the Interphone studies from the Mobile Manufacturers Forum (MMF, see note 18) and the Global System for Mobile Communication Association (GSMA) (IARC 2010). In addition to the above funds, several authors participating in the Interphone study received further funding from their national MP companies (five studies) or other private companies (three studies), such that a substantial portion of the Interphone funding came from the cell phone industry. Furthermore, other negative studies have been supported by the cell phone industry: two studies were funded by the Cellular Industry Telecommunications Association via the Wireless Technology Research, while another was funded by TeleDanmark Mobil, Sonofon and the International Epidemiology Institute – a private company operating as a cell phone industry advisor – and one by Motorola. Nevertheless, of the 17 authors of the Interphone studies, ten do not make any declaration about conflict of interests, three state 'conflict of interests: none declared' (it is not clear whether this is from the authors or from the editor), while four declare 'conflicts of interests: none' (Levis *et al.* 2011).

16 This is precisely the picture found today as regards assessment of risks correlated to the use of MPs, and more generally to residential and occupational exposure to EMF,

given that the 'confusion' arising from the production of experimental and epidemiological data and their interpretation (open to scientific discussion) is fueled by the support given to this interpretation by the extraordinary web of some authors' involvement in the agencies working in these areas, who receive financial support from the mobile telephony companies. In just one example, Prof. Anders Ahlbom, a figure of leading authority in the Interphone 'team' – set up and monitored by IARC and the EU – plays major roles in ICNIRP, SCENIHR/EC, the Swedish Radiation Protection Agency and in the WHO's EMF Project. Recently (May 2011), Prof. W. Mosgoeller, past president of ICEMS (see note 7) disclosed that Ahlbom is the co-founder of 'Gunnar Ahlbom AB', a Brussels-based lobby firm aiming to assist the telecom industry on EU regulations, public affairs and corporate communications. He created the lobby firm in 2010 together with his brother and sister-in-law. His brother, Gunnar Ahlbom, has been a telecom lobbyist in Brussels for the leading Swedish mobile phone operator TeliaSonera, among others, since the early 1990s, and was already active in this field in 1998 when Prof. Ahlbom participated in the setting of the controversial ICNIRP standards on non-ionizing radiation from different sources (see note 5). Ahlbom, professor in epidemiology at the Karolinska Institute in Sweden, is one of the leading and most influential international experts on evaluation of health risks with mobile telephony. He led an important expert evaluation for the European Commission in 2007 (Possible effects of electromagnetic fields on human health) and participated in a new expert report (SCENIHR, see note 6) to the European Commission in 2009. He has chaired every single expert investigation about possible health risks with mobile telephony and electromagnetic fields carried out in Sweden during 2003–2011 for the Swedish Radiation Protection Authority and the Swedish Council for Working Life and Social Research. Ahlbom has never mentioned his brother's work as a lobbyist for the concerned industry in his declarations of interest. Neither has he mentioned his interest in the 'Gunnar Ahlbom AB' mobile phone lobby firm. Ahlbom was appointed to chair the IARC epidemiology expert evaluation about cancer risks of mobile telephony on 24–31 May 2011. The evaluation aimed to serve as a guideline on cancer risk assessment of the mobile telephony for many years ahead. The result of the review is of utmost importance to the mobile phone industry, which sent three 'invited observers' to the meeting: Mays Swicord, CTIA (the wireless association), Joe Elder, the Mobile Manufacturers Forum (MMF) and Jack Rowley, the GSMA (see note 15). The members of the IARC scientific committee had to submit a declaration of interest, and the IARC had already barred one scientist from the committee: Dr. Alexander Lerchl from the German Radiation Protection Board, who has been questioned regarding his relations to the German mobile phone industry, and was finally not accepted onto the committee as 'an IARC Monograph is an exercise that demands complete independence from all commercial interests, and from advocates who might be perceived as advancing a pre-conceived position'. On 22–23 May 2011 Microwave News (www.microwavenews.com) communicated that: 'IARC told Ahlbom that he could still come, but only as an invited expert'. The key difference is that invited experts cannot vote on how to categorize RF radiation – say as possible or probable carcinogen. Ahlbom decided that he did not want to attend under those restrictions; therefore, in the IARC Monograph Working Group Member list, Ahlbom was quoted as an 'invited specialist (withdrew)'. The decision taken on 31 May 2011 by the IARC expert group on the evaluation of cancer risks produced by EMF/RF – including the emissions by MPs – was to allocate these agents in the 2B group as 'possible carcinogenic agents for man' (www.thelancet.com/oncology published online 22 June 2011). This decision is the same as that taken by IARC in 2001 for the ELF/EMF, unchanged despite the greatly increased amount of evidence for short- and long-term risks for human health produced by ELF/EMF that has accumulated since then. The reasons for such an ultra-conservative position by the IARC–WHO and other international scientific organizations was pointed out back in 1994 by

Tomatis and Huff (see notes 9 and 10), and there is no doubt that the same should be applied to the evaluation of the risks produced by RF/EMF and mobile phone emissions. In fact, in addition to the five members of the IARC panel on RF who declared to have conflict of interests, more than ten others members of the 30 making up the working group had conflicts, but did not declare them. Moreover, just a few days before the IARC began its evaluation of the cancer risks associated with RF radiation, French national TV accused one member of the IARC panel of trying to suppress a study indicating a health risk from cell phone use. A minority opinion was expressed by a small group of IARC panel members (Microwave News, 3 May 2011): 'Our conclusion means that there could be some risk, and therefore we need to keep a close watch for a link between cell phone and cancer risk' noted Jonathan Samet, who served as Chairman of the IARC panel on RF. Rodolfo Saracci, who also participated in the IARC panel, concluded his critical analysis of the Interphone data (Saracci 2011), stating that the 'Interphone, like other observational studies, may conceal an elevated risk under the appearance of consistently reduced risk'. Also, the Swedish Radiation Protection Agency issued a press release announcing that it was taking the Ahlbom affair very seriously and investigating whether it might affect Ahlbom's role as chairman of its own expert group, which issues an annual review of new EMF/RF research (see notes 6 and 17). As a consequence, Ahlbom was invited to resign as chairman of the agency, since he had also been a member of the Swedish Tobacco Company's Medical Research Council for a number of years. In addition, the Chair of the EU/SCENIHR working group informed the Committee that Ahlbom declared an interest view of his affiliations (http://ec.europa.eu/health/ph_risk/committees/04_schenihr/does/schenihr_mi_014.pdf). Two other members of the SCENIHR working group, D. Mattson and L. Hillert, are at the same time members of the mobile phone company TeliaSonera's scientific council (http://ollejohansen.adante.se/olle-andras-bra-saker-htm), whereas J. Schuz, who was a member of the IARC ELF and RF/EMF monograph working groups and who was recently elected president of the international Bioelectromagnetic Society, received industry funding from the Electric Power Research Institute as well as from the mobile phone industry through the EC Interphone, Cefalo and Cosmos Projects and, in addition, has consulted for an Austrian mobile phone advisory group that received funding from the Telecom companies (www.microwavenews.com, 9 June 2011). There is therefore an urgent need to review and reconsider the reports on RF health effects to the EU Commission produced by the ICNIRP and SCENIHR working groups under the chairmanship of Ahlbom and other experts with conflicts of interests.

17 This is taken from NRPB (2004), Sienkiewicz and Kowalczuk (2005), Ahlbom *et al.* (2004), European Commission and SCENIHR (2007; 2009) , Swedish Radiation Protection Authority (2006), Health Council of the Netherlands (2007), Italy's Upper Health Institute with the reports of S. Lagorio, P. Vecchia and A. Polichetti at conferences organized by the 'Consorzio Elettra 2000' and in the document on the 'Progetto Camelet', promoted and funded by the Italian Health Ministry. Other national agencies and commissions have been found to be compromised by conflicts of interests which have influenced assessment of the health risks resulting from exposure to EMF: (1) the Zmirou Commission, set up in 2001 by the French General Directorate for Health: in 2005, following the resignation of Prof. Zmirou (who, along with the other members, declared himself free from conflict of interests), successor Prof. Paillotin declared to the French Senate that the conclusions of the Commission (mobile telephony was harmless) should be considered invalid. In 2006, inquiries of the French Social Affairs and Environment General Inspectorate revealed 'inadequacies, irregularities and links between some members of the commission and the mobile telephony operators'. (2) the Royal Society of Canada produced a document held secret for a long time ('Report of the panel monitoring Ontario Hydro's electromagnetic fields risk assessment program. A panel report prepared at the request of the Royal Society

of Canada for Ontario Hydro'): this reveals that the reassuring views about EMF emissions are compromised by the interests of private companies involved in the development and management of the technologies concerned (Hydro-Quebec and Gradient Corporation). (3) There are conflicts of interests compromising WHO and ICNIRP – these are extremely serious, resulting in targeted choices of falsely reassuring data on the effects of EMF on human health. In fact, at least 50 percent of the funds for the WHO's EMF Project – which up to mid-2006 cost over $250 million – come from electricity companies and mobile telephony operators: some of these funds ($150,000 for mobile telephony alone) are collected by the MMF and sent to the Royal Adelaide Hospital in Australia (where Repacholi is based) and then transferred to the WHO. Since 2006 Repacholi has no longer led the WHO's EMF Project, but has remained as emeritus president of the ICNIRP, and was taken on as a consultant by several industries, including two American electricity companies (Connecticut Light and Powers Co. and United Illuminating Co.) to bolster support against the Connecticut Department of Public Health's initiative to lower the ELF/EMF exposure limits. These actions all conflict with the founding principles of the two organizations; the WHO in fact 'does not allow industries to participate in either setting the standards or in assessment of risks to human health'. According to the WHO,

the working groups established to set the standards may not contain industry representatives. The WHO working groups may not include anyone who has or is subject to any influence that is favorable to a given industry, in particular where assessing the effects on human health of the products of this same industry is concerned.

According to ICNIRP,

all members of the commission are independent experts' and 'they are often reminded that they must declare any interests that could compromise the principles of the statute of ICNIRP, as an independent consultation group. ICNIRP does not accept any funding from industry.

The reader is also referred to note 10 concerning report no. 238/2007 sponsored by the WHO and ICNIRP. Even though Repacholi is no longer ICNIRP president or the WHO's EMF Project leader, the workings of these two organizations has not changed: his successors, P. Vecchia (ICNIRP) and E. van Deventer (WHO's EMF Project) continue their links with the producers and operators of electricity and wireless technologies, in particular mobile telephony.

18 The aims of the MMF are set out on the website www.mmfai.org:

The MMF is an international association of telecommunications equipment manufacturers with an interest in mobile or wireless communications. Established in 1998, the association's mission is to facilitate joint funding of key research projects and cooperation on standards, regulatory issues and communications concerning the safety of wireless technology, accessibility and environmental issues. The MMF ... is currently active in more than 30 countries, as well as supporting an extensive international research program. The MMF's goal in research is to promote the highest quality independent research that furnishes relevant data for the development of sound public policy. MMF funds research addressing important scientific questions. To achieve this, the MMF has responded to the research recommendations of the WHO's EMF Project and has coordinated its global activities to correspond with these recommendations. Only by enhancing the existing scientific database relating to RF/EMF will it be possible to perform an independent health risk assessment recognized by the scientific community as well as by government and statutory bodies.... The MMF coordinates its inputs and contributes relevant expertise within standards-setting processes. The MMF commissions quality research in support of standards. The MMF's regulatory activities are focused on developing and presenting the views of the mobile industry to regulatory agencies and authorities in a globally coordinated manner. The MMF also responds to requests for information, or assistance, by national and international bodies in relation to the safety of wireless technology, accessibility and environmental issues.... The MMF supports national trade associations by providing a source of information that is based on the pooled resources and networks of our member companies.

Members of the MMF include many prestigious bodies and agencies: The MMF has links with some of the major international agencies overseeing the protection of health from the effects of EMF (WHO, EU, IARC, International Union Against Cancer, Health Council of the Netherlands, Swedish Radiation Protection Authority, Norwegian Radiation Protection Authority, UK Health Protection Agency, UK Independent Expert Group on Mobile Phones). This pool of mobile telephony industries distributes a series of information leaflets to disseminate serious and targeted misinformation, supporting an absence of risk from use of MPs, the pointlessness of taking precautionary measures even for babies, the inappropriateness of modifying the exposure limits set by ICNIRP and the need to reassure public opinion.

19 This recommendation sits well with the scientific committees that have overseen the Interphone project (see the section 'Mobile phones and head tumors') and all the other programs on EMF launched by the EU and co-funded by the mobile telephony companies (see the section 'Funding for EU programs').

20 It has been known since 2004 that no insurance company in the world is prepared to insure businesses that manufacture cell phones since they refuse to take on the risk that a user or his heirs sue for damages (see *La Nazione* of 29 January 2004, which reproduces a news item published on the front page of the *Suddeutsche Zeitung*, one of Germany's most authoritative newspapers). Instead, it is little known that, from 2010, even cell phone manufacturers have begun to include warnings in their accompanying instructions about possible risks to health that these devices could cause. Consider, for instance, the easily overlooked few lines of legalese found in the safety manual for Apple's iPhone4:

> When using iPhone near your body for voice calls or for wireless data transmission over a cellular network, keep iPhone at least 15 mm away from the body, and only use carrying cases, belt clips, or holders that do not have metal parts and that maintain at least 15 mm separation between iPhone and the body.

Similar warnings against carrying cell and smart phones in a tight pocket close to the body are found throughout the industry. The safety manual for Research in Motion's Blackberry 9000 phone tells users that: '[they] may violate Federal Communications Commission guidelines for radio-frequency energy exposure by carrying the phone outside a holster and within 2.5 cm of [their] body'. In addition, the safety manual of the Motorola W180 phone tells users to 'always keep the active device 2.54 cm (one full inch) away from [their] body, if not using a company-approved clip, holder, holster, case or body harness'. Clearly, cell phone manufacturers apply the Precautionary Principle in order to cover themselves legally, since they are aware that long-term use exceeding the standards could lead to serious adverse effects. Even more clear are the recommendations in the 'Safety and Product Information' of the BlackBerry Curve 8520 Smartphone (www.blackberry.com/docs/smartphones). It states that

> to reduce radiofrequency exposure: 1) use the BlackBerry device in areas where there is a strong wireless signal ... a reduced signal display, which might occur in areas such as an underground parking structure or if you are travelling by train or car, might indicate increased power output from your BlackBerry device as it

264   *A.G. Levis* et al.

attempts to connect to a weak signal; 2) use hands-free operation if it is available and keep the BlackBerry device at least 25 mm from your body (including the abdomen of pregnant women and the lower abdomen of teenagers) when the Blackberry device is turned on and connected to the wireless network; 3) reduce the amount of time spent on calls.

21 To this aim D.A. Carpenter (2010) concludes his review, stating that:

The benefits to society derived from electricity and wireless communications are significant, and certainly none of us is willing to return to the pre-electric age. However it is imperative that society at least acknowledges the disparities between current standards and current evidence of adverse health effects. Rigid and sudden imposition of the standards we propose is certainly unrealistic at the present time, but these levels are appropriate goals that could at least be approached by a combination of development of new technology and voluntary changes in behavior. Application of the Precautionary Principle is appropriate under the circumstances where there is a demonstrated elevation in rates of serious diseases in humans following elevated EMF exposure, but has many unanswered questions as to mechanisms responsible. We need additional research, of course, and much better exposure assessment. The evidence that we have at present is too convincing to be ignored. Our national and international standards are obsolete, and ignore evidence reported by many different investigations. The lack of certainty with regard to mechanisms and animal models is no reason to ignore studies of human health. Similar lack of certainty regarding mechanisms also exists for some chemicals, yet precautionary measures are commonly taken to reduce exposure. We need the electric and communications industries to be proactive in developing products that can be used with reduced exposures. We need governments and international organizations to set standards that are based on the evidence of whether there are hazards to humans, not on a hypothesis that is not credible based on the evidence from animal and cellular studies. Most importantly, we need individuals to understand that personal decisions will significantly impact the level to which they are exposed to both ELF and RF EMFs.

22 The 'healthy worker effect' is regularly produced in cohort studies when workers are wrongly compared to the unselected general population instead of a proper control group (non-exposed and healthy selected workers). Consequently, the worker population exhibits overall lower death (or morbidity) rates than those of the general population due to the fact that the severely ill and disabled are ordinarily excluded from employment.

References

Ahlbom, A., Day, N., Feychting, M., *et al.* (2000) 'A pooled analysis of magnetic fields and childhood leukemia', *British Journal of Cancer*, 83(5): 692–698.
Ahlbom, A., Green, A., Kheifets, L., Savitz, D. and Swerdlow, A. (2004) 'Epidemiology of health effects of radiofrequency exposure', *Environmental Health Perspectives*, 112(17): 1741–1754.
Al Mureden, E. (2010) 'I danni da uso del cellulare tra tutela previdenziale e limiti della responsabilità del produttore', *Responsabilità Civile e Previdenza*, 6: 1392–1423.
Bailar, J.C. (2006) 'How to distort the scientific record without actually lying: truth, and the arts of science', *European Journal of Oncology*, 11(4): 217–224.
Bortkiewicz, A., Gadzicka, E., Zmyslony, M. and Szymczak, W. (2006) 'Neurodegenerative disturbances in workers exposed to 50 Hz electromagnetic fields', *International Journal of Occupational Medicine and Environmental Health*, 19(1): 53–60.

Capriotti, S. (2002) 'Is there a future for cell phone litigation?', *Journal of Contemporary Health and Law Policy*, 18(2): 489–510.

Cardis, E. and Sadetzki, S. (2011) 'Indications of possible brain-tumour risk in mobile-phone studies: should we be concerned?', *Occupational and Environmental Medicine*, 68: 169–171.

Carpenter, D.A. (2010) 'Human health effects of EMFs: the cost of doing nothing', *Electromagnetic Phenomena and Health: A Continuing Controversy?*, doi: 10.1088/1755-1815/10/1/012004.

Casson, F. (2007) *La Fabbrica dei Veleni*, Trento, Italy: Sperling & Kupfer.

Davis, D. (2008) *La Storia Segreta del Cancro*, Turin, Italy: Codice.

EEA (2007/2008) 'Radiofrequency electromagnetic fields: EEA commentary on the evaluation of the evidence'. Available at: http://report.eea.europa.eu/environment_issue_report.

Egilman, D.S. and Bohme, S.R. (2005) 'Over a barrel: corporate corruption of science and its effects on workers and the environment', *International Journal of Occupational and Environmental Health*, 11: 331–337.

European Commission (2005) 'Health and electromagnetic fields: EU-funded research into the impact of electromagnetic fields and mobile telephones on health'. Available at: http://ec.europa.eu/health/archive/ph_determinants/environment/emf/brochure_en.pdf.

European Commission and SCENIHR (2007) 'Possible effects of electromagnetic fields on human health final resolution'. Available at: http://ec.europa.eu/health/ph_risk/committees/04_scenihr/docs/scenihr_o_007.pdf

European Commission and SCENIHR (2009) 'Health effects of exposure to EMF'. Available at: http://ec.europa.eu/health/ph_risk/committees/04_scenihr/docs/scenihr_o_022.pdf

Eurostat (2011) *Health Status Indicators*. Available at: http://ec.europa.eu/health/indicators/indicators/index_en.htm.

Fadel, R.A., Salem, A.H., Ali, M.H. and Abu-Saif, A.N. (2006) 'Growth assessment of children exposed to low frequency electromagnetic fields at the Abu Sultan area in Ismailia (Egypt)', *Anthropologischer Anzeiger*, 64: 211–226.

Foliart, D.E., Pollock, B.H., Mezei, G., Iriye, R., Silva, J.M., Ebi, K.L., Kheifets, L. Link, M.P. and Kavet, R. (2006) 'Magnetic field exposure and long-term survival among children with leukemia', *British Journal of Cancer*, 94: 161–164.

Gee, D. (2009) 'Late lessons from early warnings: towards realism and precaution with EMF?', *Pathophysiology*, 16: 217–231.

Gennaro, V. and Ricci, P. (2010) 'Conclusioni tranquillizzanti francamente sbagliate in epidemiologia; come capire?', *Epidemiologia & Prevenzione*, 34(5–6, suppl. 1): 231–232.

Gennaro, V. and Tomatis, L. (2005) 'Business bias: how epidemiologic studies may underestimate or fail to detect increased risks of cancer and other diseases', *International Journal of Occupational and Environmental Health*, 11: 356–359.

Gennaro, V., Ricci, P., Levis, A.G. and Czosignani, P. (2009) 'Vizi e virtù dell'epidemiologia e degli epidemiologi', *Epidemiologia & Prevenzione*, 33(4–5, suppl. 2): 49–56.

Greenland, S., Sheppard, A.R., Kaune, W.T., Poole, C and Kelsh, M.A. (2000) 'A pooled analysis of magnetic fields, wire codes, and childhood leukemia', *Epidemiology*, 11: 624–634.

Hakansson, N., Gustavsson, P., Johansen, C. and Floderus, B. (2003) 'Neurodegenerative diseases in welders and other workers exposed to high levels of magnetic fields', *Epidemiology*, 14(4): 420–426.

Hardell, L. and Carlberg, M. (2009) 'Mobile phones, cordless phones and the risk for brain tumours', *International Journal of Oncology*, 35: 5–17.

Hardell, L., Walker, M.J., Walhjalt, B., Friedman, L.S. and Richter, E.D. (2006) 'Secret ties to industry and conflicting interests in cancer research', *American Journal of Industrial Medicine*, 50(3): 227–233.

Hardell, L., Carlberg, M. and Hannsson Mild, K. (2011) 'Pooled analyses of case-control studies on malignant brain tumors and the use of mobile and cordless phones including living and deceased subjects', *International Journal of Oncology*, 38: 1465–1474.

Havas, M. (2010) 'Interphone study: it's not just brain tumors!'. Available at: www.mag-dahavas.com/2010/05/17/interphone_parotid_gland_tumors.

Health Council of the Netherlands (2007) 'No Indications for Health Effects of UMTS and DECT'. Available at: www.healthcouncil.nl.

Hernberg, S. (1981) 'Negative results in cohort studies: how to recognize fallacies', *Scandinavian Journal of Work, Environment & Health*, 7: 121–126.

Huff, J. (2002) 'IARC monographs: industry influence, and upgrading, downgrading, and under-grading chemicals', *International Journal of Occupational and Environmental Health*, 8: 249–270.

Huss, A., Egger, M., Hug, K., Huwiler-Müntener, K. and Röösli, M. (2007) 'Source of funding and results of studies of health effects of mobile phone use: systematic review of experimental studies', *Environmental Health Perspectives*, 115(1): 1–4.

Huss, A., Spoerri, A., Egger, M. and Röösli, M. (2009) 'Residence near power lines and mortality from neurodegenerative disease: longitudinal study of the Swiss population', *American Journal of Epidemiology*, 169: 167–175.

Hyland, G.J (2001) 'The physiological and environmental effects of non-ionizing electromagnetic radiation', Working Document for the STOA Panel, European Parliament/EU Directorate General for Research. Available at: www.europarl.eu.int/stoa/publi/pdf/00-07-03eu.pdp.

IARC (2002) *Monographs on the Evaluation of Carcinogenic Risks to Humans: Non-Ionizing Radiation, Part 1 – Static and Extremely-low Frequency (ELF) Electric and Magnetic Fields*, Vol. 80, pp. 1–395.

IARC (2010) 'The Interphone study'. Available at: www.iarc.fr/en/research-groups/RAD/RCAd.html.

ICNIRP (1996) 'ICNIRP statement: on health issues related to the use of hand-held radiotelephones and base transmitters', *Health Physics*, 70(4): 587–593.

ICNIRP (1998) 'Guidelines for limiting exposure to time-varying electric, magnetic, and electromagnetic fields (up to 300 GHz)', *Health Physics*, 74(4): 494–522.

IEGMP (2000) *Mobile Phones and Health*. Available at: www.iegmp.org.uk/report/text.htm

Interphone Study Group (2010) 'Brain tumour risk in relation to mobile telephone use: results of the Interphone international case-control study', *International Journal of Epidemiology*, 39: 675–694.

Krewski, D., Glickman, B.W., Habash, R.W., Habbick, B., Lotz, W.G., Mandeville, R., Prato, F.S., Salem, T. and Weaver, D.F. (2001) 'Recent advances in research on radiofrequency fields and health 2001–2003', *Journal of Toxicology & Environmental Health*, 4(4): n.p.

Lee, G.M., Neutra, R.R., Hristova, L., Yost, M. and Hiatt, R.A. (2002) 'A nested case-control study of residential and personal magnetic field measures and miscarriages', *Epidemiology*, 13: 21–31.

Levis, A.G., Minicuci, N., Ricci, P., Gennaro, V. and Garbisa, S. (2011) 'Mobile phones and head tumors: the discrepancies in cause–effect relationship in the epidemiological studies – how do they arise?', *Environmental Health*, 10: 59.

Levis, A.G., Minicuci, N., Ricci, P., Gennaro, V. and Garbisa, S. (2012a) 'Mobile phones and head tumours: a critical analysis of case-control epidemiological studies', *Open Environmental Sciences*, 6: 1–12.

Levis, A.G., Minicuci, N. and Ricci, P. (2012b) 'Statistical relationships between positive or negative results and public or private funding, in studies on EMF effects', in preparation.

Li, D.K., Odouli, R., Wi, S., Janevic, T., Golditch, I., Bracken, T.D., *et al.* (2002) 'A population-based prospective cohort study of personal exposure to magnetic fields during pregnancy and risk of miscarriage', *Epidemiology*, 13: 9–20.

Lloyd-Morgan, L. (2009) 'Estimating the risk of brain tumors from cell-phone use: published case-control studies', *Pathophysiology*, 16: 137–147.

Lloyd-Morgan, L., Barris, E., Newton, J., O'Connor, E., Philips, A., Philips, G., *et al.* (2009) 'Cellphones and brain tumors: 15 reasons for concern – science, spin and the truth behind Interphone'. Available at: www.radiationresearch.org.

Maisch, D. (2006) 'Conflict of interest and bias in health advisory committee: a case study of the WHO's EMF task group', *JACNEM*, 21(1): 15–17.

Michaels, D. (2008) *Doubt is their Product: How Industry's Assault on Science Threatens your Health*, Oxford: University Press.

Myung, S.K., Ju, W., McDonnell, D.D., Yeon, J.L., Kazinets, G., Chih-Tao, C., *et al.* (2009) 'Mobile phone use and risk of tumors: a meta-analysis', *Journal of Clinical Oncology*, 27(33): 5565–5572.

NRPB (2004) 'Review of the scientific evidence for limiting exposure to electromagnetic fields, 0–300 GHz', *NRPB*, 15(3): 1–224.

Naval Studies Board, Division of Engineering and Physical Sciences (2002) *An Assessment of Non-lethal Weapons Science and Technology*, Washington, DC: National Academies Press.

Oreskes, N. and Convay, E.M. (2010) *Merchants of Doubt: How a Handful of Scientists Obscured the Truth on the Issues from Tobacco Smoke to global Warming*, New York, Berlin and London: Bloomsbury Press.

Pawl, R. (2008) 'Cellphones more dangerous then cigarettes!', *Surgical Neurology*, 70: 445–446.

Pearce, N. (2008) 'Corporate influences on epidemiology', *International Journal of Epidemiology*, 37(1): 46–53.

Sadetzki, S., Chetrit, A., Jarus-Hakak, A., Cardis, E., Deutch, Y., Duvdevani, S., *et al.* (2008) 'Cellular phone use and risk of benign and malignant parotid gland tumors: a nationwide case-control study', *American Journal of Epidemiology*, 167: 457–467.

Sage, C. Carpenter, D. and the BioInitiative Working Group (2007) *BioInitiative Report: A Rationale for a Biologically Based Public Exposure Standard for Electromagnetic Fields: ELF and RF*. Available at: www.bioinitiative.org.

Saracci, R. (2011) 'Electromagnetic fields from wireless phones declared "possibly carcinogenic"' *Epidemiologia & Prevenzione*, 35(3–4): 171–172.

Saracci, R. and Samet, J. (2010) 'Commentary: call me on my mobile phone ... or better not? A look at the INTERPHONE study results', *International Journal of Epidemiology*, 39(3): 695–698.

Seyhan, N., Firlarer, A., Canseven, A.G. Ozden, S. and Tepe Cam, S. (2010) 'Occupational EMF exposure measurements in different work environments', *European Journal of Oncology*, 5: 379–386.

Sienkiewicz, Z.J. and Kowalczuk, C.I. (2005) 'A summary of recent reports on mobile phones and health: 2000–2004'. Available at: www.hpa.org.uk/webc/HPAwebFile/HPAweb_C/1194947376017

Svendsen, A.L., Weihkopf, T., Kaatsch, P. and Schüz, J. (2007) 'Exposure to magnetic fields and survival after diagnosis of childhood leukemia: a German cohort study', *Cancer Epidemiology, Biomarkers & Prevention*, 16(6): 1167–1171.

Swedish Radiation Protection Authority (2006) 'Recent research on EMF and health risks'. Available at: www.ssi.se.

Tomatis, L. (1965) *Il laboratorio*, Milano: Einaudi.

Tomatis, L. (2002) 'The IARC monograph program: changing attitudes towards public health', *International Journal of Occupational and Environmental Health*, 8: 114–152.

Tomatis, L. (2007) 'Percorsi e difficoltà della ricerca eziologica e della ricerca in chemioterapia', *Epidemiologia & Prevenzione*, 31(4): 197–203.

Tomatis, L. (2008) *L'Ombra del dubbio*, Milano: Sironi.

Valberg, A., van Deventer, E. and Repacholi, M. (2007) 'Workgroup report: base stations and wireless networks – radiofrequency (rf) exposures and health consequences', *Environmental Health Perspectives*, 115: 416–424.

WHO (2007) *ELF Health Criteria Monograph on Neurodegenerative Disorders*, pp. 1–187.

Zapponi, G.A. and Marcello, I. (2004) 'Recent experimental data on extremely low frequency (ELF) carcinogenic risk: open questions', *Journal of Experimental & Clinical Cancer Research*, 23: 2–16.

'Zmirou Report' (2001) *Zmirou Report to the French Health General Directorate*. Available at: www.sante.gouv.fr/index.htm

12 A crisis of freedom

Michele Cangiani

[T]he tenant said … 'It's not like lightning or earthquakes. We've got a bad thing made by men, and by God that's something we can change.'
                                                        (Steinbeck, *The Grapes of Wrath*, p. 39)

A democratic deficit affects both the institutions regulating international economies and the European Union's governance and strategies. At the level of single states, democratic representation tends to be by-passed or undermined by the so-called 'privatization of politics'. Together with the economic crisis starting in 2007–2008, a deep crisis of democracy seems to be the outcome of three decades of neoliberal policies. This topic is examined after an introductory analysis – in the section that follows – of a case in which economic and political aspects of the crisis are clearly intertwined. The combination of economic uneasiness with the decay of democracy seriously reduces the 'capabilities' of the great majority of people, and thereby, according to Amartya Sen, their 'substantive freedoms' (Sen 1999a; 1999b). The final section turns to the holistic, open-system and normative approach that has marked the radical 'institutional' economic theory in order to raise the issue of positive freedom as an issue concerning society as a whole. On one hand, in Charles Lindblom's words (2001: 190), 'people are not free' if they are excluded from important collective choices they are concerned with. On the other, in Karl Polanyi's words (1977: xliii), the very survival of human society depends on its 'freedom of creative adjustment'. The crisis gives us at least the opportunity to grasp the gravity and urgency of this issue.

An Italian case?

In June 2010 the workers of the Fiat plant located in Pomigliano d'Arco (Napoli) were asked to accept a new agreement designed by the management; otherwise, they would lose their jobs. In the referendum which was held, over 38 percent of the voters did not accept the agreement, while being aware that they were risking unemployment. The fact that this percentage has been considered surprisingly high is itself a symptom that voting was not, in this case, an expression of freedom and democracy, but a fictitious alternative submitted to blackmailed people. The old argument that links the free market to human liberty shows once more to be a fallacious inference: the evidence suggests that the lack of freedom in the actual structure and working of the market affects in a negative manner the amount of freedom society enjoys. The real free market compels (and therefore justifies) the imposition by Fiat of harder and harder conditions on its employees. On one hand, the basic features of neoliberal market globalization are the concentration of capital, the fragmentation of laboring classes and the devalorization of labor power; on the other, the automobile world market is presently saddled with an overcapacity of 35–40 percent. Both tendencies are obviously made worse by the crisis, and reinforce each other.

Planning, according to Karl Marx (*Capital*, ch. 5, § 1), characterizes human activity: as he says, it distinguishes the architect's work from the bee's. Thus human liberty realizes itself in the historical process in which human beings change themselves and, at the same time, their social and natural environment. Planning, Karl W. Kapp points out (1950b: 30), is to be considered in general as 'a prerequisite and an essential element of rational conduct', and requires 'valuation and choice'. Economic behavior does consist of valuation and choices, and therefore in planning. The problem is who chooses, what are his aims and what is the weight of his choice in comparison to choices of other actors. In fact, the freedom and scope of choosing and evaluating, and thence freedom *tout court*, are unequally distributed. Fiat workers are free to risk unemployment by voting 'no'. Fiat is free to squeeze its workers and load on them the pressure of competition.

Moreover, not only is freedom of choice unequally distributed, but the same institutional organization that produces inequality – unequal income, unequal 'capabilities', unequal power to choose – also defines the constraints that limit both choices and the evaluation of their effects for the social system as a whole. This issue is typical of the 'evolutionary' approach characterizing Thorstein Veblen's reflection and the radical tendency of institutional economics. The ground of survival 'in the competitive pecuniary struggle', Veblen points out (1901: 299), 'is fitness for pecuniary gain, not fitness for serviceability at large'. The crisis makes the constraint of 'pecuniary gain' tighter, and its opposition to 'serviceability' deeper and evident, thereby provoking opposed reactions: some claim out loud the need to question that constraint, while the defenders of the market system are willing to employ any means to preserve what they call 'market freedom', even illiberal means, including war.

Polish workers of the Fiat factory of Tychy sent their Italian colleagues a letter (http://libcom.org/news/letter-fiat-14062010) recalling that a similar alternative was imposed on them some years ago; work must be intensified in order to avoid production moving away. The results surpassed expectations, but only 40 percent of the promised productivity bonus was paid, and the threat to displace new investments to Italy or elsewhere did not vanish.

The new Pomigliano agreement includes intensification of labor, compulsory rotating shifts and overtime work, flexibility and reduction of break-times. In the document Fiat handed over to the trade unions at the end of May 2010, 19 of 36 pages are dedicated to organizational methods, improved by innovations of Japanese origin called World Class Manufacturing, allowing for both the production of different models of cars in the same line and tighter computerized control in order to minimize waste – first, waste of labor time. Full involvement of the workers is the unavoidable precondition for those innovations, which are presented as environment-friendly and aimed at increasing safety and eliminating defects, inventory and breakdowns. The only trade union resisting the agreement (FIOM, Federazione Impiegati Operai Metallurgici) was willing to discuss all this, but not further requests, such as wage reductions in case of illness or leave for union activities, and the option to dismiss workers who went on strike against the agreement. The right to strike would then be subject to constraints, while Article 40 of the Italian Constitution states that this can be done only by the law. On the whole, the requests made by Fiat tend to jeopardize the rights conquered by workers in the 1960s and confirmed by law no. 300 of 1970, named 'Statuto dei lavoratori' (the Workers' Statute). This law, which is still in force, protects workers' individual freedom, dignity and safety, and their right of free association and representation.

The events of the following months have confirmed that Fiat aims at derogating from collective agreements, in spite of their legal validity, in view of putting general collective bargaining aside. Furthermore, any autonomous labor union that would not restrict itself to complying with the management's guidelines should be defeated and possibly eliminated. In fact, in the agreement of January 2011 concerning the Fiat plant of Mirafiori in Turin a *conventio ad escludendum* was added: unions refusing to sign cannot propose their own candidates at the election of union representatives. This time, more than 45 percent of employees voted against the agreement.

Comments on the Pomigliano agreement have focused on the following issues: (1) it is a turning point in the history of industrial relations, implying heavy, general and lasting consequences in the future. In particular, trade unions are losing, together with a lot of their freedom, the remains of their social function and political relevance. However, the agreement appears to be innovative only within the Italian and European context. In fact, Fiat is itself reaping the fruits of its long-lasting global experience. The cost-cutting deal of April 2009 with the United Auto Workers and the Canadian Auto Workers (CAW), concerning Chrysler factories, contained even more severe conditions than those imposed on Pomigliano workers. The US government, in view of its financial aid, was involved in the deal, as well as Fiat, in view of its alliance with Chrysler. On that occasion, the CAW President Ken Lewenza said that the agreement was making labor costs competitive with *non-unionized* Toyota plants in Canada.

(2) High automation reduces the cost of labor to 6–7 percent of the total cost in factories directly managed by automobile corporations. But it is precisely the increase in the organic composition of capital that requires: (a) a tighter control of labor power in order to keep machines working regularly and continuously; and (b) an augmented exploitation of labor, mostly but not only through

outsourcing and delocalization. Moreover, the enhancement of competition – more precisely, of the oligopolistic struggle – on a world scale makes any minimal cost variation relevant. For all these reasons, enterprises are interested in acquiring more and even absolute power in industrial relations. Thus the agreement imposed by Fiat also has a path-breaking function: it shows the tendency of labor policy on the world scale 'without veils' (Gallino 2010: 7). Generally speaking, the current crisis, within which the episode of Pomigliano is meaningfully located, has revealed the true face of 'globalization', beyond the rhetoric of competition and growth. Social costs caused by over-accumulation are shifted to workers and the whole of society. States are induced to compete with each other for new industrial plants by offering corporations direct and indirect subsidies and low taxation. Moreover, there is by now abundant evidence that social costs, as Kapp maintains (1950a), are not simply shifted, but are *systematically produced* by the functioning of the market-capitalist mode of production; they are the main symptom of the inefficiency of that system. Workers not only have to share the burden of social costs with the generality of citizens, but are overloaded, through low wages, worse conditions of work or unemployment.

The last three decades of neoliberal globalization are, in fact, a period of continuous crisis – more or less creeping, disguised or dramatic as it has been in the course of time, more or less postponed by various 'bubbles', which eventually made the crash even more dramatic. Corporations have looked for cheap labor and convenient or, better still, inexistent labor legislation all around the world. A fragmented world labor market, though theoretically inefficient, is 'efficient' for employers, who can impose lower and lower wages and working conditions in 'central' countries as well, in the name of the need to face competition. This tendency is obviously embittered by the current crisis, together with competition; moreover, by depressing workers' purchasing power, it makes the crisis continue and grow worse. The result is a vicious circle producing social costs, shifted from big industrial and financial corporations onto many small enterprises, the greater part of citizens, public administrations and future generations.

(3) The Italian government supports this tendency in a two-fold way. First, it follows the most neoliberalist-oriented policies within the European Union, in terms of both taxation and welfare cuts, thus contributing to shifting the cost of the crisis onto laboring and poorer classes. At the same time, the government, while avoiding engaging itself and corporations in any industrial policy, has declared that the Statuto dei Lavoratori is obsolete, and that the Italian Constitution should be changed, with particular reference to its Articles 40, on the right to strike, and 41, on the limits to be imposed to free economic initiative in the case that it 'contrasts with public utility' or 'endangers security, freedom and dignity of people'.

(4) A more general weakening of the democratic system designed by the Italian Constitution results from governmental policies that undermine basic liberal and democratic principles, such as the primacy of Parliament, the separation of powers, the freedom of information and the right of every citizen to be

educated according to her/his talent. The rule of law is itself compromised because of the growing difficulty controlling the government's actions, and in particular its personalistic and populistic tendencies. We must add to this the influence that informal and even criminal powers have over decisions affecting society as a whole, and the decay of rights, institutions and opportunities allowing citizens' informed and responsible participation in political life.

We can say, in conclusion, that the Italian case is to be situated in the wider perspective of the world economic crisis, which in turn can be explained through an analysis of the development of the last three decades. Economic and political developments are evidently intertwined. A growingly concentrated and finance-oriented economy needs strong and exclusive links to politics. This is a main factor of the crisis of democracy – by now 'post-democracy' (Crouch 2003). Moreover, we are witnessing the weakening, if not the withdrawal, of such original values of Western culture as civil rights and liberal democracy. Three decades of neoliberalism, plus the crisis, have created a growing connivance between neoliberal and illiberal tendencies, such as those represented by American 'neocons' or extreme-right and racist groups in Europe.

Even more general issues would be raised, regarding the deepest causes of the crisis, with reference to the nature and dynamics of market-capitalist society. If, then, this historical mode of organizing human life on earth is to be questioned regarding its ability to realize a good or at least sustainable adaptation, the scope and method of economic theory are also at stake. There is no need to say that, in the following pages, I shall only be able to draw a very limited sketch of these themes, as related to the problem of freedom.

From development to post-democracy

Paul Krugman (2010) interprets the current deep crisis as 'the early stages' of a third depression, after the Long Depression and the Great Depression, beginning respectively in 1873 and 1929. However, it is also possible to say that the slow-down that has been going on, through some cyclical oscillations, since the 1970s has dramatically come to a head.

In the 1970s the crisis of the development era had to be acknowledged, together with the inherent contradictions of organized capitalism that postwar reconstruction and prosperity had masked. Complex analyses of the crisis – such as James O'Connor's (1973), for example – raised the issue of a necessary transformation, involving both economic and political institutions. But the change could have followed two opposite paths: either toward democracy or away from it. In reality, such alternatives constitute a crucial aspect of the history of the twentieth century, continuing, for the moment, into the twenty-first. This thesis, which implies that the relationship between the economic and political spheres is a central issue, can be found for instance in the history of 'the short Twentieth century' by Eric Hobsbawm (1994), as well as in Karl Polanyi's reflection. The major and definitive crisis of liberal capitalism, culminating in World War I, makes some change inevitable: a 'great transformation', but which way? In any case, Polanyi pointed out (1935: 367), as the solution of a radical and therefore socialist democracy could not be realized, capitalism continued its existence under a new institutional arrangement: 'in its non-Liberal, i.e., corporative forms'. The extent to which some aspects and formal rules of democracy will survive depends on economic and political conjunctures, with important geographical differences.

The Great Crisis, in Polanyi's opinion, involved the whole fabric of society; in particular, it made class conflict deeper, while cutting out economic means for a class compromise. The very need for incisive reforms led the ruling class to a stronger control of power in order to monopolize decisions about which reforms were to be implemented, and to what extent. Moreover, Polanyi contends that the diffusion of fascist regimes in many countries – and the weakening of democratic institutions in many others – revealed 'the mutual incompatibility of Democracy and Capitalism' (ibid.: 391) at that stage of their history. 'The Fascist Virus' – we read in two of Polanyi's manuscripts by the same title – is endemic in modern society, and reawakens in critical situations. Some years later, Kapp expresses himself similarly, saying the market economy 'has been accompanied by the growth of freedom (whenever it gave rise to higher standards of living) and by a return to totalitarian controls (when it produced a state of affairs which large masses of people considered intolerable)' (Kapp 1950b: 40).

The criminalization of dissent and the underrating of civil rights are a part of this general tendency, which has spread in recent years, and has been often supported by instrumental justifications, such as the 'War on Terror'.

The alternative between improvement and decay of democracy continues to be on the agenda, according to Polanyi, and becomes particularly evident in times of crisis and change. Soon after World War II, he foresaw again a possible evolution toward a 'truly democratic society', where the economy would be organized 'through the planned intervention of the producers and consumers themselves' (Polanyi 1947: 117). But he feared that the opposite tendency would prevail, supported by those who 'believe in elites and aristocracies, in managerialism and the corporation'. The resulting society would be 'more intimately adjusted to the economic system', which would remain unchanged in its basic features (ibid.), while democracy would be damaged and possibly depleted.

Otto Bauer (1936) interprets 'the crisis of democracy' after World War I as the crisis of the ruling class' hegemony. In *The Great Transformation* Polanyi speaks in the same sense of the crisis of 'the liberal state'. The *Report to the Trilateral Commission* (1975) confirms – though implicitly, through 'monetarist' arguments – that this is again the case in the 1970s: wage and normative gains obtained by unionized workers are pointed out as the cause of 'stagflation' and budget deficit. Not long before, in 1973, in Chile, the attack by Allende's government on transnational corporate power and North American rule roused a violent reaction. Augusto Pinochet took power and notoriously adopted neoliberal economic policies suggested by the Chicago School. Later, the turning point of the illiberal neoliberal solution to the crisis of the 1970s spread throughout the world. In 1978 Deng Xiaoping opened China to economic liberalization and capitalist accumulation, within an authoritarian political framework. Soon afterward, the basic purpose of both Margaret Thatcher's and Ronald Reagan's governments, starting respectively in 1979 and 1980, was to demolish the alarming power of labor, first – but not only – in industrial relations. In addition, the new 'supply-side' model of accumulation, based on the priority of profit and rent, entailed a decrease of taxation for the wealthiest strata. If, then, the 'fiscal crisis of the state' was to be faced, a greater cut of public spending was needed – the US military budget representing an important exception (plus 7 percent per year from 1981 to 1985).

Acquiring hegemony, neoliberalism asked for a 'de-regulation' of economic activity, beginning with labor and financial markets. The opening up of new fields for investment was pursued: not only financial speculation, but also scientific research, leisure activities and commodities, real estate, public utilities, health care and social services. This kind of investment generally implies rent, monopoly positions, devaluation of labor power, inequality and a further commodification of individual life and social relationships. The 'privatization' wave has not only jeopardized the 'European social model'; it has also opened new and not necessarily legal opportunities for collusion between a political patronage system and private economic interests. David Harvey points out that the main achievement of neoliberalism has been 'to redistribute, rather than to generate, wealth and income', and to generate an 'accumulation by dispossession' through various means which required state support, such as 'the use of the credit system', the commodification of land and labor power, the privatization of commons (natural resources and knowledge) (Harvey 2005: 159). In the 1980s Structural Adjustment Programs were imposed on 'developing' countries. Restrictive monetary and budget policies were also recommended to 'central' countries, the purpose remaining that of reassuring international creditors and financial investors. Profits (and losses) of the latter were to be paid for by drawing resources from wage workers and social expenditure, even at the risk of a deflationary runaway.

The 'neoliberal transformation' was achieved in the 1990s by a series of reforms. Under Bill Clinton's presidency, for example, a Welfare Reform embittering the condition of the poorest and widening the working poor area was implemented, and the final liberalization of financial markets was realized by the repealing, in 1999, of the Glass-Steagall Act of 1933. In the same year the NATO bombing of Serbia achieved 'deregulation' also in the field of international law.

The European Union – also through its enlargement, to former socialist countries in particular – has accentuated those aspects of its constitution and strategy that give its governance, and therefore its approach to the crisis, a non-democratic character: (1) technocratic and oligarchic decisional procedures set aside popular control through elected representatives; (2) there is a paradoxical fragmentation of member states' policies concerning wages, work regulations, taxation, welfare, control of financial activities and industrial strategies. Besides, restrictive monetarist policies are imposed, while neo-mercantilist attitudes are allowed, exporting unemployment to other countries; (3) privatization of public utilities and services, reduction of wages and pensions, and of taxes for higher revenues, freedom for financial investment, and a green light for delocalization of industrial activities have been allowed and often recommended; (4) there is an ideological shift from social-universalistic to individual rights, noticeable for instance in the 2007 Lisbon Treaty; (5) all this clearly coincides with the neoliberal creed to the advantage of big business, contributes to the counter-revolution against social reforms conquered by labor, increases economic and social inequality, and leads to a hierarchical structure of the market, as well as among member states.

At the world scale, 'the "democratic deficit" and the lack of political legitimacy' affecting the institutions of the 'Washington Consensus' (IMF, World Bank, WTO), as well as their 'close links' with financial interests, have been pointed out by Joseph Stiglitz (2008: 52). The tendency he names the 'post-Washington Consensus' calls not only for a radical revision of 'structural adjustment' policies, but also for reforms in global governance inspired by two basic requirements: (1) not just the increase in GDP (gross domestic product), but also environmental and social sustainability and a fairer distribution should be the goal of development policies; (2) 'countries should be given room to experiment, to use their own judgment, and explore what might work best for them' (ibid.: 54).

Walden Bello is clearly more radical than Stiglitz in criticizing the international institutions regulating neoliberal globalization. In his opinion, 'the agenda of people-oriented sustainable development can succeed only if it is evolved democratically' (Bello 2002: 117). And this presupposes a 're-empowerment of the local and national', which would only be possible within an alternative, pluralistic system of global governance – one that would be able 'to tolerate and profit from diversity' (ibid.: 114–115). But these requirements are not consistent with the maintenance of neoliberal globalization, understood as the 'unsuccessful effort to overcome the crises of overaccumulation, overproduction, and stagnation that have overtaken the central capitalist economies since the mid-1970s' (Bello 2007: n.p.).

In fact, we can say with Michel Chossudovski, and with an obvious reference to the fundamental contradiction of capitalist accumulation pointed out by Marx, that the global economic system is 'characterized by two contradictory forces: *the consolidation of a global cheap-labor economy* on the one hand and *the search for new consumer markets* on the other. The former undermines the latter' (Chossudovski 1997: 17).

Not only the analysis of the present crisis cannot be limited to its financial surface, but 'financialization' itself can only be explained with reference to the deep and contradictory dynamics of capitalism. Some consider the size and forms assumed by finance as opposed, and detrimental, to 'the real economy'. In fact, they are consistent with, and functional to, capitalist accumulation in a situation of systematic tendency to stagnation. John Bellamy Foster (2007) recalls that Harry Magdoff and Paul Sweezy raised in these terms the issue of a non-contingent shift toward finance in their 1987 book *Stagnation and Financial*

Explosion, but had already detected this tendency in the second half of the 1960s. Foster points out that the neoliberal ideology imposed itself together with 'monopoly-finance capital', and is instrumental in justifying heightened exploitation and inequality, which provide money for financial speculation and eventually to bail-out financial corporations risking failure.

Public intervention of this sort is presently commonly called 'socialism for the rich' or 'corporate welfare'. We can find a comment on a similar policy – though at a much smaller scale – in an article by Marx (1857), who, in the middle of the liberal era, ironically points out that 'this kind of communism' does appeal to capitalists.

The neoliberal transformation and the present crisis show that the economic contradiction is doubled by a political one. A rational use of resources from the point of view of social welfare and ecological equilibrium would only be possible through a democratic control of the economic system. But neoliberal society is dominated by technocratic and unaccountable institutions, while collective institutions trying to counterbalance asymmetries of power and information (e.g., trade unions) or of safety and 'capabilities' (welfare state) have greatly weakened. Big corporations and international organizations have taken decisional power away from nation states, which remain the only seat where democratic institutions traditionally developed and to some extent go on. The managerial, elitist and authoritarian aspects of post-war corporatism have increasingly taken the place of welfare policies and pluralistic 'concertation'. The structure of governance has changed. Political representative institutions are tendentially by-passed or undermined by a growing and more direct influence of economic corporate power on law-making and governmental policies.

In the interwar transformation, according to Polanyi, the need to face the irreversible decay of the nineteenth century utopia of the self-regulating markets gave rise to new institutional arrangements implying the removal of the institutional separation of the economic and political spheres. The basic feature of neoliberalism also is not, in spite of its name, a free market, but a tighter intertwining of economic and political powers. Again, the defeat of 'big labor' is a preliminary requirement, while business becomes 'bigger'. Oligopolistic competitors have become more and more involved in politics. Thus the neoliberal institutional setup enhances the role of the 'power elite' analyzed by Charles Wright Mills (1956) as the leadership by corporate, political and military vested interests in society. Capital concentration, deregulation, globalization and financialization give business an unprecedented power, not only economic, but also political, which is removed from democratic control – indeed, opposed to it.

The decay of democracy is both a means and a consequence of this process. Many authors take this tendency into consideration. Robert Reich (2007) traces it back to the 1970s and asks for a 'battle for democracy', though limiting it to a regulation of corporate lobbying and environmental damages, and to the defense of democratic procedures. These procedures are bypassed and jeopardized according to Noam Chomsky, who notoriously maintains, referring in particular to global finance, that the free flow of capital creates what is sometimes called a 'virtual senate' of lenders and investors who carry out a moment-by-moment referendum on government policies, and if they find that they are irrational, meaning they help people instead of profits, then they vote against them, by capital flight, by tax on the country, and so on. So the democratic governments have a dual constituency, their own population and the virtual senate, who typically prevails.

(www.democracynow.org/2009/7/3 noam_chomsky)

The opposition electoral control/business control concerning *The Policy-Making Process* is dealt with by Lindblom in his 1980 book so entitled, and is a central issue in a new version of the book (Lindblom and Woodhouse 1993). Here the authors also point out that the electoral control itself tends to be directly 'manipulated', and indirectly influenced by the diffusion of pro-business cultures and by the objective weight of business in economic and social conditions of life. Such influence, in reality, is only an aspect of the 'unique and powerful role' that business plays 'in the overall scope of public policy making' (ibid.: 91). This role 'renders the task of intelligent, democratic governmental policy making extremely difficult'; in particular, in 'a market-oriented society' it is difficult to restrain big economic interests, even if they cause waste and suffering (ibid.: 102–103). The conclusion, to which Lindblom and Woodhouse consistently arrive, is that 'the privileged position of business, inequality, and impaired thought' are 'tightly interconnected' (ibid.: 143). These three elements reinforce each other and 'constitute major impediments to more intelligent social problem solving' (ibid.: 141).

According to Crouch (2003: 6–7), in the current 'minimalist' model of democracy, which he calls 'post-democracy', policies are decided within the interaction between elected governments and privileged elites, which prevalently represent economic interests. From Reagan on, in Crouch's opinion, the American concept of democracy tends to be reduced to free elections – more precisely, we could add, to the right to vote, since the electorate's choice is limited, ill-informed and not necessarily respected. Furthermore, the present dominance of mass media on public opinion is highly worrying if the early remark by Schumpeter is to be taken into account, that the voters' opinion and choice cannot but be shaped, 'and the shaping of them is an essential part of the democratic process' (Schumpeter 1943: 282). Most mass media are, in fact, possessed by big corporations, and all of them depend on the huge budget corporations dedicate to advertising.

Moreover, the remains of formally democratic institutions are increasingly subjected to distortions and retrenchments, in the absence of such a substantive factor of democracy as wider, well-informed and responsible participation to political life. In fact, according to Crouch, the more the state renounces its interventions concerning common people's lives, the more people become indifferent toward politics, the more thoroughly and safely multinational corporations can exploit the community, by controlling the political agenda and manipulating public opinion (Crouch 2003: 25–26).

The recent huge public help to financial organizations risking failure has similar, indeed paradoxical, consequences: the increase of public debt not only makes a further reduction of social expenditure necessary, but it makes governments more subject to restrictions imposed by international institutions (be they located in Washington, Brussels or Frankfurt), more powerless as to the conditions imposed by corporations and even more vulnerable to speculative attacks by the same financial institutions enjoying public help.

Besides the concentration of power and the decay of representative institutions, specific state policies have also been relevant. Fiscal policy increased inequality rather than seeking to correct it through redistribution. This trend is particularly remarkable in the United States, from Reagan's 1981 Economic Recovery and Tax Act to G.W. Bush's tax reduction for revenues exceeding $200,000 (see Hacket and Pierson 2010). The rich minority could thus more easily acquire the power and safety they were looking for through the neoliberal transformation.

Income inequality, rising in the 1920s also on account of fiscal policy, is considered by John K. Galbraith (1955) as an important, perhaps the most important, cause of the Great Crisis. Krugman (2007) points out that 80 years later the situation is similar, with the richest 10 percent of the population receiving about 44 percent of US revenue. The growing economic inequality documented in Figure 12.1 is obviously also politically important, being a fundamental aspect

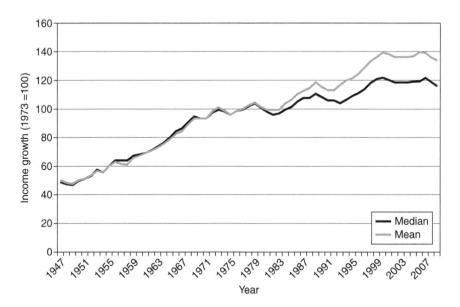

Figure 12.1 Income growth (source: Paul Krugman's blog, 'Prices and plutocrats', *New York Times*, 2 February 2011. Original source: U.S. Census Bureau).

Note
1973 = 100.

of the complex tendency denoted by the term 'plutocracy'. I made above a hint to other aspects, such as the direct and exclusive influence of economic powers on political institutions and public opinion. Also lobbyism and corruption have long since been considered as causes of the decay of democracy. The same can be said of the phenomenon described, for example, by Paul Kurtz (2000): '[the] corporate domination of the democratic process by means of campaign contributions blocks the emergence of independent voices willing to defend the public interest.'

We are thus led to a further, crucial question: Why has the democratic vote never been able to reverse this kind of social and political trend? Growing economic troubles, and the want of so-called 'citizenship rights' as a consequence of cuts affecting social policies (education, health care, poor relief) have undermined not simply the equality of opportunities, but the very 'capability' of the greater part of individuals to participate in social and political life. We must add to this the absence of real alternatives in the offer by different parties competing in the public arena, and the use of mass media and public relations techniques in view of 'manufacturing consent' (to borrow Chomsky's expression). Relevant information is concealed, and substituted by illusory representations and expectations. How would it be possible, then, to follow Bentham's 'principle of utility'? The way to 'pleasure' is difficult to find, and 'pains' are difficult to avoid. For instance, big industries try to control and address scientific information, not only to make their products attractive, but also to raise doubts about evidence of social costs and risks relative to the production and use of those products. Such 'manufacturing of doubt' is aimed at hindering public intervention and consumers' claims for damages (see the chapters by Frigato and Santos Arteaga, and Gennaro and Levis in the present volume).

Here, Kapp's observation can be usefully recalled, that in the electoral competition images of candidates and slogans are immediately adapted to the results of opinion polls. Such a misuse of voters' choice theories and of new techniques of data processing amounts to a 'manipulation of the sovereign electoral constituency by pseudodemocratic means' (Kapp 1967: 87). In fact, the immediate connection between common sense and political slogans leaves no room for the authentic public opinion formation, that is a fundamental factor of an effective policy-making process (see the above reference to Lindblom's analyses).

In his foreseeing considerations on the reduction of democracy to formal electoral procedures, Schumpeter points out the similarity between electoral competition and oligopolistic markets, adding that the consumer of political goods can be 'fooled' more easily than any other consumer (Schumpeter 1943: 264). A widening gap between elites and masses, as well as the reduction of society's capacity to solve its problems, were logically to be expected. No wonder, then, that not only elections are incapable of bringing about substantial changes, but many people do not even exert their right to vote. Thus a vicious circle of disempowerment has been set up, by which common citizens are less and less able to contribute to decision-making over issues of common interest.

In the market-capitalist system, in fact, there is a deep and permanent tendency to contrast democracy and freedom. In the neoliberal era, that tendency takes new shapes and grows stronger. In the last decades, the 'privatization' of politics and the need to support free-market principles through authoritarian attitudes and legislation have undermined both the public character of democracy and equality and self-determination, which are its basic conditions (see Lösch 2008: 221–222). A double, interdependent reduction has been accomplished: that of democracy to the formal right to vote, and that of politics to a play, or a struggle, taking place within the restricted circle of the 'power elite'. The privatization of politics is in contrast with its true, and typically modern, character: that of accomplishing the social function consisting in the acknowledgment, analysis and solution of social problems. 'Social' in the sense of problems concerning society, as a whole and as an 'open system' (see below).

Authoritarianism and inefficiency make the neoliberal order completely different from the 'truly free system', the 'competitive order' Friedrich Hayek was promoting when he founded the Mont Pelerin Society in 1947 (see Hayek 1948). His expectation that the social-democratic, Keynesian and corporatist-pluralist mood of the post-war years would be superseded by a revival of free-market orientation in the span of a generation has reached an ironic fulfillment. Hayek himself, in fact, was aware that 'many of the pretending defenders of "free enterprise" are in fact defenders of privileges and advocates of government activity in their favor' (ibid.: 107). However, he considered these to be amendable deviations in a free-market perspective. Polanyi alludes instead to structural features and inherent tendencies of capitalism when, three years before, he addresses his criticism to the liberal (free-market) conception:

> Free enterprise and private ownership are declared to be essentials of freedom.... With the liberal the idea of freedom thus degenerates into a mere advocacy of free enterprise – which is today reduced to a fiction by the hard reality of giant trusts and princely monopolies.
>
> (Polanyi 1944: 265)

Besides, differently from Hayek, who was committing his liberal utopia to the next generation, Polanyi was worried about the long-run 'universalistic' free-market strategy, which was going to characterize the *Pax Americana*. The ideology of 'liberal universalism' and the reality of 'universal capitalism' (Polanyi 1945) were to be imposed internally and internationally. This policy, and the liberal ideology supporting it, did not fade away after the end of the Cold War: on the contrary. This is convincingly shown, for instance, by Peter Gowan (1999), who also stresses the political aspect of neoliberal globalization and the influence of financial interests on US world policy.

The 'fiction' of 'free enterprise' – and the deceptive nature of free-market propaganda – have become most apparent in present times. Indeed, we feel the need to raise a radical question: What does freedom consist of, if the democratic political sphere is seriously jeopardized if not abolished? To the extent that this is the case, Polanyi points out in his essay on fascism (Polanyi 1935: 392–393), capitalism 'becomes the whole of society', and 'human beings are considered as producers, and as producers alone'. Producers without freedom. Trying to strike a historical balance of the development of our society, from World War II to neoliberal globalization, David Harvey (2005: 70) recalls 'Polanyi's fear: that the liberal (and by extension the neoliberal) utopian project could only ultimately be sustained by resort to authoritarianism.'

A demanding conception of freedom

The consequences of the crisis, and more generally of neoliberal transformation, have direct negative consequences for the living standards of the majority of people, and therefore on their 'capabilities' and their freedom. The concentration of power, of economic-financial power in particular, and the decay of democratic institutions it implies, also undermine the freedom of the great majority of citizens. Furthermore, the present crisis compels us to reflect not only on the outcomes of the neoliberal phase, but on the most general traits of our society and its basic dynamics. Is our socio-economic organization counter-adaptive? Does the economic system show its dramatic inefficiency, as soon as its effects on its human, social and ecological environment are reckoned? This leads us to a more demanding notion of freedom: the ability of human beings to arrange and transform the conditions of their lives through a purposeful and democratic control of social institutions, and, in particular, of the economic system. This notion of freedom is as important for the very survival of mankind as it is excluded from the horizon of 'manufactured consent', and, normally, of social sciences too. To what extent are citizens free to question the constraints characterizing their social organization? To what extent are citizens allowed to participate as informed and responsible persons to the formation of public opinion and public choices? This kind of freedom depends on, and at the same time is constitutive of, the degree of democracy warranted by political institutions.

The project of one world unified by development, which was designed after World War II, has resulted in a 'globalized' system where economic, social, and political inequalities tend to grow, as is documented year by year, for example, by the *Human Development Report* of the UNDP and the *World Development Report* of the World Bank. FAO reports acknowledge an increase of poverty and starvation. After that of 2007–2008, a new 'world food crisis' is coming out in 2010–2011; their origin and development have once again shown that the scarcity of food depends primarily on the social and political setup, and, in particular, on economic dynamics and the quality of public action (see McMichael 2009; and also Drèze and Sen 1989). The bright image of development has changed into that of a worldwide plunder of natural and human resources.

The present crisis suggests further reasons for criticizing the practice and ideology of development; moreover, it compels us to question the very concept of 'growth', together with the kind of 'efficiency' that characterizes the market-capitalist system and that is mirrored by conventional economics.

The counter-adaptive consequences of the economic system's dynamics on its human, social and natural environment have become more apparent in the era of neoliberal globalization. This constitutes a difference from the period of 'development' following World War II, but there are also more general and important common characteristics concerning capitalist accumulation and its contradictions. I have already alluded to the basic contradiction of capitalism – the tendency of capital over-accumulation as a consequence of the pursuit of minimum labor costs. Nor is the 'second contradiction of capitalism' analyzed by O'Connor peculiar to the neoliberal era, though in the latter, and for better reasons in times of crisis, a control on it seems more difficult, indeed precluded. Economic growth has been possible, according to O'Connor, only by depleting and damaging human, social and natural environments, without taking these costs into account. The 'second contradiction' consists of the fact that this growth strategy leads to a rise in costs within the economic system itself; the consequent need to increasingly shift costs onto the environment implies the risk of a runaway process (see O'Connor 1991).

O'Connor's political-ecological approach fits perfectly with Kapp's analysis. There is, Kapp points out, a 'growing awareness … of the essentially global and open-system character of the economic processes'. However, a closed-system perspective is generally adopted, whose 'criteria of evaluation are those in terms of which the system of business enterprise tends to evaluate its performance' (Kapp 1976: 145–146). As a result, social costs, misallocation of inputs, unfair distribution of outputs, 'deterioration and dehumanisation of the quality of living and working conditions' (ibid.: 153), and the neglect of alternative techniques of production are – at least – underrated. Thus a veil is drawn over the fact that 'the organising principles of economic systems guided by exchange values are incompatible with the requirements of ecological systems and the satisfaction of basic human needs' (ibid.: 149).

In order to satisfy these requirements, Kapp maintains, a completely new approach is needed. A complex 'system thinking' should be able to acknowledge 'discontinuous non-linear "feedback" effects which characterise the dynamic interdependencies between the different systems' (ibid.: 151). Such an open-system and interdisciplinary approach reveals, in Kapp's opinion, the need for politically stated desirable goals and norms concerning production. Furthermore, the democratic character of political institutions and processes is required, if 'justice in distribution, economic stability, full employment, efficiency in the utilization of resources, participation in decision-making' (ibid.: 154) are to be the general objective. The lack of democracy brings about insufficient information and therefore entropy; that is, Kapp specifies (ibid.: 157) 'the tendency of increasing disorganization'.

Clearly, Kapp's approach belongs to the radical tradition of institutional economics, which is characterized by its criticism of the *systematic* inefficiency of the market-capitalistic economy and of the anti-democratic concentration of economic power. The link between efficiency (in the sense of 'serviceability for society at large', that Veblen opposes to business efficiency), information and democracy is a key concept for Polanyi (see in particular Polanyi 1925). The same link has been stressed by Lindblom and Woodhouse (as we have seen), by ecological economics (e.g., Martinez-Alier 1997), and by recent proposals for an alternative economic organization.

Kapp's reflection, and more in general the systemic, institutional and ecological method, lead us to restate the polarity of open/closed. Society and its economy, as living systems drawing matter and energy from their environment, are actually *open* systems: but they are *closed* in so far as their general institutional traits impose constraints on their ability to acknowledge and process information coming from their environment, and to modify their organization accordingly. In other words, they are closed in the sense that they are insufficiently open to information and reorganization relative to the consequences of their dynamics on their environment (and on themselves).

In this sense, Polanyi writes that the capitalist mode of production, on one hand, has a 'retroactive effect on the community'. On the other hand, it lacks 'the sense organ' through which to perceive social needs and evaluation; its very (social-historical) 'nature' makes it generally refractory to be guided toward 'social utility' (Polanyi 1922: 83–84). In his analysis of land becoming a 'fictitious commodity', Polanyi raises the same problem as to the natural environment (see in particular Polanyi 1944: ch. 15).

Both the dynamics of the system and its communication with its environment depend on its organization. In the market-capitalist system, the profit motive constitutes the 'controlling factor' (Veblen) of the system, a constraint that can never be disregarded. The organization and dynamics of the system are accordingly shaped, and the interchange with its surrounding environment is bounded. In fact, as Antony Wilden says, the constraints defining the system govern 'the permissible construction of messages', making a 'greater variety of qualitatively different messages and relationships *impossible* in the system as it stands' (Wilden 1980: 228).

This is the reason why it is important for social sciences to ground their investigations on the definition of the structural features and correlative basic constraints characterizing the social system and limiting its communication with its human and natural environment. This way, these constraints – constituting the boundaries of the system – can be questioned, and either rationally accepted, if they favor the pursuit of human well-being and a non-destructive use of natural resources, or modified, if they endanger that pursuit. Otherwise, the result is a tacit, implicit assumption of the unchanging features of the existing social organization and of its constraints. Thus, adopting the viewpoint of the system, theory adopts its blindness too: we could say that it remains *closed* within it.

The closed-system perspective of conventional economics cannot question the boundaries of the economic system, because it tends to repress the question of the social-historical specificity of its organization. Thus individual economic choices and market transactions can appear as natural and rational, 'market failures' being understood as exceptions confirming the rule. The illusions of individual freedom and optimal use of resources can be nourished. At the same time, in regard to society as a whole, thoughtlessness about the feedback of the market-and-profit mechanism (preferably called 'economic growth' and even 'progress') on its environment is misrepresented as 'freedom'. The 'counter-adaptivity' of our socio-economic organization depends on its disregarding that feedback, and more generally, as Wilden points out (ibid.: 224–226), the 'elementary ecosystemic principle' of a 'hierarchically constrained universe'. We are not free to refuse to take into account the higher-order constraints arising from the natural universe, on which our life depends. We should instead be free to question the social-cultural constraints determining this refusal and that counter-adaptivity.

In François Perroux's opinion, models and concepts of conventional economics 'consider maximization as a result of supposedly rational and effective individual choices, in the context of competitive markets' and capitalist production: but they do this 'without any reference to a given form of society' (Perroux 1970: 2257, 2260 [my translation, MC]). Therefore, those models and concepts are '*implicitly* normative; they divert the attention of theorists, experts and common people from the critique of *institutions*', which is instead the 'first step towards *explicitly* normative propositions' (ibid.: 2270, 2289). The latter alone allow truly free choices.

In the open-system approach, the general organizational traits of the system, and the constraints and dynamics they imply, are included in the scope of theory. Contrary to conventional economics, institutional economics – at least, a certain kind of it – starts from 'the order of society' (Lowe 1977: 7), which always shapes economic activity, understood as 'the interchange with [man's] natural and social environment, in so far as this results in supplying him with the means of material want satisfaction' (Polanyi 1957: 243). From this viewpoint, the historical evolution of the economic system has to be considered as itself determining both wants and resources, both ceasing to be mere external data (see Löwe 1935; 1936). If, then, the social organization of the economic system determines its dynamics and changes its environment, it is necessary to widen the scope of economic science beyond rational choices that presuppose *given* ends and means, and to raise the question of the interchange between the economic system and its environment. The change the environment undergoes does constitute an economic problem, to be considered with reference to both the basic features of the system and its institutional transformations. The open-system approach takes us well beyond the boundaries of the playground of conventional economics.

As Kapp says (1976: 155), 'the formulation of social goals and objectives and the problem of collective choices can no longer be avoided'. The current crisis should for a better reason suggest, in particular, such questions as the waste and misallocation of resources, structural unemployment and inequality, the technology and organization to be adopted in productive processes, and the quality of needs to be satisfied. The problem of organizing the economic process reveals itself to be a problem of social choice, of *political* economy, and the issue of democracy reveals itself to be crucial. When applied to modern society, in fact, the wider – 'substantive' (Polanyi) and institutional – conception of economy implies the political relevance of the economic problem, and, at the same time, an upgraded conception of freedom. The emancipation of human individuals achieved by modern liberalism is to be defended and improved, but it remains an illusion if individuals are bereaved of their social, political, 'positive' liberty, consisting in the informed and responsible participation to choices concerning the organization of social life. In the last pages of *The Great Transformation*, Polanyi speaks in this sense of 'freedom in a complex society', opposing it to the liberal conception. The question is again – after the decay of liberal nineteenth-century capitalism, two world wars and fascist reaction – 'how to organize human life in a machine society'. 'The question of individual freedom', Polanyi continues, 'is only one aspect of this anxious problem' (Polanyi 1947: 109). This idea of freedom is strictly interdependent with an open-system and institutional-evolutive attitude. Polanyi himself affirms that the motive of his later comparative inquiries, concerning economic systems and the very definition of economy, is 'to enlarge our freedom of creative adjustment, and thereby improve our chances of survival' (Polanyi 1977: xliii).

The neoliberal era, and the dramatic crisis to which it has led, make this kind of freedom as relevant as it is denied, as necessary as it is repressed. So Lowe's definition of freedom, representing the starting point and deep meaning of the last among his major publications, seems of special interest. Freedom is, according to Lowe (1988: 5), 'the power of self-determination over the range open to human decision making. [Or, in other words,] the condition in which the thinking and acting of individuals and groups are not limited by external but removable constraints.'

Lowe distinguishes, then, between *private* and *public freedom*. The former consists of the part of our life space that is free from any external command. The second, which Lowe also calls *self-government*, consists of the possibility to 'codetermine with the other members [of society] the range of private freedom and also the constraints that affect other segments of our life space' (ibid.).

Two aspects of Lowe's argument are to be noted. The first is that public freedom is fundamental, because the limits, forms and means of private freedom depend on it. The second is the distinction between removable and non-removable constraints. Natural laws can be either employed for human purposes or disregarded with consequences hard to estimate, but they cannot in general be modified. The constraints pertaining to the historical, cultural, political realm, on the contrary, are – or should be – removable, in the sense that they can be modified.

We are not free to disregard our dependence on solar energy and millions of years of natural evolution. Indeed, our freedom consists of knowing as well as possible the characteristics of the system of systems which constitutes the natural environment of human society, including the physical constitution of human beings. Only by taking this knowledge into account and respecting the unavoidable constraints it reveals can we fully avail ourselves of the relative freedom these constraints allow us to enjoy, and avoid dreadful consequences (such as desertification of soil or dangers for our health).

We also cannot be absolutely free from social constraints, which, as Lowe says, limit individual freedom. Polanyi speaks in this sense of the 'reality of society'. The existence of society presupposes institutions and norms regulating social relationships and economic choices ('power and value', in Polanyi's terms – see the last pages of *The Great Transformation*). Indeed, in Polanyi's opinion, the conscience of this 'reality' constitutes the most recent and highest achievement of human liberty. This is a paradox, however, only in so far as social norms are 'naturalized', by denying their historical existence; that is, the fact that human beings make them and can change them. As Lowe points out, social norms do constitute 'external' and therefore freedom-limiting constraints for individuals, but only to the extent that they remain out of their control. Self-constraint, Lowe maintains, is not regarded as a limitation of freedom. On the contrary, 'intelligent', as he says, and democratic planning could allow a superior level of 'emancipation'.

Unfortunately, most people do not have the option to participate in the making of social norms. Such modern levels of freedom are so jealously monopolized – but also so difficult per se to be implemented – that generally individuals prefer to enjoy the limited, if not illusionary, freedom their serfdom allows.

References

Bauer, O. (1936) *Zwischen zwei Weltkriegen? Die Krise der Weltwirtschaft, der Demokratie und des Sozialismus*, Bratislava: E. Prager Verlag.

Bello, W. (2002) *Deglobalization*, London: Zed Books.

Bello, W. (2007) 'The Post-Washington Dissensus', *Focus on the Global South*, 14 September. Available at: www.waldenbello.org.

Chossudovski, M. (1997) *The Globalisation of Poverty*, London: Zed Books/Penang: Third World Network.

Crouch, C. (2003) *Postdemocrazia*, Bari: Laterza. (Enlarged version of *Coping with Postdemocracy*, The Fabian Society, 2000).

Crozier, M., Huntington, S.P. and Watanuki, J. (1975) *The Crisis of Democracy: Report on the Governability of Democracies to the Trilateral Commission*, New York: New York University Press.

Drèze, J. and Sen, A. (1989) *Hunger and Public Action*, Oxford: Clarendon Press.

Foster, J.B. (2007) 'The financialization of capitalism', *Monthly Review*, 58(11). Available at: www.monthlyreview.org/2007/04/01/the-financialization-of-capitalism.

Galbraith, J.K. (1955) *The Great Crash, 1929*, Boston, MA: Houghton Mifflin.

Gallino, L. (2010) 'La globalizzazione dell'operaio', *La Repubblica*, 14 June: 7.

Gowan, P. (1999) *The Global Gamble: Washington's Faustian Bid for World Dominance*, New York: Verso.

Hacket, J.S. and Pierson, P. (2010) *Winner-Take-All Politics*, New York: Simon & Schuster.

Harvey, D. (2005) *A Brief History of Neoliberalism*, Oxford: Oxford University Press.

Hayek, F.A. (1948 [1980]) '"Free" enterprise and competitive order', in *Individualism and Economic Order*, Chicago and London: University of Chicago Press.

Hobsbawm, E. (1994) *Age of Extremes: The Short Twentieth Century 1914–1991*, London: Michael Joseph Ltd.

Kapp, K.W. (1950a) *The Social Costs of Private Enterprise*, Cambridge, MA: Harvard University Press.

Kapp, K.W. (1950b) 'Economic planning and freedom', *Weltwirtschaftliches Archiv*, 64: 29–54.

Kapp, K.W. (1967 [1985]) 'On the problem of dehumanization of "pure theory" and social reality', in *The Humanization of the Social Sciences*, edited by John E. Ullman and Roy Preiswerk, Lanham and London: University Press of America, pp. 73–97. (First published in German: *Kyklos*, 22(1) (1967): 307–330.)

Kapp, K.W. (1976 [1985]) 'The open system character of the economy and its implications', in *The Humanization of the Social Sciences*, edited by John E. Ullman and Roy Preiswerk, Lanham and London: University Press of America, pp. 143–161. (First published in Dopfer, K. (ed.), *Economics in the Future*, London: Macmillan, ch. 6).

Krugman, P. (2007) *The Conscience of a Liberal*, New York: W.W. Norton.

Krugman, P. (2010) 'The third depression', *New York Times*, 27 June.

Kurtz, P. (2000) 'The new American plutocracy', *Free Inquiry*, 20: 4.

Lindblom, C.E. (2001) *The Market System*, New Haven and London: Yale University Press.

Lindblom, C.E. and Woodhouse, E.J. (1993) *The Policy-Making Process*, Englewood Cliffs: Prentice Hall.

Lösch, B. (2008) 'Die neoliberale Hegemonie als Gefahr für die Demokratie', in Butterwegge, C., Lösch, B. and Ptak, R. (eds.), *Kritik des Neoliberalismus*, Wiesbaden: Verlag für Sozialwissenschaften, pp. 221–283.

Löwe, A. (1935) *Economics and Sociology*, London: George Allen and Unwin.

Löwe, A. (1936) 'Economic analysis and social structure', *Manchester School of Economics and Social Studies*, 7: 18–37.

Lowe, A. (1977 [1983]) *On Economic Knowledge: Toward a Science of Political Economics*, Armonk and London: M.E. Sharpe.

Lowe, A. (1988) *Has Freedom a Future?*, New York, Westport and London: Praeger.

McMichael, P. (2009) 'The world food crisis in historical perspective', *Monthly Review*, 61(3). Available at: www.monthlyreview.org/2009/07/01/the-world-food-crisis-in-historical-perspective.

Magdoff, H. and Sweezy, P.M. (1987) *Stagnation and Financial Explosion*, New York: Monthly Review Press.

Martinez-Alier, J. (1997) 'The lack of general economic equivalency in ecological economics', in Cangiani, M. (ed.), *The Milano Papers: Essays in Societal Alternatives*, Montréal: Black Rose Books.

Marx, K. (1857) 'The financial crisis in Europe', *New York Daily Tribune*, 22 December (K. Marx and F. Engels, *Collected Works*, Moscow, London and New York: Progress Publishers, Lawrence and Wishart, 1975–2005, 15: 404–408).

Marx, K. (1979 [1867]) *Das Kapital*, vol. I, Berlin: Dietz Verlag.

Mills, C.W. (1956) *The Power Elite*, New York: Oxford University Press.

O'Connor, J. (1973) *The Fiscal Crisis of the State*, New York: St. Martin's Press.

O'Connor, J. (1991) 'On the two contradictions of capitalism', *Capitalism Nature Socialism*, 2(3):107–109.

Perroux, F. (1970) 'Les conceptualisations implicitement normatives et les limites de la modélisation en économie', *Économies et sociétés, Cahiers de l'ISEA*, 4(12): 2255–2307.

Polanyi, K. (1922 [2005]) 'Sozialistische Rechnungslegung', in *Chronik der großen Transformation*, edited by M. Cangiani, K. Polanyi-Levitt and C. Thomasberger, Marburg: Metropolis, pp. 71–113.

Polanyi, K. (1925 [2005]) 'Neue Erwägungen zu unserer Theorie und Praxis', *Der Kampf*, 18(1): 18–24. (Also in (2005) *Chronik der großen Transformation*, edited by M. Cangiani, K. Polanyi-Levitt and C. Thomasberger, Marburg: Metropolis, pp. 114–125.

Polanyi, K. (n.d. – but late 1930s) 'The fascist virus', ms, *Karl Polanyi Archive*, Montréal, file 18–28.

Polanyi, K. (1935) 'The essence of fascism', in Lewis, J., Polanyi, K. and Kitchin, D.K. (eds.), *Christianity and the Social Revolution*, London: Gollancz, pp. 359–394.

Polanyi, K. (1945) 'Universal capitalism or regional planning?', *The London Quarterly of World Affairs*, January: 1–6.

Polanyi, K. (1947) 'Our obsolete market mentality', *Commentary*, 3: 109–117.

Polanyi, K. (1957) 'The economy as instituted process', in Polanyi, K., Arensberg, C.M. and Pearson, H.W. (eds.), *Trade and Market in the Early Empires: Economies in History and Theory*, New York and London: The Free Press.

Polanyi, K. (1977) *The Livelihood of Man*, edited by H.W. Pearson, New York: Academic Press.

Polanyi, K. (1944 [2001]) *The Great Transformation*, Boston, MA: Beacon Press.

Polanyi, K. (2005) *Chronik der großen Transformation*, edited by M. Cangiani, K. Polanyi-Levitt and C. Thomasberger, Marburg: Metropolis.

Reich, R. (2007) *Supercapitalism: The Transformation of Business, Democracy, and Everyday Life*, New York: Alfred A. Knopf.

Schumpeter, J.A. (1943) *Capitalism, Socialism, and Democracy*, London: Allen and Unwin.

Sen, A. (1999a) 'The possibility of social choice', *The American Economic Review*, 89(3): 349–378.

Sen, A. (1999b) *Development as Freedom*, Oxford: Oxford University Press.

Steinbeck, J. (2006) *The Grapes of Wrath*, London: Penguin Books.

Stiglitz, J.E. (2008) 'Is there a Post-Washington Consensus consensus?', in Serra, N. and Stiglitz, J.E. (eds.), *The Washington Consensus Reconsidered*, Oxford: Oxford University Press.

Veblen, T. (1901 [1994]) 'Industrial and pecuniary employments', in *The Place of Science in Modern Civilization*, London: Routledge/Thoemmes Press.

Wilden, A. (1980) 'Changing frames of order: cybernetics and the machina mundi', in Woodward, K. (ed.), *The Myths of Information: Technology and Postindustrial Culture*, Madison: University of Wisconsin and Coda Press.

Index

Page numbers in *italics* denote tables, those in **bold** denote figures.